Lockdown

"Sobering, urgent and necessary, this is the first serious attempt to chronicle the colossal harms caused by lockdowns worldwide. Deeply researched, rich with statistics, and studded with personal testimonies from around the world, it should be compulsory reading for every policymaker, and anyone interested in a better post-pandemic world"

—Professor Lee Jones, *Professor of Political Economy and International Relations, Queen Mary, University of London, UK*

"These authors deserve the world's thanks for surveying the victims of covid lockdowns starting in March 2020. The pain communicated in the voices of victims woven into this book – from violence, anxiety, loss of love, meaning, and security, social disintegration, crushed dreams, and so much more – is enough to touch the most hardened 'neoliberal'. Presented within a well-referenced social scientific journey through the covid era, the authors' poignant condemnation of lockdowns and other covid policies that hijacked society is a welcome addition to covid policy analysis by left-wing intellectuals, most of whom – like governments worldwide – turned their backs on the victims of the madness"

—Professor Gigi Foster, *School of Economics, University of New South Wales, Sydney, Australia*

"Finally! Left-wing intellectuals writing about lockdowns who are truly on the side of the poor, the elderly, the migrants, the sick, and the young: the forgotten victims. This timely book documents how many academics and politicians fell for the illusion that one can control covid and failed to see the damage right under their nose that they were party to"

—Paul Frijters, *Emeritus Professor of Wellbeing Economics at the London School of Economics, London, UK*

"This is an absorbing account of lockdown harms, told in part through fascinating first person testimony and surveys collected throughout the pandemic from around the world. 'Lockdown' tells the global stories of moral quandries, mistrust in government and fault-lines between 'sheeple' and 'covidiots'. Bitter truths are made palatable by the engaging human stories. In one example, the bizarre management of this epidemic is illustrated in the description of a 'Covid-safe' child's party in which fun is 'broken down into sequential bouts of potential excitement followed by disappointment'. This is an essential account of lockdowns!"

—Laura Dodsworth, *author, journalist, photographer and filmmaker and author of* A State of Fear: How The UK Government Weaponised Fear During The Covid-19 Pandemic, *UK*

"As social scientists begin to interrogate the harms caused by the response to Covid-19, this book drops a bomb into the discussion which will help to demolish the myth that the destruction of so many lives and livelihoods was somehow inevitable. *Lockdown* is a brilliant analysis of the 'collateral damage' caused by the pandemic response, of the human experience of this nightmare, and of the implications for the futures of societies around the world. It is urgent, gripping, vital, and demands to be read"

—Professor Toby Green, *Professor of Precolonial and Lusophone African History and Culture, Kings College, London, UK*

Daniel Briggs · Luke Telford ·
Anthony Lloyd · Anthony Ellis · Justin Kotzé

Lockdown

Social Harm in the Covid-19 Era

Daniel Briggs
Facultad de las Ciencias Sociales y de la
Comunicación
Universidad Europea
Madrid, Spain

Anthony Lloyd
Department of Humanities & Social
Sciences, School of Social Sciences,
Humanities & Law
Teesside University
Middlesbrough, UK

Justin Kotzé
Department of Humanities & Social
Sciences, School of Social Sciences,
Humanities & Law
Teesside University
Middlesbrough, UK

Luke Telford
School of Justice, Security
and Sustainability
Staffordshire University
Stoke-on-Trent, UK

Anthony Ellis
School of Social and Political Sciences
University of Lincoln
Lincoln, UK

ISBN 978-3-030-88824-4   ISBN 978-3-030-88825-1   (eBook)
https://doi.org/10.1007/978-3-030-88825-1

This Palgrave Macmillan imprint is published by the registered company Springer Nature Switzerland
AG
The registered company address is: Gewerbestrasse 11, 6330 Cham, Switzerland

Foreword

Perhaps the biggest single error in the management of the Covid-19 pandemic has been the assumption that this is a public health problem where responses should be led by biomedical science. Pandemics challenge the whole of society and require a whole of science response, a definition of science that includes knowledge from the social sciences and humanities as much as from physics, engineering, computing or whatever. In a globally integrated world, the challenge is to the whole of global society, not just to individual nation states. An obsession with the choices of one government or another obscures the extent to which the problems to which these respond are created by global processes which, in turn, both constrain the options available and create common experiences for citizens.

The strength of this book is precisely its refusal to settle for a story about one country or another but to deal with the sources of the crisis in globalisation and the interdependencies that this has created. We should not exaggerate the novelty of these interactions—Australia was no more successful in excluding pandemic influenza in 1918 than it has been with Covid in 2021—but the acceleration of mobility in the contemporary world has greatly enhanced their impact. A virus originating in China can arrive in Europe overnight by plane rather than in weeks by steamship. The authors begin, then, with an analysis of the international division of labour, the forces that have driven it, the associated models of governance and the consequent patterns of inequality. Pandemics are a stress test for any system of social organisation—and this is no exception. Viruses find the fault lines in society. The Black Death played its part in the decline of feudal society. Will Covid-19 result in a similar shift in power or will new technologies of population control protect elites from the consequences?

The politics of the Covid-19 pandemic play out in slightly different ways in the countries studied. There are, however, notable common features, particularly in the way elite groups have seized the opportunity to entrench themselves and to remodel political discourses in their own interests. Human rights and liberties are no longer the preconditions for democracy but privileges granted by elites that may be withdrawn if inconvenient. Public assemblies of political opponents may be suppressed by invoking the language of infection control. Private spaces, such as homes, may be penetrated and policed. The Chief Medical Officer for Canada can even give advice on sexual positions that minimise the risk of transmitting infection. Public health has always had a panoptic dimension. Sometimes this can be justified in terms of protecting individuals—women and children—with limited access to the public sphere but these incursions have always been regulated by the forms of law. In the pandemic, habits of governing by decree are being formed, which will be difficult to shake off. Everyone is to be considered diseased and subject to control unless they can, repeatedly, prove their health. The basic principles of the rule of law are inverted: innocence is not assumed from the start.

Elites, however, get to opt out. Their status buys protection and privacy. This is not simply a matter of wealth, although the private jet brings a more relaxed biosecurity regime than economy class. Although the openness of biomedical career paths can be exaggerated, their meritocratic claims can be just as oppressive. If success is not an accident of birth or intergenerational wealth, then those left behind clearly deserve to be. They are the helot class, Huxley's Deltas and Epsilons, to be managed in a kindly but firm manner by those entitled to rule by virtue of superior intellect. Their fear of Covid-19 is a useful diversion from the deaths of despair engendered by globalisation, and accentuated by the pandemic—the uncounted legions of victims of suicide, cancer, heart disease, drug dependency and the like.

Medical sociologists have charted the rolling-back of biomedical imperialism since the 1960s. This has not been without struggle but the assumption that biomedical science should dictate to society had been substantially constrained. The lesson from this book is that most of those changes have been reversed in the twinkling of a historic moment. Commitments to partnership, dialogue, co-production, even to evidence-based practice have been abandoned in a resurgence of biomedical paternalism. The language of 'compliance' has re-emerged from the dark cupboards where it has been lodged for a generation.

This is a passionate book, filled with the voices of the pandemic's global victims. Like many instant books, its arguments and judgements will be subject to revision with the passage of time and the accumulation of more detailed and reflective accounts. Its importance, however, lies precisely in its passion, its anger and its provocation to think more widely and more deeply about what the management of the pandemic is doing to societies around the world, and to the values and assumptions on which they have been based for generations.

August 2021

Robert Dingwall
Nottingham Trent University
Nottingham, UK

Contents

About the Authors

Daniel Briggs, Ph.D. is a Professor of Criminology at the Universidad Europea in Madrid, Spain. As a researcher, writer and interdisciplinary academic who studies social problems, he has undertaken ethnographic research into social issues from street drug users to terminally ill patients; from refugees to prostitutes; and from gypsies to gangs and deviant youth behaviours. He also lectures across the social sciences and has published widely. One of his most recent books about the harms of drug addiction in the urban wastelands, *Dead End Lives: Drugs and Violence in the City Shadows* (Policy Press, 2017), won the Division of International Criminology's Outstanding Book Award 2018 (selected by the American Society of Criminology). Prior to the Covid-19 pandemic, his most recent book about the refugee crisis was published as *Climate Changed: Refugee Border Stories and the Business of Misery* (Routledge, 2020). In collaboration with members of an International Covid-19 research team he leads, he has just published *Researching the Covid-19 Pandemic: A Critical Blueprint for the Social Sciences* (Policy Press, 2021) and is writing *Hotel Puta: A hardcore Ethnography of a Luxury Brothel* (RJ4ALL Publications).

Luke Telford, Ph.D. is a Lecturer in Criminology at Staffordshire University. Luke is an active social scientific researcher and is co-author of *Researching the Covid-19 Pandemic: A Critical Blueprint for the Social Sciences*, and author of the forthcoming monograph entitled *English Nationalism and Its Ghost Towns*. He has published various journal articles on working-class culture, neoliberalism, political dissatisfaction, deindustrialisation, current labour market conditions and the Covid-19 pandemic.

Anthony Ellis, Ph.D. is Senior Lecturer in Criminology, University of Lincoln, UK. His research interests include male violence, homicide, social exclusion, social harms and political economy. He is the author of *Men, Masculinities and Violence: An Ethnographic Study* (Routledge), which was awarded the British Society of Criminology's Critical Criminology book prize in 2016.

Anthony Lloyd, Ph.D. is Associate Professor in Criminology and Sociology at Teesside University, UK. His research interests primarily focus on work and labour markets. His research also includes investigation of urban sociology and migration. He is particularly interested in blending analysis of the workplace with emerging theoretical frameworks around critical criminology and social harm to understand experiences of low-paid, insecure and flexible forms of labour. He has published widely in this area, his most recent book is *The Harms of Work: An Ultra-Realist Account of the Service Economy*, published by Bristol University Press (2018).

Justin Kotzé, Ph.D. is a Senior Lecturer in Criminology and Criminal Justice at Teesside University, UK. Justin's research interests are wide-ranging and he has published work on social harm; the historical sublimation of violence; the consumption of steroids; and the commodification of abstinence. He is also the author of *The Myth of the 'Crime Decline': Exploring Change and Continuity in Crime and Harm* (Routledge, 2019) and co-editor of *Zemiology: Reconnecting Crime and Social Harm* (Palgrave, 2018).

List of Figures

1

Conceptualising Covid-19 Times: Post-politics and Social Harm

The spectre of catastrophe on the horizon of popular consciousness had, until early 2020, been generally reserved for climate change and environmental disaster. Europe and North America were also experiencing extreme political polarisation, which had riven new cleavages and fault lines into a once relatively settled political landscape.[1] A global pandemic was at the forefront of very few minds. However, within a few short months in early 2020, SARS-CoV-2 (hereafter Covid-19) had fundamentally reordered political, economic and social life across much of the world.[2] Or, more accurately, the *global response* to Covid-19 had fundamentally reordered the lives of billions of people across the planet.[3] Daily press conferences announced increasingly restrictive measures, new rules on social contact, working patterns, educational activity and leisure, alongside grim updates on infection numbers, hospitalisations and deaths became commonplace. Social media debate, already liable to extreme polarisation, demonstrated further antagonisms between those seeking

---

[1] Winlow et al. (2017) and Nagle (2017).
[2] Schwab and Malleret (2020).
[3] Briggs et al. (2021).

the security of restrictions and those seeking the return of freedom. In short, Covid-19 and the global response to it not only reshaped material realities but also became firmly embedded within political, social and cultural imagination.

However, a global pandemic should not have been a surprise. History is littered with examples of pandemics and plagues and, over the last century, a surprisingly high number of epidemics and pandemics have claimed the lives of millions.[4] From the Spanish flu of 1918 through to Acquired Immune Deficiency Syndrome (AIDS), Severe acute respiratory syndrome (SARS), Middle East Respiratory Syndrome (MERS), Swine Flu, Ebola, Zika virus and more, the last 100 years have encountered new forms of disease that have often been transmitted from the animal kingdom to humans and resulted in a wide range of infection, illness and death. However, the emergence of Covid-19 in late 2019 and early 2020, principally in the Chinese province of Wuhan, seemed to catch many by surprise.[5] Within a matter of weeks, Europeans who had been aware of SARS, MERS, Zika virus and other recent pandemics—yet not directly affected in any meaningful way—went from paying little attention to news reports of a new respiratory virus in China to transferring work online, gearing up for home-schooling and preparing to enter an unprecedented lockdown. From its origins in China, Covid-19 quickly spread across trade and travel routes through to Europe and the United States of America (USA), and by 11 March 2020, the World Health Organization (WHO) had declared a global pandemic.[6] Within weeks, most countries across the world were reporting cases of the virus and governments had enacted a range of restrictive public health measures including social distancing and working from home, enshrined through emergency legislation, to prevent the spread of infection and insulate healthcare systems. For much of the world, this involved the curtailment of freedoms and liberties in unprecedented ways.

This book offers a critical account of lockdown policies and employs a social harm framework to consider the implications of sustained

---

[4] Honigsbaum (2020).
[5] Zizek (2021).
[6] World Health Organization (WHO) (2020).

restrictions. Government intervention has been framed as the careful management of risk and therefore ostensibly designed to reduce the harms of the virus, prevent hospitals and healthcare workers from being overwhelmed, reduce short-term and long-term illness, and, ultimately, deaths. However, other harms have proliferated throughout the pandemic, including rising levels of domestic abuse and child abuse,[7] hate crime,[8] increased loneliness and isolation,[9] rising levels of mental ill-health,[10] unemployment,[11] educational inequality,[12] suspected corruption[13] and fraud.[14] While not dismissing the risk of harm presented by the virus itself, we intend to shine a light on the various harms associated with the way in which governments have responded to the pandemic. We seek to explore the experiences of those across the world who have lived with the consequences of both the virus and our collective response to it.

To start this book, we feel it is important to contextualise the world before Covid-19 and offer an outline of our social harm perspective. Before we delve into this, it is important to make several points clear from the outset. First, as critical social scientists, we went to work right from the start of the crisis in March 2020 to capture public opinions on the pandemic and governmental responses.[15] We wanted to capture views from a range of people who were experiencing the pandemic in different countries with different circumstances and so we launched an international online survey, promoted via social media. Thereafter this study used other methods which we discuss later in the chapter. What we present here is based on the findings from this work.

Second, we have characterised this as a book about 'global lockdown'. 'Lockdown' has been interpreted and implemented differently across the

---

[7] Sediri et al. (2020).
[8] Gover et al. (2020).
[9] Killgore et al. (2020).
[10] Zizek (2021).
[11] Blakeley (2020).
[12] Scott et al. (2021).
[13] Abassi (2020).
[14] Grierson (2021).
[15] Briggs et al. (2020, 2021) and Ellis et al. (2021).

world and some countries followed different approaches.[16] Some countries, such as New Zealand, entered a short restrictive lockdown in early 2020 but lifted internal restrictions after only seven weeks (although more severe border restrictions were kept in place). Others, such as the United Kingdom (UK), used full national lockdowns on three occasions, as well as a regional tier system with varying degrees of restriction on travel, leisure and social interaction. 'Lockdown' here refers to restrictive 'non-pharmaceutical interventions' (NPIs) designed to prevent the spread of disease.[17] While we recognise a global study has limitations in terms of scale and the vast and diverse nature of global experience, we felt that a global pandemic required, as much as possible, a global perspective to try and identify similarities and differences in experience in a wide range of contexts. We know we cannot capture everything and we make no claims to having done so, but we have gathered over 2,000 perspectives from 59 countries. Considering the conditions under which the data was collected, we think this is pretty good going.

Finally, it reflects the rather simplistic nature of our national and international discourse on the pandemic that we even have to make this statement, but we feel it is important to state the following: we are not Covid-19 deniers. We know the virus is real. We have friends and family members who have been diagnosed with Covid-19, some experiencing mild symptoms while others experiencing more severe symptoms. Friends of friends have died with/from Covid-19. What we are saying is that our argument is not that the pandemic is somehow fake news or a conspiracy. We are also not epidemiologists, biologists or virologists. We are social scientists and, as such, are interested in the impact of social forces, including pandemics and states' responses, upon the lives of people in a range of different settings and contexts. We study and question the political, economic, cultural and social ramifications of various phenomena, including pandemics and the response of governments, political officials and media.

Our work has led us to ask critical questions that we feel have not always been sufficiently raised within academic, political or media

---

[16] Arshed et al. (2020).
[17] Flaxman et al. (2020).

spheres.[18] As critical criminologists engaged in the study of social harm, we have asked whether NPIs or lockdowns were the only available option. What harms emerge from the restrictive measures placed on people's lives throughout the pandemic, and finally, what is the balance of harm between lockdown in the name of public health and the growing list of damage experienced by individuals, families and society as a whole? When we look back on the pandemic in the future, we will ask whether the measures were worth it. Here we offer a preliminary assessment of the harms of lockdown. Before we move onto presenting the data that underpins this assessment, let us first outline life before the pandemic as the virus, and the response to it, emerged within a specific broader context.

Context

It is difficult to outline an entire global context in a few short pages but the world into which Covid-19 emerged was a world divided politically, economically, culturally and socially. Most, if not all, of the world today exists under a capitalist political economy and while 'varieties of capitalism'[19] exist, and inevitably shape countries and regions in different ways, it is reasonable to say that capitalism and its imperatives of maximising profitability and market expansion dominate the globe. China represents a form of state-managed capitalism[20] while 'developing' nations of the Global South and East provide the labour and natural resources for the advanced service and financial neoliberal economies of the Global North and West. David Harvey[21] notes the geographical element to capitalism; capital moves spatially as opportunities emerge in different parts of the world where returns on investment are more likely. When the USA and UK abandoned their productive economies in the

---

[18] Briggs et al. (2021).

[19] Hall and Soskice (2001).

[20] Liu and Tsai (2020).

[21] Harvey (2010).

1970s in favour of financial and service-based economies,[22] production was relocated to other parts of an increasingly interlinked and globalised network and supply chain. The global economy is also interconnected along lines of production and consumption. What one country produces another consumes, and this is true of both material commodities and experiences such as tourism. When we think about production and consumption, this is often underpinned by labour. Local and regional economies and labour markets rely on this interconnected network of global capitalism; what factory workers in Bangladesh make, consumers in the US purchase. What Pacific Island holiday resorts offer in employment opportunities for locals, wealthy tourists enjoy as dream holiday experiences. The interconnections of trade, production and consumption create conditions whereby the relationships between states and markets differ across the globe. The bottom line, however, is that the global capitalist economy remains a dynamic process that creates winners and losers.

In the West, neoliberalism has represented the dominant ideology for four decades.[23] Despite earlier assertions that neoliberalism represented the withering of the nation state, it would be more accurate to suggest the role of the state changed to provide the support mechanisms for global markets to emerge, consolidate and thrive.[24] The primary values of neoliberalism, both economically and ideologically, revolve around competition, individualism and the protection of private property rights. This has been evident in the UK, Europe and the USA for decades in the economic realm of trade, finance, markets, and, increasingly, the social and cultural realm, where individualism and aggressive competition for status, respect and material reward has moved to the centre of society.[25] This resulted in a focus on privatisation, outsourcing and market forces with the belief that economic competition generated both innovation and efficiency.[26]

---

[22] Varoufakis (2013).

[23] Harvey (2005).

[24] Slobodian (2019) and Mitchell and Fazi (2017).

[25] Hall et al. (2008).

[26] Lloyd (2020).

However, neoliberal capitalism has failed to maintain consistent economic growth in recent decades, despite a bloated financial sector generating huge profits uncoupled from the real economy.[27] As Wolfgang Streeck has noted, neoliberal capitalism has become increasingly volatile and unable to resolve its own contradictions.[28] The global financial crisis of 2007–08 led to a decade of austerity and deficit reduction measures in the West which further demonstrated the limits of neoliberalism and showed that the service of capital markets was more important than democracy.[29] The UK and USA imposed austerity upon its populations with devastating consequences,[30] while the European Union's (EU) anti-democratic structures demanded austerity measures from periphery nations, such as Greece and Ireland, to access loans needed to pay off bank loans.[31] While the willingness to uncouple capitalism from democracy raised some consternation in Europe, China had shown that capital markets did not necessarily go hand in hand with democracy.[32]

In Europe, the UK and the USA, these political-economic shifts hollowed out traditional manufacturing and heavy industry, outsourcing and relocating jobs to the Global South where costs and labour were cheaper.[33] The West has increasingly come to rely upon financial services, the public sector, digital technologies and traditional service economy work. Labour market polarisation has seen high-paid work in emerging sectors contrast with stagnant wages and poor conditions in the precarious service economy.[34] While unemployment fell before the pandemic, it masked the rise of insecure forms of temporary, part-time and 'nonstandard' forms of employment characterised by zero-hour contracts, gig economy work and self-employment.[35] The USA has recently witnessed

---

[27] Streeck (2016).
[28] Ibid.
[29] Ibid.
[30] O'Hara (2014).
[31] Lapavitsas (2019).
[32] So (2019).
[33] Lloyd (2013).
[34] Standing (2011).
[35] Lloyd (2018).

fights for an increased minimum wage,[36] while France saw sustained 'gilet jaunes' protests, as many people are angry at job insecurity, conditions and the overall growth of inequality in French society.[37]

As a consequence, the Global South and East have become the engine of production, but lax regulation and worker protections create profitable opportunities for multinationals while exposing workers to harsh conditions and a lack of safety that has resulted in significant workplace accidents. Factory collapses in Bangladesh[38] and a wave of suicides by jumping off Foxconn factories in China[39] serve as just two examples. It is telling that the response to the latter did not prompt a change in working conditions, but rather called for the introduction of protective netting around buildings. Pay and conditions within the formal labour market are poor while an informal and casual labour market represents a significant proportion of labour in India, Central and South America, and Africa.[40]

The Global South and East also relied on thriving tourist industries, catering to travellers from more affluent places which bolstered local labour markets; for example, luxury 'trophy hunting' holidays in Africa afford rich Westerners the chance to kill big game and simultaneously generate between $100-$400 million for the African economy and somewhere between 7,000 and 50,000 jobs.[41] Finally, labour exploitation takes place globally with different features in different parts of the world, but the interconnected nature of supply chains and trade routes facilitates the legal and illegal movement of people for the purposes of exploited labour.[42] The financial opportunities available to, for example, militias and dictators in African countries such as Democratic Republic of Congo, which control mines and their natural resources, as well as trade routes, often result in significant harms. These include the exploitation of 'workers' who effectively become slaves, huge resource extraction

[36] Pietrykowski (2017).
[37] Jetten et al. (2020).
[38] Large (2018).
[39] Chan (2013).
[40] Singhari and Madheswaran (2017), Jinnah (2017), and Milkman (2020).
[41] Smith (2019).
[42] UNODC (2016).

from local economies by corrupt political actors and global corporations, and the continuation of poverty among the local population.[43] These inequalities are interconnected while maintaining a localised imprint.

This fragmented and divisive labour market reflects a growing gap between the rich and poor that has a clear spatial context, both nationally and globally.[44] Globally, China has seen an overall reduction in poverty but a huge increase in inequality; the richest one per cent own as much wealth as the bottom half of Chinese society.[45] The USA and UK have seen wages lag over the last forty years while inequality has risen,[46] demonstrating Thomas Piketty's thesis that inequality grows when profits grow faster than wages.[47] Western countries have clear geographic wealth divides; between urban and rural communities, between North and South (in the UK) and between (and within) urban metro areas and rural communities (in the USA).[48] With those inequalities, both countries have seen increases in poverty, mental health problems, addiction and suicide.[49] These social problems are also persistent within the peripheries of Europe's great cities.[50] Economic inequality is not only reserved for middle- and lower-income nations and economies; extremes of income disparity exist in Brazil, India, South Africa and the Middle East, with the rich often comparable to Europe and the USA but with much greater poverty among those at the bottom of the income distribution.[51] Capital seeks new markets and new opportunities to reproduce. Increasingly, this involves the grossly uneven distribution of profits, resources and wealth. At the same time national and global economies continue to stagnate, masked by the success of a few businesses and sectors that enrich their shareholders.

---

43 Pitron (2020).
44 Piketty (2014) and Dorling (2015).
45 Chen (2020) and Jain-Chandra et al. (2018).
46 Blundell et al. (2018).
47 Piketty (2014).
48 Manduca (2019), Silva (2019), and Hazeldine (2020).
49 Case and Deaton (2020), Quinones (2016), and Wilkinson and Pickett (2009).
50 Briggs and Gamero (2017) and Briggs (2020).
51 Assouad et al. (2018).

Consideration of wealth disparities and global, regional and local economic inequalities sits against the backdrop of climate change and environmental concerns which have loomed on the horizon for decades. Concerns that are beginning to now materialise and are being experienced in the context of existing inequalities.[52] As carbon emissions rise, most of the scientific community agrees that the consequences for the natural environment will be significant.[53] Increasing calls for intervention demand we either slow down or reverse the potential effects of climate change, with those calls becoming louder and more panicked with each passing year.[54] Human destruction and appropriation of the natural environment has been central to our advancement as a species and civilisation, yet planetary warming since the Industrial Revolution is now beginning to affect water supplies, biodiversity, weather systems, sea levels and agriculture; not to mention the effects of melting ice caps and heating permafrost.[55] Indeed, some suggest that the increased prevalence and spread of novel viruses—from MERS, SARS and Swine Flu, to Ebola, Zika and Covid-19—stems from human encroachment into the natural environment.[56] The result is greater proximity to virus-carrying animals, such as bats, and the destruction of their natural habitat.[57]

Environmental catastrophe has generated popular protest and unrest as well as political action. The 2015 Paris Agreement committed most countries around the world to limit carbon emissions, although the USA withdrew under President Trump and re-joined under President Biden. Political disagreement also characterises the climate change debate as newly industrialised countries such as China, India and Brazil criticise the hypocrisy of those countries who commenced the Industrial Revolution and now call for curtailment of industrial expansion. Meanwhile, countries such as the UK and USA may not emit carbon through

[52] White and Heckenberg (2014) and White (2013).
[53] Klein (2014).
[54] Taylor et al. (2019).
[55] White and Heckenberg (2014).
[56] Schwab and Malleret (2020).
[57] Honigsbaum (2020).

industrial production, but their consumer societies are far from environmentally friendly,[58] leading to suggestions that we must learn to live more modestly.

In contrast, technological developments are heralded as the solution, from geoengineering[59] to net-zero economies, electric cars and hydrogen batteries.[60] However, new technologies require different natural resources, the control of which become conflict points and effectively represent a different form of natural exploitation; switching from exploiting fossil fuels to rare metals such as palladium and cobalt creates a new dependency on resources with an as-yet undetermined lifespan.[61] While climate change represents an ecological challenge, it is also a human challenge. International migration has always occurred throughout human history but today is driven by a range of factors including escalating civil war in the Middle East and North Africa, climate change and deepening economic inequality.[62] As migrants leave war zones, climate hotspots and economically marginalised spaces in search of safety and a better future, many are arriving in countries with hostile political climates and moving into spaces that are already deprived, fragmented and problematic.[63] Cultural tensions around assimilation, multiculturalism and tolerance combine with economic tensions around resources, jobs and opportunities.[64] Each of these factors requires passionate political debate and intervention, though as we explain in the next section, our current epoch represents a 'post-political' era which is ill-equipped to deal with these challenges.

---

[58] Smart (2010).
[59] Buck (2019).
[60] Schwab (2017).
[61] Pitron (2020).
[62] Parenti (2011) and Briggs (2020).
[63] Lloyd et al. (2021).
[64] Winlow et al. (2017).

Post-politics

There may be unprecedented prosperity across the world, but there is also division, inequality, poverty and the impending threat of catastrophic changes to our climate. Solutions to these challenges ordinarily emerge from politics, yet the West, in particular, has moved into an inertial state of post-politics[65] where nothing exists beyond the horizon of capitalism. Indeed, as critics from Fredric Jameson to Mark Fisher have noted, it is now easier to imagine the end of the world than the end of capitalism.[66] Politics, in its traditional sense, means the articulation of a vision for the future based on a belief system in how society could and should function.[67] However, politics has been increasingly reduced to the efficient management of the system as it exists today. Fundamental questions are rarely, if ever, asked about whether our political and economic model is the right one, with no political figures arguing for an alternative to capitalism or presenting an alternative vision. Some may argue that the Black Lives Matter protests, #MeToo movement, pro-democracy rallies in places such as Hong Kong and anti-austerity marches in the UK, France and USA represent the vibrancy of our political system. Unfortunately, this is not the case. Each of these issues is easily incorporated within the field of capitalist political economy—they do not threaten the system or call for an alternative vision, only a fairer version of what currently exists.[68] For years, Francis Fukuyama's[69] claim that liberal democratic market capitalism represented 'the end of history' was derided, while most people *acted as if it were true*.

Some may suggest that the rise of the right and a return to authoritarian government represents the return of a particular kind of alternative politics, one characterised by nationalism, populism and security. The political divisions over Donald Trump, Brexit, and the growing support for right of centre and far right parties, as well as democratic socialists

[65] Winlow et al. (2015).
[66] Fisher (2009).
[67] Badiou (2012).
[68] Winlow et al. (2015).
[69] Fukuyama (1992).

such as Bernie Sanders and Jeremy Corbyn, would seem to signal the recommencement of political division. However, before the pandemic, these divisions remained within the confines of what Fisher called 'capitalist realism' and called for, on the left, greater equality and distribution and, on the right, greater protection and security. The political fault lines in Europe now largely exist on the field of culture, rather than political economy. Issues of identity, participation and recognition are often rights-based and are easily subsumed within the capitalist system. In fact, what has emerged could be accurately described as 'anti-politics'. Issues-based movements increasingly appear to be satisfied with defeat in the political arena as long as ideological purity remains and gains are made in the cultural field. The Left appears content to lose electorally as long as they can colonise the cultural imagination and continue to criticise political leaders for not transforming society in the way they want. Political division exists but it does not, we suggest, represent the vibrancy of liberal democracy.

Instead, it demonstrates the decline of symbolic efficiency—the narrative that ideology presents to us a set of signifiers that allow us to make sense of our place in the world, a narrative that we can usually apply with a degree of consistency to our experiences in life. Neoliberalism increasingly fails to account for the reality of life in many parts of the world and the gap between that rhetoric and our realities is becoming more evident. Yet, despite this, protests continue to call for greater recognition *within the existing system* rather than a fundamental overhaul and movement to a different form of political economy.[70] It is necessary for us to acknowledge this post-political context precisely because it is within this context that governments tried to address the pandemic. Framed by the ideologies they uphold, the tools they were willing to use reflected a strong commitment to the existing system. Moreover, as we shall go on to demonstrate, our willingness to both adhere to and deviate from restrictive NPIs such as lockdowns reflected the *same* level of commitment (Chapters 6 and 10). We now turn to a brief discussion of the ultra-realist harm framework that we employ to make sense of our empirical data.

---

[70] Kotzé (2020).

Social Harm and Ultra-Realism

Our analysis here draws upon a social harm framework developed within the field of critical criminology.[71] Social harm, or zemiology, emerged from a critique of crime as a concept without firm foundation or ontological grounding.[72] Criminology had traditionally focused upon transgressions of the criminal law but the foundational concept, crime, was flawed.[73] What constitutes 'crime' is constructed by society and enshrined in laws made by us. Crime reflects wider power relations and structural dynamics that often reveal what some rather flippantly call 'petty events'.[74] While we would caution against trivialising the experiences of those who fall victim to these events, it is worth acknowledging that these incidents are generally taken up by the criminal justice system and are often punished. However, many other forms of crime and harm, often emanating from the boardroom rather than the barroom, go unreported, undetected and unpunished. Although harm has a longer history within the field of criminology, the last two decades have seen a growth in zemiological analysis and theorisation.[75] Social harm acknowledged the limitations of 'crime' as a category and recognised that wider events, processes and actions that were entirely legal could still have harmful consequences for individuals, families, communities and entire societies.[76] This positive step opened a new direction for social research which has subsequently produced work in a range of areas including work and employment,[77] climate and environment,[78] borders,[79] fashion[80] and health and safety failures.[81]

---

[71] Kotzé (2018), Lloyd (2018), and Raymen (2019).
[72] Hillyard and Tombs (2004).
[73] Pemberton (2016).
[74] Hillyard and Tombs (2004).
[75] Canning and Tombs (2021).
[76] Pemberton (2016).
[77] Lloyd (2018) and Scott (2017).
[78] White and Heckenberg (2014).
[79] Canning (2018).
[80] Large (2018).
[81] Tombs (2014).

Various harm perspectives have sought to develop typologies of harm that allow us to see the various ways in which perfectly legal processes can have profoundly negative consequences. Paddy Hillyard and Steve Tombs[82] delineated 'physical harms', 'financial and economic harms', and 'emotional and psychological harms'. Simon Pemberton[83] sought to locate 'preventable harms' across varieties of capitalism and identified 'physical and mental health harms', 'autonomy harms' and 'relational harms'. Majid Yar,[84] grounding his harm framework in the concept of 'recognition', suggested that harms represented the loss of 'respect' at a macro-level where our rights are not recognised, 'esteem' at a meso level where we are not recognised through solidarity, social identity and cultural characteristics, and 'love' at the interpersonal level where we are not recognised by family, friends and partners. Each typology offers different ways to characterise and categorise social harm across a wide variety of examples.

Simon Pemberton has argued that neoliberalism represents the most harmful form of capitalist ideology and political economy, given the exacerbation of inequality in recent decades.[85] This would indicate that the world into which Covid-19 emerged was not only divided and unequal but profoundly harmful and damaging to individuals, families and communities. While we would not disagree with this assessment, it potentially does not paint a full picture and so this represents the point where our interpretation of social harm begins to deviate from the normative social harm frameworks at the centre of this new discipline. There are undoubtedly harms that happen to us which are the result of social processes and structures. These are not necessarily intentionally harmful but do have problematic consequences. For example, deindustrialisation and globalisation are both structural processes that some may argue have positive consequences but also have negative and harmful outcomes for others. The unintentional functioning of our social

[82] Hillyard and Tombs (2004).
[83] Pemberton (2016).
[84] Yar (2012).
[85] Pemberton (2016).

system can result in harm and this can be characterised as the *negative motivation to harm.*[86]

However, we feel that this only tells half of the story and doesn't adequately explain the positive motivation to harm; in other words, the *individual's willingness to inflict harm on others for expressive or instrumental gain.*[87] Harm does not emerge from growing inequality, rather inequality stems from a willingness to inflict harm on others.[88] There are *harms done to us* by unintentional processes but also *harms inflicted by us upon each other.* Accordingly, while most harm perspectives 'look up' at social structures and macro-level processes rather than 'down' at street-level events,[89] we adopt a more integrated approach that explores both systemic *and* singular harms.[90] That is to say, we look at the harm emanating from 'up there' in the corridors of power and 'down there' on the streets.[91] From this perspective we are able to account for both the negative and positive motivation to harm. By looking at both forms of motivation we can begin to highlight their connections and understand how they feed into each other to produce both legal and illegal harms. This more integrated approach towards the study of crime and harm is informed by an ultra-realist theoretical framework. While it is not possible for us to fully explore this here, it is worth outlining some of its main components.

Ultra-realist criminology is an emerging framework on the periphery of the discipline that has made some useful contributions in relation to understanding motivation and the causes of crime and harm.[92] At its core, ultra-realism rejects the standard interpretations of subjectivity in favour of Adrian Johnston's Žižek-Lacan inspired transcendental materialism. This rejects the belief that we are rational actors or subjects of socially constructed discourse and takes us back to our biological roots, albeit in a way that shows the real dynamism between our individual

---

[86] Hall and Winlow (2015).

[87] Lloyd (2020).

[88] Hall and Winlow (2015).

[89] Canning and Tombs (2021).

[90] Kotzé (2021).

[91] Hall and Winlow (2015).

[92] Ibid., Hall (2012), and Raymen and Kuldova (2021).

agency and social and symbolic structures. The subject is constituted through 'lack', a fundamental split at the unconscious level where we pass from a state of raw nature into a state of culture.

Think here of a new-born baby: she arrives in the world that already exists yet is psychologically unable to make sense of her surroundings. That baby is bombarded by a terrifying array of stimuli. In Lacanian terms, this represents 'the Real'; an unnameable, unsymbolised world experienced as trauma. The subject, in order to stave off this trauma, unconsciously *solicits* an external 'Symbolic Order', a network of values, signs, symbols and language that allows us to make sense of our surroundings. For it to be effective, that Symbolic Order must have a degree of consistency, it must tell us a story of the world that makes sense to us and our experience of it as we make our way through life. This Symbolic Order is inscribed in our neurological circuits and, effectively, rewires the neuronal receptors in our brains. Our material being is changed by the world around us. We then act in the world and have the agency to make choices and change and adapt to our surroundings.[93]

Different Symbolic Orders exist in different parts of the world and so each individual adapts to, and is shaped by, their surroundings. The 'lack' or split at the heart of the subject creates the desire that fuels us to act in the world, seeking the 'lost object' at the centre of our being. This creates a huge current of libidinal energy that can be directed in different ways, according to political-economic systems and ideologies. For Steve Hall,[94] Western society was pseudo-pacified over centuries, channelling libidinal energy away from brigandry, violence and predation and towards economic competition and market forces that culminated with the emergence and reproduction of capitalism. Since the second half of the twentieth century, aggressive competition has emerged in the field of consumer culture and our libidinal energy has been directed towards consumer choice. While not, as critics have suggested, a direct-expression theory of crime or an economically reductionist model,[95] ultra-realism connects the reality of daily life with what critical realists call the domain

[93] Ellis (2016).
[94] Hall (2012).
[95] Wood et al. (2020).

of 'the Real'. This is an intransitive realm of depth structures, such as ideology or political economy that can shape both our subjective situations and the choices we make at both a conscious and unconscious level.[96]

For *some* subjects in possession of 'special liberty', they feel emboldened to step beyond the boundaries and rules of our social order and act in the world to further their own expressive or instrumental ends.[97] In a culture of competitive individualism, standing out from the crowd, gaining an edge over others, displaying status and avoiding symbolic or cultural annihilation, some will do whatever it takes, including harming others. This further highlights the importance of acknowledging the interconnections between the negative and positive motivation to harm and reinforces the need to adopt a framework that allows us to make sense of both. We must account for the unintended consequences of the normal functioning of political economic systems, but we must also account for the willingness of individuals to inflict harm on others. At risk of oversimplifying the matter, this is what separates our harm framework from the normative social harm frameworks that occupy the centre of the discipline. Throughout this book we draw on this framework to make sense of our data, though at times we let the rich data speak for itself to illuminate the social harms generated by lockdowns.

In analysing lockdown and the potential harmful consequences of restrictive NPIs, we want to account for the unintentional consequences of policies designed ostensibly to keep us safe and limit viral transmission, but also the opportunities that lockdown presented to those who were willing to harm others for their own ends. In the pages that follow, we suggest that there is a probabilistic causal relationship between government restrictions and a number of unintended consequences, such as mental ill-health or unemployment. At the same time, we argue that the pandemic presented others with opportunities to flout laws and restrictions to further their own ends.

---

[96] Raymen and Kuldova (2021).
[97] Hall (2012), Lloyd (2020), and Tudor (2018).

A Note on Methods

The data presented here represents the findings from an international study of the pandemic in real time, starting in March 2020. Prior to the pandemic, all five of us were ethnographers by trade; our preferred method was to undertake in-depth qualitative research and immerse ourselves in communities, cultures and settings in order to gain rich understandings.[98] Given the restrictions of lockdown in our home countries (Spain and the UK), we were forced to adapt and utilise the tools at our disposal. The data presented here comes from the following:

- Desk-based analysis of literature, reports, commentaries and data
- Semi-structured online surveys

  o Phase 1—'lockdown'—985 responses from 59 countries
  o Phase 2—'new normal'—540 responses from 40 countries
  o Phase 3—'viral hiatus'—407 responses from 33 countries
  o Phase 4—'hindsight'—450 responses from 49 countries

- Over 200 hours of digital ethnography, primarily through interaction and debate in 10 different Covid-19 Facebook forums from around the world
- 59 open-ended interviews conducted via Zoom
- Traditional ethnography, when restrictions permitted (Fig. 1.1).

As the pandemic moved into different stages, we responded accordingly and published new surveys, returned to social media forums, and issued calls for interviews. We have deliberately maintained a flexible approach to this study so we could adapt as the pandemic progressed. For example, when UK restrictions eased in summer 2020, we were able to undertake some traditional 'offline' ethnography as we could leave our homes, but the imposition of the second and third national lockdowns curtailed this activity and we reverted online. The online nature of much of the research enabled us to cast a wide net and seek experiences and opinions of people from across the globe and allowed us to consider the ways in

---

[98] Briggs (2020), Ellis (2016), Lloyd (2018), Telford (2021), and Kotzé (2019).

Fig. 1.1 Majorca normally receives around 900 flights a day early season but had only four during the lockdowns (*Photo* Daniel Briggs)

which the pandemic and government responses affected countries and citizens in different ways. We knew that the UK or Spanish experience of lockdown would be divided between what Jennie Bristow and Emma Gilland called the 'Working from Home-City' and the 'Keeping Things Going-City',[99] the divide between those who worked from home and those 'key workers' on the front line. We also knew that the UK or Spanish experience would be different to the Indian, South African, American and Argentine experience.

As such, we were able to capture perspectives from a number of countries around the world and then situate that within our desk-based analysis of those countries, their official responses and how they compared with other parts of the world. In the pages that follow, we present experiences of lockdown and the pandemic from an IT worker

---

[99] Bristow and Gilland (2021).

in Brazil, a courier in the UK, an unemployed waitress from India, a reporter from Cameroon, an American council worker and many more. Of course, comparative analysis is difficult, but they all share a common theme; they have all been impacted in one way or another by the Covid-19 pandemic and by the response from public health officials, governments and their fellow citizens. We try to situate those experiences within a wider context and contemplate where and how government restrictions impact upon their lives. We then synthesise these myriad perspectives within the social harm framework outlined here to question the balance of harm presented in the decision to utilise a range of restrictive NPIs on populations across the world.

Outline

The remainder of the book proceeds as follows. Chapter 2 critically interrogates the decision to lockdown. Crucial for us is to discuss how lockdowns became the unquestionable go-to measure even though, prior to the pandemic, they were not recommended by the governing body on global health, the WHO. In this chapter, we also wanted to interrogate the apparent domino effect of lockdowns, how country after country, regardless of their political and social circumstances, adopted this particular measure as well as look at the few who didn't follow this pathway. In Chapter 3, we look at what happened to peoples' conception of becoming ill and potentially dying of Covid-19. As countries around the world went into lockdown, we became reliant on continual media coverage and watched the viral tragedy unravel live even to the point that we were updated on every 'new case' as well as 'Covid-19 fatality'. Here we look at what this did to our conceptions of illness and mortality.

When we went into lockdown, whole economies and industries ground to a halt. The generally privileged continued about their business working from home online while precarious networks, people caught up in the informal labour sector as well as more disadvantaged and poorer groups inevitably lost out. At the same time, under lockdowns, our freedom to consume, spend and indulge was physically reduced. Instead, we relied on the digital world for these elements and in doing so contributed to the substantial wealth increase of powerful big tech companies such as Amazon and Netflix. Simultaneously, while we were being entertained and occupied by the online world, big pharma companies were mobilising quickly to capitalise on the new business providing public health material and possible vaccinations. Chapters 4 and 5 therefore, respectively, chart the people who 'lost' from the pandemic and those who 'won' or benefitted from its inception.

Chapter 6 considers how lockdowns specifically impacted Western countries and charts the inevitable division between groups who were able to continue generally economically and socially unaffected by lockdowns vs the experience of those working in frontline industries like supermarkets and health and social care. Here we make the point that the management of Covid-19 inevitably became part of particular agendas which, in turn, played a part in how it was managed in particular Western countries. Importantly, we show how government and mainstream media passed down the responsibility of this management to individual citizens and here is where we explore the aetiology of the social division and tension we now experience. For when we combine this with the ideological bombardment of public health messages, dis- and misinformation about the virus and an obsessive 24-h news reporting, the foundations were laid for societal divisions and tensions in the 'new normal'.

Chapter 7 takes a closer examination of how the lockdowns impacted the elderly and vulnerable—social groups whom governments wagered to protect as the virus spread across the world. The elderly were scared to approach hospitals for fear of infection, the disabled lost important network support while those in adult residential care homes were deprived of visits and their routines were disrupted which generally condemned them to either an early death or a miserable time before their inevitable death. While the virus clearly contributed to the death of some of these people, governments failed to protect people in care homes and we show how a lack of Personal Protective Equipment (PPE) and poor strategies to quell virus transmission also played a part in the demise of care home residents.

Chapter 8 considers how lockdowns impacted socially-forgotten groups such as prisoners, youth detainees and asylum seekers. We show

how, prior to the pandemic, these groups were already living in some kind of detention yet the lockdowns perpetuated their cell time, cut off their support and family networks and instead amplified their mental ill-health, leading some to self-harm and commit suicide. By similar measure, Chapter 9 continues to examine social groups bereft of support such as migrant workers, refugees, stateless citizens and the homeless—people who had no home to go to, no network to rely on and no element of support. When countries closed their borders and key services shut their doors, these transient groups were literally locked out.

Chapter 10 unravels important questions about if and how people were compliant with the restrictions and, if not, why? In doing so, we draw on empirical data but also consider the limited nature of research on psychological compliance to/refusal of Covid-related public health measures. We also address the issue of compliance with imposed public health restrictions and in particular what we describe as the *dichotomy of lockdowns* that appear to have split populations along lines of supposed 'compliers' and 'non-compliers'. Far from being something attributable to someone's moral outlook or psychological make up, we show how compliance was related to the continual effective deployment of ideological messaging bolstered by changes to the physical spaces to augment a sense of risk and imminent threat. On the other hand, we posit that over the course of the pandemic, in many countries, the general erosion of adherence to public health guidelines was related to:

- acting out of subjective narcissistic tendencies which trumped other social efforts to form solidarity;
- over-availability of conflicting information about the virus and its severity;
- attribution of the virus and its origins to planned 'conspiracy theories' about the remodelling of society;
- oversaturated exposure to political messaging, media fearmongering and elite special-liberty practicing, which reduced the credibility of the rationale for the measures;
- realisation—either through personal experience or through Internet research—that the virus was not as dangerous as had been indicated by governments;

- a deep-rooted subjective desire many people possessed to return to a pre-covid normal and all its consumer delights;
- reasoning that life, work, families and relationships were more important.

In Chapter 11, we discuss the residue left from lockdowns and how they have had a profound impact on society, marked by the amplification of social divisions. On the one hand, it has left some people completely dejected, distrusting of politics, and frustrated while, on the other, it has moulded others into over-cautious nervous wrecks. It has also further polarised the rich and the poor, the elite from the expanding poorer classes and precarious workers, and the digitally included from the digitally excluded. On all levels, the use of lockdowns and other public health measures have left indelible scars which, in Chapter 12, we posit are, as we write, redefining social life as we know it and creating a very different future.

References

Abassi, K. (2020). COVID-19: Politicisation, "corruption", and suppression of science. *British Medical Journal, 371,* 1–2. https://doi.org/10.1136/bmj.m4425

Arshed, N., Meo, M., & Farooq, F. (2020). Empirical assessment of government policies and flattening of the COVID19 curve. *Journal of Public Affairs 20*(4), e2333. https://dx.doi.org/10.1002%2Fpa.2333

Assouad, L., Chancel, L., & Morgan, M. (2018). Extreme inequality: Evidence from Brazil, India, the Middle East, and South Africa. *AEA Papers and Proceedings, 108,* 119–123. https://www.aeaweb.org/articles?id=10.1257/pandp.20181076

Badiou, A. (2012). *The rebirth of history.* Verso.

Blakeley, G. (2020). *The Corona crash.* Verso.

Blundell, R., Joyce, R., Keiller, A. N., & Ziliak, J. P. (2018). Income inequality and the labour market in Britain and the US. *Journal of Public Economics, 162,* 48–62. https://doi.org/10.1016/j.jpubeco.2018.04.001

Briggs, D., & Gamero, R. M. (2017). *Dead-end lives.* Policy Press.

Briggs, D. (2020). *Climate changed: Refugee border stories and the business of misery*. Routledge.

Briggs, D., Ellis, A., Lloyd, A., & Telford, L. (2021). *Researching the COVID-19 pandemic: A critical blueprint for the social sciences*. Policy Press Rapid Response Series.

Briggs, D., Ellis, A., Lloyd, A., & Telford, L. (2020). New hopes or old futures in disguise? Neoliberalism, the Covid-19 pandemic and the possibility of social change. *International Journal of Sociology and Social Policy, 40*(9/10), 831–848. https://doi.org/10.1108/IJSSP-07-2020-0268

Bristow, J., & Gilland, E. (2021). *The Corona generation*. Zero.

Buck, H. J. (2019). *After geoengineering*. Verso.

Canning, V. (2018). Zemiology at the border. In A. Boukli, & J. Kotzé (Eds.), *Zemiology: Reconnecting crime and social harm*. Palgrave Macmillan.

Canning, V., & Tombs, S. (2021). *From social harm to zemiology: A critical introduction*. Routledge.

Case, A., & Deaton, A. (2020). *Deaths of despair and the future of capitalism*. Princeton University Press.

Chan, J. (2013). A suicide survivor: The life of a Chinese worker. *New Technology, Work and Employment, 28*(2), 84–99. https://doi.org/10.1111/ntwe.12007

Chen, S. (2020, December 24). *China has a huge wealth-gap problem—And it's getting worse*. Bloomberg. https://www.bloomberg.com/news/storythreads/2020-12-24/china-has-a-huge-wealth-gap-problem-and-it-s-getting-worse

Dorling, D. (2015). *Inequality and the 1%*. Verso.

Ellis, A., Briggs, D., Lloyd, A., & Telford, L. (2021). A ticking time bomb of future harm: Lockdown, child abuse and future violence. *Abuse: An International Journal, 2*(1). https://doi.org/10.37576/abuse.2021.017

Ellis, A. (2016). *Men, masculinities and violence*. Routledge.

Fisher, M. (2009). *Capitalist realism: Is there no alternative?* Zero.

Flaxman, S., Mishra, S., Gandy, A., Unwin, H. J. T., Mellan, T. A., Coupland, H., & Bhatt, S. (2020). Estimating the effects of non-pharmaceutical interventions on COVID-19 in Europe. *Nature, 584*, 257–261. https://doi.org/10.1038/s41586-020-2405-7

Fukuyama, F. (1992). *The end of history and the last man*. The Free Press.

Gover, A. R., Harper, S. B., & Langton, L. (2020). Anti-Asian hate crime during the COVID-19 pandemic: Exploring the reproduction of inequality. *American Journal of Criminal Justice 45*, 647–667. https://link.springer.com/content/pdf/10.1007/s12103-020-09545-1.pdf

Grierson, J. (2021, May 16). Fake COVID vaccine and test certificate market is growing, researchers say. *The Guardian*. https://www.theguardian.com/world/2021/may/16/fake-covid-vaccine-and-test-certificate-market-is-gro wing-researchers-say

Hall, S., Winlow, S., & Ancrum, C. (2008). *Criminal identities and consumer culture*. Willan.

Hall, S., & Winlow, S. (2015). *Revitalizing criminological theory: Towards a New ultra- realism*. Routledge.

Hall, P. A., & Soskice, D. (2001). *Varieties of capitalism*. Oxford University Press.

Hall, S. (2012). *Theorizing crime and deviance*. Sage.

Harvey, D. (2010). *The enigma of capital*. Profile.

Harvey, D. (2005). *A brief history of neoliberalism*. Oxford University Press.

Hazeldine, T. (2020). *The Northern question*. Verso.

Hillyard, P., & Tombs, S. (2004). Beyond criminology? In P. Hillyard, C. Pantazis, S. Tombs, & D. Gordon (Eds.), *Beyond criminology: Taking harm seriously*. Pluto Press.

Honigsbaum, M. (2020). *The pandemic century: A history of global contagion from the Spanish Flu to COVID-19*. Penguin.

Jain-Chandra, M. S., Khor, N., Mano, R., Schauer, J., Wingender, M. P., & Zhuang, J. (2018). *Inequality in China: Trends, drivers and policy remedies* (IMF Working Paper. WP/18/127).

Jetten, J., Mols, F., & Selvanthan, H. P. (2020). How economic inequality fuels the rise and persistence of the yellow vest movement. *International Review of Social Psychology, 33*(1), 1–12. https://doi.org/10.5334/irsp.356

Jinnah, Z. (2017). Silence and invisibility: Exploring labour strategies of Zimbabwean farm workers in Musina, South Africa. *South African Review of Sociology, 48*(3), 46–63.

Killgore, W. D. S., Cloonan, S. A., Taylor, E. C., Miller, M. A., & Dailey, N. S. (2020). Three months of loneliness during the COVID-19 lockdown. *Psychiatry Research, 293*, 113392. https://doi.org/10.1016/j.psychres.2020.113392

Klein, N. (2014). *This changes everything: Capitalism vs the climate*. Allen Lane.

Kotzé, J. (2018). Criminology or zemiology? Yes, please! on the refusal of choice between false alternatives. In A. Boukli & Kotzé, J. (Eds.), *Zemiology: Reconnecting crime and social harm*. Palgrave Macmillan.

Kotzé, J. (2020). The commodification of abstinence. In S. Hall, T. Kuldova, & M. Horsley (Eds.), *Crime, harm and consumerism*. Routledge.

Kotzé, J. (2021). On researching harm: An ultra-realist perspective. In P. Davies, P. Leighton, & T. Wyatt (Eds.), *The Palgrave handbook of social harm*. Palgrave Macmillan.

Kotzé, J. (2019). *The myth of the 'crime decline.'* Routledge.

Lapavitsas, C. (2019). *The left case against the EU*. Polity.

Large, J. (2018). Spot the fashion victim(s): The importance of rethinking harm within the context of fashion counterfeiting. A. Boukli & J. Kotzé (Eds.), *Zemiology: Reconnecting crime and social harm*. Palgrave Macmillan.

Liu, M., & Tsai, K. S. (2020). Structural power, hegemony and state capitalism: Limits to China's global economic power. *Politics and Society, 49*(2), 235–267. https://doi.org/10.1177/0032329220950234

Lloyd, A. (2018). *The Harms of work*. Bristol University Press.

Lloyd, A. (2013). *Labour markets and identity on the post-industrial assembly line*. Ashgate.

Lloyd, A. (2020). Harm at work: Special liberty and bullying in the retail sector. *Critical Criminology, 28*(4), 669–683. https://doi.org/10.1007/s10612-019-09445-9

Lloyd, A., Devanney, C., Wattis, L., & Bell, V. (2021). "Just tensions left, right and centre": Assessing the social impact of international migration on deindustrialised locale. *Ethnic and Racial Studies, 44*(15), 2794–2815. https://doi.org/10.1080/01419870.2020.1854813

Manduca, R. A. (2019). The contribution of national income inequality to regional economic divergence. *Social Forces, 98*(2), 622–648. https://doi.org/10.1093/sf/soz013

Milkman, R. (2020). *Immigrant labor and the new precariat*. Polity.

Mitchell, W., & Fazi, T. (2017). *Reclaiming the state*. Pluto.

Nagle, A. (2017). *Kill all normies*. Zero.

O'Hara, M. (2014). *Austerity bites*. Policy Press.

Parenti, C. (2011). *Tropic of chaos: Climate change and the new geography of violence*. Basic Books.

Pemberton, S. (2016). *Harmful societies*. Policy Press.

Pietrykowski, B. (2017). Revaluing low-wage work: Service-sector skills and the fight for 15. *Review of Radical Political Economics, 49*(1), 5–29. https://doi.org/10.1177/0486613416666543

Piketty, T. (2014). *Capital in the twenty-first century*. Belknap.

Pitron, G. (2020). *The rare metals war*. Scribe.

Quinones, S. (2016). *Dreamland*. Bloomsbury.

Raymen, T., & Kuldova, T. (2021). Clarifying ultra-realism. *Continental Thought and Theory, 3*(2). http://doi.org/10.26021/10709

Raymen, T. (2019). The Enigma of social harm and the barrier of liberalism: Why zemiology needs a theory of the good. *Justice, Power and Resistance, 3*(1), 134–163.

Schwab, K., & Malleret, T. (2020). *COVID 19: The great reset*. World Economic Forum.

Schwab, K. (2017). *The fourth industrial revolution*. Penguin.

Scott, S. (2017). *Labour exploitation and work-based harm*. Policy Press.

Scott, S., McGowan, V. J., & Visram, S. (2021). 'I'm gonna tell you about how Mrs Rona has affected me': Exploring young people's experiences of the Covid-19 pandemic in North East England: A qualitative diary-based study. *International Journal of Environmental Research and Public Health, 18*, 3837. https://doi.org/10.3390/ijerph18073837

Sediri, S., Zgueb, Y., Ouanes, S., Ouali, U., Bourgou, S., Jomli, R., & Nacef, F. (2020). Women's mental health: Acute impact of COVID-19 pandemic on domestic violence. *Archives of Women's Mental Health, 23*, 749–756. https://doi.org/10.1007/s00737-020-01082-4

Silva, J. (2019). *We're still here*. Oxford University Press.

Singhari, S., & Madheswaran, S. (2017). Wage structure and wage differentials in formal and informal sectors in India. *The Indian Journal of Labour Economics, 60*, 389–414. https://doi.org/10.1007/s41027-018-0110-y

Slobodian, Q. (2019). *Globalists*. Harvard University Press.

Smart, B. (2010). *Consumer society*. Sage.

Smith, O. (2019). Luxury, tourism and harm: A deviant leisure perspective. In T. Raymen & O. Smith (Eds.), *Deviant leisure: Criminological perspectives on leisure and harm*. Palgrave Macmillan.

So, A. Y. (2019). The rise of authoritarianism in China in the early 21st century. *International Review of Modern Sociology, 45*(1), 49–70.

Standing, G. (2011). *The precariat*. Bloomsbury.

Streeck, W. (2016). *How will capitalism end?* Verso.

Taylor, M., Watts, J., & Bartlett, J. (2019, September 27). Climate crisis: 6 million people join latest wave of global protests. *The Guardian*. https://www.theguardian.com/environment/2019/sep/27/climate-crisis-6-million-people-join-latest-wave-of-worldwide-protests

Telford, L. (2021). 'There is nothing there': Deindustrialization and loss in a coastal town. *Competition & Change*. Online First. https://doi.org/10.1177/10245294211011300

Tombs, S. (2014). Health and safety 'crimes' in Britain: The great disappearing act. In P. Davies, P. Francis, & T. Wyatt (Eds.), *Invisible crimes and social harms*. Palgrave Macmillan.

Tudor, K. (2018). Toxic sovereignty: Understanding fraud as the expression of special liberty within late-capitalism. *Journal of Extreme Anthropology, 2*(2), 7–21. https://doi.org/10.5617/jea.6476

UNODC. (2016). *Global report on trafficking in persons 2016*. United Nations Publication.

Varoufakis, Y. (2013). *The global minotaur*. Zeb Books.

White, R. (2013). *Environmental harm*. Policy Press.

White, R. D., & Heckenberg, D. (2014). *Green criminology: An introduction to the study of environmental harm*. Routledge.

Wilkinson, R., & Pickett, K. (2009). *The spirit level*. Penguin.

Winlow, S., Hall, S., & Treadwell, J. (2017). *The rise of the right*. Policy Press.

Winlow, S., Hall, S., Treadwell, J., & Briggs, D. (2015). *Riots and political protest*. Routledge.

Wood, M., Anderson, B., & Richards, I. (2020). Breaking down the pseudo-pacification process: Eight critiques of ultra-realist crime causation theory. *British Journal of Criminology, 60*(3), 642–661. https://doi.org/10.1093/bjc/azz069

World Health Organization. (2020). *WHO characterises Covid-19 as a pandemic*. https://www.who.int/emergencies/diseases/novel-coronavirus-2019/events-as-they-happen

Yar, M. (2012). *Critical criminology, critical theory and social harm*. In S. Hall & S. Winlow (Eds.), *New directions in criminological theory*. Routledge.

Zizek, S. (2021). *Pandemic 2: Chronicles of a lost time*. Polity.

2

To Lockdown or Not to Lockdown? That Is the Question

Pandemics have erupted at various points throughout history, causing the tragic loss of life, multidimensional social disruption and economic chaos. The twentieth century has been branded the pandemic century,[1] with arguably one of history's most severe pandemics emerging in the final stages of World War I—the 1918–1919 Spanish flu. Widely held to have originated in a USA army camp, conditions during the war were conducive to rapid human-to-human transmission including over-crowding, relative impoverishment, a lack of sanitation and poor public health standards.[2] As a result, the virus quickly spread across the world and was estimated to have caused around 40 million deaths.[3] Indeed, the public were first informed about the virus through a newspaper in Madrid, Spain, which is why it was dubbed the Spanish flu.[4] Perhaps a more recent pandemic that is etched into popular consciousness is the 2009–2010 swine flu pandemic. First reported in Mexico, the virus

---

[1] Honigsbaum (2020).

[2] Ibid.

[3] Hilton and Hunt (2011).

[4] Liang et al. (2021).

© The Author(s), under exclusive license to Springer Nature
Switzerland AG 2021
D. Briggs et al., *Lockdown*,
https://doi.org/10.1007/978-3-030-88825-1_2

spread across much of the globe and infected hundreds of thousands of people.[5]

Perhaps it should be no surprise then that members of the WHO, including many countries across Africa, the Americas, Asia, Europe and the Western Pacific, had been preparing for pandemics for nearly thirty years before Covid-19 emerged.[6] In 2005, the WHO released international guidelines on how to curb transmission, reduce fatalities and prevent health systems from being overburdened with excess demand during viral pandemics, with hand washing, social distancing and self-isolating when one has contracted the virus all recommended.[7] There was no mention of national lockdowns.[8] Other international bodies like the EU have continued to warn about the potential of a global pandemic in the years since. Therefore, the well-trodden governmental notion that the Covid-19 pandemic embodied an unprecedented situation is not necessarily true. Nevertheless, with the rapid spread of Covid-19 across the world's seven continents including Asia, the South Pacific, Europe and the Americas, fear and panic enveloped much of the globe, with many nation states' news media reporting a daily update of 'cases', 'hospitalisations' and 'fatalities'.[9]

As mentioned, according to various thinkers, the world into which the Covid-19 pandemic emerged was one governed by the cold logic of capitalist realism: it was easier to imagine the end of the world than the end of capitalism.[10] Indeed, many people across the globe had stopped believing in the possibility of fundamental social change. However, as Žižek outlined, the Covid-19 pandemic transiently shattered the widespread sense that everything will continue to stay the same.[11] Unprecedented and unimaginable transformations were implemented as

---

[5] Hilton and Hunt (2011).
[6] Jones and Hemeiri (2021).
[7] See WHO (2005).
[8] Dodsworth (2021).
[9] Zizek (2021).
[10] Fisher (2009) and Telford and Briggs (2021).
[11] Zizek (2020).

the "*scale of the health and economic crisis*" forced "*neoliberal governments into mass intervention across the sectors of health and the economy*".[12] One of the main interventions was the use of lockdowns.

Lockdowns

There has been some geographical variation in States' responses to Covid-19. Some nations, like the USA and UK, initially delayed lockdowns in an effort to achieve immunisation,[13] but quickly shifted course. For example, on 19 March 2020, the New York governor Andrew Cuomo said he would not impose a lockdown on his State yet the next day did precisely that. Others such as India rapidly closed international borders and restricted domestic movement. Nonetheless, restrictive NPIs in the form of both national and regional lockdown measures have been used by many governments to reduce the spread of Covid-19. As Haider and colleagues outline, the definition of a lockdown is ambiguous, with some states referring to 'soft', 'hard', 'partial' and 'total' lockdowns. Haider and colleagues define lockdown as:

> A set of measures aimed at reducing transmission of COVID-19 that are mandatory, applied indiscriminately to a general population and involve some restrictions on the established pattern of social and economic life.[14]

Such measures include stay at home orders and thereby working from home where possible, avoiding unnecessary travel, prohibitions on social gatherings and the closure of non-essential stores like cinemas, restaurants, sports venues, pubs, as well as educational institutions.[15] These measures have been implemented across the world including in the USA, Honduras, Canada, UK, Belgium, Germany, Italy, India, Saudi Arabia, China, as well as in many African countries like South Africa, Uganda

---

[12] Reiner (2021, p. 154).
[13] Arshed et al. (2020).
[14] Haider et al. (2020, p. 2).
[15] Ibid.

and Ghana.[16] In January 2020, Hubei province in China became the
first region in the world to be locked down, then in March 2020 the
Italian government implemented a nationwide lockdown, followed by
many other countries like New Zealand and Croatia.

Yet lockdowns weren't the only surprise. The use of face masks was
originally discouraged by many governments such as Britain and the
USA. In fact, the Conservative government in Britain claimed their
efficacy in restricting the spread of Covid-19 was relatively limited,[17]
while the chief medical advisor to the USA's president, Dr Anthony
Fauci, suggested in March 2020 that their efficacy in slowing transmission was not clear and therefore not recommended.[18] Despite this, their
usage became commonplace in countries that enacted lockdowns. For
instance, Spain and Greece made face masks mandatory in both indoor
and outdoor public spaces, whereas in New Zealand they have been
(occasionally) mandatory on public transport (Fig. 2.1).

These restrictions placed upon civil life have been applied at different
degrees of intensity across the world since January 2020.[19] Given the
magnitude of lockdowns, and how they fundamentally restructure social
life, as well as the relationship between the state and its citizens, their efficacy and inadvertent harms ought to be debated and critiqued. However,
as we have recently highlighted,[20] so far, they have received little critical
attention within academia, politics and the media, with most mainstream
commentators simply content to regurgitate the global rhetoric of 'Stay
at Home, Protect the Health Service, Save Lives'.[21] As documented, this
has played out in a hostile political climate characterised by historic
socio-cultural divisions.[22] Emblematic of this are slandering terms like
'Covid-deniers', 'Cov-idiots' or 'Corona-clowns', which regularly appear
on social media. Such language is perhaps occasionally rightfully utilised
to describe those who espouse conspiracies about the pandemic, not least

[16] Ibid.
[17] Gov (2020).
[18] Dodsworth (2021).
[19] Briggs et al. (2021).
[20] Ibid.
[21] Miles et al. (2021, p. 1).
[22] Telford and Wistow (2020) and Winlow et al. (2017).

Fig. 2.1 A man is determined to conform to UK lockdown regulations when dining-in was prohibited (*Photo* Luke Telford)

that it is a global hoax (Chapter 6).[23] However, such terms are often used to refer to those who question the efficacy of lockdowns and their accompanying restrictions, thereby stifling important debate.[24]

Advocates of lockdown measures often provide various rationales for their usage. Indeed, Imperial College London's scientific research team published a *non-peer reviewed* article in March 2020 that provided

---

[23] Gruzd and Mai (2020).
[24] Dodsworth (2021) and Reiss and Bhakdi (2020).

the impetus for the UK lockdown.[25] They offer two ways to reduce virus transmission—suppression and mitigation, though they suggest that because of the rapid transmission of Covid-19, focusing solely on the latter would likely lead to healthcare services being overwhelmed. Therefore, they claimed that it is essential to implement various suppression measures—like lockdowns—to stem the virus and reduce fatalities. As Dodsworth and Gastroenterol highlight,[26] many policymakers and healthcare institutions across the world have occasionally sought to utilise the paper's findings to provide legitimacy for their lockdowns. However, utilising this across different contexts is potentially reductionist as it ignores each nation's healthcare capacity, the amount of intensive care beds available, and the general population's health and well-being, including the prevalence of underlying health conditions like type 2 diabetes and obesity, which would normally put an individual at increased risk of harm from Covid-19. Similar scientific advice was given by the Robert Koch Institute in Germany, which advises the German government. President of the institute, Professor Lothar Wieler, advocated the use of lockdowns to save lives, since without them he claimed that 'deaths would spiral out of control'.[27] Such forecasting was also prevalent in other countries such as South Africa, France and Switzerland.[28]

Throughout history, various NPIs like social distancing have been used by governments to try and curtail the spread of a disease. However, lockdowns *"as a public health measure of prevention and control is new in the arsenal of response"*,[29] having never been previously implemented before 2020. Ultimately, billions of people were told to stay indoors, usual routines were suspended as were several other factors of everyday life. Some advocates suggest that lockdowns cannot be imposed indefinitely; rather, they offer a transient means to dwindle transmission and lower the peak/curve of the pandemic.[30] Similarly, other proponents claim they

---

[25] Ferguson et al. (2020).

[26] Gastroenterol (2020).

[27] Reiss and Bhakdi (2020).

[28] Muller (2021) and Warren et al. (2021).

[29] Sarwal and Sarwal (2020, p. 1).

[30] Ibid.

significantly reduce transmission of Covid-19, thereby helping to contain R (reproduction number of the virus) to less than 1 and help prevent deaths associated with the disease.[31] Quite understandably, some advocated their usage at the start of the pandemic, suggesting that it was an unfortunate, but necessary, measure as scientists and governments did not know much about the disease and possessed no treatment or vaccine.

However, this was accompanied with the recommendation that they ought to be lifted when a State develops the capacity to test and contact trace on a mass scale.[32] Other arguments for lockdown include appealing to the peoples' altruism, suggesting that it is for the public good with the potential harm of not locking down far outweighing the impingement on liberties and life.[33] This provokes us to think that we should therefore do our utmost to protect the lives of others, most notably the elderly and those with underlying health conditions who are by far the most at-risk groups, by staying at home and thus reducing human contact.

However, many scientists have problematised the rationales for lockdowns. Chin and colleagues outlined how the scientific modelling utilised by research teams to provide legitimacy for lockdowns is sensitive to researcher assumptions and the data used, meaning it is not rigorous science and "highly misleading".[34] While they suggest lockdowns may have some impact on reducing the infection rate, it is difficult to isolate their impact from other public health measures like social distancing and hand washing. Some lockdown opponents suggest that forecast modelling is not reliable, often based on faulty assumptions, high sensitivity to data estimates, a lack of transparency and often the omission of contextual factors such as healthcare capacity.[35] Problems have overshadowed forecast models for some time; for instance, some scientific models predicted upwards of 65,000 deaths from the 2009 UK swine flu pandemic, yet the actual death toll was 457. It is therefore surprising that such models have maintained credibility among many governments. Relatedly, others highlight how it is impossible to separate the impact of

---

[31] Flaxman et al. (2020).
[32] Melnick and Ioannidis (2020).
[33] Barry and Lazar (2020).
[34] Chin et al. (2020).
[35] Ioannidis et al. (2020).

lockdowns from other interventions, claiming it is possible that a lengthy public events ban may have a similar impact to lockdowns on reducing transmission of Covid-19.[36]

Other scientists suggest lockdowns may have some impact on curtailing transmission, though they are not the core variable in shaping a country's infection and mortality rates.[37] Instead, *the central issue is a nation's social, cultural, and economic conditions.* Statistical analysis of the 50 countries, including China and the USA, with the highest rates of Covid-19 infections by May 2020 ascertained that those nations with a higher median age of the population, higher amount of elderly people and prevalence of obesity possessed a higher number of Covid-19 cases.[38] This was a disease which was killing the elderly and the vulnerable. Other work in the USA claimed that racial and income inequalities are important factors, since locales like Detroit, which contain a high percentage of impoverished people, have high rates of Covid-19 infections and deaths.[39] Bambra and colleagues documented how inequalities are embedded in Covid-19 cases and deaths. Essentially, locales across Europe and the USA that possess high levels of socio-economic deprivation, unemployment and problematic drug use tend to have significantly more health problems like diabetes, cancer, obesity and smoking than more affluent areas, thereby making the local population more susceptible to the disease.[40] Some scholars have pointed to the role of weather conditions, claiming it is an *"established fact that respiratory infections are more frequent during cold and low humidity conditions"*.[41] Indeed, through analysis they ascertained those nations with the highest temperatures and lowest humidity including Iran, Mexico and Ghana tended to have far fewer cases and deaths in comparison with other countries like the USA and Russia that possess low temperatures but high humidity.

Nations across the world, such as Italy and Russia, which had implemented austerity measures in the years preceding the pandemic, were

---

[36] Soltesz et al. (2020).
[37] Chaudhry et al. (2020).
[38] Ibid.
[39] Yu et al. (2021).
[40] Bambra et al. (2020).
[41] Meo et al. (2020).

also left underprepared to deal with Covid-19.[42] At the start of the pandemic, images of overcrowded hospital corridors and people on ventilators in Italian hospitals were displayed across the world's news channels, understandably engendering significant fear about the virus and providing more legitimacy for national lockdowns.[43] However, Italy's austerity history had resulted in the hollowing out of its healthcare capacity, meaning it had proportionally far fewer beds in intensive care than its European neighbours and thus reducing its capability to deal with excess demand.[44] Italy also has one of the highest smoking rates in Europe, making more people susceptible to respiratory diseases such as Covid-19. Indeed, these important contextual conditions were absent from debate in both politics and the media. In Russia, the media typically offered headlines like 'heaps of coffins', 'overloaded crematoriums' and the 'spacemen-like' masks worn by medical staff in hospitals,[45] rather than explaining how austerity had detrimentally impacted upon its health service. Indeed, with regard to Covid-19 cases and deaths, both nations have fared among the worst in the world.

Many governments across the globe also rallied around the notion that they were 'following the science', with the media often referring to a few select 'experts' and 'advisors'.[46] However, scholars have outlined how this is a gross over-simplification because one characteristic of the start of a pandemic is that there is very little knowledge about a virus's severity. Relying on one argument, one interpretation or one diagnosis also masks conflicting evidence and hides the fact that science is not a monolithic entity without disputes.[47] Perhaps the most significant example of this is The Great Barrington Declaration (GBD). Led by Professors at Stanford, Oxford and Harvard Universities, and signed by prestigious scientists and medical experts from across the world, the declaration was published in October 2020. Essentially, signatories of the act claim that the bulk of

---

[42] Ehnts and Paetz (2021) and Jones and Hemeiri (2021).
[43] Reiss and Bhakdi (2020).
[44] Briggs et al. (2021).
[45] Sharov (2020).
[46] Abassi (2020), Briggs et al. (2021), Muller (2021), Reiss and Bhakdi (2020), and Warren et al. (2021).
[47] Abassi 2020) and Warren et al. (2021).

those who have died from Covid-19 are people in the latter stages of their life with underlying health conditions, while those aged under 70 possess an infection survival rate of 99.95%.[48] Indeed, at the time of writing this book over the summer of 2021, the average global infection death rate was 0.15%.[49] Therefore, one could argue that the core governmental response across the globe—lockdown—was not proportionate to the potential harm of the disease. Instead, governments had the option to implement 'focused protection' of the most vulnerable social groups such as the elderly, which would involve temporary accommodation for older people in multi-generational housing, restricting staff rotations in care homes and providing home food deliveries for those who are shielding. Nonetheless, the GBD received little political and media attention, with a proponent of the act being labelled as an 'exorcist' and 'mass murderer' by other scientists.[50]

It is also important to note that not all countries implemented lockdowns and mandatory face masks, with Sweden being the most prominent example. Historically, the Swedish have possessed high levels of trust and faith in the government, thus the State believes that public health measures should be built on trust rather than control and punishment.[51] While Sweden didn't adopt lockdowns, they instead adhered to the WHO's pandemic preparedness plan[52] and thereby implemented some restrictive mechanisms including social distancing, limitations on social gatherings—such as a maximum of eight guests at a restaurant table—and recommendations to work from home, though 'non-essential stores' like gyms and hairdressers remained open. The country possesses a high death rate among the elderly, in part because the early mass testing and trace system was delayed for several months. However, while the country has a proportionally worse death rate than its Nordic counterparts like Finland and Iceland[53] (neither of which implemented national lockdowns), regarding deaths per 100,000 persons, Sweden has not fared

---

[48] Bhattacharya et al. (2020).
[49] Dodsworth (2021).
[50] Kulldorff (2021).
[51] Baral et al. (2021) and Josefsson (2021).
[52] Baral et al. (2021).
[53] Claeson and Hanson (2021).

as badly as Spain, Belgium and the UK who all implemented hard lock-downs and the use of face masks.[54] Like other European nations, though, deaths from Covid-19 in Sweden are much higher among those who are socio-economically deprived and who often live in overcrowded spaces.[55]

South Korea also avoided a lockdown. Buoyed by their poor handling of the MERS virus in 2015, the government reversed some of the neoliberal trends in healthcare and brought much of their health system under state control, investing heavily and building up capacity.[56] There-fore, unlike other nations that had implemented austerity, South Korea had an abundance of PPE for workers and citizens, particularly N95 masks rather than the disposable fabric masks, providing more protection against Covid-19. The State also initiated a nationwide screening proce-dure for employees in care homes, enforced social distancing, prohibited gatherings of more than 10 individuals and made masks on public trans-port mandatory.[57] The nation's response has been hailed by some because it has managed to significantly slow down transmission and thereby reduce fatalities while avoiding the collateral damage produced by lock-downs. Indeed, at the time of writing, the nation possessed 151,506 cases and 2,004 deaths from Covid-19. Perhaps this gives some credence to one of the founders of the GBD who recently claimed that lockdowns are the "*single biggest public health mistake in history*", not least because they inadvertently generate multifaceted social distress which is largely absent from countries like Sweden and South Korea which avoided lock-downs.[58] While not ignoring the potential risks posed by the virus, it is the inadvertent harms of lockdown that this book is primarily concerned with and to which we now turn our attention.

---

[54] Josefsson (2021).
[55] Baral et al. (2021).
[56] Jones and Hemeiri (2021).
[57] Chen et al. (2021).
[58] Southworth (2021).

Lockdowns: Collateral Damage

As our data reveals, the unintentional harms of lockdowns are vast and encompass rising unemployment, mental health problems, domestic violence/abuse and the intensification of social inequalities like the educational attainment and income gap between the rich and poor. The Organization for Economic Cooperation and Development (OECD) recently reported that joblessness is rising across much of the world and will stay high well into 2021. In June 2021, the unemployment rate in Spain stood at 15.6%, Turkey 13.4%, Italy 10.5%, Latvia 8% and France, 7%[59]; indeed, in the OECD area the overall unemployment level stood at 6.7%, 1.4% higher than the pre-pandemic rate.[60] Therefore, the impact of the lockdowns on unemployment is geographically variegated and often shaped by each government's financial support packages such as furlough schemes and the economic assistance available through the welfare state.[61] In Spain, Germany, France and South Africa, among other countries, the government offered social and economic support amounting to billions to businesses and self-employed individuals,[62] while in impoverished nations like Zambia and Sierra Leone, governmental support was often absent,[63] thus intensifying already high levels of joblessness.

Recent research highlights how unemployment has increased in South Asia, particularly in Bangladesh, India, Nepal and Pakistan since their economies are heavily reliant upon the agricultural industry which has been hit hard by the lockdowns (see Chapter 9).[64] In Bangladesh, the agricultural, industrial, service, and educational sectors were heavily hit by the lockdown, with unemployment and the accompanied social despair increasing.[65] While in Pakistan, over 12 million people are set to lose their jobs because of the lockdown, intensifying poverty, household

---

[59] Statista (2021).

[60] OECD (2021).

[61] Haider et al. (2020).

[62] Zizek (2021).

[63] Haider et al. (2020).

[64] Rasul et al. (2021).

[65] Begum et al. (2020).

friction and food insecurity.[66] In South Africa, during their first lock-down, nearly three million people were made redundant, intensifying socio-economic insecurity, eroding a sense of identity and exacerbating mental health problems like depression.[67] Joblessness is also on the rise in Greece, and this has accelerated depression and suicidal thoughts in people, particularly for those with fewer social support networks.[68] Similarly, lockdowns have increased unemployment in Spain, exacerbating mental ill-health and feelings of a lack of self-worth and social purpose.[69] When combined with the lack of household income from rising joblessness in other nations like Burkina Faso, Kenya, Rwanda, Ghana, Philippines and Colombia, global poverty sharply rose in 2020 in a way that possessed no historical precedent.[70]

Evidently, lockdowns have detrimentally affected peoples' mental health, with some scholars claiming they pose *"several threats to health and well-being and may even cause more overall harm than good".*[71] Indeed, the Italian lockdowns meant people endured *"an abrupt and sudden change in their habits, a sense of precariousness, the indefiniteness of the future, and a strong worry for their health".*[72] This was particularly acute in Southern Italy where unemployment, poor educational attainment and various social problems are prevalent, with young adults reporting the lowest levels of mental well-being. Rising unemployment, homelessness and poverty in India has resulted in an increase in mental ill-health, exacerbating the difficulty of breaking the cycle between socio-economic deprivation and mental health problems.[73] This has intensified the gap between the rich and the poor in India, with the lockdown impacting detrimentally on those vulnerable social groups who already live in debilitating conditions (see Chapter 9).

---

[66] Rasul et al. (2021).
[67] Posel et al. (2021).
[68] Papadopoulou et al. (2021).
[69] Castillo et al. (2021).
[70] Egger et al. (2021).
[71] Haider et al. (2020, p. 3).
[72] Epifanio et al. (2021).
[73] Golechha (2020).

Emerging evidence indicates that educational institutions' shift to online provision during the lockdowns has affected the mental well-being of both parents and children. Survey research in the UK ascertained that, during the first lockdown, school children experienced high rates of boredom and stress, while 52% indicated that they felt socially isolated.[74] Many parents also reported high levels of loneliness since they were often compelled to home-school their children on their own and thus lacked face-to-face contact with other people. The severing of children's usual school routines and face-to-face socialisation activities resulted in many children across the globe feeling low levels of motivation and high levels of anxiety about the present and their future.[75] This has been felt most acutely by children in the most impoverished countries such as India, which possesses the largest child population in the world at 472 million children. Indeed, lockdowns meant Indian children labouring in rural localities and on farms possessed no income stream, which increased their socio-economic uncertainty and had a detrimental effect upon their psychological well-being.[76]

Perhaps one of the most troubling unintentional consequences of the lockdowns has been a potential international rise in domestic violence/abuse, particularly in nations like Canada, the UK, Nepal, Italy, China and the USA.[77] Research indicates that violence against women also increased in Tunisia during the lockdown, with victims reporting intensified psychological distress like anxiety and depression.[78] Confined to their homes for sizable amounts of time, and cut adrift from social support services, many victims of domestic abuse across the world have reported feelings of abandonment and isolation.[79] During the first lockdown, calls to domestic abuse helplines also increased in France, Spain, Mexico, Colombia and Chile, particularly when the lockdown was implemented for longer periods.[80] While domestic abuse often

---

[74] El-Osta et al. (2021).
[75] Singh et al. (2020).
[76] Ibid.
[77] Ellis et al. (2021).
[78] Sediri et al. (2020).
[79] Ellis et al. (2021).
[80] Berniell and Facchini (2021).

generates physical harm, it can also lead to psychological problems, nightmares, eating disorders, suicidal thoughts and a withdrawal from society,[81] meaning the impact can have lifelong damaging effects.

Placed in this context, it is perhaps not surprising that 'deaths of despair' have increased in many parts of the world since lockdowns were implemented (see Chapter 11). Globally, suicide levels are high in comparison with previous social crises, like the 2008 global financial crash, since many people have lost hope and been unable to adjust to a new material reality.[82] Research suggests that, in Australia, there may be 1,500 extra deaths due to the lockdown, while in the USA estimates indicate that upwards of 75,000 people may die due to suicide and substance misuse.[83] Indeed, substance misuse and suicidal thoughts have increased across many states in the USA, particularly for those labouring in socially uncertain and economically insecure forms of employment.[84] Meanwhile, in Victoria, Australia, between December 2020 and May 2021, interventions to protect young people from child abuse and suicide increased by 184%, with many interventions responding to a young person's imminent intention to commit suicide.[85] Such a rise is concerning yet indicative of the sense of hopelessness some young people feel about the situation.

Important medical appointments have also been postponed or cancelled for many people across the world as hospitals made the management of Covid-19 their modus operandi. This resulted in cancellations from both the hospital and patients, as the latter often feared attending due to the risk of contracting Covid-19.[86] Survey research in India during the first lockdown discerned that 62% of cancer patients missed their hospital appointments, while 47% were unable to complete their potentially life-saving treatment.[87] Diagnosis for the most prevalent forms of cancer including breast, pancreatic, stomach, oesophagus

---

[81] Das et al. (2020).
[82] Ganesan et al. (2021).
[83] Ibid.
[84] Czeisler et al. (2020).
[85] Wootton and Mizen (2021).
[86] Briggs et al. (2021).
[87] Singh et al. (2021).

and lung cancer in the USA fell by around 50% between March and April 2020 in comparison with the previous year.[88] Although diagnosis rates had slightly risen by mid-2020, they were still significantly lower than previous years. While lockdowns have considerably disrupted patient care, they have also impacted upon important cancer research, in part because patients' willingness to take part in clinical trials has declined with many encountering difficulties in accessing the trial sites.[89] All things considered, it is likely that there will be a significant rise in premature cancer deaths in the near future. One thing is for sure, the unintended consequences of lockdowns have produced various harms experienced by many people all around the world. An ultra-realist harm perspective teaches us that harms are not only produced by the presence of something, but also by its *absence*.[90] In this context, we see the absence of support networks, employment, education, routinised and structured lifestyles, and social integration as generating a severe amount of social harm. Whether it was intended or not, there is a probabilistic causal relationship between lockdowns and an increasingly negative social reality.

Dodsworth has recently outlined another worrying aspect of lockdowns: how governments across the world have utilised fear to ensure people comply with the restrictive measures.[91] The New Zealand prime minister, Jacinda Ardern, claimed that those individuals who had to complete a government isolation period would be subjected to 14 days of 'sustained propaganda'.[92] At the same time, the Irish government's scientific advisory panel suggested that the state should search for ways to increase anxiety, uncertainty and insecurity in the general population to foster compliance. In Germany, scientific advisors encouraged the State to construct images in the peoples' minds of people choking to death in their homes to generate fear and anxiety. Perhaps most emblematic of a State-orchestrated fear campaign, however, is the example of Britain. On

[88] American Cancer Society (2021).
[89] Waterhouse et al. (2021).
[90] Lloyd (2018).
[91] Dodsworth (2021).
[92] Ibid., p. 65.

22 March 2020, the Scientific Pandemic Influenza Group on Behaviour (SPI-B), who advise the government, claimed:

> The perceived level of personal threat needs to be increased among those who are complacent, using hard-hitting emotional messaging.[93]

Britain has perhaps been a world leader in generating fear throughout the Covid-19 pandemic, with the average citizen being far more fearful of the disease than people in different countries.[94] This may be because they have been bombarded with daily updates of Covid-related 'cases' and 'deaths' rather than recoveries (see Chapters 3 and 6). Public health advertisements depict Covid-19 as posing a threat to everybody regardless of one's age and health status, and posters containing images of medical personnel wearing masks against a red and yellow background that embodies threat and danger have adorned many public places throughout the pandemic. There have even been broadcast campaigns whereby people wearing oxygen masks look directly into the camera with a narrator stating: "*Look her in the eyes, and tell her you never bend the rules*". The fear of getting ill and perhaps dying of Covid-19 has therefore been quite deliberately installed in people across the world and for many people in Western societies, this fear provokes new feelings attached to mortality.

References

Abassi, K. (2020). COVID-19: Politicisation, "corruption", and suppression of science. *British Medical Journal, 371*, 1–2. https://doi.org/10.1136/bmj.m4425

American Cancer Society. (2021). *Cancer facts & figures 2021*.

Arshed, N., Meo, M., & Farooq, F. (2020). Empirical assessment of government policies and flattening of the COVID19 curve. *Journal of Public Affairs 20*(4), e2333. https://doi.org/10.1002%2Fpa.2333

---

[93] Ibid., p. 1.

[94] Ibid.

Bambra, C., Riordan, R., Ford, J., & Matthews, F. (2020). The COVID-19 pandemic and health inequalities. *Journal of Epidemiology and Community Health, 74*(11), 964–968.

Baral, S., Chandler, R., Prieto, R., Gupta, S., Mishra, S., & Kulldorff, M. (2021). Leveraging epidemiological principles to evaluate Sweden's COVID-19 response. *Annals of Epidemiology, 54*, 21–26.

Barry, C., & Lazar, S. (2020). Justifying lockdown. *Ethics & International Affairs*, 1–7.

Begum, M., Farid, M., Alam, M., & Barau, S. (2020). COVID-19 and Bangladesh: Socio-economic analysis towards the future correspondence. *Asian Journal of Agricultural Extension, Economics & Sociology, 38*(9), 143–155.

Berniell, I., & Facchini, G. (2021). COVID-19 lockdown and domestic violence: Evidence from internet-search behavior in 11 countries. *European Economic Review, 136*, 1–13.

Bhattacharya, J., Gupta, S., & Kulldorff, M. (2020). *Focused protection: The middle ground between lockdowns and "let it rip"*. The Great Barrington Declaration. Accessed on 17 June 2021. Available at: https://gbdeclaration.org/focused-protection/

Briggs, D., Ellis, A., Lloyd, A., & Telford, L. (2021). *Researching the COVID-19 pandemic: A critical blueprint for the social sciences*. Policy Press Rapid Response Series.

Castillo, I., Mato-Diaz, F., & Alvarez-Rodriguez, A. (2021). Furloughs, teleworking and other work situations during the COVID-19 lockdown: Impact on mental well-being. *International Journal of Environmental Research and Public Health, 18*, 1–16.

Chaudhry, R., Dranitsaris, G., Mubashir, T., Bartoszko, J., & Riazbi, S. (2020). A country level analysis measuring the impact of government actions, country preparedness and socioeconomic factors on COVID-19 mortality and related health outcomes. *EClinicalMedicine, 25*, 1–8.

Chen, J., Shi, L., Zhang, Y., Wang, X., & Sun, G. (2021). A cross-country core strategy comparison in China, Japan, Singapore and South Korea during the early COVID-19 pandemic. *Globalization and Health, 17*(22), 1–10.

Chin, V., Ioannidis, J., Tanner, M., & Cripps, S. (2020). Effects of non-pharmaceutical interventions on COVID-19: A tale of three models. *medRxiv*, 1–45.

Claeson, M., & Hanson, S. (2021). Comment: COVID-19 and the Swedish enigma. *The Lancet, 397*, 260–261.

Czeisler, M., Lane, R., Petrosky, E., Wiley, J., Christensen, A., Njai, R., Weaver, M., Robbins, R., Facer- Childs, E., Barger, L., Czeisler, C., Howard, M., & Rajaratnam, S. (2020, June 24–30). Mental health, substance use, and suicidal ideation during the COVID-19 pandemic—United States. *Centers for Disease Control and Prevention: Weekly Report, 69,* 1049–1057.

Das, M., Das, A., & Mandal, A. (2020). Examining the impact of lockdown (due to COVID-19) on domestic violence (DV): An evidences from India. *Asian Journal of Psychiatry, 54,* 1–2.

Dodsworth, L. (2021). *A state of fear.* Pinter & Martin Ltd.

Egger, D., Miguel, E., Warren, S., Shenoy, A., Collins, E., Karlan, D., Parkerson, D., Mobarek, A., Fink, G . C., Walker, M., Haushofer, J., Larreboure, M., Athey, S., Lopez-Pena, P., Benhachmi, S., Humphreys, M., Lowe, L., Meriggi, N., Wabwire, A., Davis, C., … Vernot, C. (2021) Falling living standards during the COVID-19 crisis: Quantitative evidence from nine developing countries. *Science Advances, 7*(6), 1–12.

Ehnts, D., & Paetz, M. (2021). COVID-19 and its economic consequences for the Euro Area. *Eurasian Economic Review, 11,* 227–249.

Ellis, A., Briggs, D., Lloyd, A., & Telford, L. (2021). A ticking time bomb of future harm: Lockdown, child abuse and future violence. *Abuse: An International Journal, 2*(1). https://doi.org/10.37576/abuse.2021.017

El-Osta, A., Alaa, A., Webber, I., Sasco, E., Bagkeris, E., Millar, H., Vidal-Hall, C., & Majeed, A. (2021). How is the COVID-19 lockdown impacting the mental health of parents of school-age children in the UK? A cross-sectional online survey. *British Medical Journal Open, 11,* 1–11.

Epifanio, M., Andrei, F., Mancini, G., Agostini, F., Piombo, M., Spicuzza, V., Riolo, M., Lavanco, G., Trombini, E., & Grutta, S. (2021). The impact of COVID-19 pandemic and lockdown measures on quality of life among Italian general population. *Journal of Clinical Medicine, 10,* 1–19.

Ferguson, N., Laydon, D., Gilani, G., Imai, N., Ainslie, K., Baguelin, M., Bhatia, S., Boonyasiri, A., Cucunuba, Z., Dannenburg, G., Dighe, A., Dorigatti, I., Fu, H., Gaythorpe, K., Green, W., Hamlet, A., Hinsley, W., Okell, L., Elsland, S., Thompson, H. … Ghani, A. (2020). *Report 9: Impact of non-pharmaceutical interventions (NPIs) to reduce COVID-19 mortality and healthcare demand.* Imperial College COVID-19 Response Team.

Fisher, M. (2009). *Capitalist realism: Is there no alternative?* Zero.

Flaxman, S., Mishra, S., Gandy, A., Unwin, H. J. T., Mellan, T. A., Coupland, H., & Bhatt, S. (2020). Estimating the effects of non-pharmaceutical interventions on COVID-19 in Europe. *Nature, 584,* 257–261. https://doi.org/10.1038/s41586-020-2405-7

Ganesan, B., Al-Jumaily, A., Fong, K., Prasad, P., Meena, S., & Kai-Yu Tong, R. (2021). Impact of Coronavirus disease 2019 (COVID-19) outbreak quarantine, isolation, and lockdown policies on mental health and suicide. *Frontiers in Psychiatry, 12,* 1–12.

Gastroenterol, A. (2020). COVID-19: Mitigation or suppression. *Arab Journal of Gastroenterology, 21,* 1–2.

Golechha, M. (2020). COVID-19, India, lockdown and psychosocial challenges: What next? *International Journal of Social Psychiatry, 66*(8), 830–832.

GOV. (2020). *Government takes historic step towards net-zero with end of sale of new petrol and diesel cars by 2030.* Accessed 25 June 2021. Available at: https://www.gov.uk/government/news/government-takes-historic-step-towards-net-zero-with-end-of-sale-of-new-petrol-and-diesel-cars-by-2030

Gruzd, A., & Mai, P. (2020). Going viral: How a single tweet spawned a COVID-19 conspiracy theory on Twitter. *Big Data & Society, 7*(2), 1–19.

Haider, N., Osman, A., Gazekpo, A., Akipede, G., Asogun, D., Ansumana, R., Lessels, R., Khan, P., Hamid, M., Yeboah-Manu, D., Mboera, L., Shayo, E., Mmbaga, B., Urassa, M., Musoke, D., Kapata, N., Ferrand, R., Kapata, P., Stigler, F., … McCoy, D. (2020). Lockdown measures in response to COVID-19 in nine sub-Saharan African countries. *British Medical Journal Global Health, 5*(1–10), 2.

Hilton, S., & Hunt, K. (2011). UK newspapers' representations of the 2009–10 outbreak of swine flu: One health scare not over-hyped by the media? *Journal of Epidemiology and Community Health, 65,* 941–946.

Honigsbaum, M. (2020). *The pandemic century: A history of global contagion from the Spanish Flu to COVID-19.* Penguin.

Ioannidis, J., Cripps, S., & Tanner, M. (2020). Forecasting for COVID-19 has failed. *International Journal of Forecasting,* 1–16.

Jones, L., & Hemeiri, S. (2021). COVID-19 and the failure of the neoliberal regulatory state. *Review of International Political Economy,* 1–25. Online First. https://www.tandfonline.com/doi/epub/10.1080/09692290.2021.1892798?needAccess=true

Josefsson, K. (2021). Perspectives of life in Sweden during the COVID-19 pandemic. *Journal of Clinical Sport Psychology, 15,* 80–86.

Kulldorff, M., (2021). Why i spoke out against lockdowns. *Spiked.* Accessed on 17 June 2021. Available at: https://www.spiked-online.com/2021/06/04/why-i-spoke-out-against-lockdowns/

Liang, S., Liang, L., & Rosen, J. (2021). COVID-19: A comparison to the 1918 influenza and how we can defeat it. *Postgraduate Medical Journal, 97*(1147), 273–274.

Lloyd, A. (2018). *The Harms of work.* Bristol University Press.

Melnick, E., & Ioannidis, J. (2020). Head to head: Should governments continue lockdown to slow the spread of COVID-19? *British Medical Journal, 369*, 1–3.

Meo, S., Abukhalaf, A., Alomar, A., Beeshi, I. Z., Alhowikan, A., Shafi, K. M., Meo, A. S., Usmani, A. M., & Akram, J. (2020). Climate and COVID-19 pandemic: Effect of heat and humidity on the incidence and mortality in world's top ten hottest and top ten coldest countries. *European Review for Medical and Pharmacological Sciences, 24*, 8232–8238.

Miles, D., Stedman, M., & Heald, A. (2021). "Stay at home, protect the national health service, save lives": A cost benefit analysis of the lockdown in the United Kingdom. *The International Journal of Clinical Practice, 75*(3), 1–14.

Muller, S. (2021). The dangers of performative scientism as the alternative to anti-scientific policymaking: A critical, preliminary assessment of South Africa's COVID-19 response and its consequences. *World Development, 140*, 1–14.

OECD. (2021, April). *Unemployment rates.* OECD.

Papadopoulou, A., Efstathiou, V., Yotsidi, V., Pomini, V., Michopoulos, I., Markopoulou, E., Papadopoulou, M., Tsikaropoulou, E., Kalemi, G., Tournikioti, K., Douzenis, A., & Gournellis, R. (2021). Suicidal ideation during COVID-19 lockdown in Greece: Prevalence in the community, risk and protective factors. *Psychiatry Research, 297*, 1–8.

Posel, D., Oyenubi, A., & Kollamparambil, U. (2021). Job loss and mental health during the COVID- 19 lockdown: Evidence from South Africa. *PLoS ONE, 16*(3), 1–15.

Rasul, G., Nepal, A., Hussain, A., Maharjan, A., Joshi, S., Lama, A., Prakriti, G., Ahmad, F., Mishra, A., & Sharma, E. (2021). Socio-economic implications of COVID-19 pandemic in South Asia: Emerging risks and growing challenges. *Frontiers in Sociology, 6*, 1–14.

Reiner, R. (2021). *Social democratic criminology: New directions in criminology* (p. 154). Routledge.

Reiss, K., & Bhakdi, S. (2020). *Corona: False alarm?* Chelsea Green Publishing.

Sarwal, R., & Sarwal, T. (2020, March 29). *Mitigating COVID-19 with lockdowns: A possible exit strategy.* Available at SSRN https://ssrn.com/abstract=3563538 or http://dx.doi.org/10.2139/ssrn.3563538

Sediri, S., Zgueb, Y., Ouanes, S., Ouali, U., Bourgou, S., Jomli, R., & Nacef, F. (2020). Women's mental health: Acute impact of COVID-19 pandemic on domestic violence. *Archives of Women's Mental Health, 23*, 749–756. https://doi.org/10.1007/s00737-020-01082-4

Sharov, K. (2020). Adaptation to SARS-CoV-2 under stress: Role of distorted information. *European Journal of Clinical Investigation, 50*(9), 1–7.

Singh, R., Rai, C., & Ishan, R. (2021). Impact of COVID-19 lockdown on patients with cancer in North Bihar, India: A phone-based survey. *Cancer Research, Statistics and Treatment, 4*(1), 37–43.

Singh, S., Roy, D., Sinha, K., Parveen, S., Sharma, G., & Joshi, G. (2020). Impact of COVID-19 and lockdown on mental health of children and adolescents: A narrative review with recommendations. *Psychiatry Research, 293*, 1–10.

Soltesz, K., Gustafsson, F., Timpka, T., Jalden, J., Jidling, C., Heimerson, A., Schon, T., Spreco, A., Ekberg, J., Dahlstrom, O., Carlson, F., Joud, A., & Bernhardsson, B. (2020). The effect of interventions on COVID- 19. *Nature, 588*, 26–28.

Southworth, P. (2021). Lockdowns are 'the single biggest public health mistake in history', says top scientist. *The Telegraph.* Accessed on 17 June 2021. Available at https://www.telegraph.co.uk/news/2021/06/10/lockdowns-single-biggest-public-health-mistake-history-says/

Statista. (2021). *Unemployment rate in selected European countries as of April 2021.* Accessed on 17 June 2021. Available at https://www.statista.com/statistics/1115276/unemployment-in-europe-by-country/

Telford, L., & Briggs, D. (2021). Targets and overwork: Neoliberalism and the maximisation of profitability from the workplace. *Capital & Class.* Online First. https://doi.org/10.1177/03098168211022208

Telford, L., & Wistow, J. (2020). Brexit and the working class on Teesside: Moving beyond reductionism. *Capital & Class, 44*(4), 553–572.

Warren, G., Lofstedt, R., & Wardman, J. (2021). COVID-19: The winter lockdown strategy in five European nations. *Journal of Risk Research, 24*(3/4), 267–293.

Waterhouse, D., Harvey, R., Hurley, P., Levit, L., Kim, E., Klepin, H., Mileham, K., Nowakowski, G., Schenkel, C., Davis, C., Bruinooge, S., & Schilsky, R. (2021). Early impact of COVID-19 on the conduct of oncology clinical trials and long-term opportunities for transformation: Findings from an American society of clinical oncology survey. *American Society of Clinical Oncology, 16*(7), 417–422.

World Health Organization. (2005). *WHO global influenza preparedness plan: The role of WHO and recommendations for national measures before and during pandemics*. World Health Organization.

Winlow, S., Hall, S., & Treadwell, J. (2017). *The rise of the right*. Policy Press.

Wootton, H., & Mizen, R. (2021). Victorian teenage suicide threats jump 184pc amid pandemic. *Financial Review*. Accessed on 21 June 2021. Available at https://www.afr.com/policy/health-and-education/victorian-teenage-suicide-threats-jump-184pc-amid-pandemic-20210607-p57ypu

Yu, Q., Salvador, C., Melani, I., Berg, M., Neblett, E., & Kitayama, S. (2021). Racial residential segregation and economic disparity jointly exacerbate COVID-19 fatality in large American cities. *Annals of the New York Academy of Sciences, 1–14*.

Zizek, S. (2020). *Pandemic: COVID-19 shakes the world*. OR Books.

Zizek, S. (2021). *Pandemic 2: Chronicles of a lost time*. Polity.

3

Illness and Death in the Covid Epoch

This chapter looks at the collective attribution of illness and death to Covid-19. In particular, how the extensive and perpetual media coverage of transmission methods, 'new cases' and 'deaths', adoption of stay-at-home measures, social distancing and mask wearing in public, left an active ideological residue of fear and compliance which was indelibly reproduced by self-managing citizens. At first, most people became very worried about getting ill and possibly dying. Such were the levels of caution and borderline paranoia during lockdowns, that public displays of coughs and sneezes seemed to become the assumed symbolic evidence of Covid-19 illness. Perhaps this was to be expected given that, at the height of lockdowns, Covid-19 appeared to be claiming endless amounts of victims—even though, by comparison, other modes of dying were all but forgotten. As the lockdowns paved the way for the 'new normal', fears, anxieties and concerns about illness and death continued despite official Covid-19 deaths decreasing. This chapter provides a critical examination of the fear of getting ill, what it meant to be ill from Covid-19, as well as the assembly of virus statistics. Crucially, a complex interplay of hyper-individualism, the new cultural norm of 'informed patients', Covid-19 media and information saturation, produced an erosion of faith in public health services as well as belief in any adjudicating authority.

Warning: Impending Virus Alert

When measures such as lockdowns and social distancing were announced to quell the spread of Covid-19, at the time, they seemed to:

a. be based on a general lack of understanding about the virus;
b. ignore much of the reputable, established science about coronaviruses and infectious diseases;
c. be based on a series of worst-case modelling scenarios which indicated that without those measures, healthcare systems would cave under the strain and result in high rates of mortality.

Much of this was exacerbated by the contradictory and weak intervention from the world's governing body on public health, the WHO. In one way or another most countries—but not all—opted for lockdowns with a combination of social distancing, self-isolation, mask wearing and curfews. We were initially warned that the presence of one or two particular symptoms could be indicators of Covid-19 but as the pandemic evolved further signs of infection were added. Currently, according to the WHO,[1] the most 'common symptoms' of Covid-19 are:

- Fever
- Dry cough
- Fatigue

While 'other symptoms' that are less common and may affect some patients include:

---

[1] WHO (2020).

- Loss of taste or smell
- Nasal congestion
- Conjunctivitis (also known as red eyes)
- Sore throat
- Headache
- Muscle or joint pain
- Different types of skin rash
- Nausea or vomiting
- Diarrhoea
- Chills or dizziness

Yet there are also 'additional symptoms of severe Covid-19 disease' which include:

- Shortness of breath
- Loss of appetite
- Confusion
- Persistent pain or pressure in the chest
- High temperature (above 38 °C)

As well as, according to the WHO, 'other additional less common symptoms' which are:

- Irritability
- Confusion
- Reduced consciousness (sometimes associated with seizures)
- Anxiety
- Depression
- Sleep disorders

As well as more severe and rare neurological complications such as:

- Strokes
- Brain inflammation
- Delirium and nerve damage

This is quite a long list of potential ailments that large numbers of people are likely to experience at some point in the duration of a year and not necessarily as a result of Covid-19. Given the broad range of possible symptoms, it is understandable that many people became quite worried and this was certainly the case for some of our participants. Further announcements that there were possibly asymptomatic, yet still potentially infectious, Covid-19 cases, also contributed to both the sense of confusion and anxiety. One of our participants, Alex, an IT worker from Brazil, confirmed this:

> We have so little information on its mortality and it looks like a lottery, so science has not figured out what makes it kill some, and then other people have no symptoms and this is what scares me. We have an old friend, fat with diabetes and he got it, and nothing happened. Then there is this guy in the office, fit and young, and he got really sick and he was on a ventilator. It feels like a lottery which scares me the most.

Yet, as Alex notes, this information was not coming through from the Brazilian media. The scientific knowledge on Covid-19 did not seem to add up in Alex's experience and he continued to be fearful of the virus to the point where—in a country which has had relaxed measures—he and his wife were seen as "*crazy*" because they wore masks in public:

> Alex: My wife and I wear masks outside all the time, we are at the other end of the extreme, we clean all the products we buy, it's crazy man. In Brazil, people think we are crazy.
> Interviewer: Are you crazy?
> Alex: Maybe.

Conversely, across many Western countries, it was those who did not wear masks who were the ones considered 'crazy'. Though there appeared to be some doubters and naysayers, many people initially seemed to share the same concern about the disease and were in agreement with official narratives that indicated its 'random danger'—appearing to have little to no effect on some people, but potentially lethal to others. Early academic evidence, for example, linking higher probability of catching and suffering from Covid-19 to air pollution, dense, overcrowded living environments or poor health for example, were absent from media and political discourses—and to some extent this remains the case in the summer of 2021. A lack of context to how the virus was presented, coupled with the absence of context and perspective from the media, seemed to have a number of consequences. Firstly, it seemed to contribute towards increased caution about other people and thus exacerbating individualised outlooks on the world. Dimitar, a researcher from Bulgaria, suggested that:

> In a way, the pandemic taught us in a very bad way not to trust people that we even trusted before. Now you don't know where the trusted people have been. Now people are making new choices about who they want to socialise with based on things like what they think about Covid or if they have been vaccinated. In a way, we are creating new sanitised bubbles.

Secondly, it seemed to establish a stigma attached to displaying these symptoms in public, as many people sought to avoid exhibiting potential illness. Coughs were quelled, sneezes were stifled, and sniffles were silenced. The diminished amount of public life afforded to many during lockdown became about defying potential ailment as a result of the silent stigma attached to the new infectious disease.[2]

Soon into the lockdowns, however, many of our participants reported contracting the virus, and this emerging division grew even more pronounced as many who had experienced it without suffering downplayed its severity; at worst, associating it with having had a 'bad bout of flu'. Some who tested positive were convinced they had not actually had it, as their symptoms failed to match how the physiological effects of the virus were being publicly presented. For many of these people, this played a part in their *non-compliance* with public health measures. Conversely, those who experienced severe symptoms directly, or indirectly through positive cases among their acquaintances, friends and family that resulted in severe illness, tended to accept dominant political and media-generated narratives that it was indeed a potentially 'deadly virus' and this aided their compliance with the measures (Chapter 10).

---

[2] Abuhammad et al. (2020).

Illness (self-isolation) and death (predominantly at home, at hospital, or in care homes) seemed to take place quickly in private circumstances, with very few opportunities for families to 'say goodbye'. Heightened feelings about the virus were partly, it seems, the result of the lasting residual effects of traumatic illness, or the death of a loved one, which had a significant role in shaping ongoing views about restrictions and measures against it (see Chapter 11).[3] Indeed, there is evidence to suggest that people who had known someone die as a result of Covid-19 rather than through other natural or unnatural causes, experienced higher levels of prolonged grief disorder (PGD) and persistent complex bereavement disorder (PCBD).[4]

The media seemed to favour coverage of the 'case' and 'death' modelling strategies under way, some of which had been generated from non-peer reviewed papers. Under normal circumstances, credible scientific work—and academic material in general—needs to satisfy a process of peer review to ensure the interpretation of the results are accurately presented. However, as Covid-19 spread around the world these particular procedures were suspended. As mentioned, Neil Ferguson and his research team's initial epidemiological arguments for national lockdowns at the outset of the pandemic were not subject to this process. Ferguson's track record remained unquestioned even though he had previously forecast that 200 million would die from avian flu in 2005: something from which only a few hundred died. His new forecast was that without lockdowns, 500,000 people would die in the UK and two million in the USA. He reported this in mid-March 2020, yet, one month earlier in February 2020, Chinese scientists had warned:

> Importantly, in emerging viral infection outbreaks the case-fatality ratio is often overestimated in the early stages because case detection is highly biased towards the more severe cases.[5]

---

[3] Briggs et al. (2021).
[4] Eisma et al. (2020).
[5] Wang et al. (2020).

Yet, a 'case' of Covid-19 is actually a positive test result and does not guarantee that a person will develop symptoms and become ill, for some people remain 'asymptomatic'. *People with positive tests who are asymptomatic are therefore not 'cases'*.[6] Ferguson and his team were working on the 'worst-case' scenario and immediately media around the world started to report on the imminent threat. Yet, it was on this basis that political decisions were taken to lockdown whole nations (see Chapter 2). Revolving media stories showing Chinese doctors dressed in clinical suits and Italian hospitals at capacity, became fuel for hysteria and panic, reflected in a heightened sense of fear about illness and death.[7] The emerging pandemic context therefore exacerbated people's existing concerns about health while at the same time generated new and perhaps, for some, unfamiliar subjective feelings about illness and death. The successful deployment of messages and images through political discourses and mainstream media was also complemented by changes to the physical spaces, which became adorned with symbolic public health messaging around the new 'risk' and ways in which to 'protect others' by disinfecting hands, wearing masks and social distancing.[8] In some cases, direct messaging was strategically placed to warn people about the consequences of non-compliance (Fig. 3.1; Chapter 10).

Yet, in many of our ethnographic observations after the easing of lockdowns in Spain and the UK, particularly as countries entered their 'second wave', rarely did we see total adherence to these measures:

In the park, I stand and watch my daughter play between the trees as a small child nearby starts to have a tantrum because she cannot have any more sweets. Her young carer (mid 20s) offers meagre sympathy and threatens to take the child home. My daughter offers her toys to the girl and they start to play together. I stand near – but not too close – to the carer and start up a conversation. We firstly talk about the children and education and she says she cannot discipline the girl because her "*mum gives her anything she wants*" she says. She lowers her mask to scratch her nose and makes little effort to put it over her nose again. We quickly

[6] Rushworth (2021).
[7] Lazzerini (2020).
[8] Young (2021).

Fig. 3.1 Coercive compliance in the UK (*Photo* Luke Telford)

get on to the subject of coronavirus and I ask "*that mask bothering you?*" It seems so: "*yes*" she replies and continues "*the whole thing is ridiculous anyway. People die all the time and now the media are reporting on it. The virus is not that bad but our reaction has been so exaggerated*". She says all her friends doubt its seriousness and she does not understand why the country was shut down. "*Now watch what will happen and what people like me will have to do because we have to now scramble to get jobs like this one, cash in hand, to support ourselves, same for my student friends who can't find no work when they graduated this summer*" she adds. [Field notes Daniel Briggs 'Kids talk']

As highlighted in Chapter 2, it was claimed lockdowns would 'level the curve' and effectively reduce positive case numbers. Media institutions quickly aligned alongside what became frequent political messages about the dangers of the virus and that individuals should 'stay at home, save lives, and save health services'. Together, these institutions generated the ideological impetus to manoeuvre these public health messages via daily 'virus updates'. The result, seemingly, was little effective space to debate or question the implementation of lockdown measures. Simultaneously, the platform of life as we knew it had changed in our own absence during the lockdowns to emblematically reflect the 'risks' now present in public life. While updates on deaths from Covid-19 revealed the reality and potential danger of the virus, the wider social and economic context to serious illness, deaths, but crucially people's experiences of restrictions, was not always acknowledged. As one of our previously mentioned respondents, Alex, explained, his encounters with acquaintances added important layers of context to the sometimes blunt presentation of the virus's impact:

> We have a cleaning lady who comes from the favelas [extremely poor urban areas of Brazilian cities]. We talk to her about it [Covid-19] and she tells us of sad stories, people dying. This is the other side of the story but she comes from a very poor area. All in the slums. The State's help in these communities is next to nothing, almost none of these people get healthcare. This is so far from the middle-class who have private hospitals and this is a clear example of inequality. Then you have all these people running small shops or informal businesses, they lost their jobs and the unemployment shot up. People have to be creative and some started making masks, or making hand sanitisers, but many people have suffered like this even if they didn't get ill…We live in a bubble and I don't like that. Then we go out and within two miles, there is all this poverty. I don't like that man, that's shit. It is just not fair. Inequality is not like that in Europe. We try to do things to help but it doesn't work. There is something that I see about the world, it gets in my head, it makes me feel bad all the time.

From Death Data, to 'New Case' Coverage, to Variant Values

At the time of writing, over 18.5 million cases of Covid-19 had been reported in Brazil and over 500,000 deaths.[9] These represent some of the highest in the world. On reflection, one could conclude that the country was 'losing its battle' with Covid-19. Visual depictions of case numbers and deaths indicated, at the height of the country's epidemic, daily 'new case' increases and hundreds, sometimes thousands, dying of the virus each day. British media coverage of the crisis in particular highlights the failings of its prime minister, Jair Bolsonaro.[10] Despite consistent calls for the country to instigate a national lockdown, Bolsonaro refused to buckle under the pressure and kept the economy open. His cavalier attitude to the virus and approved vaccines certainly seems to have contributed to the high rate of cases and deaths but does not appear to be the sole factor.

In addition, Brazil's health infrastructure, which struggles to adequately support its middle-class electorate, has been ill-equipped to respond to the crisis. The generally poor health and overcrowded living conditions of its poorest citizens have compounded the crisis. As Taveres and Betti wrote of Covid-19's interaction with social conditions in Brazil, the country "*cannot fully implement the recommended preventive measures…because the social conditions and the healthcare system do not meet the basic requirements for avoiding preventable deaths*".[11] This not only highlights how Covid-19 exacerbated inequalities, which we consider in Chapter 4, but demonstrates how swathes of poor Brazilian communities were already highly vulnerable before the pandemic. Alex remained vaguely aware of the wider structural conditions that distribute risks from the virus unevenly and that these had insulated him and his wife somewhat from its dangers, as the excerpt from his interview earlier indicated. However, it is important to consider further what some might deem to be his slightly unfounded fears about the virus.

---

[9] Statista (2021).
[10] Guerin (2021).
[11] Tavares and Betti (2021, p. 24).

Alex's fear of illness and unlikely death is, perhaps, the product of what became an *unknown risk*, coupled with anecdotes from urban ghettos and the frequency of alarming statistics devoid of context, which depict a situation spiralling out of control: more infections, more deaths, more infections, more deaths. In our study, we noted a general pattern to media reporting which tended to follow the subsequent formula: when deaths decreased, 'new cases' received replacement attention; when 'new cases' declined, coverage converged upon the possibility of new 'variants' of the virus. Even now as we write, 'variants' are morphing into 'variants of concern'. That is possibly, until, 'deaths' and/or 'new cases' increase again likely in the autumn of 2021. Covid-19 is historically significant in this respect, as it is the first virus in the world to receive extensive 24/7 news coverage,[12] something that was not lost on some of our participants who regarded the level of coverage as excessive and unnecessary. Mike, a builder from the UK who had been made unemployed and accumulated debt during lockdowns, recognised this early on in the pandemic. About the first wave, he said:

Everyone is worried because of the media. I put on the radio and TV and it is all coronavirus, more cases, death rate, more cases, death rate, stay inside. It is brainwashing. Constantly. If you ram that on people constantly, they will start to believe it.

Later on, during the summer of 2020 as the Covid-19 case infection rate and death toll reduced dramatically, he added:

They have to make it look bad now, they [the government] can't go back on it. They brain wash you through the media. There is nothing about death rates [in the news now]. They have to justify it somehow. Flu season is at the beginning of the year and that's why its disappearing now [June] but it will pick up as the winter comes. That is why no one is dying.

Mike added how he found it "*hilarious*" many people "*believed this bull-shit*", before pointing out some of the confusing restrictions: "*funny you can get it* [the virus] *in pubs and restaurants but you can't get it from a*

Ryanair flight or from going in a supermarket". Widespread acceptance of the statistics was also used as a means of generating compliance to public health messages even if some members of the academic and scientific community quite quickly pointed out significant gaps and doubts about the figures. At this point, it's useful to remember it was these statistics which not only formed the basis for arguing for lockdowns but also contributed to the continued use of lockdowns thereafter.

There are also potential problems that have been identified with testing for Covid-19. The polymerase chain reaction, or PCR test, became the core diagnostic tool utilised to determine Covid-19 infections. Even when evidence emerged that these tests were likely to produce significant numbers of 'false positives'[13]—even as much as 17% because of contamination and human error[14]—they remained, and do so to this day, the mainstay of detecting infection numbers in many countries. Such errors can occur from incorrect data entry or when a positive sample is analysed concurrently with a negative sample thus producing contamination and the amplification of target genes.[15]

Others indicate that even if a positive test is found, it is 'inconclusive' unless it is accompanied alongside the precise parameters that were used to measure the presence of the virus.[16] Indeed, a study of hospitalised patients with Covid-19 in Wuhan found that they had tested positive for the virus on entry yet, several days later, tested negative for the virus.[17] PCR manufacturers have also made it clear that such instruments *should not be used for diagnosis* and instead only for *clinical referencing*.[18] This has resulted in some of the world's most reputable scientists contesting the accuracy of Covid-19 infection statistics largely because they could be indicating to healthy people that they have Covid-19.[19] However, conversely, PCR tests could equally

---

[13] Bamji (2020), Katz et al. (2020), and Reiss and Bhakdi (2020).

[14] Cohen et al. (2020).

[15] Li et al. (2020).

[16] Santos and Chiesa (2020).

[17] Li et al. (2020).

[18] Santos and Chiesa (2020).

[19] Cohen et al. (2020), Reiss and Bhakdi (2020), and Surkova et al. (2020).

be informing Covid-19-infected people that they have nothing whatsoever. International scientific researchers found after they had reviewed 34 international studies involving 12,057 Covid-19 cases, that there were inconsistency issues and a risk of bias thus leading to false negative test results. They recommended that repeated testing was needed because *"up to 54% of COVID-19 patients may have initial false-negatives"*.[20] Notwithstanding, in the absence of testing facilities in many countries such as India and some in Africa, *the WHO recommended people to be diagnosed as 'suspected cases' and also thus counted in the statistics.*[21]

If we recall that all along in many instances *public health policies and interventions have been based on this data*, then certain questions should emerge about the foundations for lockdown and similar decisions thereafter (Chapter 2). We find similar problems and gaps with how Covid-19-related deaths have been documented and recorded. It was modelling by researchers at London's Imperial College who suggested that at least 500,000 deaths in the UK and two million in the USA would occur without a lockdown.[22] However, significant scientific evidence tells us that in the advent of new viruses, there is a tendency to overestimate fatalities, particularly in the initial stages of the epidemic or pandemic.[23]

In this respect, the severe 'cases' were those commonly vulnerable to new respiratory-related infections—the elderly and those with compromised comorbid health issues. Research now shows how, as the pandemic evolved and a 'first wave' passed, Covid-attributed deaths in numerous countries never reached the same peak while, at the same time, excess deaths increased significantly.[24] In Denmark, it was actually the Pfizer and Moderna Covid-19 vaccine—commissioned for public use in record time after trials on generally healthy people rather than the vulnerable and elderly—that weakened the immune systems of care home residents

---

[20] Arevalo-Rodriguez et al. (2020, p. 14).
[21] Reiss and Bhakdi (2020).
[22] Ferguson et al. (2020).
[23] Wang et al. (2020, p. 471).
[24] Nørgaard et al. (2021).

after the first dose, thus contributing to their death.[25] While 'Covid-19 coronavirus' is recorded as a cause of death for people who die within 28 days of testing positive, we doubt that the 'Covid-19 vaccine' will appear in the death statistics.

Meanwhile, other pandemic-related collateral damage was being felt because Covid-19 'cases' and 'deaths' represent only a *part of the total disease, mortality and overall public health*. Further challenges were made concerning the recording of Covid-19 deaths. In the UK, for example, such deaths are counted in statistics when someone dies within 28 days of receiving a positive test from the virus. Considerable numbers of scientists have for some time now called for the distinction to be made between those who *die with Covid-19* and those who *die because of Covid-19*.[26] Similarly, early on in the pandemic, Italian researchers called for there to be some delineation recommending that:

> ...deaths with test positivity as COVID-19 deaths could be appropriate, but these deaths should be reported with all other existing medical conditions, to enable more detailed analyses of causality or association.[27]

However, to this day, this has not yet been done. It has been claimed by virologists and immunologists that "*this method of recording violated all international medical guidelines*"[28] because it was responsible for deceased individuals that had terminal illnesses such as long-term cancer having Covid-19 on their death certificate. As we now know, Covid-19 poses a serious threat to the elderly, often those with co-morbidities, and those with underlying health conditions such as type 2 diabetes and respiratory problems.[29] Many deaths could have therefore potentially been misleadingly and directly attributed to the virus. This is perhaps most starkly evident from the fact that, in the UK for example, the average age of death with/from Covid-19 (aged 82) is above the average life

[25] Moustsen-Helms et al. (2021).
[26] Reiss and Bhakdi (2020).
[27] Rao (2020, p. 298).
[28] Reiss and Bhakdi (2020, p. 16).
[29] Brandén et al. (2020) and Sanyaolu et al. (2020).

expectancy for people (aged 81.26). In Sweden—one of the few countries which decided against the lockdowns—the average age of death of someone with/of Covid-19 is 84 while the life expectancy of a Swede is 82.[30] While all deaths are naturally upsetting and generate profound distress to the deceased's family, commentators have argued that the governmental response must be proportionate to the potential risk of the virus.[31] Our participant mentioned previously, Mike, was quite blunt in his assessment of the situation:

> I haven't followed the lockdown at all. I went to see my girlfriend, I did work for elderly people and they are not bothered. They think the same thing as I do. At the end of the day, it is people who are over 85 and who have severe health problems and the rest of us have been put on house arrest for the sake of a few people who were going to die anyway.

Mike claims he is not bitter about Covid-19 because of his financial situation or work prospects, but believed the situation was unfair and unnecessary. In Peru, like many countries in Europe and the West in general, formalised political messaging about 'new cases' and 'deaths' became daily viewing material for the people in the country, who were also told to lockdown to save the country's health infrastructure (see Chapter 2, 6). Joel, a university student from Lima in Peru, recalled how it began in March 2020:

> The discourse of the president from the first day was very alarming, trying to make us fear. 90 minutes, twice a day. This was March until May 2020 and he talked to us like 'brothers don't go out' like he was our father. This created a lot of fear but after a while it had no impact at all.

Though people *"improvised with masks as they couldn't afford them"* and were *"meeting in secret"* he said, there was no mention about what he described as the country's *"decrepit health system"* which was *"poor and outdated"*. Even before the pandemic Joel said the *"people who went into*

[30] Rushworth (2021).
[31] Reiss and Bhakdi (2020) and S. Zizek (2020).

hospital were fucked and often didn't come out". As discussed, the political narrative bolstered by the media focused intently upon the reporting of 'new cases' and 'deaths', and seemed to invite potential audiences to engage with a project of panic:

> It was like cases, deaths, cases, deaths and then you looked around at the statistics and this created panic too. When the first statistics were circulated, there was speculation about the dark figure of Covid deaths: what is the method, how many cases, how are they calculated. My professors and academics at the university didn't really respond, didn't question it much. There was this weird analysis which didn't join up the dots or analyse the information like 'work and Covid' or 'penal law and Covid' and really there was not much effort to analyse the issue in its completeness. It was not clear if people died because of Covid or because of the pandemic conditions [lockdowns and other measures]. There was no such analysis. No one was allowed to see many people that died so it was very mysterious. People who were religious struggled. Then there were protocols [such as lockdowns] which I don't know if it made it better or worse.

Peru's lockdown was thought to have been one of the strictest since it combined intense policing with rigid curfews, and severe criminal justice sanctions. After some months, the men of the household could leave on alternate days to the women while, as Joel comments, *"the people working on the frontline all got Covid-19"*. This said, presenting alarmist depictions of statistics and discontinuous analysis, left absent the fundamental fact which the country's economists had quickly recognised, that *"Peru does not have a health system which can serve the needs of its people, the risk of its collapse was just a question of time"*.[32] It was asserted with confidence that 'following the measures' and 'adhering to the lockdowns' would provide suitable protection, yet Joel felt otherwise:

> People became convinced that if they followed the measures they wouldn't get ill, like masks and social distancing but it was like they were kidding themselves.

[32] Mauricio et al. (2020).

Perhaps Kisielinski et al. were right when they wrote *"the mask, which originally served a purely hygienic purpose, has been transformed into a symbol of conformity and pseudo-solidarity"*.[33] Yet by wearing a mask, governments as well as the WHO have told us, we are protecting ourselves as well as others—even despite *a lack of scientific research which can confirm their efficacy as a preventative measure in community settings*.[34] The closest study to examine the efficacy of masks in the context of Covid-19 involved 4,862 volunteers in a non-blinded randomised controlled trial undertaken in Denmark. A control group were told to wear high-quality surgical masks and the other told to go maskless for a period of a month. The difference between the two groups was minimal, with 1.8% of those wearing masks contracting the virus and 2.1% of those without them. The researchers concluded that minimal difference was due to those wearing masks not adhering properly to the rules.[35] Systematic reviews of various studies pre- and post-Covid-19 suggest:

> Face masks may slightly decrease the risk of spreading respiratory infections outside the household setting. However, it is questionable whether the effect is big enough to noticeably slow the speed at which a highly infectious disease like Covid spreads through the population.[36]

By equal measure, David, an NGO worker who travels and researches across Western, Central and Eastern countries in Africa, considers Covid-19 to be less of a threat because *"Africans are young and have strong immune systems"*. However, David, has seen the harm of the lockdowns first-hand: *"the economies have been destroyed, people have lost their work and lives and they are angry, they have protested. Africans need to be out to find work to be able to eat"*. He added:

> What I find significant is that most people who wear masks don't do it because of Covid but because they have to comply. Especially the young

[33] Kisielinski et al. (2021, p. 12).
[34] Vainshelboim (2021), Graham et al. (2020), Bakhit et al. (2021), and Reiss and Bhakdi (2020).
[35] Bundgaard et al. (2020).
[36] Rushworth (2021, p. 111).

people, they just have it in their pockets and put it on to go into a shop.
They know that without it they can't go in the shop. They want access
to the shop so they wear the mask but not because they want to prevent
Covid. In Rwanda, they do it because government is strict but they don't
do it because it is a deadly virus.

David's insights raise important questions about the extent to which
adherence reflects concern for public health or more instrumental
reasons for compliance (Chapter 10). In a situation where a country's
health infrastructure is already compromised and disadvantaged, political mobility in crisis scenarios is questionable and many of its citizens
live in abject poverty and need to be out of the house to work and earn
money to be able to eat. It is perhaps unsurprising that many citizens still
'play along' with the measures as if to almost own up to the inevitable
prospect that: (a) they will (have to) take their chances on Covid-19 and,
as a consequence, (b) illness of some sort looks set to be fairly likely (see
Chapter 6). How else would "80% of people on the frontline get infected"
said Joel. Similar issues were found in India—a country which hosts a
sixth of the world's population. We spoke to Madhuja, an unemployed
waitress who lost her job after the lockdown was initiated (Chapter 9).
Madhuja sat at home and watched the news of thousands of her fellow
countrymen and women get infected and die of Covid-19. She said to
us:

> It's as bad as it sounds. No beds in the hospitals. People lying on roads.
> It's bad. Even the vaccines which claim to be 'free' are not available. My
> parents went twice to the hospital but couldn't get vaccinated yet.

By comparison, India's first Covid-19 wave was reported as being surprisingly light despite significant discrepancies in the recording of deaths.
Here is an example of the occasional disparity when:

> Crematoriums and burial grounds were using covid-19 handling proto-
> cols not just for deaths among patients confirmed to have the viral
> infection, but also for 'suspected deaths' in which a patient shows covid-
> 19 symptoms. These are broadly based on WHO's guidelines for the
> certification of covid-19 deaths. Because laboratory testing is so limited in

India and methods such as reverse transcription PCR, which also looks for the genetic signature of the virus, and CBNAAT return false negatives, the ICMR recommends that *all suspected covid-19 deaths be reported as being from covid-19.*[37]

Another problem, equally apparent in the West, is the attribution of death to Covid-19—even if other pre-existing ailments may have already been present. In India there are millions of people in a poor state of health and living in unsanitary, air-polluted and deprived circumstances which reduce their life expectancy to just above 50. It is sadly perhaps no wonder that, pre-pandemic, around 27,000 died each day in India living in these conditions, with no access to adequate healthcare and treatment. This presented further problems for Indian medical officials:

Another problem is doctors attributing Covid-19 deaths to complications from other health conditions patients had when they contracted the virus, such as chronic hypertension, diabetes, or cancer, which make people more vulnerable to the effects of the virus.[38]

There is almost no way of separating the 'new threat' (Covid-19) from the 'pre-existing one' (the sad reality of poverty, destitution and ill-health in India). Furthermore, past viral threats seem to get no media coverage in India now. In 2018, 440,000 Indians died of Tuberculosis (TB) and there are a *"million missing cases every year that are not notified, and most remain either undiagnosed or unaccountably and inadequately diagnosed"*, states the National Strategic Plan for Tuberculosis Elimination 2017–25.[39] This is 42,000 more than the current total Covid-19 deaths recorded in India as of the summer of 2021.

---

[37] Pulla (2020).
[38] Ibid.
[39] De (2020).

In the midst of its 'second wave' during April and May 2021, and despite these recording discrepancies, the arrival of its traditional respiratory illness season and with a substandard public healthcare system, India is now reporting tens of thousands of Covid-19 'cases' each day and hundreds of deaths. In the absence of rising 'case numbers' and 'deaths' at present in numerous Western countries during the same period, media and political attention turned to India. With economies and social life starting to open up in the West at this time, the India situation provides the political impetus to temporarily *remove the visible immediate concern of Covid-19* while, at the same time, placate it with *an invisible subtle reminder of its likely return.*

A Marriage Made in Heaven: New Fears of Illness and Death

On the subject of return:

It's been over a year since I saw Luis who is the father of one of my daughter's friends at her school. Since the lockdown of March 2020 the only time he left his 70m2 squared flat for a period of six months was to take the rubbish out. "*It stresses me out when I am outside and there are lots of people you know*" he says from beneath his mask which jolts around with his words. "*I am used to the mask now, I don't go out, I don't want to be ill; I don't want to die*" he adds when I ask him if he sees any of his friends or those of his son. "*I don't go to bars or restaurants, no need, I can't be in those places anymore, I am fucked*" he says.
We get on to the subject of his work and he shakes his head. Prior to Covid-19 Luis was working in the HR department of a care home service in Madrid, Spain. "*The residents lived above us and we were the operations team really…well they pretty much all died, and even some of the carers too. No one knew what it was, no one was prepared, we had no masks, gowns, no protocols, no way of knowing how to deal with it*" he continues as he also shakes his head. "*One guy who was 50 years old, a carer, died…too much Covid-19 around and he got it, was in hospital and didn't come out…I don't know who is worse off*" he says as he comes back to me. "*What do you mean?*" I say before he starts bemoaning what it is like at our children's

school. Both his son and my daughter attend with the mask on all day, they sit individually on a desk which is surrounded by plastic sheets and the windows are left open all day. At playtime, they have to keep within 'bubbles' and cannot socialise with their allocated friendship group. Luis' son, however, has developed some mental health problems and is seeing a child psychologist because he thinks the *"virus is in the wind"* and is developing a phobia of outdoor spaces. [Field notes Daniel Briggs 'The return']

These field notes taken from Madrid in March of 2021 highlight several important features of new fears of illness and death. There is the notably personal experience Luis had having worked in the care home without adequate PPE, as well as guidance and international research that shows that these unfortunate disadvantages were likely to play a part in his current fear of the illness and compliance with the measures (Chapter 10). He said he couldn't *"escape the news"* and even though he tried to distract himself through following Real Madrid, he said he often found himself *"lying awake at night thinking of Covid-19"*. The fear still dominates his thoughts impeding a return to having a social life.

The *direct experience of being around death* associated with Luis' fear of illness and death is complemented by continual mainstream media expositions of the threat and daily doses of Covid-19 'new case' and 'death' statistics. Sadly, however, his son is also impacted as well. Luis' son didn't leave the flat for the same period, not even to go down to the communal gardens. The fact that Luis doesn't see friends or arrange social visits for his son means his son is also affected, augmented by the symbolic presence of both subtle and instructive ideological public health messages and protocols which are bolstered by the staff's preoccupation in his son's school. Countries such as Spain and the UK had prevention campaigns which saddled the potential responsibility of infecting others on to children's shoulders. His son fears participation in public life, burdened by the possibility of becoming infected or infecting and potentially 'killing someone'—something which other children in Spain have been found to experience.[40]

---

[40] Gómez-Beccara et al. (2020).

We have to question how this has come to be the case given that the virus only tends to be particularly dangerous for the elderly and/vulnerable (Chapter 2) and as considerable international scientific evidence has indicated—from very early on in the pandemic until as recently as May 2021—that most children develop no symptoms of illness and remain at an extremely low risk of death from Covid-19.[41] Moreover, schools have not been found to be transmission hubs for the virus.[42] Yet, and perhaps it could be argued unfairly, children have been exposed to changes in social life, and in the context of a pandemic lockdown, absorbed all the advice given to them from politicians, their families, teachers and everyone around them. In China, almost a quarter (22%) of children from a survey sample (n = 320) were worried about contracting Covid-19 and infecting other adults, particularly older family members.[43] In India, evidence is emerging of young people from economically-distressed families suffering as a consequence of lockdowns and/or lockdown-related pressures, such as fear of Covid-19 or obtaining a positive Covid-19 status, harming family members[44] and/or committing suicide.[45]

The consequences of these pressures for children and young people we explore in detail throughout the book, but the point we want to make here is that *the political framing of Covid-19 and its public health measures generate additional mental anxiety that endorse an elevated preoccupation with personal health, particularly the potential for infection, transmission and death.* Psychologists and Psychiatrists internationally have found strong links between news and social media consumption with elevated Covid-19-related anxiety and depression.[46] One study concluded that this may lead to 'high-health anxiety' which is potentially responsible for:

[41] Bhopal et al. (2021).
[42] European Centre for Disease Prevention and Control (2020).
[43] Jiao et al. (2020).
[44] Mamun et al. (2020).
[45] Dsouza et al. (2020).
[46] Brendau et al. (2021) and Cullen et al. (2020).

…a variety of other maladaptive safety behaviours. In the context of viral outbreaks, this may include excessive handwashing, social withdrawal, and panic purchasing. It is noteworthy that all of these behaviours are consistent with public health recommendations for managing epidemics and pandemics; however, in the case of those with high health anxiety, they are taken to an extreme that can have negative consequences to the individual and their community.[47]

Many times, we witnessed examples of such behaviours in public spaces in both the UK and Spain since the advent of the 'new normal':

I take a seat on the plane which is, once again, half empty. The journeys between Madrid and Majorca have not been the same since Covid-19. My seat is on the aisle and to my left, with a healthy gap between us, is a young man in his early 30s. The man gets out the disinfectant cloth given to us by the plane staff and proceeds to wipe his hands, his phone, his keys, his laptop and the table and seat around him. He then sits back for a minute or two. He looks at his watch and reaches for the bag below the seat in front to get some more disinfecting gel. He gets it out and applies it to his hands before reaching in the same bag and pulling out a drink. It is only when he proceeds to remove his mask that I see another mask underneath. Perhaps to be on the safe side, he turns his head towards the window, thus reducing the space he can drink, and removes the second mask and drinks as quickly as possible before concealing his face with both masks and disinfecting his hands once again. [Field notes Daniel Briggs 'Disinfecting']

We explore the application and rejection of these measures in more detail later on in the book (see Chapter 10), but here we have to reference them as they play a significant role in the *fear of illness and possible death*. There are other numerous and more extreme international examples reported in news media which exemplify this exaggerated concern for personal welfare and health in a time of pandemic fears:

An American couple Patrick Jesernik (aged 54) and partner Cheryl Schriefer (aged 59) – were involved in a Covid-19-related murder-suicide.

---

[47] Asmundson and Taylor (2020).

Patrick shot Cheryl (who had been suffering from severe breathing problems) before killing himself. He was fearful that Cheryl, his girlfriend, had been infected with Covid-19. While both had been tested for the virus neither had received their results before their deaths yet the autopsies showed that neither was infected with the disease.[48]

A Malaysian couple – Subramaniam (aged 65) and his wife Lalitha (aged 55) – both attempted suicide together by swallowing sleeping pills because they were not provided seats on a special Covid-19 rescue flight back to their home country of Malaysia. They were told by airport officials that their names were not listed on the flight and were distraught by the responses from embassy officials and attempted to take their own lives.[49]

A young couple from Bangladesh – Shamim (aged 30) and wife Renoka Begum (aged 24) – committed suicide together by hanging themselves in their house. They had a three-year old child and were experiencing financial problems as a result of lockdown.[50]

One man from Bihar, India – Ramesh Shah – committed suicide by hanging himself after his wife Suman, committed suicide by setting herself on fire. The couple were unable to pay back a loan on a truck they had bought because they were unable to work during the Covid-19 lockdown. After an argument concerning their finances, Suman deliberately set herself on fire. Ramesh tried to save his wife but she died at hospital. He was so distraught from the experience that he killed himself. The couple left behind two young children aged 7 and 10 respectively.[51]

Zikri, an IT worker from Malaysia, described to us how two of his closest friends, both working in the hotel and hospitality sector, had committed suicide because of *"debt and depression"*. *"One jumped from the 19th floor of the hotel where he worked because he was in debt"* while the other *"gassed himself at home because he was laid off by the hotel"* he said. In Malaysia, public health restrictions, including the sporadic use of lockdowns, had been used to counter potential infections in 2020, which in the main remained low. Borders were closed, businesses were shut and

[48] BBC (2020).
[49] Indian Express (2020).
[50] Zamin (2020).
[51] Kumar (2020).

services were run at a minimum for some months. Millions of people like Zikri's friends working in the hospitality sector lost their jobs and businesses as tourism ground to a halt.[52] When the country's economy did start to resume service in June 2020, it was according to strict health protocols and this was not enough to kickstart any economic recovery, even less so when Zikri informs us that the government as a substitute *"give people $50 a month"* which is about $1.60 a day. *"How can you live on that?"* he says with disgust. Like numerous countries in the Far East which, as we write during the summer of 2021, are now experiencing increases in 'cases', hospitalisations and deaths because of the reported 'Delta variant',[53] Malaysia is now once again subject to a strict lockdown. Zikri now does all his work online and doesn't leave his flat because his *"health app"* says there are *"40 infections within a 1 km radius of where he lives"* and because the *"army are stopping infected people from leaving the neighbourhoods"*.

Fear of illness coupled with debt and/or a shut down on economic opportunity can pull the trigger on already fragile feelings, particularly for those living in poverty, debt and disadvantage. Joseph, a reporter for a small media organisation in Yaoundé in Cameroon, watched on as his prime minister started to shut down the country fearing the healthcare system would be overwhelmed. Like many other countries pre-pandemic, Cameroon's health system had suffered significantly over the last four decades because of structural adjustment, corruption and limited investment.[54] Joseph wrote at the time how there was *"lots of fear of the white man's disease"* as it was known and how it became real—not because of skyrocketing virus 'cases' or 'deaths'—but because *"all ports and airports shut, educational, public and private was shut down"* he said. *"By 6 pm every day, streets were deserted"* he remembers. The closure of borders, travel and business between neighbouring countries in the modern and informal economies had immediate ramifications and tens of thousands of people, particularly women, lost work. The closure

---

[52] Hanafiah et al. (2021).
[53] Choudhary (2021).
[54] Ojong (2020).

of these institutions and the mandatory use of face masks, he wrote, changed the way people practiced public life:

> All of a sudden, distribution of hand sanitizer and masks are everywhere but most were improvised 'pieces of cloth' as people are too poor and the government don't give us things like this. Go to market put on mask, bank put on mask, supermarket put on mask, even mask on black market.

The Cameroon government were granted a loan of $226 million from the International Monetary Fund (IMF) to deal with the unfolding crisis and, aside from asking its primary healthcare facilities to donate to what it called the *Special Fund of National Solidarity*, also asked its own citizens to make a contribution.[55] *"It was necessary, health has no price"* commented Joseph, adding:

> The more you treat people with Covid-19, the more people fear going to public hospitals for normal illnesses. The more 'cases', the more money they pour in because, for example, since coronavirus, AIDS funding has been redirected.

In Cameroon, people are required to contribute to healthcare in the country but nearly two-thirds of its population cannot afford it and for that reason rarely present at primary healthcare facilities or hospitals. The advent of Covid-19 exacerbated that fear. Mathematicians from universities in Douala and Yaoundé in Cameroon hypothesised that *"the eradication of the pandemic is highly dependent on the control measures taken by government"* and endorsed the continued use of lockdowns, curfews, social distancing and mask wearing[56]—even if it continues to cause economic turmoil, social discontent and fear of illness and death among its people.

As of June 2021, around 80,000 'cases' and 1,330 people had died in Cameroon with/of Covid-19, though the death rate is thought to be higher because of discrepancies in recording. Yet, questions started to emerge concerning where the funds had gone for hospitals. Healthcare

---

[55] Human Rights Watch (2021).
[56] Nkwayep et al. (2020, p. 25).

workers reported shortages in basic hospital goods, including thermometers, disinfectants, and medicines, as well as ventilators and oxygen, and protective clothing for doctors and nurses, such as masks, gloves and glasses. When members of the opposition party started to provide disinfectant and masks free of charge to people, they were arrested and charged with the crime of *rebellion*. Even though the IMF have now loaned $382 million to the Cameroon government to assist with implementing Covid-19 interventions, it is unknown how this money has been spent.

Hyper-Individualism and the Subjective Distance from Mortality

In contrast, during the pandemic, many people in the West were suddenly confronted with the increased visibility and proximity of both 'real' illness and death. While Western populations routinely consume and view images of pain and suffering, this is largely at a distance through screens.[57] Imagery associated with Covid-19 was much 'closer to home' in the sense that it was happening in the communities, care homes and hospitals of their respective nations—it was happening 'here and now' and we were 'watching it live' if you like. Our data reinforces the point, in that, many people we spoke to had direct experience of what was being broadcast daily, whether directly or indirectly. Pre-pandemic though, for many, illness and mortality did not generally intrude into their everyday lives in such a dramatic and spectacular fashion: graphical depictions of cases of infection or deaths from diseases were not so routinely shared in news media, nor were distressing images of suffering and dying from inside hospitals and intensive care units. Incremental rises in living standards and advances in medicine across the twentieth century have brought unprecedented comfort and extended life spans for many in affluent societies. As a result, death is becoming the province of old age across, particularly, Western nations[58] and something which,

---

[57] Atkinson and Rogers (2016).
[58] Walter (2017).

some have argued, has been gradually hidden from public view, regarded as a proximally distant event, and therefore "*pushed back into the darker corners of our minds*".[59]

Indeed, the various maladies and frailties that develop in old age are often managed and contained within nursing homes and private dwellings, away from public view. While with well-resourced healthcare systems, comparative to many States in the Global South for example, even if they were in fact reeling from the fallout of austerity measures (Chapter 2), the prospect of them being suddenly 'overwhelmed' represented new and frightening territory. Similarly, catastrophes that engender considerable suffering, such as war, mass violence, famine and pandemics of dangerous diseases that result in high numbers of deaths, have been in recent history relatively absent from many affluent Western societies (see the account of Osama in Chapter 9). As mentioned, such events are now more likely to be simulated for Western audiences who view and consume them. This has led some to suggest that social numbness results from this and individuals increasingly resist a confrontation with the reality of death and harm.[60] With the advent of Covid-19, to some degree, many in the West experienced this *subjective distance* from death and suffering reduce quite suddenly and dramatically. We were not able to leave our homes, were not able to meet people, go to shops or restaurants, we could not meet relatives in care homes. Taken for granted aspects of our lives pre-pandemic were halted and many were left only with the daily briefing bombardment of 'new cases' and 'deaths', the 24/7 media coverage of the crisis, and consumer distractions to get through it.[61]

Paul, a student in his late 20s residing in Northern England, typified this. After describing how he was "*sick of the word Covid*" after the first wave, he was relieved to see how things were "*going back to normal, pubs open and things gradually returning to how they were*". This was after people he had known through friends had passed away from the virus:

---

[59] Mellor and Shilling (1993).
[60] Atkinson and Rogers (2016).
[61] Briggs et al. (2020).

Auntie has Covid and whole household but she was worst affected and started to lose her hair which no one talks about as a side effect. My partner's dad has friends who died, at least one definitely had it. In his case, they tested him after he had gone in and they took ages with the test and then when they called him when he was already back in hospital but he died in the end. He had some pre-existing conditions though.

After confessing he was *"following it"* during the 'first wave', Paul describes how, with the decrease in reported 'cases' and 'deaths' in the UK during 2020 he *"doesn't really think about it"*. In the end, with *"all the statistics and stuff"*, he thought there was *"so much conflicting information that you end up casting it to one side"*. This *reverse process of over-saturation*, in part, produces his distance from potential illness and eliminates concern about him dying, but what completes it is the reasoning that something like Covid-19 is not that dangerous to him and that there are far more important things to look forward to when the restrictions disappear (see Chapter 6):

I think at the start there was a lot of pseudo solidarity, clapping for the carers and 'we're all in it together'. I feel that was just piecemeal and temporary. Everyone was asked to volunteer to help vulnerable people but this was surely what the government should have been doing in the first place! All the solidarity has been lost now. We just want to enjoy ourselves as much as possible now, go shopping and spend money. I am just as bad, I wanted that too, I had money to spend and I held off for so long but the consumer in me was just too powerful.

Paul *"expects the virus to come back"* because he says he has *"done the research"* on the issue representing what is known as the *informed patient*. For some years, and because of austerity politics, health systems have been passing on the responsibility for welfare through 'responsible behaviour' and 'responsible choices'. When people are made responsible for their health they rely on accurate information to be able to act accordingly.[62] However, in a context where those very health systems need to advise on a new virus which is seemingly killing people quickly,

---

[62] Parker (2006).

combined with Covid-19 media saturation, the *informed patient* seeks to investigate themselves. In Paul's case, self-evaluations of the risk of the virus produce his distance from mortality and diminish his concern about illness. Paul is young and has worked out that this is not something he should be worried about. Yet, this pressure on people to be responsible for their own health can also have reverse consequences.

One of our participants, María from Madrid in Spain, was always concerned throughout the first lockdown in Spain: "*it is terrible what is happening*", she told us, "*so many people getting ill and dying*". In Spain, the lockdowns have been notoriously harsh and heavily policed. Social distancing and public health messages are everywhere and even mask wearing in public has been enshrined in law since May 2020 while only recently relaxed in June 2021. Having the comfort of working from home and the space of a garden, she said she "*weathered the lockdown*" but towards the end of it—when the case numbers and deaths desisted—reported feeling ill with fever and headaches. Although the guidance in Spain recommends her self-quarantine, she went a step further by wearing a mask at home around her family and slept in a separate bedroom to her husband, who was not in a high-risk category. She became so worried that she paid €250 for two separate Covid-19 tests—both were negative—yet insisted on a further period of self-isolation and continued to wear a mask at home for another month. Maria's actions seem to reflect a *silent stigma attached to Covid-19 illness*, which was often juxtaposed in the Facebook forums where anonymous individuals confessed to being ill/dying or being fearful about being ill/dying from Covid-19. Many testimonies not only reflected the dominant narrative on Covid-19 (pro-lockdown, in support of measures, wearing masks and social distancing) but acted like a warning to others. Here, Stewart, a man in his late 40s recounts for the fifth time his experience with Covid-19 in the Facebook forums:

It was six weeks ago tonight. I started a slight cough, got tested next day and got a positive result on the Tuesday. In the last few days, I seem to have more or less fully recovered. It did linger with me, the breathlessness and wheezing, but I'm practically back to normal. I'm 47, bit overweight, diabetes (well controlled) and slightly high blood pressure. It was a worrying time but thankfully it was mild and, even with lingering symptoms, I seem to be over it now.

Although I was lucky and had no serious issues, unfortunately some people do have issues. For that reason, I still stand fully with my masking, social distancing and hygiene. I honestly believe it was because of my standards and practices that meant that when I did catch the virus, I only had mild symptoms.

Please everyone respect the lockdown measures and do every bit you can to keep that extra little bit of distance away from others. I know its tough and people are getting exhausted of rules, but the virus is not getting bored or exhausted. Also we need to protect the NHS for other people who need them with issues that are not Covid-related.

There could not have been a better endorsement for what the government was doing than from Stewart. Important factors such as his diabetes and weight are played down even though they are variables which could lead to heart disease—something which, pre-Covid-19, led to an average of 450 deaths each day or one every three minutes in the UK.[63] Related to this, in a post-Covid-19 world, other modes of dying are mixed up with Covid-19—which has become the dominant factor in the cause of death. Yet, other feelings are also at play here which perpetuate the potential for suffering. Take Ben, for example, who was made redundant during the first UK lockdown. He was angry but, by the summer of 2020, had started his own makeshift business cleaning windows and things started to improve. He was amazed how his father, aged 91, had survived the outbreaks of the virus in care homes since he suffered from dementia. After the New Year, however—and with the advent of the second Covid-19 wave—his dad fell ill the morning of 10 January 2021:

> Unfortunately, poor dad has the Covid. Two members of staff at the care home got it and many residents have come down with it. I think he's in his final hours as he is not in good health. It's looking very bleak. He was feeling bad, got a bit better but now has had a sudden downturn. I think he has given up the fight. He has had a good life. It brings the reality of the virus home.

---

63 British Heart Foundation (2021).

Ben's short dialogue here is almost a preparation for the inevitable but note how the main attribution of his father's likely death is made to Covid-19. Would he have said the same if his dad would have died from just dementia and old age? It wouldn't be the same if his words were 'it brings the reality of dementia and old age home'. What if he had died of flu—which may have been possible during 2018 and 2019? Evidence from numerous European countries including France, Spain, UK, Italy to name a few indicates that previously less intense flu seasons left a surplus number of people who didn't—but would have—passed away under a normal flu strain.[64] The fact that this cohort of people didn't die meant that when a stronger viral strain came along, it contributed to their otherwise natural demise. Only Ben does not recognise his father's death as 'natural' because of the *ideological tumult around Covid-19*. Six hours later at 7 pm:

> Dad passed away. We got to speak to him as a family although he couldn't reply of course as he couldn't hear. That was at 6.50pm. He was a good man who lived a happy life. Covid took him in the end.

Covid-19 is responsible for shortening what would otherwise be *a natural means of dying*—even if the means of death is actually entirely natural—but how much longer would his father have lived? Same for Harry, an insurance worker, who seemed now to attribute all illness, suffering and death to Covid-19. Harry has had "*many friends*" affected by Covid-19, several hospitalised who now "*remain physically and mentally affected by the experience*" he says. Some of his friends, he adds, "*have lost their elderly parents to the virus*". The suffering seems to be all around him for, at the time of interview, three days previously, two of his neighbours had been rushed to hospital, one of whom was on a ventilator. "*Three days ago, two of my neighbours living either side of my house were rushed into hospital*". When we probed further in the interview, it turned out that all these people had underlying health issues or were elderly, but for Harry "*it didn't matter, it was still Covid*".

---

[64] Hope (2020).

This kind of 'death anxiety'[65] has recently been shown to predict anxiety-related disorders to Covid-19 but also to play a causal role in various mental health conditions aggravated by the existence of the virus and the potential to be infected from it. There is emerging evidence now that people who know someone die of/with Covid-19 experience higher levels of Prolonged Grief Disorder and Persistent Complex Bereavement Disorder (PCBD) in comparison with those who die of other natural or unnatural causes.[66] Fear, illness and death are seemingly high on the public health agenda in a post-Covid-19 world and this creates the opportunity for particular industries to step in and capitalise (Chapter 5) while others simply collapse and fold, causing simultaneous, irreparable parallel damage.

References

Abuhammad, S., Alzoubi, K., & Khabour, O. (2020). Fear of COVID-19 and stigmatization towards infected people among Jordanian people. *International Journal of Clinical Practice, 75*(4), e13899.

Arevalo-Rodriguez, I., Buitrago-Garcia, D., Simancas-Racines, D., Zambrano-Achig, P., Del Campo, R., Ciapponi, A., Sued, O., Martinez-Garcia, L., Rutjes, A. W., Low, N., Bossuyt, P. M., Perez-Molina, J. A., & Zamora, J. (2020). False-negative results of initial RT-PCR assays for COVID-19: A systematic review. *PLoS One 15*(12), 14. e0242958. https://doi.org/10.1371/journal.pone.0242958

Asmundson, G., & Taylor, S. (2020). How health anxiety influences responses to viral outbreaks like COVID-19: What all decision makers, health authorities, and healthcare professionals need to know. *Journal of Anxiety Disorders, 71*, 1–2.

Atkinson, R., & Rogers, T. (2016). Pleasure zones and murder boxes: Online pornography and violent video games as cultural zones of exception. *British Journal of Criminology, 56*(6), 1291–1307.

Bakhit, M., Krzyzaniak, N., Scott, A. M., Clark, J., Glasziou, P., & Del Mar, C. (2021). Downsides of face masks and possible mitigation strategies: A

---

[65] Menzies and Menzies (2020).
[66] Eisma et al. (2020).

systematic review and meta-analysis. *BMJ Open, 11*(2), e044364. https://doi.org/10.1136/bmjopen-2020-044364

Bamji, A. (2020). COVID-19: What's going wrong with testing in the UK? *British Medical Journal, 370.* https://doi.org/10.1136/bmj.m3678

BBC. (2020, April 5). *Coronavirus fears linked to Illinois pair's murder-suicide.* Cited online at https://www.bbc.com/news/world-us-canada-52192842

Bhopal, S., Bagaria, J., Olabi, B., & Bhopal, R. (2021). Children and young people remain at low risk of COVID-19 mortality. *The Lancet Child and Adolescent Health.* Published online 10 March 2021. https://doi.org/10.1016/S2352-4642(21)00066-3

Brandén, M., Aradhya, S., Kolk, M., Drefahl, S., Malmberg, B., Cederström, A., Andersson, G., & Mussino, E. (2020). Residential context and COVID-19 mortality among adults aged 70 years and older in Stockholm: A population-based, observational study using individual-level data. *Lancet Healthy Longevity, 1*(2), e80-88. https://doi.org/10.1016/S2666-7568(20)30016-7

Brendau, A., Petzold, M., Pyrkosch, L., Maricic, L., Betzler, F., Rogoll, J., Große, J., Ströhle, A., & Plag, J. (2021). Associations between COVID-19 related media consumption and symptoms of anxiety, depression and COVID-19 related fear in the general population in Germany. *European Archives of Psychiatry and Clinical Neuroscience, 271,* 283–291.

Briggs, D., Ellis, A., Lloyd, A., & Telford, L. (2020). New hopes or old futures in disguise? Neoliberalism, the Covid-19 pandemic and the possibility of social change. *International Journal of Sociology and Social Policy, 40*(9/10), 831–848. https://doi.org/10.1108/IJSSP-07-2020-0268

Briggs, D., Ellis, A., Lloyd, A., & Telford, L. (2021). *Researching the COVID-19 pandemic: A critical blueprint for the social sciences.* Policy Press Rapid Response Series.

British Heart Foundation. (2021). *UK Factsheet.* British Heart Foundation.

Bundgaard, H., Bundgaard, J. S., Raaschou-Pedersen, D. E. T., von Buchwald, C., Todsen, T., Norsk, J. B., Pries-Heje, M. M., Vissing, C. R., Nielsen, P. B., Winsløw, U. C., Fogh, K., Hasselbalch, R., Krisrtensen, J. H., Ringgaard, A., Andersen, M. P., Goecke, N. B., Trebbien, R., Skovgaard, K., Benfield, T., … Iversen, K. (2020, November). Effectiveness of adding a mask recommendation to other public health measures to prevent SARS-CoV-2 infection in Danish mask wearers: A randomized controlled trial. *Annals of Internal Medicine.* https://doi.org/10.7326/M20-6817

Chaiuk, T., & Dunaievska, O. (2020). Producing the fear culture in media: An examination of Coronavirus discourse. *Journal of History, Culture and Art Research, 9*(2), 184–194. https://doi.org/10.7596/taksad.v8i4.2316

Choudhary, S. (2021, August 9). *Charts show that COVID is hitting parts of Asia harder now than when the pandemic began.* CNBC. Cited online at https://www.cnbc.com/2021/08/10/covid-is-hitting-parts-of-asia-harder-now-than-beginning-of-pandemic.html

Cohen, A., Kessel, B., & Milgroom, M. (2020). Diagnosing COVID-19 infection: The danger of over- reliance on positive test results. *medRxiv: The Preprint Server for Health Sciences*, 1–11. https://doi.org/10.1101/2020.04.26.20080911

Cullen, W., Gulati, G., & Kelly, B. (2020). Mental health in the COVID-19 pandemic. *QJM: An International Journal of Medicine, 113*, 311–312.

De, A. (2020, April 17). India's top infectious disease killed over 440,000 people in 2018. *Indian Express.* Cited online at https://indianexpress.com/article/india/coronavirus-india-top-infectious-disease-tuberculosis-6365732/

Dsouza, D. D., Quadros, S., Hyderabadwala, Z. J., & Mamun, M. A. (2020). Aggregated COVID-19 suicide incidences in India: Fear of COVID-19 infection is the prominent causative factor. *Psychiatry Research*, 113145. https://doi.org/10.1016/j.psychres.2020.113145

Eisma, M. C., Boelen, P. A., & Lenferink, L. I. M. (2020). Prolonged grief disorder following the Coronavirus (COVID-19) pandemic. *Psychiatry Research, 288*, 113031. https://dx.doi.org/10.1016%2Fj.psychres.2020.113031

European Centre for Disease Prevention and Control. (2020). *COVID-19 in children and the role of school settings in transmission—First update.*

Ferguson, N., Laydon, D., Nedjati-Gilani, G., Imai, N., Ainslie, K., Baguelin, M., Bhatia, S., Boonyasiri, A., Cucunuba, Z., Dannenburg, G., Dighe, A., Dorigatti, I., Fu, H., Gaythorpe, K., Green, W., Hamlet, A., Hinsley, W., Okell, L., Elsland, S., Thompson, H. … Ghani, A. (2020). *Report 9: Impact of non-pharmaceutical interventions (NPIs) to reduce COVID-19 mortality and healthcare demand.* Imperial College COVID-19 Response Team.

Gómez-Beccara, I., Flujas, J., Andrés, M., Sánchez-López, P., & Fernández-Torres, M. (2020, September). Evolución del estado psicológico y el miedo en la infancia y adolescencia durante el confinamiento por la COVID-19. *Revista de Psicología Clínica con Niños y Adolescentes, 7*(3), 11–18.

Graham, P., Martin, E. H., McCartney, M., & Dingwall, R. (2020). Science, society, and policy in the face of uncertainty: Reflections on the debate around face coverings for the public during COVID-19. *Critical Public Health, 30*(5), 501–508. https://doi.org/10.1080/09581596.2020.1797997

Guerin, O. (2021). *COVID-19 pandemic: Everything you should not do, Brazil has done.* https://www.bbc.co.uk/news/world-latin-america-57733540

Hanafiah, M. H., Balasingam, A. S., Nair, V., Jamaluddin, M. R., & Zahari, M. S. M. (2021). Implications of COVID-19 on tourism businesses in Malaysia: Evidence from a preliminary industry survey. *Asia-Pacific Journal of Innovation in Hospitality and Tourism, 10*(1), 81–94.

Hope, C. (2020). *COVID-19 death rate is higher in European countries with a low flu intensity since 2018.* Cambridge University Press.

Human Rights Watch. (2021, April 23). *Cameroon: Ensure credible inquiry on COVID-19 funds.* Cited online at https://www.hrw.org/news/2021/04/23/cameroon-ensure-credible-inquiry-covid-19-funds

Indian Express. (2020, April 5). *No seats in special rescue flight, Malaysian couple attempts suicide.* Cited online at https://www.newindianexpress.com/states/tamil-nadu/2020/apr/05/no-seats-in-special-rescue-flight-malaysian-couple-attempts-suicide-2125937.html

Jiao, W. Y., Wang, L. N., Liu, J., Fang, S. F., Jiao, F. Y., Pettoello-Mantovani, M., & Somekh, E. (2020). (Behavioral and emotional disorders in children during the COVID-19 epidemic. *The Journal of Pediatrics, 221*, 264–266.

Katz, A. P., Civantos, F. J., Sargi, Z., Leibowitz, J. M., Nicolli, E. A., Weed, D., Moskovitz, A. E., Civantos, A. M., Andrews, D. M., Martinez, O., & Thomas, G. R. (2020). False-positive reverse transcriptase polymerase chain reaction screening for SARS-CoV-2 in the setting of urgent head and neck surgery and otolaryngologic emergencies during the pandemic: Clinical implications. *Head & Neck, 42*, 1–8. https://doi.org/10.1002%2Fhed.26317

Kisielinski, K., Giboni, P., Prescher, A., Klosterhalfen, B., Graessel, D., Funken, S., Kempski, O., & Hirsch, O. (2021). Is a mask that covers the mouth and nose free from undesirable side effects in everyday use and free of potential hazards? *International Journal Environment Research Public Health, 18*(8), 4344. https://doi.org/10.3390/ijerph18084344

Kumar, A. (2020, May 4). *Coronavirus lockdown 3.0: Unable to repay loan, couple commits suicide in Bihar.* Cited online at https://www.deccanher

ald.com/national/east-and-northeast/coronavirus-lockdown-30-unable-to-repay-loan-couple-commits-suicide-in-bihar-833285.html

Lazzerini, M. (2020). Delayed access or provision of care in Italy resulting from fear of COVID-19. *The Lancet Child & Adolescent Health, 4*(5), e11-12.

Li, Y., Yao, L., Jiawei, L., Lei, C., Song, Y., Cai, Z., & Yang, C. (2020). Stability issues of RT- PCR testing of SARS-CoV-2 for hospitalized patients clinically diagnosed with COVID-19. *Journal of Medical Virology, 92*(7), 903–908. https://doi.org/10.1002/jmv.25786

Mamun, M., Bhuiyan, A., & Manzar, M. (2020). The first COVID-19 infanticide-suicide case: Financial crisis and fear of COVID-19 infection are the causative factors. *Asian Journal of Psychiatry, 54,* 102365. https://doi.org/10.1016/j.ajp.2020.102365

Mauricio, J., Pereyra, A., & Carbajal, D. (2020, July–December). Análisis de políticas públicas en el Peru ante la crisis derivada de la COVID-19. *Semestre Económico, 23*(55), 113–138.

Mellor, P., & Shilling, C. (1993). Modernity, self-identity and the sequestration of death. *Sociology, 27*(3), 411–431.

Menzies, R. E., & Menzies, R. G. (2020). Death anxiety in the time of COVID-19: Theoretical explanations and clinical implications. *The Cognitive Behaviour Therapist, 13*(e19), 1–11. https://doi.org/10.1017%2FS175 4470X20000215

Moustsen-Helms, I. R., Emborg, H.-D., Nielsen, J., Nielsen, K. F., Krause, T. G., Mølbak, K., Møller, K. L., Berthelsen, A.-S.N., & Valentiner-Branth, P. (2021). Vaccine effectiveness after 1st and 2nd dose of the BNT162b2 mRNA Covid-19 vaccine in long-term care facility residents and healthcare workers—A Danish cohort study. *MedRxiv.* https://doi.org/10.1101/2021. 03.08.21252200

Nkwayep, C., Bowong, S., tewa, T., & Kurths, J. (2020). Short-term forecasts of the COVID-19 pandemic: A study case of Cameroon. *Chaos, Solitons and Fractals, 140,* , , 110106. https://doi.org/10.1016/j.chaos.2020.110106

Nørgaard, S., Vestergaard, L., Nielson, J., Richter, L., Schmid, D., Bustos, N., Brave, T., Athanasiadou, M., Lytras, T., Denissov, G., Veideman, T., Luomala, O., Möttönen, T., Fouillet, A., Caserio-Schönemann, C., Heiden, M. A. D., Uphoff, H., Gkolfinopoulou, K., Bobvos, J., ... Mølbak, K. (2021). Real- time monitoring shows substantial excess all-cause mortality during second wave of COVID-19 in Europe, October to December 2020. *Euro Surveillance, 26*(2). https://doi.org/10.2807/1560-7917.ES.2021.26.1. 2002023

Ojong, N. (2020). The COVID-19 pandemic and the pathology of the economic and political architecture in Cameroon. *Healthcare, 8*, 176. https://doi.org/10.3390/healthcare8020176

Parker, R. M. (2006, December 24). What an informed patient means for the future of healthcare. *Pharmacoeconomics, 2*, 29–33. https://doi.org/10.2165/00019053-200624002-00004. PMID: 23389486.

Pulla, P. (2020). What counts as a COVID-19 death? *British Medical Journal*. https://doi.org/10.1136/bmj.m2859

Rao, C. (2020). Medical certification of cause of death for COVID-19. *Bulletin World Health Organisation, 98*(5), 298. https://www.who.int/bulletin/volumes/98/5/20-257600.pdf

Reiss, K., & Bhakdi, S. (2020). *Corona: False alarm?* Chelsea Green Publishing.

Rushworth, S. (2021). *COVID: Why most of what you know is wrong*. Karneval Publishing.

Santos, S., & Chiesa, M. (2020). *PCR positives: What do they mean?* The Centre for Evidence- Based Medicine. https://www.cebm.net/covid-19/pcr-positives-what-do-they-mean/

Sanyaolu, A., Okorie, C., Marinkovic, A., Patidar, R., Younis, K., Desai, P., Hosein, Z., Padda, I., Mangat, J., & Altaf, M. (2020). Comorbidity and its impact on Patients with COVID-19. *SN Comprehensive Clinical Medicine*, 1–8. https://doi.org/10.1007%2Fs42399-020-00363-4

Statista. (2021). *Coronavirus (COVID-19) in Brazil*. Statista.

Surkova, E., Nikolayevskyy, V., & Drobniewski, F. (2020). False-positive COVID-19 results: Hidden problems and costs. *The Lancet, 8*, 1167–1168. https://doi.org/10.1016/s2213-2600(20)30453-7

Tavares, F., & Betti, G. (2021). The pandemic of poverty, vulnerability, and COVID-19: Evidence from a fuzzy multidimensional analysis of deprivations in Brazil. *World Development, 139*, 24.

Vainshelboim, B. (2021). Facemasks in the COVID-19 era: A health hypothesis. *Medical Hypotheses, 146*, 110411.

Walter, T. (2017). *What death means now: Thinking critically about dying and grieving*. Policy.

Wang, C., Horby, P. W., Hayden, F. G., & Gao, G. F. (2020). A novel coronavirus outbreak of global health concern. *The Lancet, 395*(10223), 470–473. https://doi.org/10.1016/S0140-6736(20)30185-9

World Health Organization. (2020). *WHO characterises Covid-19 as a pandemic*. https://www.who.int/emergencies/diseases/novel-coronavirus-2019/events-as-they-happen

Young, A. (2021). Locked-down city. *Crime, Media and Culture, 17*(1), 21–25.

Zamin, M. (2020, April 24). *Marido y mujer se suicidan con una cuerda en Keshabpur*. Cited online at https://mzamin.com/article.php?mzamin= 223588

Zizek, S. (2020). *Pandemic: COVID-19 shakes the world*. OR Books.

4

Lockdown Inequalities: Covid-19 Losers

As we noted earlier, the world into which the pandemic entered was vastly unequal and rife with fault lines, tensions and divisions. This not only characterised the risk associated with catching Covid-19, but also the chances of adequate healthcare treatment, survival rates, and, more recently, chances of receiving approved Covid-19 vaccines.[1] While inequalities existed in terms of income, health, housing, food, employment, status, class, gender, age and a range of other characteristics prior to the pandemic, Covid-19 has also exacerbated existing—and created new—forms of inequality. For example, the IMF estimates that income inequality grew more sharply in 2020 than in any previous crisis.[2] Here we consider a range of lockdown inequalities and draw attention to those who have lost the most during the pandemic before looking at the lockdown 'winners' in the next chapter. We can broadly define three groups across the two chapters:

---

[1] Bambra et al. (2021).

[2] Romei (2020).

© The Author(s), under exclusive license to Springer Nature Switzerland AG 2021
D. Briggs et al., *Lockdown*,
https://doi.org/10.1007/978-3-030-88825-1_4

1. the 'truly disadvantaged' (borrowing from William J. Wilson) who were reliant on crumbling welfare regimes, informal labour markets, charity, and lived insecure lives before the pandemic;
2. the 'newly precarious' who were forced to stay at home, saw life chances diminish through educational inequalities and collapsing labour markets;
3. and the 'lockdown winners' who at one end of the extreme saw their savings rise, their lives slow down as they enjoyed the advantages lockdown afforded and, at the other, among the billionaires, millionaires and sectors where profits exploded and shares of wealth and power became more heavily concentrated.

This chapter is framed geographically, presenting evidence across continents. Here we discuss the first two groups, with the much smaller group of pandemic winners addressed in the following chapter. The global financial crisis of 2007–2008 offers a useful template for the pandemic in terms of spread, response and inequality in that, *like the virus*, the crisis quickly spread across the (financial) trade routes of the world, hit some places sooner than others, caused more damage in places more vulnerable to this threat, and showed the limitations of neoliberal capitalism and its governance structures.[3] The response to the crisis also demonstrated the ideological limits of those in positions of power, willing to pull certain economic levers to save the capitalist system yet unwilling to countenance more radical surgery for a patient on life support.[4]

Similar to the Covid-19 pandemic, the crisis itself also exacerbated and generated rampant inequalities as thousands of foreclosures cost people their homes, savings and futures.[5] Foodbank use entered popular consciousness in an unprecedented manner.[6] Unemployment and the growth of precarious, insecure 'non-standard' forms of work became the 'new normal'.[7] The austerity agenda, designed to fix the damage wrought by the crash, facilitated the service of capital markets, but heightened

3 Harvey (2010).
4 Mitchell and Fazi (2017).
5 Desmond (2017).
6 Garthwaite (2016).
7 Lloyd (2018).

inequality,[8] has been linked to rising violence and unrest[9] and increasingly demonstrated the waning symbolic efficiency of a neoliberal model unable to offer a coherent narrative that chimed with the lived experience of millions around the world.[10]

By the time Covid-19 and the associated measures charged with its management arrived, these issues hadn't been adequately resolved, instead they further entrenched the 'already unequal'. Like the financial crisis, some benefitted handsomely from the chaos and were able to further entrench and solidify their position.[11] So, in many ways, as we alluded to in Chapter 1, the financial crisis and the decade that preceded Covid-19 represent the context behind the pandemic and its inequalities. We will now consider evidence from around the world to offer a preliminary analysis of those global inequalities that emerged from, and those which were exacerbated by, the pandemic. Each section will take us on a tour of different continents to show the range of outcomes and impacts. However, where relevant, we also refer to other nation state contexts within sections to highlight consistent threads between countries.

Africa

The truly disadvantaged represent those for whom inequality was a fact of life pre-Covid-19. The pandemic and range of lockdown measures have exacerbated and entrenched economic insecurity, health outcomes and social and cultural tensions. For example, South Africa implemented lockdown in March 2020 with instructions for individuals to stay at home except under exceptional circumstances. Essential services continued so some people could go to work, and restrictions were placed on where and how income could be spent. All non-essential industries

---

[8] Streeck (2016).
[9] Ellis (2019).
[10] Hall and Winlow (2015).
[11] Harvey (2010).

closed, leading to declines in production and increases in unemployment.[12] The five-week lockdown was so severe that estimates suggest only 40% of people were able to continue working and that includes those working from home.[13] The informal food sector in South Africa—street vendors, spaza shops (operating from a residence) and bakkie traders (operating from the back of a pickup truck)—accounts for 40–50% of sales. It is worth around R360 billion ($20 billion) and is central to the supply chain.[14] The South African government's initial Covid-19 lockdown measures prevented informal traders from working and forced residents to use more expensive supermarkets where social distancing was harder. The extra expense came at a time where, as Jain and colleagues showed,[15] many were experiencing job terminations, income reductions and were unable to access social protection payments. Informal vendors were eventually allowed to restart trade but only with permits. Some regions had no system in place to supply permits and those who did receive accreditation were harassed by security services who either didn't know or care about the permits. Although some traders reported being back in business and making a living, others were struggling. This situation is not unique to South Africa. While contextual variations are important to acknowledge, we can see similar economic precarity in places like Bulgaria. For example, Dimitar, a Bulgarian researcher, told us that:

> Many families are worse off than they were before the pandemic, even those working in the black market or grey economy. But what is more problematic is that there is no hope for them to get back into some form of employment – even if it is in informal sectors.

South Africa's economy relied heavily on tourism with over 10 million international visitors in 2016 which generated over R102 billion in revenue (around $7 billion). The pandemic not only imperils this sector overall, but this is experienced spatially within South Africa. The top

---

[12] Arndt et al. (2020).

[13] Bhorat et al. (2021).

[14] Wegerif (2020).

[15] Jain et al. (2020).

20 leading tourist destinations in South Africa account for nearly 50% of all revenue.[16] A collapse in tourism may not affect the most visited destinations but will affect particular local areas where the centrality of tourism and hospitality to the local economy created a dependency that has been removed by the pandemic. Like other countries, the South African government introduced emergency social insurance but this did not reach all affected workers, with around 20% of those temporarily prevented from working and one-third of the newly unemployed unable to access any significant form of social protection.[17] Already insecure labour markets and workers have been severely affected by South Africa's lockdown measures and the gaps in its social protection payments. Again, returning to Dimitar, we can see a similar situation in Bulgaria:

> We are talking about totally insecure work, people who rely on their personal networks every day to get work, perhaps even just to get work every couple of days to survive. These people may be lucky to get €100 a month which is really in the poverty bracket. These people have nothing now and in Bulgaria there are many of them. Many, many of them.

Of course, the public health consequences of a viral outbreak can be significant, and lockdown has attempted to prevent that, but the evidence points to significant deepening of harmful social outcomes like inequality and poverty. From a harm perspective, the absence of work and effective social protection creates an instability and insecurity that prevents people from supporting their family and having the economic foundations to forge a livelihood. The economic shock caused by lockdowns has splintered already insecure labour markets and this has led to an increase in food insecurity in many countries across Africa.[18]

In Kenya, for example, prior to the pandemic, malnutrition among the general population was a problem: agriculture and informal activity were central to the economy and the export of commodities was crucial in accessing foreign currency; the government had limited fiscal space to tackle the pandemic. Pre-Covid-19, one in three people in Kenya

---

[16] Rogerson and Rogerson (2020).
[17] Jain et al. (2020).
[18] Nechifor et al. (2021).

did not meet their daily calorie requirement and therefore food poverty was a significant problem, particularly in rural areas where 35.8% of the population (over 10 million) live below the poverty line. Government's spending on the pandemic has been focused on mitigating the impact on the economy and household income, yet recovery has been uneven. Sub-Saharan Africa was not only affected by their own government's measures; lockdowns in China, Europe and the USA impacted on the international movement of goods and people which not only affected tourism and trade but heightened all four pillars of food insecurity—availability, accessibility, utilisation and stability. If harm represents the inability to flourish and strive towards a 'good life', food insecurity is a clear barrier to this goal.

News on how Covid-19 measures were impacting areas in the Global South rarely entered public consciousness in the West. Almost nothing is written or reported in Western media on what has taken place in Uganda for example, where Papsher, an artist, runs a child refugee music charity in Kampala. After attending some of his online events, we kept in touch and sent him two packages with pens, pencils and paper for the refugee children in April 2021. He wasn't able to collect the packages because in Kampala "*tear gas was in town like you couldn't imagine*" because "*people protested against the government lockdown and curfew time they put at 6 pm*". Prior to the arrival of Covid-19, Uganda had a complex political situation with Yoweri Museveni having reigned the presidency for over 30 years. Inheriting a broken, corrupt and violent country in the wake of the Idi Amin regime, he pledged to bring back formal economies and secure political stability. In his time, however, he has not achieved this having been accused of perpetuating corruption and inequality in the country through the privatisation of public assets and siphoning off foreign aid meant for the people.

Opposition leaders, such as Robert Kyagulanyi, had grown in popularity before Covid-19 and his rallies were seen as visible and credible threats to the regime. Like many African countries with high numbers of young populations and low numbers of elderly, Covid-19 cases and deaths have stayed low, around 90,000 and 2,400, respectively, in a country where the population is 44 million. However, the arrival of pandemic conditions meant that public health measures—in particular a strict lockdown—resulted in a high proportion of the population being subject to violence and/or discrimination.[19] By June 2020, there had also been 21,260 cases of child neglect, sexual and physical abuse across the country—a substantial increase on the previous year.[20] This trauma, however, is not on the political radar because *Covid-19 measures have essentially been exercised to quell the possibility for political change*. While many countries in the West have had social distancing restrictions put in place which prohibit meetings of between 4 and 6 people, it is the gatherings of more than 200 people which are illegal in Uganda and this has very much been used to deter political opposition rallies. Papsher elaborated:

> People cannot work. There is not enough time in the day to make money so people are angry. We are under lockdown and curfew but the government don't contribute anything to its people, they just want to stop their circulation. This is not about a virus. I saw lots of violence and human rights neglected.

The absence of work during the lockdowns brought about harmful conditions including violent activity and the lack of governmental focus on basic human rights and liberties, engendering social discontent. Indeed, the leader of the opposition party, Robert Kyagulanyi, was recently arrested for breaking Covid-19 conditions because of the rallies and charged by the government. This marked the violence that Papsher witnessed in May 2021. As Uganda now recovers from its 'second wave', resources are scarce and the vaccines have run out. Not that this even makes the news for people in Western countries.

---

[19] Katana et al. (2021).
[20] Ejang (2020).

South and Central America

Most of South America has suffered a similar form of neglect from mainstream media aside from controversial Brazil—whose government decided against a lockdown. Regularly cited in the Western press as evidence of the failure of far-right leader Jair Bolsonaro to manage the pandemic, as pointed out in the previous chapter, it is important to look at Brazil in context. Access to Brazilian healthcare is vastly unequal and therefore deaths from Covid-19 are significantly high. Moreover, risk of Covid-19 death is disproportionately high among indigenous black Brazilians compared to white Brazilians—62% higher. Nearly half (48%) of hospitalised indigenous Brazilians have died during the pandemic compared to 28% of their white counterparts in the same circumstances.[21] Indigenous communities have also been actively omitted from protective measures implemented to mitigate the virus as an authoritarian government continues its neoliberal reforms and attempts to claim territory through 'the politics of extermination'. Covid-19 intensified harmful conflicts between communities and the authorities and political acts of resistance have increased. Meanwhile, Peru enacted a full lockdown ten days after the first case was reported within its borders. The lockdown restrictions lasted until September 2020 and although restrictions remained in place in the most affected regions, the virus continued to spread. Estimates suggest 70% of Peru's workforce are informal workers who received no income during this quarantine period and their economic necessity triggered a collapse in sanitary measures.[22]

At times, it is difficult to imagine the reality of hardship beyond our own contexts, but if we are to fully appreciate the myriad harms generated by lockdowns, we must consider how its consequences cut across geographical space and social class. Located further North in Central America, Leonardo, a UN worker in Costa Rica, makes the point well by noting that:

---

[21] Menton et al. (2021).
[22] Neyra-Leon et al. (2021).

There is a need to compare our middle-class lockdown and its impacts with those who are in real poverty, without access to space, internet, food, water, remote work and healthcare. This virus is shown in some social media as a lovely street party creator but also is creating huge inequality and risk for those who are not so fortunate, and it is to these people we should focus our efforts on helping.

This focus should also be extended to Peru's healthcare workforce, 50% of whom serve in Lima. The country lacks specialised laboratories, PPE and intensive care units. The healthcare workforce itself has become central to the spread of the virus with significant numbers of cases and deaths among physicians. Moreover, high levels of harmful mental distress like anxiety are reported among Peruvian healthcare workers, particularly those working in and around Lima.[23]

Nations around the world enacted stricter border controls in the name of public health protection but in places across Central and South America this has exacerbated inequalities and tensions around migrant workers. Chile and Peru both had existing immigration issues, particularly with growing numbers from other South and Central American countries.[24] Chile's immigration policy involves issuing visas based on a number of checks but still has a significant undocumented or irregular migrant population. The pandemic response involved Emergency Family Income and other measures targeting the most vulnerable populations but required recipients to have a valid Chilean ID and be included on the Social Registry of Homes. Irregular migrants and those with expired IDs cannot access benefits, including those who had begun the process of regularisation but had not yet received their official identification. Additionally, rhetoric around illegal immigration has hardened through a public health focus on tighter border restrictions designed to prevent importation of the virus. Anti-immigrant sentiment existed within Chilean society pre-pandemic and the virus has exacerbated this issue with reported incidents against Haitian and Venezuelan migrants, as well as Asian communities.[25]

---

[23] Yanez et al. (2020).
[24] Freier and Espinoza (2021).
[25] Ibid.

The tensions generated over rights to citizenship, access to support services and vaccinations risk further polarising already fractured communities. We found evidence of similar issues in other parts of the world too. In Spain, for example, a housing worker named Gonzalo believed that *"we will see a much more polarised society; more violence and racism"*. He also told us that *"in Madrid they are taking decisions on confinement in poor parts of the city. The data reflects that the virus has more impact there. This is polarising society"*. In Peru, the migration of Venezuelans over the last decade has been heavily politicised with 850,000 arrivals since 2008. The profile of migrants has trended towards lower socio-economic status, fewer skills and lower education level, and hostility within Peru has seen a tightening of restrictions. Venezuelans need to apply for a visa at home (requiring a passport and clean criminal record). Peru's response to the pandemic has included financial support but this is limited to those with a national ID and thus excluded immigrants and refugees. Already precarious and insecure workers are further harmed by policies designed to prevent the spread of Covid-19.

Oceania

In Australia, many of the 'losers' include young people who were already suffering in a neoliberalised economy littered by precarious forms of employment. Recent research documented how between February–October 2020, around 800,000 jobs in Australia had been lost, particularly in the service industries like accommodation, food and recreation as demand decreased dramatically during the lockdowns.[26] Other scholars have highlighted how New Zealand's first lockdown engendered unintentional harmful outcomes, not least a 6% increase in suicidal thoughts particularly for those aged between 18–24, perhaps because they tend to endure poverty more and labour in more precarious forms of work than other age groups.[27] First world issues such as not being able to go shopping or go out to a pub compared starkly to how the Covid-19

---

[26] Churchill (2020).
[27] Every-Palmer et al. (2020).

lockdowns and subsequent economic downturn have affected developing nations, particularly those dependent on global economic opportunities such as tourism. Kelly, a UNICEF worker from New Zealand, was concerned about the Pacific Island Countries, where 2.3 million people reside. She said:

> Many Pacific Islands rely heavily on tourism and, as that has dried up, there are significant challenges for communities. The Solomon Islands, for example, have higher rates of malnutrition than Sub-Saharan Africa but it rarely features in global headlines. Now Covid-19 has hit the world and there is no tourism. No tourism, no work; no work, no future.

As Kelly says, these realities, however, rarely feature in the news but the almost inevitable closure of borders, lockdowns and social distancing have shattered the isolated tranquillity of the Pacific Islands resulting in severe economic and, as a result, social hardship.[28] At the time of writing, across the Pacific Islands, there were low Covid-19 cases and deaths— 453 people had died with/from Covid-19 in total.[29] Yet almost all of the islands ground to a halt and enforced strict lockdowns. By the summer of 2020, on Vanuatu, the number of employees in the tourism industry declined by about 64% during the Covid-19 crisis. While in June 2020, unemployment had nearly tripled in Fiji compared with levels in 2019.[30] The halt to the economy also saw additional harmful job losses in other tourism-related sectors such as the retail and food service industry.

This severely impacted the islanders' mental health as opportunities seemingly disappeared and the future became increasingly uncertain. Family violence increased and stigma associated with seeking help for mental health prevented many islanders from accessing services. Indeed, suicides in some places reached the same levels as Covid-19 deaths. For example, on 5 September 2020, the number of suicides in Guam equalled the number of Covid-19 deaths which was 15.[31] By late September 2020, by which time there had been 1,758 cases and 21

---

[28] Filho et al. (2020).
[29] Pacific Community (2021).
[30] Arahan et al. (2021).
[31] Pacific News Centre (2020).

deaths in Guam, widespread protests took place against government measures with references to '174 days with no hope' and 'it should be the people that decide [about which measures they adopt]'.[32] In Fiji, the hospitals were not filling up with Covid-19 patients but mentally broken young people as Empower Pacific Mental Health Specialist, Prem Singh, reported a *"spike in young people being admitted in most of the hospitals across Fiji for deliberate self-harm or attempted suicide"*.[33]

Even into 2021, some islands like Papua New Guinea (PNG) remained drastically unprepared for a viral outbreak. Initially, the PNG government only instigated a two-week lockdown but, given that a high proportion of the population—between 50–70%—rely on rural farming and local trade, it was counterproductive in the end. The country is poor, health infrastructure is limited, and there are often various diseases which keep the life expectancy low as Jess, a teacher posted out in a rural PNG community, explained to us in January 2021:

> There are no ventilators or hospitals which are equipped and no one wears masks in town so no one is prepared. It makes sense to be careful given that there really is no health infrastructure. But here we are used to death. The average life expectancy [in this poor community] is like about 45 here and the average for the country is about 60. The country is rural and poor. People who are ill have to walk for hours to get a basic treatment in a nearby village. Maybe there is a trained doctor but really they are only able to tell you if you have dengue fever or malaria. So here you live a hard life and you die from something in your 40s or 50s. If you make it to 60, that is considered to be old and wise. Here you are going to die, it doesn't matter: you are old, you died. Equally, something will kill you.

Jess explains that the locals think Covid-19 is a *"white persons disease"* and don't understand or seem interested in the concept of social distancing or mask wearing. However, in a country where 50% of the population lived below the income poverty line of $3.20 a day in 2019, it seemed almost inevitable that Covid-19 restrictions would have some impact.

---

[32] Kaur (2020).

[33] Nanuqa (2021).

While reported infections and deaths remained low throughout 2020, the country felt the after-effects of its own national lockdown as well as those from other countries including border closures. A report by the United Nations Development Programme (UNDP) found that in 2020, PNG experienced the following:

> Travel and tourism are the worst affected with a decline of about 97% of business. The Services sector, as well as labor-intensive manufacturing and industry, saw 90% layoffs. Manufacturing witnessed an 18% decline as major companies suspended or significantly reduced operations in several manufacturing facilities/factories. The entertainment industry and sporting events saw a 95% decline in business. Agriculture reported a 12% sharp fall in production and fresh food markets, food supply chains, seed supply, livestock, and agribusiness.[34]

Up until February 2021, PNG folk had to live in these harmful economic and social circumstances yet tended not to see the problem of Covid-19 until reported 'cases' started to increase and infection spread. Despite this, some people thought they were dying because of sorcery or black magic[35] or, as Jess says, *"from the way people cook food which often involves heavy smoke so it's common to get respiratory illnesses so people wouldn't know if they had Covid or not"*. By June 2021, there was a reported 17,500 'cases' and 191 deaths with/of Covid-19. However, in many instances, there are extremely low levels of testing in PNG and infected patients don't generally seek treatment, and so, as Jess concurred, fatalities aren't identified with the virus.

Asia

Like some of the islands of Oceania, the poorest sections of society in Asia have been hit hardest by the pandemic. South Asian economies such as India, Nepal and Sri Lanka have relied on remittances—monies sent back by international migrant workers, particularly those working in the

---

34 UNDP (2020).
35 Mercer (2021).

oil-rich Gulf States—instead of building up internal labour markets and sectors.[36] Remittances accounted for $554 billion worldwide in 2019 and these three countries have benefited considerably. Covid-19 has collapsed economies and forced international migrants to either return home or curtail remittance payments. This has significant implications for regional and national economies as significant shortfalls exist due to the absence of remittance payments. Furthermore, the repatriation of hundreds of thousands of now jobless workers exacerbates financial inequalities, damages economic health and creates further inequalities and demands on already stretched state services.

In early 2021, India became the epicentre of a media storm as cases and deaths skyrocketed following the emergence of the 'Delta' variant. However, the pandemic's unequal impact on India had been highlighted well before the second wave. Levels of homelessness are unclear and include the mentally ill, street children, migrant workers and others.[37] Research indicates that many informally paid migrant workers often slept on the sidewalks and were paid cash in hand by businesses forced to shut down as part of the initial pandemic response. The workers were stranded and many continued to live on the streets. Other homeless populations live in poor conditions and lack information and testing facilities to protect themselves from the virus. Those internal migrant workers within India's informal economy were susceptible to the double trauma of the pandemic and occupational uncertainty.[38] Around 100 million people are internal migrant workers who work often on a seasonal or temporary basis and move from region to region. Work is often unskilled, low paid and economically vulnerable (see Chapter 9). Meanwhile, predictions estimated 38 million jobs lost in India's hospitality sector, around 70% of the hospitality workforce[39] such as Madhuja who we met in Chapter 3. One study interviewed senior hospitality workers who saw a need to remain optimistic about the future, but the harmful impact of such high

---

[36] Withers et al. (2021).

[37] Banerjee and Bhattacharya (2021).

[38] Choudhari, R. (2020) COVID-19 pandemic: Mental health challenges of internal migrant workers of India. *Asian Journal of Psychiatry, 54*. 102,254. https://doi.org/10.1016/j.ajp.2020. 102254

[39] Kaushal and Srivastava (2021).

levels of unemployment is evident in a country with already polarised economic inequalities and significant levels of poverty.[40] Unemployment can be framed as harmful by considering the barrier it presents to stability, security and flourishing. Accordingly, unemployment on this scale represents significant harm to individuals, families, communities and the wider economy.

Europe

In Europe, pre-existing inequalities were also exacerbated by the economic shock of lockdown orders. In Portugal, for example, findings suggest asymmetric impacts that disproportionately affect those working in tourism and hospitality, young people and female workers. This is partly due to existing labour market conditions whereby young people and female workers are more likely to have worked in unstable and temporary forms of employment that have been hit hard by the pandemic and the state of emergency declared at the outset. The national data covered the first half of 2020 and preliminary investigation indicates that the termination of the state of emergency in early May 2020 did not have an immediate effect on the recovery of employment.[41]

In Romania, survey research ascertained that the lockdowns intensified already existing mental distress, particularly among younger people at university. Confined to their domestic dwelling for lengthy periods of time, many university students endured an increase in stress brought by having their daily routines suspended and thereby spending more time on their phone and watching the media's coverage of the pandemic.[42] As Romanians' lives dramatically and rapidly changed, many individuals reported losing their jobs/having it temporarily suspended, while others indicated an increased sense of social isolation brought by being

---

[40] Ibid.
[41] Almeida and Duarte Santos (2020).
[42] Dumitrache et al. (2021).

ordered to stay at home.[43] Similarly, survey research in Poland ascertained that many people who lived in cities and were compelled to work at home during the lockdown reported a harmful increase in alcohol consumption, particularly of wine among young people and women, in part because of increased boredom and a lack of social interaction.[44] Mirroring research in other countries during the lockdowns, mental ill-health like depression and anxiety, as well as a heightened sense of social fear, was most pronounced in younger people in Poland.[45]

The UK saw one of the worst case and fatality rates in Europe, despite three national lockdowns and a range of tiered and localised restrictions. As with other countries like Portugal, Romania and Poland, existing inequalities were reinforced by what Bambra, Lynch and Smith referred to as an 'unequal pandemic'.[46] Even in its earliest phase, Covid-19 reflected existing socio-economic and health inequalities in terms of those who contracted the virus and those who died. Some suggest that Covid-19 is a 'syndemic pandemic'—Covid-19 intertwines with and feeds off, in a cumulative way, existing epidemics of chronic disease as well as the social determinants of health, while the lockdown restrictions and economic downturn that followed also disproportionately affect those at the bottom of the social hierarchy.[47] This demonstrates a consistent thread between many countries. Indeed, cutting through the "*incessant chatter without any meaning*" associated with the 'new normal' rhetoric, Vasil, a teacher from Bulgaria, raises similar concerns regarding the consequences of mounting inequality: "*I am concerned about the more than obvious escalation of poverty and social inequality in my country*".

The Covid-19 mortality rate in the UK has been higher among Black, Asian and other minority groups, as well as those living in deprived areas, overcrowded conditions and those who work in high-risk occupations.[48] During the UK's first wave of Covid-19 (March–July 2020), the mortality rate was higher in the North of England compared to the

---

[43] Catana et al. (2020).

[44] Szajnoga et al. (2021).

[45] Gambin et al. (2021).

[46] Bambra et al. (2021).

[47] Ibid.

[48] Marmot et al. (2020).

South. An extra 12.4 people per 100,000 died of Covid-19 and an extra 57.7 per 100,000 died of all causes during this period, with an estimated cost to the UK economy in lost productivity of around £6.86bn. Unemployment rates hit the Northern Powerhouse much harder than the rest of the UK and poor mental and financial well-being, including loneliness, was also higher. This comes in the context of austerity, also disproportionately affecting the North, and, combined with the social, health and economic consequences of the pandemic, is expected to further widen the productivity gap in the UK.[49] For Karen, a UK social worker, this should hardly come as a surprise because *"in Britain our politicians play to the Middle and Upper classes, and inequality is actively encouraged. Why? because Capitalism works best when there is division and inequality"*.

Although the UK government enacted unprecedented measures to provide financial support, the growth in economic inequality has been clear. Unemployment has increased, furlough has paid a percentage of wages while others have earned full income working from home. 'Key workers' who went to work throughout the pandemic are largely low-paid and insecure workers—delivery drivers, couriers, supermarket workers, nurses, care home staff—and they were inevitably at greater risk of catching Covid-19 (see Chapters 6 and 7 for more detail). While staying at home has been beneficial for some, being locked down has had severe consequences for others. In the first month of the UK lockdown, calls to Refuge, a domestic abuse charity, increased 25% (a picture replicated across many countries).[50] Moreover, school closures forced children to stay home.

By April 2020, 138 countries worldwide had closed schools in order to reduce transmission of Covid-19 and an estimated 80% of children worldwide were no longer physically present in class. Van Lancker and Parolin[51] argue that extended closure of schools would exacerbate food insecurity and educational inequality. Indeed, 5.5% of UK households with children and 6.6% of those in the EU couldn't afford a meal with

---

[49] Bambra et al. (2020).
[50] Nicola et al. (2020); Dlamini (2021).
[51] Van Lancker and Parolin (2020).

meat, fish or a vegetarian equivalent every second day. Estimates in the USA place this at 14%. In the UK, this was highlighted by professional footballer Marcus Rashford's campaign to ensure food security for children unable to receive free school meals due to lockdown and school closures.[52] In terms of educational inequality, socio-economic disadvantage includes the absence of appropriate technology in the home, adequate heating, outdoor leisure or access to books. Indeed, children, particularly those from disadvantaged families, have been greatly affected by lockdowns and this is the case across a number of countries. Hilda, a PhD student from Germany, for example, explains how *"the most vulnerable groups - children from low-educated low-income families - were largely neglected"*. What is more, they were often publicly shamed for *"seeking social contact while older generations had other options to meet in disguise which fuelled intergenerational conflict"*.

A qualitative study of 31 young people (13–17) in North-East England used 'lockdown diaries' and telephone interviews to understand the experiences of young people living through the pandemic.[53] Findings showed that the disruption to normal life generated feelings of uncertainty, loss and grief. They also found ambivalent feelings about school, including initial relief at a 'break' from school in the first lockdown, hope and anticipation about returning to school mixed with apprehension at how different it would be with masks, social distancing and 'bubbles'. While annoyance was expressed at the seemingly contradictory implementation of social distancing, some felt they had fallen behind educationally, particularly in exam years. Mental health and well-being were affected by the pandemic and the government's response, and we could argue this represents the 'newly precarious'. We say this because the pandemic has created harmful outcomes including fear, anxiety, mental ill-health and educational inequality, all of which will have long-term consequences across the life-course.

[52] Shields (2021).
[53] Scott et al. (2021).

North America

In the USA, the Trump administration was initially dismissive of the pandemic in public while Trump himself apparently acknowledged its severity in private.[54] However, his administration floundered in its response.[55] Although the USA passed the Coronavirus Aid, Relief and Economic Security (CARES) Act to support those newly unemployed as a result of the economic shutdown, the impact of lockdown changed the circumstances of millions. A national survey by the Urban Institute[56] with over 4,000 responses throughout May 2020 showed that 43.4% of respondents (over 2/5) reported job or income loss because of the economic impact of Covid-19 and the 'stay at home' order. These losses disproportionately affected families of adults with lower incomes and Hispanic people. The overall working population dropped by 3%, from 68 to 65%, with Hispanic and non-Hispanic white adults reporting significant declines in employment. Among adults whose families suffered job losses, 36% had received Unemployment Insurance (UI) benefits in the 30 days before the survey. An additional 17% had applied for UI but had not received payment. Most adults who had applied but not received payment reported the process as difficult to navigate. There were more than 42 million new unemployment insurance claims between March and May 2020 with 21.5 million fewer people in employment in May 2020 compared with February. As we saw in Africa, job loss and insecurity also create food insecurity. A longitudinal study in the USA found that almost 50% of over 2,000 respondents experienced unemployment and of that group 37% reported food insecurity while 39% reported eating less due to financial constraints. The findings suggested that expanding the amount and duration of unemployment insurance would be an effective way of reducing both food insecurity and its associated harmful social outcomes.[57]

---

[54] Woodward (2020).

[55] Lewis (2021).

[56] Acs and Karpman (2020).

[57] Raifman and Venkataramani (2021).

The truly disadvantaged, those already unequal in economic and health-terms, were statistically more likely to catch Covid-19 and die from the disease.[58] Racial inequality was also present in the USA; socio-economic and racial segregation, particularly the concentration of black families in poor neighbourhoods, has historically been related to poor health outcomes and other health epidemics and in recent research a correlation between concentrated disadvantage and Covid-19 mortality was evident.[59] This follows other negative health outcomes dispro-portionately affecting those in disadvantaged areas, particularly black communities. While this research relies on official death data that we critiqued earlier, given the body of evidence related to social determi-nants of health and spatial concentration, there is no reason to suggest Covid-19 doesn't disproportionately affect poor black communities in the USA. As Daniel, an IT software supervisor from the USA, puts it: *"was life prior to this crisis amazing for most people? Or had our neoliberal economy created vast inequality and misery for the masses? Only the elites were benefiting"*.

The newly precarious also fared more unequally in North America as depression and anxiety grew among college students impacted by pandemic-related unemployment and financial insecurity.[60] These all represent harmful consequences of lockdown policies as well as the pandemic itself. Although survival rates were high, particularly among younger populations, government messaging and media reporting have increased fear and anxiety dramatically which adds further harm.[61] These all represent what we might call the unintended harmful consequences of the pandemic response. Further American research shows an additional inequality that we can characterise as the positive motivation to harm; the increase in anti-Asian hate crime.[62] Covid-19's Chinese origins has led some angry and frightened Americans to target Asians as the source of the disruption and upheaval they have faced. They have demonstrated

---

[58] Oronce et al. (2020).

[59] Khanijahani and Tomassoni (2021) and Dalsania et al. (2021).

[60] Rudenstine et al. (2021).

[61] Dodsworth (2021).

[62] Gover et al. (2020).

a willingness to inflict harm on those they wrongly see as the cause of their woes.

This concludes our mini-world tour of those hit hardest by lockdown inequalities though the truth is there is more to come. Although we do not cover every country, in other chapters, the socially harmful consequences of lockdowns are graphically revealed, and the emerging evidence tells a similar story. Existing forms of inequality, particularly related to the social determinants of health as well as low-paid, insecure and informal work, exposed certain groups to the virus more than others. The poor, the marginalised and the precarious were at greater risk of the virus, in terms of transmission, hospitalisation and death. Lockdowns and other non-pharmaceutical interventions created economic challenges that further exacerbated those existing inequalities. Stay-at-home orders curtailed much economic activity, particularly in hospitality, tourism and informal sectors that shut down overnight. This created significant unemployment and required unprecedented government support that was in many cases slow to arrive, hard to navigate and further exacerbated anxiety, stress and economic uncertainty. Whether bar workers in the USA or food vendors in South Africa, the absence of work and the bureaucratic challenge in accessing government assistance catapulted many towards poverty, increased mental ill-health and created food insecurity. These issues clearly indicate unintended yet harmful consequences of the pandemic response.

Additional inequalities include hardening attitudes towards migrant workers—seen in Europe, South America and Asia—where borders close, government assistance is exclusionary, and cultural tensions emerge. Local and regional economies that have relied on migrant labour have seen a dismissal of those workers who now become the virus-carrying 'other'. Rising levels of domestic violence and child abuse also demonstrate significant disparities in experience of lockdown and represent further inequality. These cultural inequalities have consequences. Meanwhile, worldwide school closures create and widen inequalities in educational achievement and learning as access to technology, suitable home environments and the practicalities of remote learning disproportionately favour middle-class children over working-class children, or those from low-income families. School closures also increase inequalities in food security as children from low-income homes went hungry. The highly publicised campaign by footballer Marcus Rashford is just the most visible example of charity and community responses to food poverty in the UK and elsewhere.

Finally, growing anxiety, stress and fear represent an additional inequality that relates to the others listed here. A global mental health crisis is inevitably on the horizon as many have faced significant challenges, disadvantages and inequalities since early 2020. The harms associated with these inequalities are legion and can all be characterised by the impediments to individual and collective flourishing. The absence of stability and security removes the foundations upon which people build lives. Although implemented to protect against a harmful virus, lockdown has stacked up harms on the other side of the balance sheet. However, while the truly disadvantaged and the newly precarious have had to find ways to cope with the inequalities of lockdown, a much smaller group have thrived.

References

Acs, G., & Karpman, M. (2020, June). *Employment, income, and unemployment insurance during the COVID-19 pandemic* (Urban Institute Report).

Almeida, F., & Duarte Santos, J. (2020). The effects of COVID-19 on job security and unemployment in Portugal. *International Journal of Sociology and Social Policy, 40*(9/10), 995–1003. https://doi.org/10.1108/IJSSP-07-2020-0291

Arahan, R., Doan, D., Dornan, M., Muñoz, A., Parsons, K., Yi, S., & Vergara-Hegi, D. (2021). *Pacific Island countries in the era of Covid-19*. World Bank Group.

Arndt, C., Davies, R., Gabriel, S., Harris, L., Makrelov, K., Robinson, S., Levy, S., Simbanegavi, W., Van Seventer, D., & Anderson, L. (2020). COVID-19 lockdowns, income distribution, and food security: An analysis for South Africa. *Global Food Security, 26,* 100410. https://doi.org/10.1016/j.gfs.2020.100410

Bambra, C., Munford, L., Alexandros, L., Barr, A., Brown, H., Davies, H., Konstantinos, D., Mason, K., Pickett, K., Taylor, C., Taylor-Robinson,

D., & Wickham, S. (2020). *COVID-19 and the Northern powerhouse.* Northern Health Science Alliance.

Bambra, C., Lynch, J., & Smith, K. E. (2021). *The unequal pandemic.* Policy Press.

Banerjee, D., & Bhattacharya, P., (2021). The hidden vulnerability of homelessness in the COVID-19 pandemic: Perspectives from India. *International Journal of Social Psychiatry, 67*(1), 3–6. https://doi.org/10.1177%2F0020 764020922890

Bhorat, H., Oosthuizen, M., & Stanwix, B. (2021). Social assistance amidst the COVID-19 epidemic in South Africa: A policy assessment. *South African Journal of Economics, 89*(1), 63–81. https://doi.org/10.1111/saje.12277

Catana, S., Toma, S., & Gradinaru, C. (2020). The economic and social impact of COVID-19 pandemic: Evidence from Romania. *University Annals, Economic Sciences Series, 20*(2), 273–277.

Churchill, B. (2020). COVID-19 and the immediate impact on young people and employment in Australia: A gendered analysis. *Gender, Work & Organization, 28*(2), 783–794.

Dalsania, A. K., Fastiggi, M. J., Kahlam, A., Shah, R., Patel, K., Shiau, S., Rokicki, S., & DallaPiazza, M. (2021). The relationship between social determinants of health and racial disparities in COVID-19 mortality. *Journal of Racial and Ethnic Health Disparities.* Online First. https://doi. org/10.1007%2Fs40615-020-00952-y

Desmond, M. (2017). *Evicted: Poverty and profit in the American city.* Penguin.

Dlamini, J. (2021). Gender-based violence, twin pandemic to COVID-19. *Critical Sociology, 47*(4/5), 583–590. https://doi.org/10.1177%2F0896920 520975465

Dodsworth, L. (2021). *A state of fear.* Pinter & Martin Ltd.

Dumitrache, L., Stanculescu, E., Nae, M., Dumbraveanu, D., Simion, G., Talos, M., & Mareci, A. (2021). Post-lockdown effects on students' mental health in Romania: Perceived Stress—The Impact of Missing Daily Social Interactions and Boredom Proneness. *Preprints.* https://doi.org/10.20944/ preprints202107.0473.v1

Ejang, H. M. (2020). *Protecting children from a distance: An ongoing experience in virtual child protection during COVID-19.* UNICEF.

Ellis, A. (2019). A decivilizing reversal or system normal? Rising lethal violence in post-recession austerity United Kingdom. *The British Journal of Criminology, 59*(4), 862–878. https://doi.org/10.1093/bjc/azz001

Every-Palmer, S., Jenkins, M., Gendall, P., Hoek, J., Beaglehole, B., Bell, C., Williman, J., Rapsey, C., & Stanley, J. (2020). Psychological distress, anxiety, family violence, suicidality, and wellbeing in New Zealand during the COVID-19 lockdown: A cross sectional study. *PLoS ONE, 15*(11), 1–19.

Filho, W., Lütz, J., Sattler, D., & Nunn, D. (2020). Coronavirus: COVID-19 transmission in Pacific small island developing states. *International Journal of Environmental Research on Public Health, 17*, 5409. https://doi.org/10.3390/ijerph17155409

Freier, L. F., & Espinoza, M. V. (2021). COVID-19 and immigrants' increased exclusion: The politics of immigrant integration in Chile and Peru. *Frontiers in Human Dynamics, 3*, 6. https://doi.org/10.3389/fhumd.2021.606871

Gambin, M., Sekowski, M., Wozniak-Prus, M., Wnuk, A., Tomasz, O., Cudo, A., Hansen, K., Huflejt-Lukasik, M., Kubicka, K., Lys, A., Gorgol, J., Holas, P., Kmita, G., Lojek, E., & Maison, D. (2021). Generalized anxiety and depressive symptoms in various age groups during the COVID-19 lockdown in Poland. Specific predictors and differences in symptoms severity. *Comprehensive Psychiatry, 105*, 1–10.

Garthwaite, K. (2016). *Hunger pains*. Policy Press.

Gover, A. R., Harper, S. B., & Langton, L. (2020). Anti-Asian hate crime during the COVID-19 pandemic: Exploring the reproduction of inequality. *American Journal of Criminal Justice 45*, 647–667. https://link.springer.com/content/pdf/10.1007/s12103-020-09545-1.pdf

Hall, S., & Winlow, S. (2015). *Revitalizing criminological theory: Towards a New ultra- realism*. Routledge.

Harvey, D. (2010). *The enigma of capital*. Profile.

Jain, R., Budlender, J., Zizzamia, R., & Bassier, I. (2020). *The labor market and poverty impacts of COVID-19 in South Africa*. (SALDRU Working Paper No. 264). Saldru.

Katana, E., Amodan, B. O., Bulage, L., Ario, A. R., Fodjo, J. N. S., Colebunders, R., & Wanyenze, R. K. (2021). Violence and discrimination among Ugandan residents during the COVID-19 lockdown. *BMC Public Health, 21*(1), 467. https://doi.org/10.1186/s12889-021-10532-2

Kaur, A. (2020, September 20). Residents against COVID-19 lockdown protest again. *Pacific Daily News*. Cited online at https://eu.guampdn.com/story/news/local/2020/09/10/residents-against-covid-19-lockdown-protest-again/5765533002/

Kaushal, V., & Srivastava, S. (2021). Hospitality and tourism amid COVID-19 pandemic: Perspectives on challenges and learnings from India. *International Journal of Hospitality Management, 92*, 102707. https://doi.org/10.1016/j.ijhm.2020.102707

Khanijahani, A., & Tomassoni, L. (2021). Socioeconomic and racial segregation and COVID-19: Concentrated disadvantage and black concentration in association with COVID-19 deaths in the USA. *Journal of Racial and Ethnic Health Disparities*, 1–9. Online First. https://doi.org/10.1007/s40 615-021-00965-1

Lewis, M. (2021). *The premonition: A pandemic story*. Allen Lane.

Lloyd, A. (2018). *The harms of work*. University Press.

Marmot, M., Allen, J., Goldblatt, P., Herd, E., & Morrison, J. (2020). *Build back fairer: The COVID-19 Marmot review: The pandemic, socioeconomic and health inequalities in England*. Institute of Health Equity.

Menton, M., Milanez, F., de Andrade Souza, J. M., & Cruz, F. S. M. (2021). The COVID-19 pandemic intensified resource conflicts and indigenous resistance in Brazil. *World Development, 138*, 105222. https://doi.org/10. 1016/j.worlddev.2020.105222

Mercer, P. (2021, May 3). Papua New Guinea Covid-19: Mistrust fuels crisis as infections rise. *BBC*. Cited online at https://www.bbc.com/news/world-asia-56926131

Mitchell, W., & Fazi, T. (2017). *Reclaiming the state*. Pluto.

Nanuqa, J. (2021, March 16). Social issues major cause of suicide. *FBC News*. Cited online at https://www.fbcnews.com.fj/news/social-issues-major-cause-of-suicide/

Nechifor, V., Ramos, M. P., Ferrari, E., Laichena, J., Kihiu, E., Omanyo, D., Musamali, R., & Kiriga, B. (2021). Food security and welfare changes under COVID-19 in Sub-Saharan Africa: Impacts and responses in Kenya. *Global Food Security, 28*, 100514.

Neyra-Leon, J., Huancahuari-Nunez, J., Diaz-Monge, J. C., & Pinto, J. A. (2021). The impact of COVID-19 in the healthcare workforce in Peru. *Journal of Public Health Policy, 42*, 182–184. https://doi.org/10.1057/s41 271-020-00259-6

Nicola, M., Alsafi, Z., Sohrabi, C., Kerwan, A., Al-Jabir, A., Losifidis, C., Agha, M., & Agha, R. (2020). The socio-economic implications of the Coronavirus pandemic (COVID- 19): A review. *International Journal of Surgery, 78*, 185–193. https://doi.org/10.1016/j.ijsu.2020.04.018

Oronce, C. I., Scannell, C. A., Kawachi, I., & Tsugawa, Y. (2020). Association between state-level income inequality and COVID-19 cases and mortality in the USA. *Journal of General Internal Medicine, 35*(9), 2791–2973. https://doi.org/10.1007/s11606-020-05971-3

Pacific Community. (2021, May 24). *COVID-19: Pacific community updates.* Cited online at Updates https://www.spc.int/updates/blog/2021/05/covid-19-pacific-community-updates

Pacific News Centre. (2020, September 5). *15 suicides on Guam in the past three months of COVID year.* Cited online at https://www.pncguam.com/15-suicides-on-guam-in-the-past-three-months-of-covid-year/

Raifman, J., Bor, J., & Venkataramani, A. (2021). Association between receipt of unemployment insurance and food insecurity among people who lost employment during the COVID-19 pandemic in the United States. *JAMA, 4*(1), e2035884 . .. https://jama.jamanetwork.com/article.aspx?doi=10.1001/jamanetworkopen.2020.35884&utm_campaign=articlePDF%26utm_medium=articlePDFlink%26utm_source=articlePDF%26utm_content=jamanetworkopen.2020.35884

Rogerson, C. M., & Rogerson, J. M. (2020). COVID-19 and tourism spaces of vulnerability in South Africa. *African Journal of Hospitality, Tourism and Leisure, 9*(4), 382–401.

Romei, V. (2020, December 31). How the pandemic is worsening inequality. *Financial Times.* https://www.ft.com/content/cd075d91-fafa-47c8-a295-85bbd7a36b50

Rudenstine, S., McNeal, K., Schulder, T., Ettman, C. K., Hernandez, M., Gvozdieva, K., & Galea, S. (2021). Depression and anxiety during the COVID- 19 pandemic in an urban, low-income public university sample. *Journal of Traumatic Stress, 34*(1), 12–22. https://doi.org/10.1002/jts.22600

Scott, S., McGowan, V. J., & Visram, S. (2021). 'I'm gonna tell you about how Mrs Rona has affected me': Exploring young people's experiences of the Covid-19 pandemic in North East England: A qualitative diary-based study. *International Journal of Environmental Research and Public Health, 18,* 3837. https://doi.org/10.3390/ijerph18073837

Shields, K. (2021). Free school meals and governmental responsibility for food provision. *Edinburgh Law Review, 25*(1), 111–117. https://doi.org/10.3366/elr.2021.0678

Streeck, W. (2016). *How will capitalism end?* Verso.

Szajnoga, D., Klimen-Tulwin, M., & Piekut, A. (2021). COVID-19 lockdown leads to changes in alcohol consumption patterns. Results from the Polish national survey. *Journal of Addictive Diseases, 39*(2), 215–225.

UNDP. (2020). *Socio-economic impact assessment of COVID-19 on Papua New Guinea* (p. 8). UNDP.

Van Lancker, W., & Parolin, Z. (2020). COVID-19, school closures and child poverty: A social crisis in the making. *The Lancet Public Health, 5*(5), e243-244. https://doi.org/10.1016/S2468-2667(20)30084-0

Wegerif, M. C. A. (2020). 'Informal' food traders and food security: Experiences from the COVID-19 response in South Africa. *Food Security, 12*(4), 797–800. https://doi.org/10.1007/s12571-020-01078-z

Withers, M., Henderson, S., & Shivakoti, R. (2021). International migration, remittances and COVID-19: Economic implications and policy options for South Asia. *Journal of Asian Public Policy.* https://doi.org/10.1080/175 16234.2021.1880047

Woodward, B. (2020). *Rage.* Simon and Schuster.

Yanez, J. A., Jahanshahi, A. A., Alvarez-Risco, A., Li, J., & Zhang, S. X. (2020). Anxiety, distress and turnover intention of healthcare workers in Peru by their distance to the epicenter during the COVID-19 crisis. *American Journal of Tropical Medicine and Hygiene, 103*(4), 1614–1620. https://doi.org/10.4269/ajtmh.20-0800

5

Pandemic Winners: Unlocking the Wealth Industries

As is well known, capitalism's structural crises produce both winners and losers. Some people, particularly those at the top of the social structure, emerge with more economic stability, wealth and material comfort. Others are often made unemployed and lose their livelihood, while the world's destitute often witness their precarious situation worsen (Chapter 1). The lockdowns initiated by governments across the world to try and reduce transmission of Covid-19 and contain excess fatalities have had similar effects. As demonstrated, the response to the pandemic has generated various inadvertent consequences, not least a potential international rise in domestic violence/abuse, joblessness, mental health problems like anxiety and depression, disruption to many children's education and brazen totalitarianism[1] (see Chapters 6, 7, 8 and 9). These unintentional consequences perhaps embody the *tip of the iceberg*.

---

[1] For example, see: Ellis et al. (2021), Golechha (2020), Haider et al. (2020), and Posel et al. (2021).

While many industries have endured declining fortunes throughout the pandemic, some like Pharma, digital, health insurance, as well as the globe's largest online retailer, Amazon, have flourished. It is to these 'pandemic winners' that we now turn our attention.

The World's Super-Rich

The transient 'corona-economy'[2] or 'corona-capitalism'[3] has seen many of the richest members of society increase their wealth to a historically unprecedented level. Perhaps the most evident example of this is Jeff Bezos, the founder of the multinational conglomerate Amazon. Despite Amazon adopting what have been described as draconian working conditions under neoliberalism—including the excessive use of targets, surveillance and monitoring of employees' movements, non-unionisation and poor wages[4]—sales in the first quarter of 2021 rose by 44% to $108 billion.[5] While this was no doubt aided by paying no corporation tax in Europe in 2020,[6] the upshot is that Bezos' personal wealth now stands at around $200 billion. In 2020, Amazon employed around 180,000 additional workers in the USA to cope with rising demand during the pandemic, though many are employed on temporary contracts and can be easily disposed of once demand desists.[7] Such working practices are not new and have enabled Bezos' wealth to perpetually increase for several years now. Between January and April 2020, his wealth increased by $25 billion,[8] setting him on track to be the world's first trillionaire. Bezos' surge in wealth during the pandemic has also partially been enabled by the closure of many small businesses, who did not possess the financial reserves required to stay afloat in the corona-economy, allowing

[2] Žižek (2021, p. 30).
[3] Žižek (2021, p. 29).
[4] Bloodworth (2019).
[5] Day (2021).
[6] Neate (2021).
[7] Blakeley (2020).
[8] Collins et al. (2020).

Amazon to monopolise their market share and thereby intensify social inequality.

Bezos' financial stardom, though, is emblematic of the world's billionaire class, many of whom have generally done well throughout the pandemic, with nearly 50% of them increasing their wealth.[9] Elon Musk, CEO of electric car company Tesla, has also witnessed his affluence blossom, gaining around $8 billion in one month between March and April 2020.[10] Indeed, many of the globe's super-rich had already attained ostentatious wealth under neoliberalism, with London being the home for many of them, possessing the most 5* hotels and Michelin star restaurants in the world.[11] With London temporarily out of bounds during the lockdowns, many of the world's billionaires, particularly from the Middle East and America, instead acquired stately homes including castles across England.[12] Many of these homes had gardeners, butlers, wine cellars and tennis courts and often cost over £15 million, providing a peaceful escape from the stress of life during the lockdowns.

However, the vast majority of those forced to stay at home didn't enjoy such luxury (Chapter 6), even less so if they were living by more precarious circumstances (Chapters 4, 8 and 9). Instead, for the majority of the reasonably well off, dining rooms became offices, kitchens became classrooms where parents tried their best to home-school, and any vestige of privacy all but left the home. Indeed, Dimitar, the Bulgarian researcher who we met in the previous chapter, notes how public and private space have merged: *"Now there is no private space, it is public because we are always on the laptop or computer, and you can't even take a shit because you are on your mobile"*. With some now working from home indefinitely, Dimitar sees this as a change, or rather a development, to *"the outsourcing industry"*:

> Neoliberal companies will feel good about this as they are not obliged to pay rent any more so no flashy offices, people can work more hours,

---

[9] Collins et al. (2020).
[10] Ibid.
[11] Atkinson (2020).
[12] Briggs et al. (2020).

there is no excuse as they are working at home. They can save money and make more profit. This is a worrying trend.

While lockdown has conflated public–private space for many, this has certainly not been the case for the world's super-rich. Many of these individuals, as Atkinson outlines,[13] have sought to escape social life, its restrictions, and civil obligations through acquiring property protected by large securitised gates and holidaying in remote locations. This certainly adds credible weight to those who claim that the dreams of the rich involve escaping society, mimicking the dystopian film *Elysium* whereby the super-rich live on a distant and prosperous artificial world away from the poor, conflictive and diseased masses.[14] Perhaps there is some parallel as billionaires such as Branson and Bezos flex their profit muscles by taking their holidays in outer space. Yet, this disconnect has intensified during the pandemic, with many of the wealthy escaping to their second properties in relatively remote areas like the USA's Mountain resort Jackson Hole, as well as Martha's Vineyard Island off the USA's East Coast.[15] Similarly, while the commercial aviation industry almost came to a complete halt, operating at significantly reduced capacity since the pandemic emerged, sales of private jets increased. Many of the world's super-rich simply opt for medium and large jets, enabling them to travel long distances to remote locations.[16] Unlike commercial planes, private jets are allowed to miss several touchpoints on their journeys, meaning some of the global rich have continued to fly while limiting their contact with other people. Perhaps we are now beginning to see the full extent of the social atomisation fostered by neoliberalism as lockdowns intensify neoliberalism's harmful post-social tendencies. Although some members of the billionaire class have done well during the pandemic, the global demand for medical equipment and vaccines has meant the pharmaceutical industry has also boomed.

---

[13] Atkinson (2020).
[14] Žižek (2021).
[15] Collins (2020).
[16] Leigh (2020).

Pharma

Like Bezos and friends, parts of the private healthcare and pharmaceutical industry have enjoyed significant enhancements in their profit margins during the Covid-19 pandemic. For instance, the multinational conglomerate and manufacturer of medical equipment, pharmaceuticals and PPE—Johnson & Johnson—increased its revenue by 6% to $82 billion in 2020. Indeed, scholars have highlighted how the use of respiratory medicines and sedatives increased between 100 and 700% in the initial months of the pandemic.[17] We saw this reflected in countries like Germany, where the desire to individually protect oneself at the expense of others likely led to the panic buying of medical products such as antidepressants, sedatives and betablockers,[18] with similar consumer patterns mirrored across the world including in Spain, Australia, Japan, UK, USA and Italy.[19] This is emblematic of the positive motivation to harm whereby any concern for others is overridden in the pursuit of self-interest. With the hollowing out of state capacities through neoliberal ideology in the West, and the underdevelopment of many nations in the Global South, there was a sizable shortage of both medicines and PPE in Africa (Chapter 4), the Middle East, several EU countries and the USA in the early stages of the pandemic.[20]

In many states like the UK, the response to crises partially generated by neoliberalism has been to rely upon more neoliberal mechanisms,[21] creating what Jones and Hameiri have described as *"an enormous bonanza for private-sector contractors"*.[22] Emblematic of this is how firms like PA Consulting and Deloitte were tasked by the UK government to manufacture 30,000 ventilators within two weeks. Instead of liaising with small domestic manufacturers, they joined together with other inexperienced global conglomerates and delivered a mere 344 ventilators before the first Covid-19 wave peaked. Such a dependence upon the private sector has

---

[17] Kostev and Lauterbach (2020).
[18] Ibid.
[19] Sim et al. (2020).
[20] Ayati et al. (2020).
[21] Schalkwyk et al. (2021).
[22] Jones and Hameiri (2021, p. 18).

potentially led to corruption, with over £10.5 billion worth of contracts involving the emergency procurement of vital supplies given without competitive tender. It is estimated that over 500 firms were given high-priority contracts without proper tendering, in part because of their links to senior government officials. This point is driven home well by Samuel, a writer from the UK:

> The government have lied and been totally incompetent since the beginning of the pandemic. They have treated the public with utter contempt along with making lots of their friends far wealthier by awarding them contracts without the right and proper tendering.

Such crisis conditions create new illicit opportunities. Indeed, the EU anti-fraud office identified nearly €300m in misused public funds in 2020 which was spent on counterfeit items, including face masks, hand sanitiser, testing kits and vaccines, many of them posing a risk to peoples' health.[23] Rather than helping the rich to line their pockets, Susan, a UK primary school teacher, stressed that *we need to place more value on our health service and other frontline services*. She was hopeful that *people will see that society's wealth and resources need to be more evenly distributed for the benefit of all*.

Although it usually takes between five to ten years to develop an effective vaccine, the race to secure a vaccine against Covid-19 was won quickly in 2020. States directed billions of funding in the form of both loans and grants towards multinational pharmaceutical companies, as well as world-leading universities, to develop an effective vaccine, including the European Corona Vaccine Trial Accelerator Platform (VACCELERATE) which received around £12 million in research monies from the EU.[24] By the summer of 2020, before the second and third waves, Moderna and Pfizer had emerged as the leaders in the race to vaccinate the world, holding several trials which were regarded as a success in 2020 on July 14th (Moderna) and August 12th (Pfizer). At the time of writing, various other vaccines have also been approved

---

[23] Euronews (2021).
[24] European Commission (2020).

to provide protection against Covid-19 including ones by AstraZeneca and Sinovac. As a result of winning the vaccine race, Pfizer/BioNTech is expecting between $15 and $30 billion in sales in 2021.[25] Moreover, various governments across the globe have purchased the Moderna vaccine, including the USA, Japan, Switzerland, Colombia, Canada, Israel, Taiwan, Singapore and Qatar, equating to over 640 million doses.[26] Accordingly, the company's forecast for sales in 2021 stands at nearly $19 billion, with its share price increasing by 372% between 2020 and 2021.[27] Relatedly, the AstraZeneca vaccine was developed by researchers at Oxford University in the UK, with over 400 million doses being ordered across the EU. However, they charge far less for the doses, meaning they are expecting less profit than other providers in 2021—a mere $3 billion.[28]

Considering the sizeable sums of money involved in the sale of Covid-19 vaccinations, it is perhaps understandable that some people are a bit sceptical. Our Facebook forum data revealed much in this regard. For example, Anne, a community access worker in the UK, said *"no thanks to the vaccine or other measures"*. Her view was that big pharmaceutical and tech companies *"are all interconnected and trying to get us to comply with their experiments"*. Anne's narrative may sound a bit like a conspiracy theory, but we will leave it up to the reader to decide. Another example comes from Paul, an environmental analyst from New Zealand, who told us that *"there's a lot of corrupt paid astroturfing going on in Facebook groups, with believable but fake profiles, to try and convince people they need to have this vaccine to do things"*. Astroturfing is where messages from sponsors or organisations are masked and made to look as though they came from unaffiliated, and therefore trusted, sources—such as your average 'Jane' or 'Joe'. According to Paul, *"this is going on all over Facebook right now"*. He went on to explain that:

---

[25] Kollewe (2021).
[26] Moderna (2021).
[27] Kollewe, J (2021).
[28] Ibid.

Rich, powerful organisations such as big pharma use this paid deceit all the time to further their agendas and to try and swing public opinion, and to discredit movements, and discredit the key people in them with 'casual' smears: always by posing as 'one of the people' hiding behind very convincing Facebook profiles. This way they infiltrate groups and public posts to create mistrust, division and increase and foment ridicule of the targeted group/movement.

Pharmaceutical companies are not the only pandemic winners for health-care insurance providers have also been one of the few industries to flourish during the pandemic, further intensifying harmful levels of socio-economic inequality. Of course, more unequal societies often engender more harmful social outcomes, not least criminal activity, an educational attainment gap between the rich and poor and more precarious forms of work. In the USA, the private healthcare provider UnitedHealth Group's income grew from around $3 billion in 2019 to nearly $7 billion in 2020.[29] However, millions of people do not have health insurance in the USA, leaving them potentially vulnerable if they contract Covid-19.[30] Many of those fortunate enough to possess an insurance policy must often pay a high deductible (excess in the UK) cost before they can access medical treatment, meaning many Americans are not accessing vital treatment when they become seriously ill with Covid-19. Moreover, in Australia, between January and March 2020, 50,000 people signed up to a private medical insurance provider, ensuring the industry enjoyed a before-tax profit for the first quarter of 2020 of $366 million.[31] In Spain, nearly 500,000 people acquired health insurance in 2020, increasing by 47% in comparison to 2019, while in Germany, private health insurance increased by 1.8% in 2020, ensuring the industry enjoyed a profit of 42 billion Euros.[32] As with many members of the world's super-rich, the pharmaceutical and private healthcare industries have flourished during the pandemic. Meanwhile, the virtual world has crept further into social life.

---

[29] Plott et al. (2020).

[30] Huff (2020), and Kolmes (2020).

[31] ABC Australia (2012).

[32] Landauro (2021).

Digitalisation

Confined to their homes for a lengthy period, the lockdowns curtailed usual routines and created a stationary global population. Our previous research demonstrated how many people were ensnared in a repetitive and harmful cycle of *depressive* hedonia; furloughed from work they had little else to do but embrace consumerism's virtual reality and seek individualised gratification.[33] Rather than learning a new musical instrument, a different language or thinking deeply about the society in which they live, many people further embraced social media, gaming and Netflix, while following the non-stop unravelling of the Covid-19 pandemic on the news media. Bombarded with daily updates of 'cases', 'hospitalisations' and 'fatalities' (Chapter 3), many people had nowhere else to go but consumerism's surrogate social world to temporarily alleviate their sense of frustration, uncertainty and insecurity. One of our participants, Steve, gave a perceptively accurate assessment of the situation noting that *"the pandemic has accelerated our reliance on digital industries"*. The big data expert from South Africa went on to note that:

> Microsoft, Google, Apple, any of these tech giants, or any cloud-based services which are rapidly consumed, have got their stuff together with regard to their user experience and enhancing work collaborations online. Netflix, Amazon, Zoom, have all seen exponential growth and these industries won't want to let go of this boom.

Steve went on to explain that he feels there is no way back from this mass digitalisation, *"It is in everything, I think we are extinct as a species. We have come to the end of evolution"*. For Steve, we have become so inured with technology and integrated with 'smart devices' that *"we are already cyborgs"* and have seen *"the last of the free-range humans"*. Indeed, there is no denying that the digitalised world has continued to tighten its grip on peoples' lives. Netflix and its abundance of movies, documentaries and television series appealed to many during the first lockdown, with around 16 million people signing up between January and March

---

[33] See Briggs et al. (2020).

2020.[34] In the Czech Republic, survey research ascertained that many people, particularly during the first wave of the pandemic, opted for online retail and home food deliveries for the first time, thus triggering rapid changes in consumer behaviour.[35] Interestingly, internet search terms that have increased exponentially during the Covid-19 pandemic include 'dumbbells', 'yoga mats' and 'indoor activities',[36] as gym closures during lockdowns meant sales of indoor fitness equipment skyrocketed. For instance, sales of Peloton's fitness bikes and treadmills increased by 172% in 2020, despite the bike being relatively expensive at a cost of around £2,000.[37] Recent UK survey research found that nearly 50% of respondents exercised more during the first lockdown, in part because of the evisceration of often lengthy and stressful commutes to work.[38] This perhaps also demonstrates the deep commitment to a highly commodified body image outlined by previous research.[39] Lockdowns may take our freedom but not the aesthetic pleasure of a primed and tuned body, especially when this pleasure can be virtualised to enhance one's 'Instafame'.[40] This virtualisation of aesthetic pleasure feeds into and further intensifies neoliberalism's socially harmful and corrosive values of competition and egotistical individualism.

Indeed, as gyms closed in France, fitness influencers on social media platforms like Instagram witnessed a rise in their popularity.[41] Many fitness influencers broadcasted live fitness classes on their social media page, often involving a 'fit week' whereby they would inform their audience that the lockdown could be utilised for the enhancement of their health and physical well-being, suggesting they should only get to watch Netflix after 'working out'. Survey research in Germany during the second lockdown also ascertained a rise in the use of home fitness equipment to exercise indoors, with the most popular online classes including

[34] Briggs et al. (2020).
[35] Eger et al. (2021).
[36] Hasanbayli (2021).
[37] BBC (2020b).
[38] Robinson et al. (2020).
[39] For example, see: Kotzé and Antonopoulos (2019), and Kotzé et al. (2020).
[40] Kotzé et al. (2020).
[41] Godefroy (2020).

circuit and full body training.[42] However, those that were older and with less space in their homes, were the least likely to participate in online fitness classes, further exposing societal inequalities that have been central to the Covid-19 pandemic (Chapter 4).

In this context, it is perhaps not surprising that the big global tech companies including Amazon, Apple, Microsoft, Google and Facebook increased their market share by 52% during 2020.[43] As people have been confined to their homes, many have been compelled to work from home on online platforms often provided by Microsoft such as 'Teams', as well as Zoom who increased their pre-tax profits by 4,000% during the pandemic.[44] As many people have been socially isolated, social media has often filled the void and helped to assuage peoples' boredom, particularly for the younger generation. Consumption of social media outlets like Facebook and WhatsApp increased by around 40% in 2020, with some teenagers staying up all night to communicate online, profoundly disrupting their sleep pattern and potentially harming their health and well-being (see Chapter 8 for how this plays out).[45] This further exemplifies the depressive hedonia that has been a core part of some peoples' lives during the lockdowns.[46]

However, some argue that much of this online communication is no adequate substitute for face-to-face interaction, potentially intensifying feelings of isolation and loneliness.[47] As Žižek outlined, the intensification of virtual reality has perhaps amplified de-socialisation, or what might be identified as post-social tendencies[48]—whereby adequate socialisation is absent, and individualism is pervasive—since many people did not see anybody face-to-face outside of their own home during the lockdowns.[49] Recent research in the UK found that many people utilised social media productively during the first lockdown

---

[42] Mutz et al. (2021).
[43] Calcea (2021).
[44] Massie (2021).
[45] Grigg-Damberger and Yeager (2020).
[46] Briggs et al. (2020).
[47] Altena et al. (2020).
[48] Winlow and Hall (2013).
[49] Žižek (2021).

to watch videos on food recipes and physical workouts, while others aimlessly scrolled through WhatsApp, YouTube and Facebook for hours each day.[50] With many digital industries benefiting from the confinement of large numbers of people to private dwellings, a reduction in car journeys and aviation during lockdowns has provided an opportunity to re-think and make the case for alternative forms of energy. Green energy, in particular, has emerged as a potential pandemic winner and it is to this industry that we now turn in the final section of this chapter.

Green Energy

As mentioned, many have argued that both structural crises and pandemics throughout history have often catalysed the restructuring of society, economy and culture.[51] Of course, the combination of structural conditions like The Great Depression and World War II helped to bring about a period of relative affluence and stability in the West in the post-war epoch.[52] Likewise, the 2008 global financial crash ushered in an age of austerity and accelerated social inequalities like the ever-widening gap between the rich and poor (Chapter 1). However, the current crisis has provided a *unique window of opportunity*[53] for the world to significantly tackle global warming, which is arguably the biggest threat to the future of humanity. The continual burning of fossil fuels, most notably gas, coal and oil, and the subsequent release of carbon dioxide into the atmosphere is trapping heat on an unprecedented scale, leading to rising global temperatures. Indeed, we are set to pass two degrees warming by 2050, which would lead to the extinction of various species and the submersion of parts of the world under water, making certain nations unliveable and thereby leading to the mass movement of people from the

[50] Kaur et al. (2020).
[51] Schwab and Malleret (2020).
[52] Lloyd (2018), and Telford and Lloyd (2020).
[53] Schwab and Malleret (2020, p. 144).

Global South to the West, potentially fuelling harmful tensions between various social groups.[54]

Investors, governments and key figures at important global institutions such as the WEF have spoken about the need for an environmental reset, or, indeed, the Fourth Industrial Revolution.[55] Over the last few decades, transformations to the biological, digital, social, economic, cultural and environmental have begun to take place to engender a shift towards green, renewable energy.[56] While this shift has been slowly underway for some time, it has been intensified by the pandemic.[57] In June 2020, BP slashed the value of its oil and gas assets by $17 billion, claiming that the company needed to move to renewable energy.[58] Investments in renewable energy, particularly solar and wind, increased exponentially in 2020, with global wind capacity intensifying by over 90% during 2020. The year the pandemic emerged also coincided with the largest global renewable energy capacity increase since 1999, jumping by around 45%.[59] Global investors in green energy have also announced that they will increase their investments in renewables from around 4% to over 8% within the next five years, claiming the pandemic must be utilised to shift to a greener future.[60]

President of the USA, Joe Biden, has also suggested that the G7 nations including Germany, UK, Canada, France, Japan and Italy will agree to end government support for coal by the end of 2021, providing significant investments in green energy markets which involves a Climate Investment Fund of $2 billion to support the energy transition.[61] The UK government has spoken about a Green Industrial Revolution, providing £12 billion in funding for renewable energy projects, promising to create around 60,000 employment opportunities in the

---

[54] Chomski and Pollin (2020).
[55] Schwab (2017).
[56] Ibid.
[57] Briggs et al. (2021).
[58] Schwab and Malleret (2020).
[59] International Energy Agency (2021).
[60] Ambrose (2020).
[61] The White House (2021) Room.

wind sector and 50,000 jobs in carbon capture.[62] Part of these ongoing plans involves significant investment in economically abandoned areas like Teesside in Northeast England, forming part of the area's 'Net Zero' project. The project seeks to capture carbon and thereby make Teesside's cluster of industrial domains the UK's first decarbonised industrial conglomeration. The project is being led by a consortium of five key members including BP and Shell.[63] Accordingly, many of the key ecological polluters like these fossil fuel companies have now pledged to be at the forefront of a net-zero emissions future.[64]

Sales of electric or hybrid vehicles have also surged over the past 17 months, particularly in Iceland, Germany, the Netherlands, Denmark, UK, Norway and Austria.[65] In 2020, sales of electric cars globally rose by 43%, with Europe leading the way for sales.[66] Such growth has been supported by many governments across the world—for instance, in Germany, the state offered a subsidy on each newly purchased electric vehicle, amounting to a $9,000 customer discount.[67] In November 2020, the UK government also announced a ban on the sale of new diesel and petrol vehicles by 2030 to ease the transition to electric cars.[68] This has been accompanied by a £1.3 billion investment in electric vehicle charge points for private residences, streets and motorways across the nation, providing the economic fuel for an infrastructural transformation.[69] While these transformations are certainly positive, we must not be naïve nor complacent. As we noted in Chapter 1, new technologies require different natural resources and the control of these often creates harmful points of conflict. Moreover, substituting fossil fuels for rare metals like palladium and cobalt to produce electronic products and batteries still constitutes the exploitation of natural resources.

[62] HM Treasury (2021).
[63] Net Zero Teesside (2020).
[64] See, for example: Shell (2020).
[65] Campbell and Miller (2021).
[66] Carrington (2021).
[67] Campbell and Miller (2021).
[68] GOV (2020).
[69] Ibid.

Nevertheless, at various stages of the pandemic bouts of optimism about the potential for change permeated online discussion forums. Yet, for now, at least, aspiration for a reconfigured future has by and large given way to a resolute commitment to existing consumer lifestyles.[70] It seems that the desire for change and the willingness to act towards it are not in constant alignment, as Monique, a public servant from Belgium, points out:

> I was hoping for a paradigm change in our society, which unfortunately doesn't seem to have happened. We have shown how much could be done when old wealthy men are at risk because governments order a complete 'lockdown'! Then it's sad to see how any changes to the system which is ruining the environment, driving masses into slave-like working conditions etc. still seem impossible. All because of the way we're heading is not threatening the old white rich men.

Far from constituting a doorway to a better future in which we inhabit a more just world, the global response to the pandemic has simply reinforced a commitment to the present; one which is perhaps already operating out of time. Some of our survey respondents were vocal in their frustration about the gravity of our current situation. For example, Maria, a self-employed resident of Spain, commented that:

> People are going out to dance and celebrate the quarantine. I say celebrate because that is what it looks like with so much partying from the balconies. They are not aware of what is happening, and this is a lack of respect to the thousands of people who are dying from the virus but also the other damage being done to society [through lockdowns].

The disparity between the pandemic winners and losers is stark. While the former have benefitted handsomely, the latter have experienced hardships that are likely to have long-lasting effects. We are not suggesting that Covid-19 is the product of the super-rich's desire to further fatten their coffers. Nor are we suggesting that the fallout generated by government responses was somehow premeditated. What we are trying to point

---

[70] Briggs et al. (2020).

out is that the unintended harms of lockdowns have exacerbated existing inequalities and even created new fault-lines that further disadvantage the most vulnerable members of society. In the next chapter, we see how this all plays out by examining how lockdown was experienced by those in Western society.

References

ABC Australia. (2012). Another 50,000 Australians take out private health cover. *International Journal of Health Care Quality Assurance, 25*(7). https://doi.org/10.1108/ijhcqa.2012.06225gaa.006

Altena, E., Baglioni, C., Espie, C., Ellis, J., Gavriloff, D., Holzinger, B., Schlarb, A., Frase, L., Jernelov, S., & Riemann, D. (2020). Dealing with sleep problems during home confinement due to the COVID- 19 outbreak: Practical recommendations from a task force of the European CBT-I Academy. *Journal of Sleep Research, 29*(4), 1–7.

Ambrose, J. (2020). Investors plan major move into renewable energy infrastructure. *The Guardian.* Accessed on 25 June 2021. Available at https://www.theguardian.com/environment/2020/nov/23/investors-plan-major-move-into-renewable-energy-infrastructure

Ayati, N., Saiyarsarai, P., & Nikfar, S. (2020). Short and long term impacts of COVID-19 on the pharmaceutical sector. *DARU Journal of Pharmaceutical Sciences, 28*, 799–805.

Atkinson, R. (2020). *Alpha City.* Verso.

BBC. (2021b, March 17). *COVID-19 disruptions killed 228,000 children in South Asia, says UN report. BBC.* Cited online at https://www.bbc.com/news/world-asia-56425115

Blakeley, G. (2020). *The Corona crash.* Verso.

Bloodworth, J. (2019). *Hired: Six months undercover in low-wage Britain.* Atlantic Books.

Briggs, D., Ellis, A., Lloyd, A., & Telford, L. (2020). New hopes or old futures in disguise? Neoliberalism, the Covid-19 pandemic and the possibility of social change. *International Journal of Sociology and Social Policy, 40*(9/10), 831–848. https://doi.org/10.1108/IJSSP-07-2020-0268

Briggs, D., Ellis, A., Lloyd, A., & Telford, L. (2021). *Researching the COVID-19 pandemic: A critical blueprint for the social sciences*. Policy Press Rapid Response Series.

Calcea, N. (2021). Pandemic winners and losers: How Big Tech's gains mask a struggling economy. *New Statesman.* Accessed on 23 June 2021. Available at: https://www.newstatesman.com/politics/2021/02/pandemic-winners-and-losers-how-big-techs-gains-mask-struggling-economy

Campbell, P., & Miller, J. (2021). Electric cars surge in popularity after manufacturers' late dash.*Financial Times.* Accessed on 25 June 2021. Available at: https://www.ft.com/content/e9a6aa4f-4a8b-4c80-a89b-3e8fbde2c43

Carrington, D. (2021). Global sales of electric cars accelerate fast in 2020 despite pandemic. *The Guardian.* Accessed on 25 June 2021. Available at: https://www.theguardian.com/environment/2021/jan/19/global-sales-of-electric-cars-accelerate-fast-in-2020-despite-covid-pandemic

Chomsky, N., & Pollin, R. (2020). *Climate crisis and the global green new deal*. Verso.

Collins, C. (2020). Let's stop pretending billionaires are in the same boat as us during the pandemic. *The Guardian.* Accessed on 22 June 2021. Available at: https://www.theguardian.com/commentisfree/2020/apr/24/billionaires-coronavirus-not-in-the-same-boat

Collins, C., Ocampo, O., & Paslaski, S. (2020). *Billionaire bonanza 2020: Wealth windfalls, tumbling taxes, and pandemic profiteers*. Institute for Policy Studies.

Day, M. (2021). Amazon sales skyrocket as pandemic shopping habits persist. *Al Jazeera.* Accessed on 22 June 2021. Available at: https://www.aljazeera.com/economy/2021/4/29/amazon-sales-skyrocket-as-pandemic-shopping-habits-persist

Eger, L. K., Egerova, L., Micik, D., & M,. (2021). The effect of COVID-19 on consumer shopping behaviour: Generational cohort perspective. *Journal of Retailing and Consumer Services, 61,* 1–11.

Ellis, A., Briggs, D., Lloyd, A., & Telford, L. (2021). A ticking time bomb of future harm: Lockdown, child abuse and future violence. *Abuse: An International Journal, 2*(1). https://doi.org/10.37576/abuse.2021.017

Euronews. (2021, June 10). EU anti-fraud office identified nearly €300m in misused public funds last year. *Euronews.* Cited online at https://www.euronews.com/2021/06/10/eu-anti-fraud-office-identified-nearly-300m-in-misused-public-funds-last-year

European Commission. (2020). *EU support for vaccines.* Accessed on 24 June 2021. Available at: https://ec.europa.eu/info/research-and-innovation/res

earch-area/health-research-and-innovation/coronavirus-research-and-innova
tion/vaccines_en

Godefroy, J. (2020). Recommending physical activity during the COVID-19 health crisis. Fitness Influencers on Instagram. *Frontiers in Sports and Active Living, 2*, 1–7.

Golechha, M. (2020). COVID-19, India, lockdown and psychosocial challenges: What next? *International Journal of Social Psychiatry, 66*(8), 830–832.

GOV. (2020). *Government takes historic step towards net-zero with end of sale of new petrol and diesel cars by 2030*. Accessed 25 June 2021. Available at: https://www.gov.uk/government/news/government-takes-historic-step-towards-net-zero-with-end-of-sale-of-new-petrol-and-diesel-cars-by-2030

Grigg-Damberger, M., & Yeager, K. (2020). Bedtime screen use in middle-aged and older adults growing during pandemic. *Journal of Clinical Sleep Medicine, 16*(1), 25–26.

Haider, N., Osman, A., Gazekpo, A., Akipede, G., Asogun, D., Ansumana, R., Lessels, R., Khan, P., Hamid, M., Yeboah-Manu, D., Mboera, L., Shayo, E., Mmbaga, B., Urassa, M., Musoke, D., Kapata, N., Ferrand, R., Kapata, P., Stigler, F., … McCoy, D (2020). Lockdown measures in response to COVID-19 in nine sub-Saharan African countries. *British Medical Journal Global Health, 5*(1–10), 2.

Hasanbayli, A. (2021). Nascent consumer behaviors in the platform economy during covid-19 pandemic. *7th ITEM Conference—"Innovation, Technology, Education and Management"*. 80–89

HM Treasury. (2021). *Build back better: Our plan for growth*.

Huff, C. (2020). Covid 19: Americans afraid to seek treatment because of the steep cost of their high deductible insurance plans. *The British Medical Journal. 371*, 1–2.

International Energy Agency. (2021). *Renewable energy market update: Outlook for 2021 and 2022*. IEA.

Jones, L., & Hemeiri, S. (2021). COVID-19 and the failure of the neoliberal regulatory state. *Review of International Political Economy*, 1–25. Online First. https://www.tandfonline.com/doi/epub/10.1080/09692290.2021.1892798?needAccess=true

Kaur, H. S., Arya, T., & Y Mittal, S,. (2020). Physical fitness and exercise during the COVID- 19 pandemic: A qualitative enquiry. *Frontiers in Psychology., 11*, 1–10.

Kollewe, J. (2021). From Pfizer to Moderna: Who's making billions from COVID-19 vaccines? *The Guardian*. Accessed on 24 June 2021. Available at: https://www.theguardian.com/business/2021/mar/06/from-pfizer-to-moderna-whos-making-billions-from-covid-vaccines

Kolmes, S. (2020). Employment-based, for-profit health care in a pandemic. *The Hastings Center Report, 50*(3), 22–22.

Kostev, K., & Lauterbach, S. (2020). Panic buying or good adherence? Increased pharmacy purchases of drugs from wholesalers in the last week prior to Covid-19 lockdown. *Journal of Psychiatry Research., 130*, 19–21.

Kotzé, J., & Antonopoulos, G. A. (2019). Boosting bodily capital: Maintaining masculinity, aesthetic pleasure and instrumental utility through the consumption of steroids. *Journal of Consumer Culture*. https://doi.org/10.1177/1469540519846196

Kotzé, J., Richardson, A., & Antonopoulos, G. A. (2020). Looking 'acceptably' feminine: A single case study of a female bodybuilder's use of steroids. *Performance Enhancement and Health*. https://doi.org/10.1016/j.peh.2020.100174

Landauro, I. (2021). *Health policies a shot in the arm for west European insurers hit by COVID-19*. Reuters. Accessed on 24 June 2021. Available at: https://www.reuters.com/article/us-health-coronavirus-insurance-idUSKBN2AW0KE

Leigh, G. (2020). Why private are all the rage during a pandemic. *Forces*. Accessed on 22 June 2021. Available at: https://www.forbes.com/sites/gabrielleigh/2020/08/25/why-private-jets-are-all-the-rage-during-a-pandemic/?sh=744d7ae778f7

Lloyd, A. (2018). *The harms of work*. University Press.

Massie, G. (2021). Zoom increased profits by 4000 per cent during pandemic but paid no income tax, report says. *The Independent*. Accessed on 25 June 2021. Available at https://www.independent.co.uk/news/world/americas/zoom-pandemic-profit-income-tax-b1820281.html

Moderna. (2021). *U.S government purchases additional 100 million doses of Moderna's COVID-19 Vaccine*. Moderna. Accessed on 24 June 2021. Available at https://investors.modernatx.com/node/10991/pdf

Mutz, M., Muller, J., & Reimers, A. (2021). Use of digital media for home-based sports activities during the COVID-19 pandemic: Results from the German SPOVID survey. *International Journal of Environmental Research and Public Health, 18*(9), 4409.

Neate, R. (2021). Amazon had sales income of £44bn in Europe in 2020 but paid no corporation tax. *The Guardian*. Accessed on 22 June

2021. Available at: https://www.theguardian.com/technology/2021/may/04/amazon-sales-income-europe-corporation-tax-luxembourg

Net Zero Teesside. (2020). *System value to the UK power market of carbon capture and storage.* Net Zero Teesside.

Plott, C., Kachalia, A., & Sharfsterin, J. (2020). Unexpected health insurance profits and the COVID- 19 crisis. *Journal of the American Medical Association, 324*(17), 1713–1714.

Posel, D., Oyenubi, A., & Kollamparambil, U. (2021). Job loss and mental health during the COVID- 19 lockdown: Evidence from South Africa. *PLoS ONE, 16*(3), 1–15.

Reuters. (2020, June10). *Denmark sees no rise in COVID-19 cases after further easing of lockdown.* Cited online at https://www.reuters.com/article/us-health-coronavirus-denmark-idUSKBN23H1DU

Robinson, E. G., & S & Jones, A,. (2020). Weight-related lifestyle behaviours and the COVID- 19 crisis: An online survey study of UK adults during social lockdown. *Obesity, Science and Practice, 6*(6), 735–740.

Schalkwyk, M., Maani, N., & McKee, M. (2021). Public health emergency or opportunity to profit? The two faces of the COVID-19 pandemic. *The Lancet: Diabetes & Endocrinology, 9*(2), 61–63.

Schwab, K. (2017). *The fourth industrial revolution.* Penguin.

Schwab, K. & Malleret, T. (2020). *Covid 19: The great reset.* World Economic Forum.

Shell. (2020). *Responsible energy: Sustainability report 2020.* Shell.

Sim, K., Chua, H., Vieta, E., & Fernandez, G. (2020). The anatomy of panic buying related to the current COVID-19 pandemic. *Psychiatry Research, 280,* 113015.

Telford, L., & Lloyd, A. (2020). From "infant hercules" to "ghost town: Industrial collapse and social harm in Teesside. *Critical Criminology, 28,* 595–611.

The White House. (2021). *Fact sheet: G7 to announce joint actions to end public support for overseas unabated coal generation by end of 2021.* Briefing Room. Accessed on 25 June 2021. Available at https://www.whitehouse.gov/briefing-room/statements-releases/2021/06/12/fact-sheet-g7-to-announce-joint-actions-to-end-public-support-for-overseas-unabated-coal-generation-by-end-of-2021/

Winlow, S., & Hall, S. (2013). *Rethinking social exclusion.* Sage.

Žižek, S. (2021). *Pandemic 2: Chronicles of a Lost Time.* Polity.

6

Locked Down—Western Society

As lockdowns were implemented, the personal freedoms that many people in Western societies took for granted were suddenly withdrawn. There was no social life, no eating out and no travel. Everyone was sent home and told to remain there. Across the West, children were home-schooled and those fortunate to keep their jobs worked from home. Time at home was stressful for many and saw increased mental anguish and anxiety, pacified, for some, through increased indulgence with digital products and services. This digital demand was almost inevitable given that, pre-pandemic, people across Western countries had come to rely on consumer goods as part of their daily lives and leisure existence. Under lockdown conditions, peoples' emotional and habitual attachment to digital modes of communication increased and this *anesthetised the prevailing change to life as we know it*—in short, it comforted them and gave them security, and thus confined them subjectively.

Investment in a general pro-lockdown stance meant subservience to government public health ideologies at the expense of any space to accept the potential for their harms. When we combine this digital commitment with the ideological bombardment of public health messages, dis- and misinformation about the virus and an obsessive 24 hours news

© The Author(s), under exclusive license to Springer Nature Switzerland AG 2021
D. Briggs et al., *Lockdown*,
https://doi.org/10.1007/978-3-030-88825-1_6

reporting, the foundations were laid for societal divisions and tensions in the 'new normal'. A frightened and distracted electorate embroiled in disagreements about who was and who wasn't following the rules, and who would and wouldn't get vaccinated while, at the same time, were glued to digital entertainment. All this diminished the potential to question how Covid-19 had become entangled in particular political agendas.

Viral Politics

> I feel like Covid is more like a present or a gift for the elite. You can accept it, open it and use it. If you don't, it is like a wasted opportunity. If ever politics wanted to implement something in law or on society or in economic practice, and I'm not saying Covid was made, but it does feel like it has been used like a weapon and that politics has used it to its advantage.

The above quote comes from Panni who sells shoes in Switzerland. Panni felt that political leaders and parties have used Covid-19 to serve particular agendas. He thinks it is important to recognise that the (in)actions of governments and the decisions they make about what their respective citizens should or shouldn't do, have a key role to play in the transmission trajectory of a virus. It is not that a virus simply passes naturally among a community, infecting random people. A virus has to exist and be active and additional external variables very often either stimulate or repress it. Since Covid-19 emerged in Wuhan, China, decisions and interventions (or the lack of them) played a part in its global transmission. We know and recognise now that perhaps the most controversial intervention used by nation states were lockdowns (Chapters 1 and 2). However, it is important to recognise that governments were thrust into making decisions about how to control and reduce the risk of the virus while balancing public health against the economic functioning of their respective countries. At the same time, governments had political agendas that didn't simply disappear with the arrival of Covid-19.

Governments around the world had to respond to Covid-19; however, as discussed in the case of Cameroon in Chapter 3, they have used it for political purposes. Like a *"political weapon"*, as Panni puts it in the previous quote. Even if many countries around the world have engaged in following the same Covid-19 measures such as lockdowns, social distancing and mask wearing, an additional consequence is that it has become immersed in the way in which politics operate in different countries. The pandemic has therefore become *politicised in particular agendas*. For example, in New Zealand, due process has often been compromised because of the rushed use of remote court technologies while prisoners have been kept in their cells often for over 24 hours.[1] In Hong Kong, new Covid-19 regulations have been weaponised in response to high levels of political protest at the proposed extradition of criminal suspects to Mainland China.[2] The refusal of the Australian state to include refugees, people seeking asylum, and other non-citizens in the urgent national public health response to the pandemic, thus perpetuated the suffering of this already-politically abandoned group.[3] Similarly, in the UK, political pledges were made to protect and support the vulnerable, something which John, a young student, claimed had not been effective enough:

> The necessary measures were put in place but far too late. This is reflected in the overall number of deaths...I think once these steps were taken, they were effective, but would have been more so if implemented earlier. I don't think enough was done to economically protect and support those most vulnerable during this crisis...many were forced to put themselves at risk in order to work. The virus has greatly exacerbated the already existing situation here because the poor and vulnerable have inevitably suffered the most... I feel like *the worst is yet to come*. I don't have any faith in the government effectively handling the economic crisis in the aftermath of the virus.

---

[1] Stanley and Bradley (2020).
[2] Ismangil and Lee (2021).
[3] Vogl et al. (2020).

It is precisely the elderly and vulnerable who have been most affected in the UK and this also seems to be the case across the world.[4] In Armenia, a country impacted by what was considered to be a short national lockdown, the government was eager to avoid paralysing economic activity. When the country reopened, politicians were criticised as infections and deaths increased, and the subsequent lockdown had left greater unemployment and job insecurity.[5] Dalita, a young Armenian self-employed woman said: *"they could have taken better preventive measures but, since it is a populist government, they carried on with their political agenda"*. For other countries such as Serbia, Poland and the USA, Covid-19 was seen to be a good excuse to assist/prevent certain political processes:

> *Petra:* Our government manipulated the information and the situation for the sake of political elections, they used the Covid situation to blame protesters who went out on the streets to protest against political corruption. On the other hand, there were some good measures but those were more on an operative level. (Serbia, Female, Self-employed)
>
> *Aleksandra:* My country [Poland] was one of the first introducing very hard measures. It affected us badly with the online classes for children. But then the government officials broke their own restrictions by meeting other reluctant world leaders openly. Additionally, there were planned elections during the lockdown which were downplayed by the government as they were losing in the polls. (Poland, Female, Self-employed)
>
> *Sean:* In America, there are two views, and they are completely opposite. In general, the mainline news outlets are doing a great job. The right wing, conservative group which support Trump are giving false information about the virus to try and make him look better. (USA, male, Aviation worker)

Donald Trump, who had started the process of defending his Republican presidency at the beginning of 2020, suddenly found that much of the work he had done to try to improve economic opportunity for Americans was being jeopardised by Covid-19. Trump downplayed the

---

[4] Guilmoto (2020).

[5] CRRC (2020).

gravity of the virus in an attempt to retain electoral advantage, and logistical deficiencies in testing paraphernalia led to a gross underreporting of tests.[6] He and his political aides were quoted in interviews stating the virus was *"contained and it's — going to be just fine", "it will go away" "it is flulike"*,[7] suggesting that Covid-19 not only reflects existing political divisions, but also creates new ones. Jeff, a researcher from Baltimore, said:

> Trump was warned in December or January and ignored it and minimised it and we could have imposed measures similar to New Zealand, and he knew that if he could play the waiting game and use this to mask the issue of cultural politics, we would be able to make an issue in his campaign.

With confusion at the top, mainly deriving from an ambition to avoid undoing the economic progress during his presidency with lockdowns, division ensued among different States about how best to mitigate the damage and harm of Covid-19. Jeff continued:

> Governors in many states now ravaged by Covid, particularly Republican, didn't want to implement anything like closing bars and restaurants to minimise Covid. They didn't want to do that. Trump went to rallies, very few were wearing masks and he encouraged it as much as possible and it was a shitshow and this is a result of that, open-air meetings, football games, rallies, universities open. It has been a clusterfuck of utmost proportions.

To this day, the schism existing across the USA is related to economic activity and whether to subdue or accelerate it. Should people work from home or continue with their business? But, as we know, certain jobs can't be undertaken in a home environment.

---

[6] Balogun (2020).

[7] Greenberg (2020).

Lockdown Polarities Part 1: Online vs. Frontline

Distinct polarities emerged between social groups through the imposition of lockdowns. Importantly, divisions emerged among citizens in Western countries between the nature of their working practices during the pandemic. Firstly, there were those who could maintain their jobs in an online setting and work from home, or were put on furlough schemes and remained at home receiving recompense. Secondly, and by contrast, were those unable to transition to online and home working, and with little option but to face the potential of the 'viral risk' through continuing to work. Susan, a self-employed woman from the UK, seemed to be part of the first category:

> Ah many [advantages of lockdown]! I love the quiet. I love working from home. I love spending time with my husband. Just the pace of life being much slower and just focusing in on the essentials. Speaking to people much more and having a shared problem. The feeling that the country has pulled together after the awful Brexit years... Ability to do things in the house that have been put off. Less need to consume so saving a lot of money. Time to reflect. I've just decided to work with a Career Coach to help me think about my long-term career future... More time for hobbies. Less pressure at work. Not having to see people has advantages! The fact the environment is improving and there is less pollution in London! The fact that people are valuing migrants and low-paid workers and see the importance of the NHS. If it wasn't for the hideous killer virus, I would love this lifestyle.

Despite the untold damages that lockdowns were creating for billions of people, life seems to still be pretty good for Susan. With the transfer of their life and work online, the first lockdown for people like Susan was considered novel and exciting, permitting experience and exploration of new opportunities. Equally Simon, an IT manager from the UK, was fortunate:

> Luckily I am still able to work from home, so for now largely as before just with no commute. There is less socialising, less frequent but larger

shopping trips and we don't go out as a family at weekends. Now it's all online learning and online shopping. There is also more time with kids in garden on trampoline, playing video games, attempting (and mostly failing) to teach them things.

Simon's socio-economic position, the space within his property and his continued access to pre-Covid-19 consumer experiences fundamentally shaped his experience of lockdown. Life changed, but not in ways that caused significant damage or trauma. However, even for those with jobs, the added pressure of the incessant news media coverage of Covid-19, of home-schooling, and the lack of freedom, had harmful effects on peoples' mental health:

> *Sandra:* You are closed off from seeing anyone in person, you grow tired of seeing the same people in your household everyday. There are only so many chores to complete. We are also stressed because of unemployment (husband), school and the situation itself so anxiety and depression are through the roof as well. (Female, part-time Childcare assistant, USA)
>
> *Debra:* In the gap between the two lockdowns, I kept socialising to a minimum and found it as saddening and depressing as ever. In practical terms, life changed hugely; I lost work (paid and unpaid) and my partner changed jobs (because of poor corona-related working conditions). The children were elated at being able to go to playgrounds with their friends again but are very sad that they'll have to stop this again with a second lockdown. In general terms, I'm just very sad and fed up of the whole thing. (Female, pre-school assistant after losing her job as a freelance musician and music teacher, UK)

This was the reverse experience for workers on the frontline. Branded as 'heroes' by the political elite, 'key workers' were instrumental in ensuring that countries continued to function. While many worked from home, in and outpatients were cared for, hospitals were cleaned, police officers continued to patrol and respond to incidents, supermarket shelves were restocked, takeaways and deliveries were made. For some, their recognition was well received to start with, as Katie, an NHS Pharmacist, remembers:

Early on, it was so much recognition, the clapping on the doorsteps and while you were shopping people would congratulate you or smile or comment at you. It was so rewarding as when you delivered the treatments, people were so thankful, so grateful. One or two people would leave me chocolates. One man applauded me from his conservatory. When I delivered one elderly lady's son's medication who had a severe learning difficulty, and she put a thing on Facebook, shared and tracked me down and sent me a personal message and sent a card to the department. It encouraged me to carry on, we were making a difference. We were somehow supporting very vulnerable people.

However, as the lockdowns went on, these feelings disappeared as she recalled:

People are fed up with it. We were encouraged to eat out to help out but then the second wave came and people just went back to normal. So people think 'we locked up and it came back' then 'we went back to normal and it came back.' People are getting bored and found ways around it during the first lockdown. There was a guy in the supermarket the other day who got abusive because he was told he could only have four toilet rolls. I feel there is a lot of frustration. It was never really enforced properly [the first lockdown]. I mean playgrounds are supposed to be closed but everything around where I am is heaving with kids.

The solidarity that some respondents described was prevalent early in lockdowns but seemed to dissipate as an underlying tension came to the surface and frontline workers experienced the brunt of it, as Katie recognised. Indeed, throughout our time between the lockdowns and bouts of 'new normal' in both the UK and Spain, we have also witnessed this:

I am sitting on the front step with a glass of water, cooling down from my run. The regular courier who delivers to our street approached the front gate and announces he has a parcel for me. The front gardens in our terraced street are small and the fences are low so it's possible to have conversations from the street. The gate is ten feet from the front door so I say, *"just throw it over, it's not fragile"*. He does so but then replies, *"you know, some people are funny about things like that. "Oh be careful, it's got glass in it"*, like there aren't more important things going on in the world."

I ask him if he has been busier during lockdown, *"Oh yeah, I'd say two and a half times as busy as I used to be. I'm really starting to feel it now, I'm more tired than normal."*
As we talk about his work during lockdown, he says he usually doesn't finish until around 7.30pm each day. I ask him how people have been with him during lockdown and he says it is a real mix. He's found some people have been kinder – *"not bowing down before me for bringing their stuff but definitely friendlier"* – but he's also seen an increase in the number of people who are nasty towards him – *"some people I think just want to take their aggression or frustration out on someone. I get people swearing at me, calling me all sorts. Even on this street, there's a mix of people. Some are lovely, very friendly, others are really aggressive and always give me shit."* I am surprised and tell him, *"I thought everyone would love you – stuck in their houses and you're bringing them all the stuff they've ordered".* Apparently not. He says that it's funny how people judge others – he has a dishevelled appearance but while people just see a scruffy courier, he actually has a degree in maths. He thinks that working as a courier is good for him as he's learning how to handle different attitudes and behaviours.
We talked about the lockdown and he touches on politics, *"If I was running the country, there'd be 20,000 less dead."* I reply that just about anyone other than Boris Johnson would have managed the crisis better and he agrees. *"I voted for him. I really shouldn't have but I voted for this government and look where that got us."* We go back to talking about the people in our neighbourhood that he encounters in his work. He observes that some people follow social distancing very well and go out of their way to stay more than two metres away but a lot of people, particularly young people, show no consideration and make no attempt to socially distance, even if it meant old people had to walk around them. He's been delivering parcels to our house for three or four years and this is the first time we have had a conversation longer than the transactional encounter related to his work and our delivery. [Field notes Anthony Lloyd 'Delivery']

Despite the use of furlough schemes—in which governments paid a percentage of workers' wages—in 2020, 114 million jobs were lost across the world.[8] These two unemployed people from the UK were feeling the newfound pressure of losing their jobs:

> *Ashley:* I am submitting job applications every day and hoping after the lockdown I get a job. I am definitely listening less to any news on Covid-19 as it is depressing and trying to think positive, preventing negative thoughts wearing me down.
>
> *Marcus:* I feel so much isolation, depression, I am unable to shop for clothes and have to do it online while swelling with anxiety on being a victim of cyber theft and fraud.

Ashley had become reliant upon her own personal resilience and test of will to get through what had become a challenging period of her life. Marcus meanwhile found little comfort or distraction from his feelings of anxiety. Isolation, loneliness, worries about personal health or the health of others, restrictions on movement, as well as concerns about work and financial security, converted into high levels of collective anxiety, distress and depression. A Centre for Disease Control (CDC) survey in December 2020, for example, found that 42% of Americans reported anxiety or depression symptoms which represented an increase of over 200% from the 2019 average.[9] Meanwhile, in the UK, 31% of people responding to a survey in September 2020 had developed depression severe enough to qualify for 'high-intensity psychological support'.[10] In France, which, at the time of writing, had experienced three national lockdowns, nearly a quarter of young people 18–24 couldn't find work, while depression among this group had nearly doubled during April to November 2020.[11] The rapid spread of the virus seemed to generate collective fear and insecurity for some, as one of our interviewees Michael—a Greek man working in Belgium—explained *"everyone became just as vulnerable as the disadvantaged...through the consequences of 'social distancing,' people around the globe can now experience the same vulnerability that was before only felt by some".*

---

[8] International Labour Organisation (ILO) (2021).
[9] CDC (2021).
[10] Jia et al. (2020).
[11] Associated Press (2021).

Old Attachments, New Habits and Subjective Shrinkage

As we discussed in the previous chapter, the immediate consequence of many of the lockdowns was that much of the world's population increased their reliance on digital modes of communication and entertainment (Chapter 5). With nowhere to go, no one to see, no means of travel permissible, many people relied on news media as a means to follow the developments. However, quite quickly, it became clear that many of the mainstream news channels aligned with governmental messaging and rarely posed critical questions or debates about alternatives to lockdowns—thus aiding in processes of compliance.[12] People also increased their affiliations with social media and internet-communicative platforms such as Skype, Zoom and WhatsApp to name a few. UK residents' daily internet usage time, for example, increased from an average of 3.5 hour in 2019 to 4 hour a day during lockdown, and during the same period Netflix subscriptions increased by 16 million, as did the number of livestream gamers from 2.3 million in January 2020 to 4.2 million in April 2020.[13] Some of those we spoke to reflected on the excitement of going through entire series on HBO or Netflix before watching films and playing online games. The seemingly endless possibilities of the online world, conversely, troubled others like Peter, a secondary school teacher from the UK:

> I feel more disconnected from others at the moment and think that many people have retired into their own microspheres which I find very worrying and wonder whether face-to-face communication - which was already being seriously eroded in a post-social age of online-oriented communication - will ever recover.

---

[12] See Briggs et al. (2021).
[13] Ibid.

Peter is concerned that increased allegiance to online industries does harm to people on both a social and subjective level. Without face-to-face contact, Lina—a German youth worker—says relationships suffer and technology doesn't seem to be enough to fulfil people:

> [In lockdowns] Physical contact is missing and the online world is not enough to fully experience (human) emotions. People are losing their jobs, they are getting lonely and depressed. Relationships are getting worse because of too much limitations on movement and socialising. Some people will be excluded even more if they are not able to use the technology or don't even have the devices to participate. That, and also the economy will be destroyed.

But it may be too late as we have documented in previous research.[14] Panni, our shoe salesman from Switzerland, believes that the pandemic has irreversibly exacerbated our reliance on digital goods and industries. He sees a future where masks become fashion accessories (see Fig. 6.1 and Fig. 6.3) and one where digitalisation continues to dismember collectivity and commercially embed itself in our way of life, forcing us increasingly into post-social tendencies. He said:

> We will enter a new fashion like Gucci and Prada masks, and people will want to look nice with masks, people will start to disbelieve the governments and what they are saying and will want to fight the system but will realise it is futile. And the best thing which will come will be the economic crisis. Because they are handing money out all the time to every person who can't work. Where is this money coming from? When people think the worst is gone like the virus, then that's when the worst will really come. It won't change, the virus is part of our lives now. Besides technology makes peoples' lives easy, they are lazy and people won't want to remove themselves from that loop, the comforts, Amazon, etc. I feel sometimes like I am on autopilot and I am just passing each day automatically. That is the feeling for many people at the moment. I think people wanted a reason to be anti-social anyway, to isolate themselves from other people, go online, do shopping, check Facebook and this will mark the disintegration of the human race.

---

[14] See Briggs et al. (2020).

Fig. 6.1 Fashion markets for masks[15]

Many of those we spoke to via Facebook forums seemed unable to tear themselves away from digital platforms where furious and continuous debates ensued about the 'rights' and 'wrongs' of lockdowns, while appearing intermittently in the background where elements of what Panni had identified: it seems some people in Western societies don't mind being 'anti-social', staying at home and immersing themselves in a digital social life. In one such status:

---

[15] Photo courtesy of Jeff, an American participant.

> *Ruth:* Will Amazon orders etc. stop now then [with more lock-
> downs]? Argh what am I going to do without impulse buying!?

Vicky, an online betting employee, here celebrates the quick convenience
of all the consumer indulgences:

> Amazon prime is now available in our area and yesterday, we got
> Morrisons [supermarket] delivered within three and a half hours of
> ordering! This totally saved our Friday night live!! 🍺🍷 Cheers!

Here Liam, a sales assistant from the UK, tries to convince the thousands
of other people in his anonymous Facebook forum about the social and
moral value of lockdown, as well as the additional benefits:

> *Liam:* We have smart phones, the internet, online deliveries, virtual
> GPs, Netflix, Amazon Prime, 100s of TV channels, Skype, etc. Yes,
> isolation can be difficult to cope with at times – and I don't even
> have a garden - but we have it easy. Let's stick to social distancing
> and isolating to avoid a second wave.
> *Paul:* (in response): I'll just get in touch with my overseas family and
> tell them I don't wanna see them anymore because I have Netflix
> shall I?
> *Liam:* You could Skype them and then watch something on Netflix
> together Zoom is great for family quizzes too.
> *Paul:* Fuck off!

Indeed, even as we write—and life remains fairly stationary—we read
about the WEF recommendations to resolve the inability and unavail-
ability of holiday tourism via 'virtual tourism'. The future, according to
Anu Pillai, a Consultant to the aviation and hospitality sector, is going on
holiday from your living room via virtual reality. He passionately writes
this world is:

> … a human-centric designed, interactive space online that makes a desti-
> nation accessible and so real for a sightseer with sound captured by
> electro-acoustic researchers. You could view holiday sites in a video or
> through self-navigation using voice or joystick controls, interact with
> people using video-calling platforms, travel through the streets of said

location, eavesdrop on local music and much more. This could be stitched together in a single platform individually or in silos on the internet and further enhanced by setting up physical experience tourism centres locally. Such a setup would allow tourist guides, artisans, craftspeople, hoteliers and transport businesses to create their own digital and virtual offerings and interact with possible customers.[16]

Paul, who took exception to Liam's embrace of the digital, would probably also say 'fuck off' to this as well. Such digital, post-social futures took several steps closer during the lockdowns and now seem to be quickly taking hold but bring other problems as this pandemic has also seen.

Alert! Covid-19 Dis/mis/information Overload

Even though, in many instances, most of the mainstream media very much aligned with governmental policies around the world, some people still developed questions during the lockdowns and, more so, in their aftermath in the 'new normal'. The world had essentially been sent home and were subject to an onslaught of the 'Covid-19 danger' and never-ending 'new cases' and 'death' statistics (Chapter 3). While compliance was achieved to some degree through these mediums and bolstered by online news forums and social media posts, some people still had doubts (Chapter 10). These people sought to confirm or deepen their knowledge about what they were being told.[17] However, wading through much of this additional information was overwhelming so a surplus unforeseen consequence of this exposure to continual online digital media was the inability to distinguish scientific fact from scientific fiction, reliable information from sensation and manipulation. An indicator of this doubt was in the high rates of scepticism about the Covid-19 statistics and government legitimacy.[18]

---

[16] Pillai (2021).
[17] See Briggs et al. (2021).
[18] Ibid.

Researchers examining the distribution of 'misinformation' about Covid-19 in the UK, Spain, Ireland, USA and Mexico found a paradox: that many people find it 'highly reliable' while, at the same time, a smaller group find factual information about the virus 'highly unreliable'.[19] When these people tried to vocalise their doubts in online platforms such as YouTube and Facebook, they were met with significant opposition confirming that these spaces didn't want to host such questions. 'Karen'—as she calls herself—endured hostile opposition in one global Covid-19 forum when she initiated debates. After having some of her posts removed and her account regularly suspended, she tried to come to some common ground with thousands of other people in the forum:

Surely, we can all agree with this?

If our government and media had earned themselves adequate credibility, then freedom of speech would pose little threat to them. If people in the West are turning away from government and news media in order to seek the truth elsewhere, then that is because they have lost trust in government and news media. Nor will trust be restored by censorship. Credibility seems to have hit an all time low. Why is this? Why have they lost credibility? Finding the honest answer to that is the first step. Rectifying it is the next. (2 likes)

Karen's statement, however, was met with a strong reaction:

George: I'm not turning away from news media. I seem to remember from past posts, you seem very paranoid towards news outlets. Also, when you talk about credibility, I question the credibility of most of the things you post about 😐 (17 likes)

Harry: I'm sorry but the freedom of speech you are referring to here does not pose a threat to the government etc. It is more of a threat to the general public. Those with a lesser understanding, a lower IQ etc being subjected to ridiculous conspiracy theories and dangerous misinformation being peddled by a select few relatively intelligent individuals for personal gain. Whether that be

---

[19] Roozenbeek et al. (2020).

monetary or simply just for kicks. It then gets spread and passed on from there. So no, I don't agree. No threat to the government and powers that be. Just a serious threat to Jo public. (100 likes)

Joe: I think that it's a minority who are turning away from legitimate media and looking for less credible news sources that fit a certain narrative and that's up to them to be honest. I certainly have absolutely zero faith in our government, however I still fully support the science that has been acted upon too late. Some people are clearly more comfortable with obvious misinformation. This is not a threat to the government at all, the only danger they pose is to themselves and those that they influence. (60 likes)

Given that in many countries protesting had been banned because of 'public health risks', this left only online platforms as a space to contest things. Posts—which were permitted by the Administrators—were repeatedly uploaded about contradictory reports, interviews and data which went against the general messages governments were trying to transmit. Those messages were often met with sarcastic memes, abuse and, in some cases, threats. Chat Administrators frequently patrolled the forums, closing off exchanges and banning members for persisting in potentially 'offending' people or just those who had an alternative point of view. Indeed, YouTube have a policy to take down content which contravenes WHO guidance, and Facebook donate money to 'independent factcheckers' to moderate the content which is shared on its sites. The online space people thought was available to debate these issues during the lockdowns was, in fact, heavily policed and this led to forum users utilising code words like 'Jibby Jab'—meaning vaccine—so the 'bots' could not detect the posts. Kenny, a taxi driver, wrote a status update in frustration noting how:

Facebook bots go back through your old posts and check to see if you have said anything that goes against the narrative they are pushing. They removed three of my comments saying they were spam. I thought spam was when someone posted the same thing over and over again? (Fig. 6.2).

No wonder they were removed: Kenny was examining the correlations between death rates and vaccination rates.

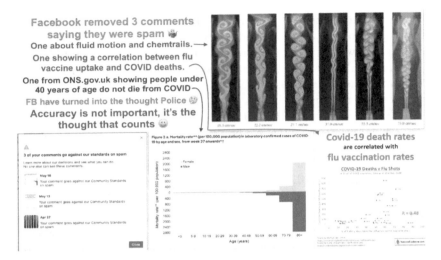

Fig. 6.2 Kenny's own research into the pandemic

Lockdown Polarities Part 2: Sheep/le vs Covid Denier/Covidiot/Conspiracy Theorist

The second part to lockdown polarities relate to a clear-cut divide in the placement of trust: those who invested trust in the government and media and thus followed the government public health measures, as opposed to those who tended to be more sceptical about these respective institutions and their advice. However, for the former group, there were even people who secretly doubted their credentials. The media were *"unprepared, no fact checking"* said Antonia, a Bulgarian factory worker in her 40s. Rahul, an Indian ticket inspector, said *"the media is full of bullshit"*. Hilda, a playschool teacher in her 30s from the Netherlands, said the constant reference to Covid-19 was about *"intended fear as a tool to control the masses' behaviour"*, while Agata, a young shop assistant from Slovakia claimed the *"shock value seemed more important than facts"*. In a balanced reflection, Paula, a Spanish receptionist suggested:

> I believe that not all measures taken by the Spanish government have been effective. The media make it worse. I believe that there must be some way

to reconcile the economy and social life with this virus, since because of these restrictions many businesses have been forced to close. On the other hand, I believe that the psychological burden that this pandemic carries is going to mean a considerable increase in psychological consultations and the government is not taking this into account. I understand that this is a difficult situation to address but I feel that public opinion is never taken into account when taking action and that there should be a place of debate where the citizen can at least set out his point of view and be heard.

People linked feelings of high levels of harmful anxiety and high media consumption. This self-employed French translator in his 40s said of the media coverage that it was *"appalling. I stopped watching news* [during lockdown] *due to the constantly contradicting 'expert' opinions. I found news coverage too anxiety-inducing - as I have found it to be during other events (yellow vest movement in France, terrorist attacks, etc.)"* As discussed in Chapter 3, this anxiety negatively affected many people's mental health. This, combined with the continued oversaturation of 'virus warnings' and 'fearmongering statistics', however, did not seem to convert some people who took it upon themselves to rigorously research and inform themselves about things like epidemiology, virology and immunology. Because mainstream information avenues did not convince them, much of this research and information they found went against the general scientific evidence and advice that many governments were using to argue for lockdowns. In the main, it was these people who started to doubt fundamental elements of the pandemic.

At the extreme end of the spectrum, a minority of members of this group were denying the existence of the virus and regarded the whole issue as a smokescreen under which other more sinister plans were being put into action by the powerful elite. Laura, a British woman working as a receptionist for a Spanish car hire company, said:

It's gone perfectly for them. World's ten richest men even more disgustingly rich than they were before [the pandemic]. All members of WEF donate to the WHO, meet in Davos and either directly benefit from lockdown or have shares in vaccine companies, they donate to many news channels including the BBC, newspapers like the Guardian, the Independent etc. Bill Gates had it all planned (Event 201) just before it happened, what a great coincidence, he was there to provide the solution when the problem came along (vaccines AND ID2020).

However, for the majority of others, they simply had doubts and disagreed. Yet, like these people, we too also noticed that with the advent of lockdowns and the establishment of Covid-19 Facebook forums, it became increasingly difficult to have alternative debates which contravened government public health messages. In one public forum, dominated in the main by thousands of pro-lockdown participants, messages or posts projecting anything other than positive messages supporting the health service or in favour of the vaccine were quickly dismissed. Stephanie, a young female Croatian artist living in the UK, said:

> *Stephanie:* I see 'saving lives' the same rhetoric as 'saving the planet.' 'So, you don't believe there is a virus' is the same as someone calling you a 'denier'. It's there to stop any debate. Or anti vaxxer. It's been the same since the beginning: tow the party line or else. Deifying of the NHS. There has been lots of scare mongering throughout, whilst defending all restrictions and demanding more of it. Any dissenting voice treated with contempt. And now when it's about the vaccine, they're up in arms and calling out on 'fear mongering' if you dare to question the narrative. And when I come on here there are lots of members talking of getting the jab and 'feeling great'.
>
> *Interviewer:* Do you think people have completely submitted to the ideology or do you think it's more that certain characters have an ulterior motive in the forums?
>
> *Stephanie:* I would say it's more of the latter. I have no proof, but it is my instinct. When I post something, it could be a long read or a video or whatever. And laughing at emojis and dissing of the content comes with speed. It's like they have a job to do.

Such forums become the spaces where much of the government public health ideologies are aggressively reproduced and reinforced emotively in high frequency by a voluntary collaborative intent on ousting the virus heretics, or as we came to know quickly, the 'Covid deniers'. In one Facebook forum, David, a young unemployed fitness trainer from the USA who had lost his job during lockdown, was regularly targeted by other members of the group for being critical of the public health messages associated with Covid-19. He said:

> Covid-19 represents the complete destruction of humanity. Not a human being to talk to. People are freaked out about meeting someone they don't know (so how does a person meet anyone?) No public events (so how does a person meet anyone?) I think an entire generation has been driven to hopelessness, to the point where death may be more appealing than life, all due to government stupidity over a fraud. Take the masks for example. Their purpose is emotional isolation, dehumanization and the erasing of identity. If you put a muzzle on a dog, it suppresses free will. That is the only purpose of the masks. I sometimes refuse to wear the mask when shopping, and I see people give me dirty looks, or walk wide around me like I'm a leper for having a face. Even if in the most vulnerable age range, there is only a 0.0056% chance of death if infected, and my State has 0 to 5% infection according to PCR tests which are known to be 80% false positives.

David was so concerned about masks he sent us an image of the new 'masks' on sale in the USA (Fig. 6.3). An unemployed man from the UK also questioned the severity of Covid-19 and what he believed were the real motivations behind the 'measures':

> *Mick:* No one ever trusted a politician, or the media. But for some strange reason they all trust them 190% now [because of Covid]…Hahaha, can't make this shit up, pal. I keep getting banned and deleted by Facebook because of it.
>
> *Interviewer:* Why?
>
> *Mick:* Broadcasting the truth. Why are people trying to contain a virus which everyone is going to get? This is the fourth industrial revolution. In ten years' time, there will be no work mate. It's agenda 2030.

Consequently, people such as Mick, who challenged the narratives of established bodies like the WHO or respective government institutions and criticised measures were either branded 'deniers', 'covidiots'

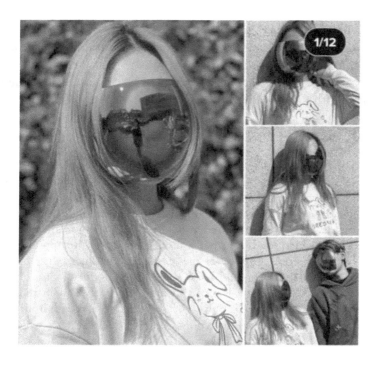

2021 Fashion OVERSIZED Huge Big MASK
SHIELD FULL FACE Polarized Large MIRROR
Sunglasses Outdoor Sports Cycling Sunglasses
★ ★ ★ ★ ☆   (31)

Fig. 6.3 "A leper for having a face?"[20]

or 'conspiracy theorists'. Agenda 2030 refers to the UN's 2015 pledge to reconfigure the way life works on the planet by eliminating poverty, enhancing prosperity and limiting environmental damage. Mick believes that societies around the world are being reconfigured economically, politically and ecologically along these lines. For his penance for having these views on Facebook, however, he is now using his third Facebook

---

[20] Photo courtesy of David, an American participant.

account as the two previous ones were closed eight times before being permanently erased. Certain elements of the Agenda 2030, and the more recent WEF publication of 'the Great Reset',[21] are being discussed and considered as potentially viable changes. It is not necessarily pure conspiracy, as there will inevitably be unemployment in the fallout of the pandemic and this will require governments to rethink how societies operate. In the absence of a job following the impact upon some industries like the hospitality and aviation sectors, in a potentially 'greener world', Universal Basic Income (UBI) is one possible option and we are increasingly seeing discussions about this in the news media. UBI, for example, is central to the WEF's recent publications and was trialled pre-Covid-19 in places like Finland[22] and there is increased support for such initiatives in the UK and USA.[23]

As was Stephanie's experience, those raising questions about what changes may be enforced in the wake of the pandemic were often met with quite rampant hostility. However, in the Facebook forums, a minority of people labelled those complicit in following preventative measures such as lockdowns, social distancing and mask wearing as 'sheep'—because they just did what they were told and followed the masses. We witnessed, however, through the phases of our study, more and more people question what was taking place and what the future may look like. Oona, a Finnish secondary school teacher, was perplexed at the disproportionate governmental public health measures against what she described as *"almost non-existent Covid numbers"* in her country:

> The measures are lighter in Finland than in many other countries in Europe, as there are not many people who got Covid. The virus is almost non-existent, Covid numbers here, there is no need for wearing a mask or social distancing. There is a virus but it's not as dangerous as the manipulated media state. There is a lot of big business-big money plans behind all this story.

---

[21] Schwab and Malleret (2020).
[22] Patel and Kariel (2021).
[23] Nettle et al. (2021).

She went on to add how *"people don't believe me or dismiss me when I have this view, they think I deny it all."* Oona was seen as a 'covid-denier' without a doubt. Bill, an unemployed UK chef, unable to work in his restaurant, said: *"I do not believe life will ever return to how it was before as I think Covid-19 was used as a smoke screen to keep the public occupied while governments collaborated to change laws and monetary systems"*: Bill was also labelled a 'conspiracy theorist'. When people referred to Mick as a 'denier' or 'conspiracy theorist' he retorted condescendingly *"I just laugh at them…Some people you just can't help… They are in their little secure bubbles, bless em"*.

Yet, these are the bubbles which *secure people's subjective commitment to digital platforms and reduce their capacity to question.* Such conversations and debates on social media were often generated from the charts and graphs shown on the Covid-19 daily news briefings and continued media reporting about the numbers of people dying. Even in these forums, there were frantic debates over the credibility of the statistics. James, an American librarian, posted this in one Facebook forum made up of 150 thousand people in December 2020 at the height of many second waves across the world:

I'm curious.

To all the people that believe the novel 2019 Coronavirus is similar to the flu/a hoax/fake, what number of daily deaths would it take to change your minds about the severity of this pandemic?

Yesterday we just had the first 3,000+ day of reported COVID-19 deaths. September 11 had 2,996 deaths. Cancer kills an average of 1,642 people a day in the US. Heart disease takes an average of 1,796. The flu kills an average of 93 people a day.

What number would change your mind regarding the severity of this pandemic?

The responses to this post highlight the division and conflict over the issue. Here are just a few from the 500+ comments:

Marina: All those deaths aren't just Covid though. They are inflating the numbers. Anybody dies now or is sick and they say it's Covid. If you believe the government doesn't lie to us, I feel sorry for you. (29 likes)

Hazza: They want you to believe it. They want you to fear. They want you to beg for the vaccine. (11 likes)

Kara: I can tell you from having Covid myself a very healthy fit individual, it stresses every major system in your body above anything I have ever had and for a much longer time period. It undoubtedly would cause issues that you normally would not experience. The virus works in strange ways and presents differently from person to person. For those that don't believe, hopefully you will not have to experience it to believe it - I wouldn't wish it on anyone. (4 likes)

Sarah: The number doesn't matter!!! People die! I'm not saying I don't mourn for those lost and I'm not saying I'm not scared a little bit about how my family would fair if we caught it since we've had two bad colds since March in my family so hey we might have had it but we don't test we just isolated and stayed home. BUT we must also look at the numbers of other things as a result of this lockdown to 'save lives'....what about the children and teenagers committing suicide, what about the adults committing suicide? What about the kids stuck at home with abusive parents or the women stuck at home with an abusive partner and vice versa? What about all the families losing their houses and jobs and livelihoods? What about everyone ending up homeless because of all the rules and lack of work? People can't be so worked up about JUST COVID. If you care so much, then you must care about the other side of this too. Covid isn't the only thing you should care about and if it is then I'm sorry you might deserve to suffer more than anyone. This virtue signalling is garbage. (3 likes)

Michele: I've been sick since 11/20 and was hospitalized because of it. For me it was NOT like the flu at all. I'm still not better. It felt foreign to me and like something my body had never fought. I'm 43. My sisters and nieces caught it as well. My young niece of 25 got really sick but didn't have to be hospitalized like me. However, my older sister with tons of health issues was asymptomatic. With this virus you don't know how or who it's going to affect badly. Being in healthcare I've been tested routinely since April-negatives and no false positives. I knew the moment I caught it in Nov. that what I caught was different it was unlike anything I've had before and it's been a tough go of it. Some people are not going to believe it until it affects them or someone they love sadly. And there are still flu cases and reports; not everything is classified as Covid. 🙂 (3 likes)

Ashley: Covid has taken my great grandfather to hospice. Anyone who believes it's a scam is a fucking idiot. (7 likes)

Larry: This virus is so bad. It knows when you are in a pub not eating its going to get you. It's so clever it's going away for five days over Christmas. I could go on and on but reading the 'it isn't a hoax bores me'. Where have all the flu deaths gone this year? (0 likes)

The final comment from Larry highlights what many believed were the contradictions and the ambiguity of the different measures applied by governments to prevent transmission, which were also a source of further conflict over the most appropriate way to respond to the virus. In some cases, this ambiguity was evident within the same country and even the same city as Lara, a Slovenian woman noticed:

I am Slovenian but live in Belgium. The reaction here is very uncoordinated, meaning that different rules apply to different communes within one city (depending on the mayor). For instance, in the city centre, masks are not obligatory, not even in shops. Yet a couple of metro stops further, in another commune, you get fined for not wearing the mask in a street!

Lockdown Polarities Part 3: Responsible Citizen vs. Negligent Citizen

For people who had followed strict lockdowns in the 'new normal', those identified as 'deniers' and potential 'conspiracy theorists' were believed to be 'jeopardising the progress made'. Nieves, a young Spanish student, said *"it's pretty alarming the spread of pseudoscientific and conspiracy ideas amongst the populace. It contributed to worsening the pandemic outcome."* In contrast to 'reckless others', people like Nieves believed that they were acting responsibly, with discipline and displaying compassion for others. They reported following arrows on the floor directing individuals around shopping centres and workplaces, washing their hands regularly, wearing masks (replacing disposable ones every four hours as recommended), maintaining social distancing and were at home when told to be according to curfews. Like Nieves, many had similar things to say about their conduct during the pandemic:

> *Ivan:* I have become more responsible as my role in society. I must do whatever I can to avoid large gatherings so as to avoid the further spread of the virus. (Bulgaria, Male, Call Centre worker)
>
> *Marja:* I am more careful and adhere to social distancing as best as I can (except for when meeting with my parents). I am more tuned in to other peoples' attitude towards the pandemic. I still wash my hands regularly, more than before the pandemic. My social circle has shrunk dramatically though. (Netherlands, Female, Secondary School teacher)
>
> *Kadri:* Society is wearing masks and I am wiping everything with alcohol and there is no physical contact with anyone. (Turkey, Female, Teacher)
>
> *Brad:* Everyone should wear a mask, should respect, and practice social distance, and use hand sanitizers. They should get the vaccine and not jump the line in front of front-line workers or the elderly. (USA, Male, Mechanic)

In our study, we found a high proportion of those reporting strict adherence to measures had remained employed during the pandemic; had experienced, by comparison, little change in the quality of their lives; and, because of this, questioned why others around them could not do the same. Like Nieves mentioned previously, many were critical of whom they saw as, what we call, *negligent citizens*. This *us-vs-them* mentality represents an extension of these previous polarities coming to fruition and seemed to be particularly destructive to collective efforts to curb the transmission of the virus. Rocio, from Madrid in Spain, for example, was fortunate to retain her work during the lockdown, having established her own practice. On arriving home every-day from work, she would disinfect her shoes and shower before greeting anyone in the family. She took pride, she says, in *"being responsible"*. While she was critical of the government and media, saying: *"they had lied from start to finish"*, she was similarly critical of some of her fellow citizens because *"people need to be responsible and not break the rules otherwise they risk the health of everyone else"*. In a similar case, Mara, a Serbian youth worker, trainer and online yoga teacher who had already adapted her work online during the lockdown described herself as *"ready for the digital future"*, and during the lockdown wanted *"people in my country to be more responsible, in solidarity and focused on making things become better in Covid situation"*.

While the sense of a division between *responsible* and *negligent* citizens was evident in virtual spaces, we observed, once public spaces re-opened, such tensions emerging in face-to-face interactions. The encounter described through the field notes below occurred in a large high street store:

> The socially-distanced queue snakes away from the counter and is so long it extends beyond the extendable barriers that mark out the queuing aisle. The sudden sound of raised voices draws the attention of most people waiting to pay for their items. A middle-aged woman at the back of the queue is engaged in a heated argument with a young man and his two friends who are several places in front of her. He isn't wearing a face mask and it quickly becomes clear that this is the reason for the confrontation: *"I just want him to put his mask on that's all"* the middle-aged woman says to one of the other young men with him. The young man without a face mask retorts sarcastically, *"Oh yeah you think you are better than me cos you have a mask on. It's none of your business if I have a mask on or not."* The middle-aged woman replies defiantly: *"Yes I am better than you because I am thinking of others and wearing my mask, you are not"* The young man becomes visibly frustrated and the exchange begins to escalate. He raises his voice to a shout and throws his arms up in the air in frustration: *"We are better people than you...go away I don't want to talk to you, you stupid lady"*. *"Oh what don't you like being challenged by a woman?"* the woman replies. By this point the confrontation has attracted the attention of everyone queuing and others in the shop who begin to stop and observe. Several staff begin to make their way over to intervene. A young woman, wearing a mask, who has just finished being served at the counter approaches the young man without a mask and tells him to

calm down and that the middle-aged woman is *"just trying to wind you up now"*. Another person waiting in the queue interjects into the confrontation and asks *"Can you calm down please there are children present"*. As the young woman wearing a mask walks away from the counter having paid for her items, she passes the older woman involved in the confrontation and says to her: *"Who are you anyway? Mask police?*" She then utters *"Weirdo"* at the older woman as she walks away. [Field notes Anthony Ellis 'Mask police']

Some of those who displayed strong commitment to the restrictions had a strong desire to return to life as they knew it pre-Covid. Their belief was that if everyone worked together, the virus would prove a temporary blip to the functioning of social life, which would return to normal quicker if everyone complied. Blocking their path to freedom, however, were *negligent citizens* who, in their eyes, jeopardised the future by exercising special liberty and demonstrating a blatant disregard for the health of other people:

> *Matt:* It's probably people not wearing masks properly that I find particularly infuriating. Some people just appear to have the attitude that it doesn't matter, or that they are in some way special so the rules don't apply to them. It pisses me off because obviously nobody wants to wear masks, but we do it. I think there's a real arrogance in their choosing to pull it down below their chin or simply take it off. Of course, this frustration isn't levied at those who have a legitimate reason not to wear a mask. (Student, UK)
>
> *Rob:* It is regrettable because we have made sacrifices to protect them [other people who don't follow the restrictions] and society in general. It is unfortunate that their level of social consciousness is so low as to not think about their "neighbours". (Retired Engineer, Canada)
>
> *Tiago:* It makes me anxious and irritated when people don't follow the rules. (NGO worker, Honduras)
>
> *Arjun:* It makes me angry, anxious and disgusted at the utter negligence of the people who do not follow the government advice. (IT supervisor, India)
>
> *Sergio:* I don't like it. Rules are there for a reason. If nobody respected rules everything would be a mess. (Physiotherapist, Spain)

Lisette: I wish some of them would get Covid to know what they might be inflicting on others. I used to get very upset in the beginning about others not being careful, but there have been too many incidences of incivility and I can't be bothered to get upset now. (Retired, France)

These divisions, however, have become further complicated with the advent of available approved vaccines which, scientists, politicians and journalists, have claimed to represent the potential route out of the pandemic and imposed restrictions.

Lockdown Polarities Part 4: Pro-Vaccine vs. Anti-Vaxxers

Quite quickly into the pandemic, and alongside public health measures such as lockdowns, social distancing and mask wearing, governmental action was taken to initiate a rapid programme of research into possible vaccines. Within months, possible vaccines were under trial, and a process which normally takes at least several years was fast-tracked. The resulting billion-dollar investment in pharmacological solutions to the Covid-19 crisis paid off as countries battled to order the vaccines in an effort to get their country protected first, thus protecting vulnerable people from possible infection and death as well as restarting their respective economies. As a result, some politicians claimed that consenting to a vaccination—*even if all the pharmacological companies would be legally exempt from possible prosecution*—could act as a trade-off for the return of pre-Covid freedoms. Suddenly, in many Western countries, there was a sense of hope among *responsible citizens* and a utopian forecast of 'things returning to normal'. However, this was seen to be jeopardised—once again—by the Covid 'deniers' and 'conspiracy theorists', and *negligent citizens*, through their irresponsible behaviour and dismissive attitudes towards the vaccine:

Hugo: I feel very frustrated because their refusal has a direct effect on everybody else's health and restriction on what we can do in society. (Retired, UK)

Viktoria: The short of it is that they are idiots. The long of it is that somewhere along the way, discussions about public health (i.e. what it means, how it is managed, what steps and negotiations are involved etc.) got muddled in a big way. I mean historically not just in the moment, hence no negotiated common ground was established nor a sufficient long-term process of education along such lines. (Lecturer, Bulgaria)

Jane: I think its a rather selfish attitude, although every case should be judged individually. I understand the uncertainty because it's new [the virus and measures] and we don't know what the effects will be for years to come; however, at the moment it is the best chance of getting through the pandemic so it should be compulsory. (Police Officer, UK)

Carl: They're not helping us to build up immunity. They're being ignorant. They'll soon use the NHS if they get ill with COVID. (Teacher, UK)

Orla: I understand but do not agree. The impact on society and public is too high. Those who refuse - not because of a medical 'can't' - should lose the right to use public services such as public transport, should not be allowed in shops and only use online shopping. (Data scientist, Ireland)

Demands for vaccine take up have further intensified following the evolution and high-frequency reporting of new 'more infectious variants' of the virus, such as those from Kent, South Africa, Brazil and, as we write, India, though associating these variants with these countries is thought to cause stigma and generate racism so the WHO uses more neutral names like Alpha, Beta and Delta. The possibility of the envisaged pathway back to 'freedom' begins to narrow once again and consumer possibilities, such as luxury holidays, become distant once more. In one Facebook forum, Michelle reflected these fears:

I would love to go to Kassiopi, it looks quaint. We have only been to Paleokastritsa. We love Corfu and thinking of going to Kassiopi and seeing the north maybe for another holiday when things are back to normal. If only people would adhere to the rules, get the vaccine and we could all get back to doing these things.

Disinformation and misinformation about the vaccine, or perhaps just general doubts, subdue what appears to be a global programme towards mass vaccination. The extent to which governments have gone to achieve herd immunity via vaccination has led to some nations using a mix of (a) fear-inducing, and (b) incentivising methods to convince citizens to 'get vaccinated'. With regard to the former, in the UK, the reported rapid spread of the Delta variant in late April and early May 2021, for example, alerted the governmental Scientific advisors Scientific Advisory Group for Emergencies (SAGE) to project—as they have throughout the pandemic—in a 'worst case scenario' that up to 10,000 people per day could be hospitalised should the Delta variant prove to be more transmissible than that of the Alpha.[24] Highly publicised hospitalisations from the Delta variant of people who had 'refused the vaccine' were noted in Bolton, a town in the north of England, which led to a surge in vaccinations.[25]

With regards to the latter, the American State of Ohio attempted to incentivise vaccination by offering registered and vaccinated voters automatic entry into a weekly lottery draw for $1 million. However, those who are not vaccinated cannot access this potential jackpot. For those under 18, specifically aged 12–17, there are similar draws for funding for full-state scholarship to a college or university. However, those who have not had the vaccine are not eligible for the prize.[26] Equally, low uptake of vaccinations in the State of New Jersey has prompted the Governor, Phil Murphy, to target a younger audience by offering 'free beers and shots' after vaccination.[27] To boost London's low vaccine rate in June 2021, Sadiq Khan—the Mayor—said that he would lottery out two tickets to the Euro football finals and 50 pairs of tickets to the Trafalgar Square Fan Zone.[28]

---

[24] Blanchard (2021).
[25] Clarke (2021).
[26] Brown (2021).
[27] Kott (2021).
[28] BBC (2021c).

The New Fault Lines of Social Divisions in the 'new Normal'

The end result of the pandemic experience has been a 'new normal' of increasing division along several lines as outlined above in this chapter, where there are paradoxes of a desire for complete relaxation of restrictions among some, against a sense of rampant anxiety of fully opening up among others (also see Chapter 11). There is fear on the one hand of re-entering shared public space among others, alongside a yearning for a return to populated public spaces devoid of distancing. While considerable numbers of people constantly evaluate their own, and others, behaviour for signifiers of responsible or negligent commitment to the cause. Scared to return to the public realm, Gema, a student in her early 20s, had only been out of her house twice in the three months after the first lockdown in the UK:

> *Interviewer:* Are you worried about going out in public?
> *Gema:* Oh yeah, yes definitely. I took a bus into the city and was quite nervous. I wore a mask, and I wouldn't have done that a few months ago. Walking around I got nervous people who didn't have them or who came into my space. It was more random people coming into my space.
> *Interviewer:* Do you avoid going out?
> *Gema:* Yes. I mean I have only been out twice in three months. But it's ok if I am around people I know and trust.
> *Interviewer:* But isn't there the same risk? I mean you don't know where they have been, and they could have gone out.
> *Gema:* Yes, I realise this. I have only been near one person though.

As Gema sees it, the 'careless' and 'selfish' people that jeopardise her safety and psychological security are returning to pre-Covid practices, while she must remain cautious. New expectations and procedures, which now govern the 'new normal', reveal a new digital apartheid as Emma recounted through a recent experience:

> I took my dad, he's 88 walks with walking aid and is deaf, to Dunhelm [large high street store] yesterday for a few things for his newly decorated

bedroom. Whilst in there my dad needed a rest so decided to take him for a sit down and a cup of tea in the cafe. As we walked in a woman from behind the counter shouted, *"wait there to be seated"*, my dad didn't hear her obviously and he carried on walking, she shouted again so I shouted back *"he's deaf"*. She came running out with a notebook and pen. *"Name address and phone number!!!"* I said, *"what for?"* *"Track and trace"* she replied, I said *"he doesn't have a phone number and as I've just explained he's deaf and lip reads so could you remove your mask please"*, she didn't. *"I said are you refusing him service because he doesn't have a phone number?"* At this point she called for a manager, they wouldn't allow my dad to sit whilst he waited, in comes the manager, I explained the situation to her, she said *"we need a phone number"*, I said *"he hasn't got one so are you refusing him service?"* She said, *"yes we are just following orders."*

As Emma's experience with her father indicates, increasingly, shops, restaurants, bars and other venues subscribe to new modes of digital surveillance as a means of tracking possible virus outbreaks. This leaves many important questions about the dynamics of inclusion and exclusion which we start to analyse in the following chapters in more detail in the context of the elderly and vulnerable (Chapter 7), prisoners, asylum seekers and youth detainees (Chapter 8) and migrant workers, refugees and stateless citizens and the homeless (Chapter 9).

References

Associated Press. (2021, February 2021). *As the COVID-19 crisis drags on, hard-hit French youth struggle.* cited online at https://www.euronews.com/2021/02/16/as-the-covid-19-crisis-drags-on-hard-hit-french-youth-struggle

Balogun, J. (2020). Lessons from the USA delayed response to the COVID-19 pandemic. *African Journal of Reproductive Health, 24*(1), 14–21.

BBC. (2021c). *COVID: Sydney city centre and Bondi beach to enter lockdown.* https://www.bbc.co.uk/news/world-australia-57590969 (last accessed 25 June 2021).

Blanchard, S. (2021, May 14). Sage models warn COVID hospital admissions could be higher than second wave if Indian variant is 40% more infectious than Kent strain as UK cases double in a week. *Daily Mail.* Cited online at https://www.dailymail.co.uk/news/article-9578503/Coronavirus-SAGE-models-warn-hospital-admissions-soar-India-variant-infectious.html

Briggs, D., Ellis, A., Lloyd, A., & Telford, L. (2020). New hopes or old futures in disguise? Neoliberalism, the Covid-19 pandemic and the possibility of social change. *International Journal of Sociology and Social Policy., 40*(9/10), 831–848. https://doi.org/10.1108/IJSSP-07-2020-0268

Briggs, D., Ellis, A., Lloyd, A., & Telford, L. (2021). *Researching the Covid-19 pandemic: A critical blueprint for the social sciences.* Policy Press Rapid Response Series.

Brown, H. (2021, May 14). *Ohio's $1 million Covid vaccine lottery is bribery at its best.* MSNBC News Online. Cited online at https://www.msnbc.com/opinion/ohio-s-1-million-covid-vaccine-lottery-bribery-its-best-n1267276

CDC. (2021). *Symptoms of anxiety or depressive disorder and use of mental health care among adults during the Covid-19 pandemic—United States, August 2020–February 2021.* CDC.

Clarke, L. (2021, May 18). Covid Bolton: Vaccine surge as Indian variant remains a concern. *The Bolton News.* Cited online at https://www.thebolton news.co.uk/news/19309873.covid-bolton-vaccine-surge-indian-variant-rem ains-concern/

CRRC. (2020). *Armenia: Citizens' perceptions on COVID-19 pandemic.* The World Bank.

Greenberg, J. (2020, March 20). Timeline: How Donald Trump responded to the Coronavirus pandemic. *PolitiFact.* https://www.politifact.com/art icle/2020/mar/20/howdonald-trump-responded-coronavirus-pandemic/. Accessed April 3, 2020

Guilmoto, C. (2020). *COVID-19 death rates by age and sex and the resulting mortality vulnerability of countries and regions in the world.* CEPED Université de Paris.

International Labour Organisation (ILO). (2021). *ILO Monitor: COVID-19 and the world of work* (7th ed.). Geneva.

Ismangil, M., & Lee, M. (2021). Protests in Hong Kong during the Covid-19 pandemic. *Crime, Media and Culture, 17*(1), 17–20. https://doi.org/10.1177%2F1741659020946229

Jia, R., Ayling, K., Chalder, T., Massey, A., Broadbent, E., Coupland, C., & Vedhara, K. (2020). Mental health in the UK during the COVID-19 pandemic: Cross-sectional analyses from a community cohort study. *BMJ Open, 10,* e040620. doi: https://doi.org/10.1136/bmjopen-2020-040620

Kott, M. (2021, May 7). Free beer offered as US vaccine drive turns to bribes. *The Sydney Morning Herald.* Cited online at https://www.smh.com.au/

world/north-america/pots-shots-and-pot-for-shots-us-vaccine-drive-turns-to-bribes-20210507-p57pom.html

Nettle, D., Johnson, E., Johnson, M., Saxe, R. (2021). Why has the COVID-19 pandemic increased support for universal basic income? *Humanities and Social Sciences Communication, 8*(79). https://doi.org/10.1057/s41599-021-00760-7

Patel, S., & Kariel, J. (2021). Universal basic income and Covid-19 pandemic. *British Medical Journal, 372.* https://doi.org/10.1136/bmj.n193

Pillai, A. (2021, May 21). *How virtual tourism can rebuild travel for a post pandemic world.* World Economic Forum. Cited online at https://www.weforum.org/agenda/2021/05/covid-19-travel-tourism-virtual-reality/

Roozenbeek, J., Schneider, C., Dryhurst, S., Kerr, J., Freeman, A., & van der Bles, S. (2020). Susceptibility to misinformation about COVID 19 around the world. *Royal Society of Open Science, 7*, 1–15. https://doi.org/10.1098/rsos.201199

Schwab, K., & Malleret, T. (2020). *COVID 19: The great reset.* World Economic Forum.

Stanley, E., & Bradley, T. (2020). Pandemic policing: Preparing a new pathway for Māori? *Crime, Media and Culture, 17*(1), 53–58. https://doi.org/10.1177%2F1741659020946228

Vogl, A., Fleay, C., Loughnan, C., Murray, P., & Dehm, S. (2020). COVID-19 and the relentless harms of Australia's punitive immigration detention regime. *Crime, Media and Culture, 17*(1), 43– 51. https://doi.org/10.1177%2F1741659020946178

7

Locked in: The Elderly and Vulnerable

While the lockdown was an economic gift for some of the world's super-rich, for others, it became a living nightmare. Most prominently, and despite continual political promises, some of the elderly and vulnerable in adult care homes were condemned to either an early death or a miserable time before their inevitable death. Lockdowns and social distancing meant that stringent measures changed their routines and banned them from seeing loved ones. Yet, at no point were the elderly consulted about their own 'vulnerability' or even if they wanted to stay in their rooms and be able to take the risk to see their families. In these facilities, staff got ill while others refused to work with the elderly. Equally, when we were told to enter into lockdowns to preserve the burden on healthcare systems, retired people already wedded to important medical procedures and treatment processes were restricted, some even dying at home by themselves too scared to seek help for ailments which, in the end, were fatal. The mental health of disabled people and vulnerable adults deteriorated significantly under lockdowns while women and vulnerable children were suddenly further exposed to neglect or abuse at home. No one knew what went on behind closed doors, and all doors were closed.

© The Author(s), under exclusive license to Springer Nature
Switzerland AG 2021
D. Briggs et al., *Lockdown*,
https://doi.org/10.1007/978-3-030-88825-1_7

This chapter examines the experiences of these groups of people essentially 'locked in' against their will but, as they were told, for their own good and for the good of others.

Absent Questions, Silent Answers: Austerity and Depleted Healthcare Systems

Initially, governments argued measures such as lockdowns, social distancing, curfews and mask wearing were partially enacted to ensure healthcare facilities, such as primary care and hospitals, were not overloaded with Covid-19 patients. Anticipating a barrage of patients, numerous countries erected extra-field hospitals at the cost of billions only for them to be quietly dismantled without use. Interrogation into why this took place to this day remains absent, as do key questions about *why healthcare systems were unprepared to deal with these challenges in the first place.* To us, it has seemed strange that such questions have escaped the lips of thousands of journalists when they attended government briefings as it seemed to, at the same time, escape both mainstream media and political discussion. Instead of investing in robust healthcare systems which can support every citizen, energy and money were invested in alerting the public to the very real risks posed by Covid-19, and to urge them to comply with public health measures to quell and control the transmission of the virus (Chapters 2 and 3).

As the virus circulated, one by one it exposed the inadequacies of the world's crumbling health systems, particularly in countries that had neoliberalised. Italy was one of the first countries charged with responding to the increasing 'case numbers' and 'deaths' but even before the arrival of Covid-19, the stage had been set for problems. From 2010 to 2019, the Italian health service had suffered €37 billion cuts and experienced a gradual privatisation of services[1] and continual neglect for investment.[2] Furthermore, in Italy, local authorities are responsible for healthcare strategy meaning the national government has little

---

[1] Cartabellotta et al. (2019).
[2] Ricci et al. (2020).

influence, so when Covid-19 started to spread and kill predominantly elderly people in the region of Lombardy—an area prone to air pollution and disproportionately populated by elderly people—there was only capacity for 724 beds. Yet, within weeks of the outbreak, thousands of patients would need that treatment and the national government had little involvement.[3] No lessons seemed to have been learned from the flu seasons of 2014–2015 and 2016–2017 which had killed 40,000 Italians because there had been no further investment in the health system.[4]

In the USA, which saw millions of infections and hundreds of thousands of Covid-19-related deaths, almost no attention had been given to the fact that between 2002 and 2019, public health funding of the American health system had been reduced from 3.21% to 2.45% of national spending which saw the loss of 50,000 public-health-related jobs. Such a reduction disproportionately affected those from poor and minority ethnic backgrounds in ghetto urban areas. Furthermore, diminishing life expectancy because of these structural shortfalls—something also absent from political discussion and media publication—had meant that 461,000 people had their lives 'shortened' leading to hundreds of thousands of avoidable deaths over the same period.[5]

Unanimously, it was found that even countries with a 'gold standard' healthcare system were poorly equipped for such a pandemic.[6] We suspect now that such questions about the readiness and robustness of healthcare systems were glossed over as part of relentless attempts to ensure compliance with public health measures. Indeed, very few people we spoke to even recognised it as an issue. Lana, a university lecturer in Serbia was one of the few to make this observation nonetheless:

The health system in Serbia has been neglected for at least three decades. It currently has poor infrastructure (health centres, hospitals etc.), poor equipment, and medical workers are emigrating in thousands etc. And also it took weeks for the government to take the threat seriously although the virus was present for weeks in Europe. The government have applied

---

[3] Armocida et al. (2020).
[4] Conticini et al. (2020).
[5] Blumenthal and Hamburg (2021).
[6] Dalglish (2020), Razavi et al. (2020, p. 5), and Lal et al. (2021).

curfews from 5pm to 5am and all weekends, while people over 65 are not allowed to leave their homes at all for over a month. There are still improvisations and failures in procedures, so the virus has entered homes for elderly and some hospitals. Comparably, a lot of medical workers have died as well as the elderly.

Lana recognises that the structural hindrances in healthcare investment had a direct impact upon the management of the virus, as well as the level of exposure faced by vulnerable and frontline healthcare staff. Political decisions made in a pandemic context had consequences for other health-related treatments. National health systems in Africa were automatically at a disadvantage since many already suffer from civil wars, hunger, as well as diseases like AIDS and TB and, in recent years, Ebola outbreaks[7] from which more than 11,000 people had died.[8] However, in March 2020, when WHO recommended the temporary suspension of mass vaccination campaigns and restriction of routine immunisation services in settings where community transmission of Covid-19 has been established, this had a catastrophic impact on basic vaccinations for millions of people. This decision alone meant that the routine vaccination of diseases such as diphtheria, measles and polio were disrupted for at least 80 million children at risk of contracting them.[9] Summer 2020 also saw marked reductions in immunisation encounters, including cancer-preventive vaccination against Hepatitis B Virus and Human papillomavirus (HPV) in 89% of countries in the WHO African region.[10] Covid-19 may not be much of a direct threat to Africa because of the general young age of the population, but certainly decisions to endorse public health measures such as lockdowns and social distancing seem to be doing other forms of social harm (Chapter 4).

Of the numerous examples, here we highlight something closer to home by analysing the UK adult social care sector ('care sector' hereafter) as one such case. Pre-pandemic, working conditions in the UK care sector under austerity were characterised as degrading and poorly

---

[7] Dzinamarira et al. (2020).

[8] CDC (2016).

[9] WHO (2020b).

[10] Nnaji and Moodley (2021).

paid. Morale was low among care workers and attitudes of individualised responsibility prevailed over a team ethos.[11] Given that it is increasingly a system which functions by privatisation, many private care homes employed migrants from Eastern Europe, maximising profitability for the private provider because they were hired cheaply through an agency on insecure and uncertain employment contracts.[12] Care workers also often possess little knowledge of their working rights and the UK's history of trade unionisation. They also work long and unsociable hours and suffer high levels of burnout.[13] As a result, staff turnover rates are high and standards of care are distinctly poor. Although these structural conditions left the care sector underprepared to deal with the virus, subsequent governmental mismanagement compounded these issues, and most importantly, the distress of care workers and elderly people was the result of this systematic negligence.

No Country for Old People: The Systemic Failure of Covid-19 Management in UK Care Homes

> Every new policy they enact proves that their previous policies were ineffective, their entire political history (but most especially right now) lacks any thought towards elderly and vulnerable people and, because of this, lacks human empathy.

Like many other participants, Whitney—a non-binary law administration officer in the UK—was particularly critical of the UK government's management of Covid-19 in care homes during the lockdown and intervallic periods afterwards. And rightly so, because even as we write, there has been little if any mention of how and why so many elderly vulnerable people died in care homes. Even if the UK government knew about

---

[11] Robbins et al. (2013).
[12] Shutes (2012).
[13] Costello et al. (2020).

who the virus was most likely to kill, why were the elderly not protected? If we remember back to March 2020, the core governmental messaging was *"stay at home, save lives, protect the NHS"* and resulting campaigns ran in tandem like the 'clap-for-carers' initiative.[14] Questions about the state of the health system were not asked and instead efforts to galvanise members of the public in solidarity gestures were encouraged: perhaps the most significant being when members of the public stood outside their houses at 8 pm each night, making a collective salute to people working on the pandemic's frontline.[15] This was supposed to recognise the work of NHS doctors and nurses and other related hospital/medical staff but, in time, its remit expanded to include adult social healthcare workers—after all, these people deserved recognition as they too were charged with saving lives. Glaring facts confirming how the elderly are most vulnerable to respiratory illnesses must have been at the centre of government planning as the health officials made promises to ensure that elderly care home residents were appropriately shielded and protected.[16]

Yet, even as virus cases started to increase in the UK in March 2020, basic public health protocols had not even formulated in care home strategy.[17] The absence of a strategy resulted in the botched organisation and mobilisation of the care sector and this inadvertently engendered myriad harm, leaving elderly residents unprotected in both care homes and end-of-life care facilities.[18] In the beginning, Covid-19 testing capacity was limited meaning it was near impossible to identify positive cases and there was a lack of PPE to minimise virus transmission. Without these provisions, when the transfer of thousands of hospital patients to care homes took place, no testing or prevention work could be done to reduce the likelihood of Covid-19 infection.[19] What further complicated matters was that Covid-19 among generally frail care home residents could result in the presentation of atypical symptoms:

[14] Wood and Skeggs (2020).
[15] See Briggs et al. (2020).
[16] Oliver (2020).
[17] Daly (2020).
[18] Amnesty International (2020a).
[19] Devi et al. (2020).

COVID-19 frequently presents atypically in care home residents. Pyrexia, diarrhoea and delirium are common presentations, frequently in advance or absence of respiratory symptoms. Non-specific symptoms such as anorexia and decreased mobility may be the only presenting features but have next to no specificity for COVID-19, since they are common presentations of many illnesses in older people.[20]

It can be difficult to attribute Covid-19 infection to other common ailments among elderly care home residents. Nevertheless, the government seemed concerned with freeing up bed space within austerity-crippled hospitals in preparation for the potential arrival of numerous Covid-19 patients. However, because of this urgency, usual funding assessment protocols associated with care home placement were disregarded which essentially sped up the discharges from hospital to care home. The result was that those patients who had tested positive for Covid-19 in hospital infected others in care home settings.[21]

Lack of bed space derived from an already-austerity hit healthcare system which, as recently as 2019, had been cut back even further. Curiously, the warmer winters over the previous years in as many as 32 European countries had seen a decrease in flu-related and respiratory-difficulties in many countries including the UK.[22] For example, the ONS (2020a) indicated that excess winter deaths were at their lowest in 2018 to 2019 with 23,200 in England and Wales, the lowest since the winter of 2013 to 2014. This meant that people who perhaps would have died under normal winter conditions actually lived on. One Cambridge Professor put it like this:

In the UK, there are about 20,000 excess deaths from influenza in a typical year. However in 2018/19, there were only about 1,700 excess deaths, and there is anecdotal and statistical evidence that the 2019/20 flu season was very mild in the UK as well. This implies that there were over 30,000 people alive in the UK at the start of the COVID-19 pandemic who would have been expected to die in the previous two flu seasons.

---

[20] See Gordon et al. (2020, p. 2).

[21] Hanratty et al. (2020).

[22] Hope (2020).

These people are likely to have been predominantly elderly, and in poor health as "most influenza-related deaths occur in the elderly (65 years of age and older) and in those with underlying cardiovascular and respiratory comorbidities".[23]

Indeed, these are the people who have been found to be at highest risk of dying if infected with Covid-19. However, this reduction in demand led NHS trust managers—continually under pressure to look for places to make 'efficiency savings'[24]—to cut services. The Guardian journalist, Denis Campbell wrote in November 2019 how *"17,000 beds have been cut from the 144,455 that existed in 2010 leaving only 127,225".*[25] As a result:

> The NHS entered the pandemic with one of the lowest numbers of acute beds per capita among developed nations and was already struggling to meet waiting time standards for emergency departments, surgery, or outpatients.[26]

The sudden governmental scurry to clear bed space in hospitals at the inception of the pandemic is therefore attributable to diminished capacity. Yet, the issue of care homes does not appear to have been discussed at length as part of the pandemic response. It was reported that the government's SAGE discussed care homes only twice in their meetings during the first five months of 2020[27]—as the first wave hit, peaked and diminished. Elderly people were dying—not only with/of Covid-19 but of neglect, delirium and loneliness—and the government seemed to be unmoved.[28] Between 2nd March and 12th June 2020, there were 66,112 deaths of care home residents in England and Wales, of which 19,394 (or 29%) were officially attributed to Covid-19.[29] Even

---

[23] Ibid.
[24] Carter (2016).
[25] Campbell (2019).
[26] Oliver (2020).
[27] Lintern (2020).
[28] Briggs et al. (2021).
[29] ONS (2020a).

now, the attribution of these deaths directly to the virus has been questioned, largely because those dying with or from Covid-19 were not distinguished.[30]

The people working on the care home frontline that participated in this study recognised these discrepancies and were heavily critical of the government and the healthcare institution charged with their management, Public Health England. The pressure to create NHS bed space also resulted in the blanket use of Do Not Resuscitate (DNRs) policies, and some of the care workers we spoke to said that doctors and GPs were issuing DNRs without the consent of the patients or their families. This meant that if they were ill, they would not be taken to hospital for life-saving care. Sarah, for example, who only entered the care sector in August 2020 because she was made redundant from an admin job at the start of the first lockdown, was *"deeply affected"* by this. Even towards the end of 2020, during the UK's second wave, she observed that this practice was still being used—despite being under investigation from the Care Quality Commission. She said:

> There were people coming in from hospital that said 'Do Not Resuscitate' but there was nothing in the box which would say if the family had been contacted or it had been discussed with them. The hospitals were just putting DNR on these patients because they wanted to clear the beds in the NHS. The senior was then charged with phoning these families and telling them. The families were turning up and crying outside and they couldn't come in because of social distancing. It should be agreed by the families and the doctors should consult them, but it was all being done behind their backs as these people have dementia and things. That for me was very sinister, this was not right. I have had to keep quiet and it breaks me every day. We had 17 come in for respite from hospital in October and November 2020 and they all had DNR on them. They all died.

Furthermore, there was no suggestion that these 17 residents had the virus. Donna also noticed how DNRs were irregularly assigned *"people were having DNRs on their files against their will. They were doing it to*

---

[30] See Chapter 3.

everyone, even to disabled people, younger people with severe disabilities" she said. Moreover, Sarah relayed how the first wave did not really impact upon the care home, but the advent of new public health measures like social distancing, which changed the delivery of care practice and banned families from physical visits, significantly weakened the residents. Another worker, Carmen, recognised this too:

> It wasn't all down to Covid though [dying]. It was more that the families couldn't come in. When they stopped, that's when our residents went downhill. That was heart-breaking. You knew that link had gone. I had an elderly woman who was very loved and had visits from family who came up every week, drove 130 miles, but when they stopped coming you could see it in her eyes and body language. She went downhill quick because the connection, they didn't want to eat or drink, they became weak. Once Covid came in it just took them out, one then two a day. They were already weak, they had given up many of them. I could see them wanting their family. There was nothing we could do, we put the music on, you knew they were going to die with a broken heart. They had Zoom calls but they didn't understand, there was no physical presence. Other times there were maybe visits in a tent outside but they didn't recognise their family as they had masks on, white suits, and they didn't understand.

Evidently, restrictive measures accompanying the lockdown caused myriad harm to some of the UK's most vulnerable elderly people, who were cut adrift from essential support networks. Carmen suggested that this made *"their immune system so low because when flu comes it can do the same. I have seen that from some who passed away that they put Covid on their death certificates, but they had not been tested".* Donna reported similarly that adding Covid-19 onto death certificates *"happened all the time".* Donna gave the example of a resident in very poor health who *"was dying anyway"* and was *"expected to die soon".* After being rushed into hospital, the resident passed away with Covid-19 added to their death certificate. However, Donna remained sceptical given the very poor health of this resident, but also others, arguing that *"we can't say they died of Covid, can we".*

Relatedly, experts recognised that care home residents, who were also subject to lockdown and social distancing measures, were generally confined to their rooms which increased the chances of morbidity and raised safety and staffing concerns.[31] In the context of the public health restrictions on already-fragile care home residents, this meant that less contact with their families and carers equated to more deaths. It was not until the summer months of 2020 that the UK government devised a full care home strategy.[32] Not only have they refused to publish detailed data of how care-home deaths from the preceding months had occurred but deferred calls for a public enquiry. Instead, Prime Minister Boris Johnson has blamed the care sector for *"not following the procedures"*.[33] By July 2020, a national testing programme had been implemented in UK care homes, with weekly swabbing for staff and four-weekly swabbing for residents. Although decreased cases in the summer months were attributed to improvements in virus detection and prevention measures, residential care homes remained at significant risk of exposure to further outbreaks. As the second wave hit the UK, thousands of care home residents died once again—about 1,000 more than the first wave.[34]

A recent national survey of care workers (N = 1,194) found that they endured harmful consequences of the lockdown, including feeling stigmatised, lonely, unsupported by management and lacked support during these waves of Covid-19 infection.[35] In one care home, Rebecca remembered how, one by one, staff started to test positive and/or self-isolate because of Covid-19 symptoms. She was one of five workers faced with caring for 34 residents. She was compelled to move and live in the care home as she attempted to provide as much support as possible. Under normal circumstances, the workforce would have been 31 but 26, including the cook and cleaner, had either contracted the virus or were self-isolating. Rebecca noted how *"Public Health England never sent anyone else, no one came"*. These frontline workers had to balance their home lives with extremely difficult working conditions. During the

---

[31] Gordon et al. (2020).
[32] See Daly (2020), and Devi et al. (2020).
[33] BBC (2020).
[34] Duncan (2021).
[35] Greene et al. (2021).

"second or third" Covid-19 wave at the beginning of 2021, Carmen found herself in an almost impossible situation; she had to work, home-school her children and support her elderly parents:

> When the second or third wave whatever it was, they got it in one wing so we shut that down. Staff had to wash hands, gloves, temperature taking and it was quick. We didn't get Covid until October or even November 2020. It was hard as I was home-schooling, the kids stayed at home, I was going out to the shops and doing work, and it was hard as I am a single mum. No one was out. I couldn't see my mum who has Alzheimer's and lives with my dad. That was difficult.

As the second UK lockdown continued, there were further unintended harms for her eldest daughter who tried to take her own life:

> As a family thing, my daughter took a turn for the worst as she has mental health problems and she couldn't be left alone. She is 16 and has always had depression but lockdown made it a lot worse. She had too much. Like a lot of children her age, lockdown has done damage to them. My daughter took an overdose while I was at work during the Covid-19 in January, so I rang her and paramedics answered. I had to take time off work but my colleagues helped me through it.

In this respect, care workers were not only balancing work on the frontline but also the constant pressures of the lockdown experience as we discussed in Chapter 6. Just like Mandy, an experienced care worker in her 50s, life had been turned upside down given she was caring for her frail parents who could be exposed to the virus but also managing the impact of the lockdowns on her children's mental health and future:

> … my sons are depressed, my parents are depressed as they know that they will die if they get it and they are not ready to leave yet. It's destroyed everything, my son has no work prospects, no money coming in. [Covid-19] it has destroyed everything.

Abandonados: Care Home Desertion in Spain

During an interview, Barbara, a financial consultant from Madrid, Spain, offered a scathing assessment of the Spanish government's management of the pandemic:

> Society should have been informed earlier and a state of alarm should have been declared when the WHO had been saying so since January/February. The government have not protected health care workers or elderly people's homes, the latter being the people most at risk. They are trying to control what is said in the media and social networks. We have no way to protect ourselves to go shopping at the supermarket, there is no material. And when they have wanted to buy it the government goes to a company that rips them off not once, but twice. We are the laughingstock of Europe, they have been mismanaging it from the beginning.

Barbara's anger seemed to be fuelled by the fact that both her parents were living in care homes in March 2020. As rapid lockdown measures closed down the capital and, in doing so, all the care homes, she had no opportunity to see them, could not speak to them, and when she tried to see them, she was told she would be breaking the lockdown law and was told to stay at home. One month later, both had died and were found abandoned and dead in the care home by the Spanish army who were brought in to deal with the situation. Barbara was not even sure if her parents had Covid-19 at the time of their deaths. As a result, she understandably has questions concerning the manner of their deaths. Like our care workers in the UK, she felt there were irregularities. Firstly, as she said, *"the people working in the care home were not at work, almost all of them, because they were self-isolating"* which led her to question who exactly was taking care of her elderly parents. Secondly, when she offered to take them to hospital, she was told *"they won't allow them in because the hospitals are too full"*. Lastly, the private company managing the home, refused to answer her calls or emails which made her *"mad with rage yet helpless"* because Barbara felt that *"they don't really care about my parents because they only want to make money from them"*, adding *"the most I could get from them was that they thought they died from Covid-19 because the virus was in the care home – but no tests were done".*

Like the UK, Spain's healthcare system had been reeling from austerity cuts, leaving its adult-care infrastructure already debilitated when Covid-19 started to spread. The care home sector is all but privatised in Spain and it is common for firms to make savings on running costs so that a profit can be made—often coming at the expense of the quality of care. Even before the pandemic, it was common for there to be staffing shortages and a lack of equipment across the sector. However, when the virus started to spread, the lack of PPE and government strategy meant many care workers fell ill, and because of the volume of viral exposure, some died. This, in turn, had implications for the care of the elderly in care homes.[36] In December 2020, an Amnesty International report found that:

> The effects of the dismantling of the public health care system have been felt in Madrid and Catalonia in the care of older people in residential homes during the peak of the first wave of the pandemic (in March and early April) in several ways: on the one hand, the lack of protection for the staff working there, who were not provided with PPE or PCR tests. And on the other hand, many of the care home residents did not have adequate health assistance, were excluded from referrals to hospitals across the board and did not receive the assistance they needed in the care homes either, despite the 'medicalisation' announced by the authorities. In addition, many care home residents have been virtually cut off from the outside world and their families for weeks on end.[37]

It has been difficult to get a purchase on how many elderly people have died in care homes in Spain over the course of the pandemic, as the government has revised up and revised down the death toll. For example, in May 2020, it removed 1,918 people from the death count (leaving it at 26,834) because of 'double counting' before adding another 1,700 to the toll the following month (at 28,313). It was explained that *"many fatalities were not properly recorded at the time when Spain was most severely*

---

[36] Faggioni et al. (2021).
[37] Amnesty International (2020b).

hit by the pandemic".[38] At the time, however, there were another 15,000 deaths unexplained. One year later, in May 2021, government figures estimated 100,000 people had died with/of Covid-19 but this was then downgraded to 79,853 in June the following month.[39]

It took one year for the Spanish government to provide an indication of the number of elderly residents that had died during the first wave. In March 2021, it was announced that 29,408 people died during the first four months of the pandemic *"with confirmed Covid or compatible symptoms"* in residential homes.[40] Suspected Covid-19 diagnosis and the lack of separation between 'confirmed' and 'compatible' symptoms in these figures still leaves room for uncertainty. Indeed, Luna, a young Spanish student who *"spent the lockdown looking out of my small flat each day and getting depressed"* believed that:

> The media is overstating everything that is happening related to Covid-19. The statistics about everything are a mess, about for example, how many people are infected and how many people died. We don't know. It seems that nothing else is happening in the world right now. There is no domestic violence, no cases of child abuse, nothing else, only Covid-19 deaths.

Silent Victims and the Fostering of Future Harms: Domestic Violence and Child Abuse

During the second quarter of 2020, when the first lockdown was implemented in Spain, researchers found that emergency calls reporting domestic violence, and the subsequent issuing of protection orders, increased in areas experiencing higher rates of unemployment.[41] These two main factors, lockdown and unemployment, have now been directly associated with the 23% increase in intimate partner violence towards

---

[38] Catalan News (2020).
[39] ECDC (2021).
[40] Troya (2021).
[41] Vives-Cases et al. (2021).

Number of calls to "016"

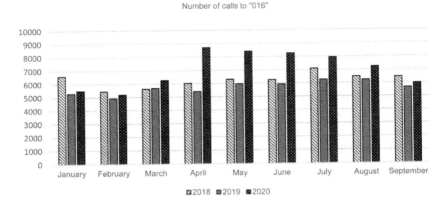

Fig. 7.1 Number of calls to 016, Spain's domestic violence hotline[44]

women in Spain during the first lockdown.[42] Even one month into the lockdown, in April 2020, there was a 47% increase in calls to Spain's domestic violence helpline in comparison with the same month in 2019[43] and even when the deaths and Covid-19 case rate diminished into the summer of 2020, levels of domestic violence reports remained high (see Fig. 7.1).

Even though the authorities have sought to keep courts open to hear cases relating to domestic violence, this appears to have made no difference. The distress resulting from confinement to dwellings, work uncertainty and unemployment appears to have led to increased abuse of women. Over the course of 2020, calls to the emergency number 016 rose 15% in comparison to 2019, while emails increased more than 230% on the previous year, but this was often where things ended. As lockdowns enforced cohabitation, it frequently pressed women to seek help in secret in an effort to avoid their partners' reprisals.[45] Decreased reporting may also indicate increased abuse. Before the pandemic in the USA, one in four women were found to have experienced intimate

---

[42] Esther Arenas-Arroyo et al. (2021).

[43] Burgen (2020).

[44] Ministry of Equality (2020).

[45] Laudette, C. (2021).

partner violence which is classified as physical, emotional, psychological or sexual abuse.[46] However, with the advent of Covid-19 and the lockdowns in some areas of America, reporting of such abuse dropped by more than 50%.[47]

Sonya, a young peoples' sexual health manager from Portugal, *"struggled with lockdown personally because it was isolating"* spending most of it *"trying to support a family member to escape domestic abuse"*. She said, *"it was impossible, all we had was the secret WhatsApp calls and even then there were long periods when she wasn't in touch with me, I was so, so worried about her…It doesn't help that she has no job or no other education"*. One of the main problems has been that the lockdowns have intensified some women's economic dependence upon abusive partners. Without an alternative form of income, escaping violence is made even more difficult. Some women were left with little to no options. Public health restrictions reduced the possibility of seeking alternative support with friends or family, while some safe accommodation for women during the lockdowns were operating on a reduced capacity or were closed.

Children have also faced escalating risks in familial homes. Prior to the Covid-19 pandemic, it was estimated that around one billion children and young people (aged 2–17) across the world had experienced physical, sexual or emotional violence or neglect.[48] Political decisions to lockdown whole countries and societies and confine people to their homes have meant that such measures have the potential to exacerbate this number, both in the short term (during the pandemic, in particular lockdowns) and the medium to long term (as the trauma experienced by many of these children and young people will likely later manifest itself in a reproduction of violence). This reflects what Peter Green calls the *"secondary pandemic of child neglect and abuse"* or the *"secondary harm being done to the adults of the future"*.[49]

Available information gathered from global studies, albeit subject to caution due to widely acknowledged limitations in recording and

---

[46] Smith et al. (2018).
[47] Fielding (2020).
[48] Hillis (2016).
[49] Green (2020).

reporting mechanisms, largely support these forecasts. For example, during the first lockdown in Croatia from March to May 2020 reported rates of family violence in which children were victims rose 35% to 502%.[50] Childline South Africa reported a 400% increase in calls within the first week of its lockdown and identified a 62% increase in child abuse and neglect cases.[51] Before the pandemic, it had been estimated that 53% of Indian children had experienced different kinds of abuse, such as nude photography, assault, inappropriate touching and abuse. However, during the country's lockdown Childline India Foundation reported a 50% increase in calls for assistance.[52] In the cases which reached prosecution in the Indian courts during the same period, 93% were relatives or known individuals.[53]

Chinese researchers analysed over one million tweets regarding family violence such as child abuse, assault, coercive control and physical aggression during the first lockdown, specifically from April–July 2020. They concluded that family violence was increasing since many of the tweets outlined how vulnerable individuals were more at risk because of financial constraints and quarantine rules.[54] Other researchers indicated that increases in family violence took place across China during the lockdown and were principally perpetrated by men, yet, as support services closed, the needs of child victims of violence were neglected.[55] Such pressures relating to lockdowns had even reached low-crime countries such as New Zealand, where a survey undertaken during the country's lockdown found 1 in 10 respondents had endured family violence such as physical abuse and sexual assault during lockdown.[56]

In Uganda, a country that experienced one of the world's strictest lockdowns, there was a 13-fold increase in the number of child abuse and neglect calls made to the Uganda Child Helpline (from on average

---

[50] Dapić et al. (2020).

[51] Bega et al. (2020).

[52] Podder and Mukherjee (2020).

[53] Unni (2020).

[54] Xue et al. (2020).

[55] Zhang (2020).

[56] Every-Palmer (2020).

100 calls a day to 1369) during the lockdown period.[57] In the UK, police-recorded-crime data showed an increase in domestic-abuse related offences during the lockdown even if it was acknowledged that this may be reflective of changes in police recording practices for such offences.[58] Nevertheless, it has since been recognised that vulnerable children in the UK were subject to a *"prolonged exposure to potential harm"*, since both access to protective services and time spent outside the household contracted.[59]

However, like rates of domestic violence, we have to remain cautious because lockdowns perpetuate the difficulties in reporting children's suffering, particularly, if abusive adults also have control over, and can monitor, children's communications as well as their movements. For example, an American study has highlighted a decrease in the reporting of child abuse during the lockdowns because *"of fewer opportunities for detection"* rather than an actual drop in cases.[60] The three-month lockdown in Nepal, from March 24th to June 14th, resulted in 885 young women and girls making complaints of abuse: twice the number received from the previous quarter of December 2019 to February 2020; although this was presumed to be vastly underreported.[61] German studies,[62] as well as American[63] and Canadian[64] research, found statistical decreases in child abuse and neglect reporting, but the researchers conclude this is the case because of closures and restrictions placed on child-welfare agencies to undertake frontline face-to-face work and thereby identify cases of abuse. Lockdowns then, while engaged to protect health services and vulnerable populations, have not only been detrimental to elderly care home residents, but also created additional risk for already vulnerable children. This was confirmed by one of our participants, Fiona, an experienced Child Protection Officer based in the North West of

---

[57] Seerwanja et al. (2020).

[58] ONS (2020b).

[59] Romanou and Belton (2020).

[60] Campbell (2020).

[61] Dahel et al. (2020).

[62] Hell et al. (2020); Mairhofer, et al. (2020).

[63] Baron et al. (2020).

[64] Zussman (2020).

England. Fiona was sceptical about the necessity for lockdowns, particularly because it meant *"the public sector shut its doors"*. Fiona felt that Covid-19 measures and protocols had been detrimental to the aim of protecting children:

> The general consensus is that children are more at risk from Covid but I think the service has used Covid as a reason or excuse to shut down. Parents or risky carers have used it as an excuse to keep us at arm's length, and there is no legislation to help us to continue to do our job. It's just closed doors in our faces.

She recalls when the first lockdown was announced how email directives and office politics revolved around *"putting up Covid signs in the office and getting alcohol stations installed"*, something which distracted her and her colleagues from *"focussing on child protection"*. Fiona felt uncomfortable about *"an obsession with handwashing"* saying *"for God's sake, we are educated to degree and Masters level, we know how to wash our hands"*. Such a context affected relationships with colleagues at her office:

> The divide is what you'd see in normal society. There are a small band like me who are sceptical [about the virus severity], and we come into the office, we come in do our job and try and work around the government legislation, and health and safety. But then there are people who are taking advantage of an easy life situation. It gives them an easy quiet life in child protection. Then there are people who are scared, who worship the vaccine, who are obsessed with gloves, masks, PPE, etc. In the end, we have lost sight of children who are vulnerable. This is not a blanket disease which will kill everybody, and the hysteria connected with that! It has swept through the department and changed working relations and what we do with the children. It has massively impacted on the work we do. We depend on health professionals and they are the ears and eyes for us, and they shut down.

Such *"hysteria"*, as she puts it, was followed by the closure of some of the offices from which Fiona and her colleagues delivered their services. Subsequently, remote online working became the predominant means of service delivery. Fiona was critical of this because *"it is not the same as face-to-face working, thrashing out difficult decisions about a child's welfare was done well face-to-face*". Relatedly, she adds that this made her more motivated to attend the office because she felt "*the risk of Covid should not outweigh the risk the children are exposed to like parental drug use, sexual abuse, etc.*". The minority of workers in her office who complained at the move to online service delivery were granted permission to go in. She did this knowing that it was important to see colleagues, to share information effectively by phone and through face-to-face meetings, otherwise:

> Communications break down – if it is all put on email but there is a time delay – when kids end up injured or dead it is down to poor communication. We had to come together and refuse to do what we were being told. The ones that come in like me are the ones who are resistant to it. It [Lockdown] was limiting our role.

She continued to "*put child protection before Covid*" because it was not what she "*signed up for*" insisting that she wanted to "*be in the office, have my phone, and challenge unsafe situations and see our children to help them*". Despite this small victory, she continued to feel impotent with regards to wider service delivery, since she was restricted to, at best, "*doorstep visits*" or at worst "*virtual visits*": the latter being a ten-minute online consultation while the former being the physical presentation of the child in front of them on the doorstep. This made Fiona immensely frustrated:

> If parents won't open the door then they wave through the window and that is the box ticked. Parents tell us they have tested positive and we can't go in if we are concerned about neglect.

Under the new conditions of work, Fiona saw her caseload drop. This was not necessarily a good thing since many of the staff did not receive referrals as they used to pre-Covid. Instead, and likely because of the impediments to prevention work, they now saw many of their cases appearing as escalated police incidents:

> Before we would have between 40–50 new cases between seven workers; but this comes down to 20 now [under lockdown] and the complexity is more difficult as they are not at school, so we don't have that contact.

> Where I live and work there is a lot of gun and gang crime, so we are just getting direct referrals from the police now. Teenagers out and about in the community, not at school, not supported by the services and they are vulnerable.

This challenge was made more complicated by the fact that there was a high turnover of staff. The advent of the pandemic and subsequent lockdown had resulted in some of the more experienced staff moving on. *"Some giving up, changing to charity work, moving on"* said Fiona as she noted that this was having an impact on service delivery:

> The service is stripping itself down. Newly qualified staff are from the agency, so they are inexperienced, and their attitude is much different. They can't deal with this sort of thing [the complexity]. The kids need high-level oversight and court intervention, but the workers don't have this experience.

Fiona lambasted the new online service delivery for this reason as she noted that the new agency staff were not prepared to take risks and *"deviate from the rules"* to deliver services. Instead, she felt this made the service more static and less responsive. Again, the critique was directed towards the government, the lack of legislation and the persistence with technology as the new, efficient alternative:

> I am most troubled by cases where we know something is going on behind closed doors and we cannot do anything about it. We can't get in; we have no power. The government thinks technology has the answer, but we can't do a thing about this. We are no longer a prevention service. We are just reacting.

In the time since the first lockdown, Fiona had not only witnessed the complexity of cases increase but the consequences present in increased police referrals from drug county lines and gang cases. In some other examples, she felt utterly powerless when presented with such complex cases and being reconciled to a 'doorstep visit' because of Covid-19 restrictions:

We have a sexual exploitation case of two girls: the mum and dad are benefitting [deleted for confidentiality reasons] so they close the door. There is no school attendance this is not mandatory, and dad says he is vulnerable because he has [deleted for confidentiality reasons]. We do a doorstep visit and nothing else. One of the girls, a recent referral, she has overdosed. She has suicidal tendencies, she is making allegations of physical assault from her dad, he is denying it and it is all there and we can't do anything. She told a hospital worker she sells drugs and funds her own habit. We have a meeting next week, but these teenagers are running amok and they don't want them at home and no legislation can sort all this out.

While there is some office resistance and resilience, Fiona found it more difficult with no legislation, concluding that *"lockdown has had a massive impact on how we operate and because of that how we help (or don't) the kids"*. She feels the children are now at further risk of harm and, *"by working comfortably online"*, the professionals have added to that risk because of the dearth of frontline action and support. Indeed, she said: *"this has become very normalised and acceptable"* and:

I feel like we joke about the new mini team we have created because we are the same people who turn up every day and we are seen as the 'rule breakers' because we actually do the visits when we shouldn't. PPE makes our life so difficult. It's utter rubbish. We are 'rule breakers' because we want to do our job. The priorities of people are backward and many of my colleagues are not visiting because of the Covid rules.

Her criticism of colleagues extended to their missed meetings and work-days which were often to seek ways to get the vaccine. *"Healthy, fit people"* said Fiona who *"did not turn up for work because they were in the vaccine queue, but they are not vulnerable?"* Although she added how she would consider the vaccine when it was her turn, she threw her arms in the air when she summarised:

In child protection, we have been distracted by Covid. Now people are arguing about if we should have the sodding vaccine and in the end, we lose time working and doing things for the children. Children and young people have been forgotten and Covid, handwashing and masks have become more important. I feel like everyone is walking around brainwashed and have lost their autonomy. Nothing will change and this feels like it is the future. The service has realised cost benefits of doing things like virtual work but the frontline then changes. Cost trumps the protection of the child and this will be worse for the children. This is a silver lining for local authorities because they are already in massive debt.

In this respect, lockdowns also harmfully impact on the operations of social services as well as specialist child services. Their transition from home visits to 'online support' is now also thought to possibly reduce the potential for abuse cases to come to light at a time when there is an increased demand for services. With limited space for reprieve due to school, library and church closures, as well as restrictions on accessing outdoor spaces, Covid-19 public health measures have inadvertently intensified the potential for children to experience abuse. Other pressures caused by the pandemic, such as the amplification of stress due to unemployment, reduced or limited income, restricted support and social interaction in general, also render them more vulnerable.[65]

Home Alone: Solitary Confinement and Lonely Graves

Alexandra lost her job in Spain as a result of the first lockdowns. For a few months, her company paid her as part of the government funded furlough scheme before it went into administration. In anger, she started researching for herself about the virus and came to the following conclusions.

COVID-19 has an overall recovery rate of 99.9%. It is extremely rare for a child to contract the virus or lose their life from this disease so it did not warrant school closures. The average age of death for those with COVID is 82 (this is 1 year higher than average life expectancy!) You are no more or less at risk in a supermarket than you are being on the

---

[65] De Cao and Sandner (2020).

premises of a small/medium business. You would need to keep at least 30 feet away from another person to prevent/reduce risk of transmission. Despite what the public have been told, asymptomatic transmission in coronaviruses is virtually non-existent and according to FAUCI *"is not the driver of pandemics"*. Also masks have been proven not to work.

Another example of the *informed patient* (Chapter 3), Alexandra seems to align with much of the unconsidered science. Her main grievance, however, is not her job loss, but the damage the lockdowns are doing to the vulnerable and elderly. She continued:

> Many have lost their lives due to an inability to access life-saving/sustaining treatments. Suicide rates have increased. Our elderly and disabled are dying of loneliness and isolation at home and in our care homes, without visits from loved ones.

We have already addressed residential care home management of the virus, but here we look at those who were too afraid to present themselves to healthcare services in particular hospitals. At this point, it is important to remember how, throughout the pandemic, *governments wanted to protect already-depleted healthcare systems and devised campaigns that deterred people from attending for fear of overwhelming inadequately prepared health facilities and hospitals*. In addition, with healthcare systems and protocols seemingly all redirected to the Covid-19 cause, everything else—such as fundamental screening, appointments and routine treatments for disabled people and for those with ailments such as heart disease and cancer—was pretty much suspended.

For disabled and vulnerable adults across the world, routine health-care and rehabilitation were put on hold. Essential health services, already suffering from austerity cuts or general lack of investment, suddenly became more difficult for people with disabilities to access due to Covid-19 restrictions. People with existing mental health difficulties—particularly vulnerable to social isolation—saw their routine appointments cancelled.[66] Notwithstanding those with disabilities who had already died with/of Covid-19, decisions to impose lockdowns and

---

[66] Flaherty et al. (2020).

social distancing resulted in negative impacts on disabled people such as fear of going out, reduced visiting and access to public space which, inadvertently, impacted on their personal wellbeing.[67] Without access to the care they need, people with disabilities can see their health status worsening, risking complications and additional permanent difficulties or reduced functional ability. Wendy, a self-employed worker from the UK, was quickly feeling the impact of the lockdowns and subsequent hospital appointment postponements:

> I am disabled and my pain levels have been a lot higher. I can't get access to my treatments and my hospital appointments have been cancelled.

In the UK, cardiology presentations for routine heart-related-problems reduced 50% during the lockdowns while in Scotland, it was 40% less than it would be otherwise.[68] In the context of cancer screening and treatment, lockdowns and social distancing measures inadvertently meant:

- increased waiting time for cancer screening appointments due to strain on the healthcare systems caused by Covid-19;
- cancellation of cancer related surgery; and
- weakened immune systems of cancer patients potentially leaving them more vulnerable to serious Covid-19 symptoms.

Across the world, routine screening as well as vital treatments were suspended. Early analysis suggests that this will result in the death of millions of other people.[69] For example, Petia, a Bulgarian waitress, told us:

> I watched friends of mine go broke [during the lockdowns], my uncle lived in great pain for the hospital delayed his operation for months, I lost track of my schedule completely and had to go work abroad as soon as possible because I needed money, and needed to send them money to survive.

---

[67] Sayce (2021).
[68] Fersia et al. (2020).
[69] Richards et al. (2020).

This does not discount the number of people fearful of obtaining medical intervention—be it for basic primary care or more serious assistance. For example, in June 2020 in the USA, because of concerns about Covid-19, an estimated 41% of American adults had delayed or avoided medical care, including urgent or emergency care (12%) and routine care (32%).[70] As we found in the UK, some felt a sense of dedication and moral obligation to the people they cared for—particularly unpaid adult care workers—even if they felt exploited by their governments. Ronald, an 80-year-old-man from the USA said:

> The media gave lots of space to presenting the views of the government, although not necessarily endorsing them. I would have appreciated more coverage from independent public health experts. There was one news programme which I never missed which presented findings made by active journalists. It was from that programme that I became aware of the concept of excess deaths - i.e. people who had died as a result of the circumstances of the pandemic (e.g. delayed operations), although not necessarily from COVID itself.

Early into the pandemic, we were told that excess deaths were related to those who had caught Covid-19 and died without making it to the hospital. Yet, 'excess deaths' are considered to be those that stem from a pandemic situation regardless of whether they are as a direct consequence of the virus and so therefore encompass other forms of mortality. According to the WHO (2020):

> Excess mortality is defined as the difference in the total number of deaths in a crisis compared to those expected under normal conditions. COVID-19 excess mortality accounts for both the total number of deaths directly attributed to the virus as well as the indirect impact, such as disruption to essential health services or travel disruptions.[71]

---

[70] Czeisler et al. (2020).
[71] WHO (2020c).

However, as discussed in Chapter 3, there are large discrepancies in the reporting and categorisation of Covid-19 deaths. The WHO recommended death classifications to report *suspected Covid-19 virus-related deaths* as well and some countries include these people in the death count. The problems continue, however, because:

- Some countries only report Covid-19 deaths in hospitals meaning those that die at home from the virus may not appear in the statistics;
- Some countries only report Covid-19 deaths after a test has confirmed that a patient was infected with the virus meaning those who have not received/been tested may not appear in the figures;
- In poorer countries, the modes of recording mortality may be inadequate.

All of which are true but more specifically in the context of what we are saying in this chapter is that:

- The pandemic may also produce increased deaths from other causes for a number of reasons including weakened healthcare systems; fewer people seeking treatment for other health risks; less available funding and treatment for other diseases (e.g. HIV/AIDS, malaria, tuberculosis); or the halting of treatment/vaccination programmes;
- Fewer deaths may occur from more common viruses like the flu because of public health measures to reduce the spread of Covid-19 but equally Covid-19 could now cause death for those who otherwise would have died from the flu.

In the first 30 weeks of the pandemic in England and Wales:

There were 62,321 excess deaths. Of these, 46,221 were attributable to respiratory causes, including COVID-19, and 16,100 to other causes.[72]

As there had been in Germany[73] and Brazil[74], deaths for this time of year were above what they would normally be. Clearly, there is a pandemic impact. Indeed, throughout 2020, in 29 high-income countries, there were one million excess deaths which *"substantially exceeded reported*

---

[72] Kontopantelis et al. (2021).

[73] Andreas et al. (2020).

[74] Brant et al. (2020).

deaths from covid-19", however, *"long term data on the cause of deaths will be needed to fully examine the effects, because lockdown may have had other unintended consequences".*[75] As discussed in Chapter 3, there is difficulty in separating Covid-19 deaths from other deaths attributed to respiratory problems. Even then, just over a third have nothing to do with the virus it seems. Similarly, American research published in July 2020 that used data from the evolving first wave in the States suggests:

> There were approximately 781,000 total deaths in the USA from March 1 to May 30, 2020, representing 122,300 more deaths than would typically be expected at that time of year. There were 95,235 reported deaths officially attributed to COVID-19 from March 1 to May 30, 2020. The number of excess all-cause deaths was 28% higher than the official tally of COVID-19–reported deaths during that period. In several states, these deaths occurred before increases in the availability of COVID-19 diagnostic tests and were not counted in official COVID-19 death records. There was substantial variability between states in the difference between official COVID-19 deaths and the estimated burden of excess deaths.[76]

The USA was also drastically underprepared for Covid-19. Brad, an American nurse, summarised how there was *"limited PPE in stockpile, my hospital still only has N95s for the Covid unit and only 1 mask per staff per 5 days. The President is more worried about money than lives".* It is tempting to think that the States that did not lockdown had a higher mortality rate. However, evidence indicates it was the reverse: the States that locked down appeared to have a higher number of excess deaths. In New York—a State which a day before lockdown declared it would not lockdown—fears arose about the potential death toll if the virus could not be suppressed. By mid-March 2020, a combination of Weill Cornell Medicine, the consulting firm McKinsey & Company, and the CDC, were all predicting high numbers of deaths.

Yet, more severe warnings about the need for ventilators and hospital beds were made on the 26th March 2020 when further advice came from the Institute of Health Metrics and Evaluation (IHME), which had

---

[75] Islam et al. (2020).
[76] Weinberger et al. (2021).

recently been funded $279 million over 10 years by the Gates Foundation to investigate the *"world's most costly health problems"*.[77] The IHME forecast became the central reference point for modelling in the States—even if its projections largely were based on every state locking down. By April 5th, the IHME was claiming that New York would need 69,000 hospital beds and 10,000 ventilators even if on that day only 16,500 were in hospitals—only 4,000 of which were on ventilators. Like Neil Ferguson and colleagues at Imperial College, the modelling had failed because these epidemiologists were convinced lockdowns were the only way to manage the pandemic (Chapter 2).

In Italy, some people turning up at hospitals had Covid-19 but others had presented out of caution due to other flu-like symptoms. Some had presented because they were fearful and this increased congregation in hospitals—even at a time when people were discouraged to use them—further assisting in the virus spread. Those that did not die at home from other ailments such as strokes or heart attacks and become part of the 'excess death statistics', likely improved their chances of catching Covid-19 by presenting to hospitals—one of the main epicentres of viral transmission—and thus became part of the 'Covid-19 death' statistics.[78]

Evidence from Denmark concluded that as lockdown eased cases of Covid-19 did not rise.[79] In the US, public pressure mounted, particularly among Conservative supporters, to end restrictions. Southern States started to re-open and there were no spikes in 'reported cases'. Three States in particular, however, saw some sharp increases in the summer of 2020. From June to mid-July, in Arizona, Texas and Florida hospitalisations increased from 1,000 to 3,500, 2,000 to 11,000 and from 2,000 to 9,000, respectively.[80] While deaths occurred—and having discussed the disparities in the recording and interpretation of Covid-19-related deaths—they occurred at a far lower level than many of the North-Eastern States such as New York. Hospitalisations thereafter

[77] IHME (2020).
[78] King (2020).
[79] Reuters (2020).
[80] Berenson (2020).

rapidly declined by mid-July and *none of these three States had re-imposed lockdowns or mandated mask-wearing as obligatory practice.*[81]

As was discussed in Chapter 3, it seems that in many of the countries discussed, a novel and new virus has mostly taken the lives of the most elderly and most vulnerable, before entering into endemic status. In the nineteenth century, William Farr—an epidemiologist at the time working in the UK—concluded that during viral epidemics, death rates act in a particular manner: appearing high like a bell curve before tailing off. Even then, at the time, Farr had noted how the most vulnerable tend to die in these instances. The excess deaths now appear concerning and perhaps attributable to decisions made to lockdown social life, paralyse work and travel, postpone and cancel life-saving hospital and medical treatments. The evidence presented here suggests they have not adequately protected the elderly and vulnerable and, as we will see, they also seem to do further damage to those right at the bottom of the social scale.

References

Amnesty International. (2020a). *As if expendable: The UK government's failure to protect older people in care homes during the Covid-19 pandemic.*

Amnesty International. (2020b). *Spain: Older people in care homes abandoned during COVID19 pandemic.* Amnesty International.

Arenas-Arroyo, E., Fernandez-Kranz, D., & Nollenberger, N. (2021). Intimate partner violence under forced cohabitation and economic stress: Evidence from the COVID-19 pandemic. *Journal of Public Economics, 194,* 04350.

Armocida, B., Formenti, B., Ussai, S., & Missoni, E. (2020). The Italian health system and the COVID-19 challenge. *The Lancet Public Health.* https://doi.org/10.1016/S2468-2667(20)30074-8

Baron, E. J., Goldstein, E. G., & Wallace, C. T. (2020). Suffering in silence: How COVID-19 school closures inhibit the reporting of child maltreatment. *Journal of Public Economics, 190,* Article 10425. https://doi.org/10.1016/j.jpubeco.2020.104258

---

[81] Ibid.

Bega, S., Smillie, S., & Ajam, K. (2020, May 16). *Spike in child abandonments and the physical abuse of youngsters during lockdown.* IOL. https://www.iol.co.za/saturday-star/news/spike-in-child-abandonments-and-the-physical-abuse-ofyoungsters-during-lockdown-48012964

BBC. (2020d, July 7). *Coronavirus: Boris Johnson criticised over 'cowardly' care home comments'.* Cited online at https://www.bbc.com/news/uk-politics-533 15178

Berenson, A. (2020). *Unreported truths about Covid-19.* Amazon.

Blumenthal, D., & Hamburg, M. (2021). February 20). US health and health care are a mess: Now what? *The Lancet, 397*, 647–648.

Brant, L. C. C., Nascimento, B. R., Teixeira, R. A., Lopez, M. A. C. Q., Malta, D. C., Oliveira, G. M. M., & Ribeiro, A. L. P. (2020). Excess of cardiovascular deaths during the COVID-19 pandemic in Brazilian capital cities. *Heart, 106*, 1898–1905.

Briggs, D. (2020). *Climate changed: Refugee border stories and the business of misery.* Routledge.

Briggs, D., Ellis, A., Telford, L., & Lloyd, A. (2021). *Working, living, and dying in Covid times: Perspectives from frontline residential care workers in the UK' in safer communities.* https://doi.org/10.1108/SC-04-2021-0013

Burgen, S. (2020, April 28). Women killed in Spain as coronavirus lockdown sees rise in domestic violence. *The Guardian.* Cited online at https://www.theguardian.com/global-development/2020/apr/28/three-women-killed-in-spain-as-coronavirus-lockdown-sees-rise-in-domestic-violence

Campbell, D. (2019, November 25). Hospital beds at record low in England as NHS struggles with demand. *The Guardian.* Cited online at https://www.theguardian.com/politics/2019/nov/25/hospital-beds-at-record-low-in-england-as-nhs-struggles-with-demand

Campbell, A. (2020). An increasing risk of family violence during the Covid 19 pandemic: Strengthening community collaborations to save lives. *Forensic Science International: Reports, 2,* Article 100089. https://doi.org/10.1016/j.fsir.2020.100089

Cartabellotta, N., Cottafava, E., Luceri, R., & Mosti, M. (2019, September). *Il definanziamento 2010–2019 del Servizio Sanitario Nazionale.* https://www.gimbe.org/osservatorio/Report_Osservatorio_GIMBE_2019.07_Def inanziamento_SSN.pdf (accessed March 20, 2020).

Carter, P. (2016). *Operational productivity and performance in English NHS Acute hospitals: Unwarranted variations. independent report for the department of health.* Accessed from https://www.gov.uk/government/publications/productivity-in-nhs-hospitals.

Catalan News. (2020, June 19). Spain's Covid-19 death toll revised up by 1,177 to 28,313. *Catalan News*. Cited online at https://www.catalannews.com/soc iety-science/item/spain-s-covid-19-death-toll-revised-up-by-1177-to-28313

CDC. (2016). *2014–2016 Ebola Outbreak in West Africa*. Cited online at https://www.cdc.gov/vhf/ebola/history/2014-2016-outbreak/index.html

Conticini, E., Frediani, B., & Caro, D. (2020). Can atmospheric pollution be considered a co- factor in extremely high level of SARS-CoV-2 lethality in Northern Italy? *Environmental Pollution, 261,* 114465.

Costello, H., Cooper, C., Marston, L., & Livingston, G. (2020). Burnout in UK care home staff and its effect on staff turnover: MARQUE English national care home longitudinal study. *Age and Ageing, 49*(1), 74–81.

Czeisler, M., Lane, R., Petrosky, E., Wiley, J., Christensen, A., Njai, R., Weaver, M., Robbins, R., Facer-Childs, E., Barger, L., Czeisler, C., Howard, M., & Rajaratnam, S. (2020, June 24–30). Mental health, substance use, and suicidal ideation during the Covid-19 pandemic—United States. *Centers for Disease Control and Prevention: Weekly Report, 69,* 1049–1057.

Dahel, M., Khanal, P., Maharajan, S., Panthi, B., & Nepal, S. (2020). Miti- gating violence against young women and girls during Covid 19 induced lockdown in Nepal: A wake up call. *Globalisation and Health, 16,* Article 84, https://doi.org/10.1186/s12992-020-00616-w

Dalglish, S. L. (2020). COVID-19 gives the lie to global health expertise. *Lancet, 395,* 1189.

Daly, M. (2020). COVID-19 and care homes in England: What happened and why? *Social Policy Administration, 54*(7), 985–998.

Dapić, M., Flander, G., & Prijatelj, K. (2020). Children behind closed doors due to COVID-19 isolation: Abuse, neglect and domestic violence. *Archives of Psychiatry Research, 56*(2), 181–192. https://doi.org/10.20471/dec.2020. 56.02.06

De Cao, E., & Sandner, M. (2020, May 8). *The potential impact of the COVID- 19 on child abuse and neglect: The role of childcare and unemployment.* Vox Eu CEPR. Retrieved from: https://voxeu.org/article/potential-impact-covid- 19-child-abuse-and-neglect

Devi, R., Hinsliff-Smith, K., Goodman, C., & Gordon, A. (2020). The Covid- 19 pandemic in care homes—Revealing the cracks in the system. *The Journal of Nursing Home Research Sciences, 6,* 58–60.

Duncan, P. (2021, May 11). More care home residents died of Covid in second wave than first in England and Wales. *The Guardian*.cited online on https://www.theguardian.com/world/2021/may/11/more-care-home-res idents-died-of-covid-in-second-wave-than-first-in-england-and-wales

Dzinamarira, T., Dzobo, M., & Chitungo, I. (2020). COVID-19: A perspective on Africa's capacity and response. *Journal of Medical Virology, 92*(11), 2465–2472. https://doi.org/10.1002/jmv.26159

ECDC. (2021, June 4). *COVID-19 situation update for the EU/EEA.* Geneva.

Every-Palmer, S., Jenkins, M., Gendall, P., Hoek, J., Beaglehole, B., Bell, C., Williman, J., Rapsey, C., & Stanley, J. (2020). Psychological distress, anxiety, family violence, suicidality, and wellbeing in New Zealand during the COVID-19 lockdown: A cross sectional study. *PLoS ONE, 15*(11), 1–19.

Faggioni, M., Melado, F., & Di Pietro, M. (2021). National health system cuts and triage decisions during the COVID-19 pandemic in Italy and Spain: Ethical implications. *Journal of Medical Ethics, 47*, 300–307.

Fersia, O., Bryant, S., Nicholson, R., (2020). The impact of the COVID-19 pandemic on cardiology services. *Open Heart, 7*, e001359. https://doi.org/10.1136/openhrt-2020-001359

Fielding, S. (2020, April 3). In quarantine with an abuser: Surge in domestic violence reports linked to coronavirus. *The Guardian.* https://www.theguardian.com/us-news/2020/apr/03/coronavirus-quarantine-abuse-domestic-violence

Flaherty, G. T., Hession, P., & Liew, C. H. (2020). COVID-19 in adult patients with pre-existing chronic cardiac, respiratory and metabolic disease: A critical literature review with clinical recommendations. *Trop Dis Travel Med Vaccines, 6*, 16. https://doi.org/10.1186/s40794-020-00118-y

Gordon, A., Goodman, C., Achterberg, W., Barker, R., Burns, E., Hanratty, B., Martin, F. C., Meyer, J., O'Neill, D., Schols, J., & Spilsbury, K. (2020). Commentary: COVID in care homes—Challenges and dilemmas in healthcare delivery. *Age and Ageing, 49*(5), 701–705.

Green, P. (2020). Risks to children and young people during COVID-19 pandemic. *British Medical Journal, 369*(8244), https://doi.org/10.1136/bmj.m1669

Greene, T., Harju-Seppänen, J., Adeniji, M., Steel, C., Grey, N., Brewin, C. R., Bloomfield, M. A., & Billings, J. (2021). Predictors and rates of PTSD, depression and anxiety in UK frontline health and social care workers during COVID-19. *European Journal of Psychotraumatology, 12*(1), 1882781. https://doi.org/10.1080/20008198.2021.1882781

Hanratty, B., Burton, J., Goodman, C., Gordon, A., & Spilsbury, K. (2020). Covid-19 and the lack of linked datasets for care homes. *British Medical Journal, 369*, m2463.

Hell, A., Kampf, L., Kaulet, M., & Kohrsal, C. (2020, May 6). Hausliche Gewalt in der CoronaKrise. Wenn das Kind verborgen bleibt. *Süddeutsche Zeitung.* www.sueddeutsche.de/politik/coronavirus-haeusliche-gewalt-jugendaemter-1.4899381

Hillis, S., Mercy, J., Amobi, A., & Kress, H. (2016). Global prevalence of past-year violence against children: A systematic review and minimum estimates. *Pediatrics, 137.* e20154079. https://doi.org/10.1542/peds.2015-4079

Hope, C. (2020). *COVID-19 death rate is higher in European countries with a low flu intensity since 2018.* Cambridge University Press.

IHME COVID-19 Health Service Utilization Forecasting Team. (2020, March 26). Forecasting COVID-19 impact on hospital bed-days, ICU-days, ventilator days and deaths by US state in the next 4 months. *MedRxiv.* https://doi.org/10.1101/2020.03.27.20043752.

Islam, N., Shkolnikov, V. M., Acosta, R. J., Klimkin, I., Kawachi, I., Irizarry, R. A., Alicandro, G., Khunti, K., Yates, T., Jdanov, D. A., White, M., Lewington, S., Lacey, B. (2021). Excess deaths associated with covid-19 pandemic in 2020: Age and sex disaggregated time series analysis in 29 high income countries *BMJ, 373*, n1137. https://doi.org/10.1136/bmj.n1137

King, E. (2020). Rapid response: COVID-19: Science, conflicts and the elephant in the room. *BMJ, 371*, m4425.

Kontopantelis, E., et al. (2021). Excess deaths from COVID-19 and other causes by region, neighbourhood deprivation level and place of death during the first 30 weeks of the pandemic in England and Wales: A retrospective registry study. *The Lancet Regional Health—Europe.* https://doi.org/10.1016/j.lanepe.2021.100144

Lal, A., Erondu, N., Heymann, D., Gitachi, G., & Yates, R. (2021). Fragmented health systems in COVID-19: Rectifying the misalignment between global health security and universal health coverage. *The Lancet, 397*, 61–67.

Laudette, C. (2021, January 20). *The silent epidemic: Abuse against Spanish women rises during lockdown.* Cited online at https://www.reuters.com/article/us-health-coronavirus-spain-women-idUSKBN29P1WU

Lintern, S. (2020, May 31). Coronavirus: Care homes mentioned only twice in five months of Sage minutes. *The Independent.* Cited online at https://www.independent.co.uk/news/health/coronavirus-sagemeetings-care-homes-a9541321.html

Mairhofer, A., Peucker, C. H., Pluto, L., van Santen, E., & Seckinger, M. (2020). *Kinder- und Jugendhilfe in Zeiten der Corona-Pandemie.* DJI Publication.

Ministry of Equality. (2020). *GBV helpline calls*. Data obtained from the website of the Ministry of Equality of Spain.

Nnaji, C. A., & Moodley, J. (2021). Impact of the COVID-19 pandemic on cancer diagnosis, treatment and research in African health systems: A review of current evidence and contextual perspectives. *Ecancermedicalscience, 15,* 1170. Published 2021 January 14. https://doi.org/10.3332/ecancer.2021.1170

Oliver, D. (2020). Let's not forget care homes when COVID-19 is over. *British Medical Journal, 369,* 1629.

ONS. (2020a). *Excess winter mortality in England and Wales: 2018 to 2019 (provisional) and 2017 to 2018 (final).* ONS.

ONS. (2020b, November). *Domestic abuse during the Coronavirus (COVID-19) pandemic, England and Wales.* https://www.ons.gov.uk/peoplepopulationandcommunity/crimeandjustice/articles/domesticabuseduringthecoronaviruscovid19pandemicenglandandwales/november2020

Podder, S., & Mukherjee, U. (2020). Ascending child sexual abuse statistics in India during COVID-19 lockdown: A darker reality and alarming mental health concerns. *Indian Journal of Psychological Medicine, 42*(5), 491–493. https://doi.org/10.1177%2F0253717620951391

Seerwanja, A., Kawuki, J., & Kim, J. (2020). Increased child abuse in Uganda amidst COVID-19 pandemic. *Journal of Paediatrics and Child Health.* Advance Online Publication. https://doi.org/10.1111/jpc.15289

Smith, S. G., Zhang, X., Basile, K. C., Merrick, M. T., Wang, J., Kresnow, M., & Chen, J. (2018). *The National Intimate Partner and Sexual Violence Survey (NISVS): 2015 data brief—Updated release.* National Center for Injury Prevention and Control, Centers for Disease Control and Prevention.

Razavi, A., Erondu, N., Okereke, E. (2020). The global health security index: What value does it add? *BMJ Glob Health, 5,* e002477

Reuters. (2020, June10). *Denmark sees no rise in COVID-19 cases after further easing of lockdown.* Cited online at https://www.reuters.com/article/us-health-coronavirus-denmark-idUSKBN23H1DU

Ricci, G., Pallotta, G., Sirignano, A., Amenta, F., & Nittari, G. (2020). Consequences of COVID-19 outbreak in Italy: Medical responsibilities and governmental measures. *Frontiers in Public Health, 8,* 588852. https://doi.org/10.3389/fpubh.2020.588852

Richards, M., Anderson, M., Carter, P., Ebert, B. L., & Mossialos, E. (2020). The impact of the COVID-19 pandemic on cancer care. *Nature Cancer, 1*(6), 565–567. https://doi.org/10.1038/s43018-020-0074-y

Robbins, I., Gordon, A., Dyas, J., Logan, P., & Gladman, J. (2013). Explaining the barriers to and tensions in delivering effective health in UK care homes: A qualitative study. *British Medical Journal Open, 3*, 1–9.

Romanou, E., & Belton, E. (2020). *Isolated and struggling: National society for the prevention of cruelty to children*. NSPCC. https://learning.nspcc.org.uk/media/2246/isolated-and-struggling-social-isolation-risk-child-maltreatment-lockdown-and-beyond.pdf

Sayce, L. (2021, February 21). *The forgotten crisis: Exploring the disproportionate impact of the pandemic on disabled people*. The Health Foundation. Cited online at https://www.health.org.uk/news-and-comment/blogs/the-forgotten-crisis-exploring-the-disproportionate-impact-of-the-pandemic

Shutes, I. (2012). The employment of migrant workers in long-term care. *Journal of Social Policy, 41*(1), 43–59.

Stang, A., Standl, F., Kowall, B., Brune, B., Böttcher, J., Brinkmann, M., Dittmer, U., & Jöckel, K.-H. (2020). Excess mortality due to COVID-19 in Germany. *Journal of Infection, 81*(5), 797–801.

Troya, M. (2021, March 2). *El Gobierno certifica que 29.408 personas han muerto por coronavirus en residencias desde el inicio de la pandemia*. La Sociedad. Cited online at https://elpais.com/sociedad/2021-03-02/en-espana-han-muerto-29408-mayores-que-vivian-en-residencias-desde-el-inicio-de-la-pandemia.html

Unni, J. (2020). Social effects of Covid-19 pandemic on children in India. *Indian Journal of Practicing Pediatricians, 22*(2), 102–104.

Vives-Cases, C., Parra-Casado, D. L., Estévez, J. F., Torrubiano-Domínguez, J., & Sanz-Barbero, B. (2021). Intimate partner violence against women during the COVID-19 lockdown in Spain. *International Journal Environment Research and Public Health, 18*, 4698. https://doi.org/10.3390/ijerph18094698

Weinberger, D., Chen, J., Cohen, T., Crawford, F., Mostashari, F., Olson, D., Pitzer, V. E., Reich, N. G., Russi, M., Simonsen, L., & Watkins, A. (2021). Estimation of excess deaths associated with the COVID-19 pandemic in the United States, March to May 2020. *JAMA Internal Medicine, 180*(10), 1336–1344. doi:https://doi.org/10.1001/jamainternmed.2020.3391 Published online July 1, 2020.

WHO. (2020b, May 22). *At least 80 million children under one at risk of diseases such as diphtheria, measles and polio as COVID-19 disrupts routine vaccination efforts, warn Gavi, WHO and UNICEF*. Cited online https://www.who.int/news/item/22-05-2020-at-least-80-million-children-under-

one-at-risk-of-diseases-such-as-diphtheria-measles-and-polio-as-covid-19-dis
rupts-routine-vaccination-efforts-warn-gavi-who-and-unicef

WHO. (2020c, June 8). *The true death toll of COVID-19.* Cited
online at https://www.who.int/data/stories/the-true-death-toll-of-covid-19-
estimating-global-excess-mortality

Wood, H., & Skeggs, B. (2020). Clap for carers? For care gratitude to care
justice. *European Journal of Cultural Studies, 23*(4), 641–647. https://doi.
org/10.1177%2F1367549420928362

Xue, J., Chen, J., Chen, C., Hu, R., & Zhu, T. (2020). The Hidden pandemic
of family violence during COVID-19: Unsupervised learning of tweets.
Journal of Medical Internet Research, 22(11), e24361. https://doi.org/10.
2196/24361

Zhang, H. (2020). The influence of the ongoing COVID-19 pandemic on
family violence in China. *Journal of Family Violence.* Advance Online
Publication. https://doi.org/10.1007/s10896-020-00196-8

Zussman, R. (2020. May 11). Reports of child abuse down amid COVID-19,
as B.C. advocates remind public of duty to report. *Global News.*https://glo
balnews.ca/news/6929622/child-abuse-reporting-coronavirus

8

Locked Up: Prisoners, Youth Detainees and Asylum Seekers

While the West was experiencing an existential threat, and the elderly and vulnerable were neglected, also absent from the news and general attention were those people already 'locked up' in prisons and detention centres. How was the virus impacting their lives? What did public health measures do to those already confined to some form of detention? As the virus permeated prisons, many inmates were inevitably confined to cells often without adequate support, locked up in solitary confinement in substandard conditions for long periods as institutions adopted public health measures such as lockdowns, social distancing and self-isolation. Youth detainees, already vulnerable having experienced troubled childhoods, were left in some instances with no interaction in their cells for up to 23 hours a day with no formal psychological or social intervention. Asylum seekers saw their applications delayed and, in some cases, their deportation elevated, causing them immense distress and anxiety. Here, we examine these experiences in detail.

© The Author(s), under exclusive license to Springer Nature Switzerland AG 2021
D. Briggs et al., *Lockdown*,
https://doi.org/10.1007/978-3-030-88825-1_8

Thrown Away Keys: Locked Up Prisoners

The spread of Covid-19 in prisons around the world had the potential to not only aggravate existing pressures present in carceral facilities but also to introduce new ones. In Brazil, for example, where there are around 760,000 people in prison, cultural life and conditions in the prison system pre-pandemic were already described as 'medieval' because of the high prevalence of violence. Only in January 2017, almost 150 prisoners were killed as rival gangs battled each other in several prisons in northern and north-eastern Brazil. In one such violent skirmish in Manaus, 57 inmates were killed, some of whom were decapitated and thrown over prison walls.[1] So when Covid-19 spread across the country and the president decided to do very little in favour of keeping its economy buoyant, this left prisons on the frontline for contracting the virus. In just over a year from its inception, the Brazilian prison system—already riddled with these challenges of violence, overcrowding and poor sanitary—had 43,957 confirmed Covid-19 infections and 135 deaths among inmates. Low numbers one could say but perhaps high given that only 10% of the prison population were tested for Covid-19: in this way, this very much disguises the real impact of the virus.

Like Brazil, Thailand has one of the world's highest prison populations and one of our participants, Sunan, is in the fourth week of his new job working for an international human rights agency which monitors the treatment of prisoners across the country. Having studied Psychology at university, he had been interested for some time in the state of Thailand's incarcerated population. *"In prison there is no human rights, less so in Thailand where people practically sleep on top of each other and are treated like dogs"* he reflects initially as he shakes his head on our patchy Zoom call. Today, well over 307,000 people are incarcerated in Thailand which is three times its legal capacity. No surprise this then represents the largest prison population in Southeast Asia. The majority of its populace, around 80%, have committed crimes relating to possession or potential to sell small quantities of 'yaba' or 'shabu' which is a type of methamphetamine, thus highlighting the country's harsh approach to petty drug

---

[1] Kelly and Slattery (2020).

possession. Yet, the Thailand Institute of Justice observes that one of the main drivers of over-incarceration is the remarkably low threshold amount of drugs that defines 'intent to sell' when a person is caught with possession of methamphetamine. For example, 375 mg or more of pure substance can result in a sentence between four years to life imprisonment.[2]

Having seemingly dodged the Covid-19 waves experienced by many western countries in March 2020 and the turn of new year, by the spring and into the summer of 2021, infection rates rapidly increased in Thailand. However, this was not reflected in the death rate statistics perhaps because anyone testing positive for the virus was hospitalised—even if they were asymptomatic or had just mild symptoms. Essentially, this meant that the chain of transmission never really arrived to very vulnerable people.[3] Additional factors influencing this low rate were related to the low incidences of obesity, hypertension and diabetes among the population: all of which play a part in a higher chance of Covid-19 mortality (Chapters 2 and 3).

Yet, even though the infections remained low in 2020 and early into 2021, the country's government still implemented restrictions, in the main attributed to border controls which consequently stopped the flow of people leaving and entering the country. For example, since March 2020, entering into Thailand requires a 14-day quarantine in special facilities as well as a series of Covid-19 tests thereafter. Given that the economy relies significantly on tourism, the measures to halt infections have proved economically devastating for the country. Millions of people working in both the formal and informal tourism sectors have lost their jobs. The politically instigated lockdown which ran from March to June 2020 immediately put at risk 8.4 million jobs in the formal sector on top of the precarious existence of the six million farmers already impacted by drought.[4] But it is the other 20 million people working in informal sectors—almost half of Thailand's population—that were more sharply affected. For example, the loss of income among this group pushed them

---

[2] TIJ (2021).
[3] Ratcliffe (2021).
[4] ILO (2020).

into the poverty threshold, reducing daily wages below 60 Thai Bahts which is just $1.90 per day. This resulted in the number of working poor doubling from 4.7% to at least 11% in 2020.[5]

Naturally, these harmful economic pressures do detriment to peoples' lives, welfares and futures which is why it should perhaps be no surprise that it proved too much for some people working in industries impacted by the lockdowns. Samaritans in Thailand, who offer emotional support to people contemplating suicide, received 10,000 calls in 2019, but the lockdown restrictions resulted in a doubling of their call volume. While pre-pandemic, Thailand had the highest rate of suicide among Southeast Asia when it was estimated that one person tried to kill themselves every 10 minutes, the advent of economic pressures resulting from lockdowns saw suicides jump 11% from 2019 to the end of 2020, from 4,581 to 5,085 deaths.[6]

As we write, around 240,000 people have been infected with Covid-19 in Thailand yet only 1,870 have died. While this sounds like an overwhelming success when set against countries like the USA and the UK, "*it doesn't tell the whole story*" says Sunan because "*these are formal, 'recorded' numbers, and from when I am going into prisons in Bangkok, I am seeing many more infections and deaths from other things as well as Covid which do not form part of these statistics*". In April 2021, a decree formalised the suspension of prison visits as the government watched on as Covid-19 infections increased. Knowing that closed spaces—more so those densely and extremely overcrowded such as the country's prisons—would likely suffer the worst, the government came under pressure to release 50,000 people to ease the burden on the penal system and reduce overcrowding.

They never did this, even though international evidence from 10 different countries indicates that reducing prison populations—precisely because of pressure generated from public health measures—were an important objective to achieve to reduce Covid-19 infection transmission.[7] By early May 2021, there were a reported 5,000 infections in three

---

[5] Poonsab et al. (2020).

[6] Taylor and Siradapuvadol (2021).

[7] Fair and Jacobson (2021).

Thailand prisons but the issue only gathered momentum and media coverage because of complaints from a high-profile former detainee—protest leader Panusaya "Rung" Sithijirawattanakul, who was released on bail and had said she caught the virus while in prison. *"I remember seeing it on closed social media networks, she had made the issue public because of her testimony, and in the prisons there was relief about this because otherwise nothing would have been said"* said Sunan. This set in motion new measures in prison relating to two-week mandatory staff testing, prisoners isolation after court or hospital attendance and increased tele-conferencing of the former. Inmates were even encouraged to wear masks even when they slept next to each other in grossly overcrowded conditions. In Facebook forums, we found the words of Chuvit Kamolvisit, a former businessman and politician who had been imprisoned three times at Bangkok Remand Prison:

> In prison, not a second goes by when prisoners are more than a step away from one another. They eat together, bathe together, stay together and lie down next to one another 15 hours a day from 3pm to 6am.

Sunan confirmed this when he told us that in many of these prisons *"during peak times, a cell of four by ten metres can hold as many as 60–70 people which is about two per square metre - less space to sleep than the inside of a coffin…it is a dire situation sir, but this is the way the powerful treat the poor in my country"*. Indeed, the Ozone Foundation—one of the largest NGO providers of health services for drug users in Thailand—in collaboration with the International Drug Policy Consortium (IDPC) found in a report on female incarceration that the majority of women in prison for such drug offences generally have no education and, at best, basic literacy. Most are also mothers and almost half of them had no legal representation during their trial when they were sentenced to prison.[8] Why would government attitudes to overcrowding change even in the event of a public health crisis in the country's prisons? Well, they didn't. Even with the publication of a timely UN Report which called for the decriminalisation of minor drug offences and, instead, see them

---

[8] IDPC (2018).

replaced with evidence-based and voluntary drug treatment as a means to ease overcrowding issues.[9] By the third week of May 2021, infections were reported to have increased to 11,000 in 13 of the country's prisons, meaning Thailand has one of the world's highest number of Covid-19 cases in prisons only superseded by Brazil, Colombia, India and the USA.[10] A week later, this was reported to have doubled to 22,000[11] and another week later it was 30,000.[12] Low numbers were said to have died in prison—in some reports as little as two—but Sunan said:

> Of course, they don't want to show it in the statistics that they have done almost nothing for these people. I can tell you many died because they already had vulnerable health for some had Aids, Hepatitis C, compromised health which means that Covid-19 did more damage. At least I think, I cannot be sure because the healthcare was withdrawn from many people so they may have died of their previous problems going untreated…but many things happen in prison don't come to light. Why would they [the government] worry about prison deaths if there are already too many prisoners?

By mid-June 2021, the scale of infections reached such a level that the United Nations Office on Drugs and Crime (UNODC) stepped in and donated 1,500,000 surgical masks to the Thai Department of Corrections.[13] The WHO remain ambiguous on their advice for how long such masks should be worn before being discarded but sources from our study indicate that this could be as little as every '4 hours' and as much as 'after each day'. If there are 307,000 people in prison in Thailand, then this supply meant that each prisoner had a new mask every day for just under five days. June 2021 also marked the beginning of a vaccination programme only thanks to, as Sunan calls it, *"the issue being forced by activists"* otherwise, he says, *"there would have been no such knowledge of Covid-19 in our prison system"*.

---

[9] UN (2021).
[10] Lai (2021).
[11] CNA (2021).
[12] Thawan (2021).
[13] UNODC (2021).

Indeed, it should be no surprise that many governments around the world attempted to supress information about the spread and impact of Covid-19 in prisons.[14] Researchers reviewing governments' approaches to managing Covid-19 in Argentina, Colombia, Mexico and Chile found that overcrowding drastically impeded strategic responses to managing the virus while at the same time exposed weak prison infrastructures and poor-health procedures. Furthermore, the same academics found that public health restrictions such as those made by the WHO and CDC which the governors attempted to implement all but paralysed prison work and study, and negatively impacted on the already-fragile mental health of the inmates.[15] Thus, Covid-19-related measures exacerbate existing problems of overcrowding and poor-health systems and accentuate the deprivations and vulnerabilities of the prisoners. The amplification of these stresses and pressures have resulted in discontent and riots. American anthropologist and prison ethnographer, James Scott, wrote how midway through 2020 there were "*as many as 40 prison uprisings in places as diverse as Italy, Thailand, Iran, Colombia and the USA. With densely populated cell blocks, poorly circulated air, and substandard water and food supplies, prisons are the worst places to be during a pandemic*".[16]

In Canada, however, one the few countries which eased the burden of its prison population by diverting offenders from custody and/or placing them on early release, things were managed differently. Knowing that prisons were places vulnerable to disease outbreaks, Canadian authorities worked hard to ensure prisoners were not infected. Early into the lockdowns, from March to May 2020, for example, in a study of 50 prison facilities, the average infection rate was far lower than that among the Canadian public.[17] But this was not of immediate concern for Peter, a Canadian prison chaplain working out of Ottawa. Until March 2020, Peter used to visit youth detainees as well as serious male offenders in the local prison. Though he was extremely concerned that people like him

---

[14] Byrne et al. (2020) and Rapisarda and Byrne (2021).
[15] Marmolejo et al. (2020).
[16] Scott (2020).
[17] Blair et al. (2021).

had not been able to support the prisoners, lockdowns had prevented much of his community work with the vulnerable elderly. Similar to the care workers in the previous chapter, he was also firstly extremely critical of the lack of protection for the vulnerable in general, and particularly the elderly (Chapter 7). In December 2020, he said:

> There have been around 11,000 deaths in Canada and 80% of them were in care homes. Sitting ducks, so sad to see them suffer so quick. There was a crisis in care homes as staff went off sick, so why would you go back when they are barely paid the minimum wage and work in such poor conditions. They were locked out from seeing their loved ones, couldn't hold hands, no one could go in, and these poor people had mental issues which got worse because their families weren't there and some people in those homes were not getting food until 9pm at night. Their families had to meet them through the window, that's it, can you imagine that? In Canada of all nations. The worst thing is many of these homes are private and there is little transparency and you don't know how bad it is until the ambulances come and the body bags leave.

Lockdowns not only meant he could not work in the local community and visit these homes but they also impeded his pastoral support for the prisoners. He tended to be positive that the local prison had worked hard to ensure people did not pile up in prison when he said how:

> The occupancy levels of the prison have been down (to about just 30% of capacity) quite a bit due to the provincial practice of 'diversion from custodial sentencing' so there should be good buffering for safety.

However, in the autumn and winter of 2020, further Covid-19 outbreaks occurred as a second wave gripped the prison population. By the end of March 2021, of 40,000 incarcerated Canadians, 1,540 inmates were infected across the country's facilities—although discrepancies in testing make this number unlikely to be accurate. Of concern, were principally the poor air ventilation and difficulties of social distancing[18] and the fact that many prisoners had still not been offered the vaccine—even though

---

[18] Rodriguez (2021).

the general Canadian public had.[19] Even as we write during the summer of 2021, Covid-19 public health measures prevent Peter from being able to return to his duties in the prison as well as deny other key welfare support services and families. Naturally, he was worried about the mental health of the prisoners, particularly the young detainees, whom in this time had received no visits:

> Some of these kids are just 12-17 years of age, some committed capital murder, they are in maximum security prison and you hear their stories and you think why is he here, and then you hear his trauma, all the shit they go through and it causes them to veer off into areas where they don't want to. In the prison, they were concerned about Covid getting into the prison, it is congested in there. In the adult section, there are six minimum security pods or dorms with 30 men per dorm and people can barely live in these conditions, bunks are so close and you hit the other guy then there is another one over there. Once it is in a prison system, the staff get sick and this compromises the whole unit and things fall apart. So, I get the need to ensure the virus doesn't get in there but on the other hand everything else has been suspended, no visits, no support and no one really knows how they are feeling or fairing up inside now.

As we write, there is next to no empirical data available on exactly how measures to manage Covid-19 as well as isolation, discontinuation of prison visits and reduced mental health services are harmfully impacting on the mental health of Canadian prisoners. Peter hopes to be allowed to return to prison in the Autumn 2021, though, perhaps like the general trajectory of this pandemic and public health measures used for its management, there is no guarantee.

Under Lock and Key: Youth Detainees

Like adult prisons, as Peter was alluding too, facilities holding children and young people were also too significantly affected by the implementation of lockdowns. The sudden withdrawal of support and social visits

---

[19] Oullet (2021).

contributed to the rapid deterioration of already-fragile minors. One of our participants, Martyna, never thought she would end up working with such groups but with the advent of the pandemic, she too found herself on the frontline (Chapters 6 and 7). Although she has a Masters in Psychology, she had to start working in the most basic, low-paid jobs when she moved to the UK in 2018: she had no choice, it seems as she had two children to support. This is often the experience for economic migrants in the UK in that they have to automatically assume rank in neoliberalism's exploitative service or social care sector.

Indeed, Martyna applied for a job as a cleaner in a Children's secure unit while her partner got a job in a pizza take-away. When she started the job, she was working nights but because of a high staff turnover was quickly asked if she would apply for a care role. By 2019, she was working every day with very troubled girls and boys aged 12–17, many of whom she described as having *"a history of abuse, sexually exploited, groomed or were working on the county drug lines, difficult kids with difficult pasts. They are not evil, but they are troubled"*, The staff outnumbers the 20 minors that stay in the unit because of the challenges the young people pose. All have their own rooms with bathrooms and, within reason, can come and go as they please if they are not on a curfew. The first immediate difference Martyna noted as the country started to lockdown was the introduction of mask wearing which quickly dented her ability to have good relationships with the young people in the unit:

> Before Covid, it was never easy but now it is much, much harder. We have to wear masks now but I don't as I am exempt as the mask gives me distress and gives me panic attacks, so I wear a plastic thing. I have been more nervous about masks than the kids who might hit me! The kids don't have to wear masks but we do struggle with communicating with the kids, they get more angry as they can't hear properly and can't see our face, they want to trust from the facial expressions but we now have that shut off from them. We can't smile, we can't reassure them, it makes the relationships more distant and we have more problems.

Pre-pandemic under perhaps more normal circumstances, there were occasions when the young people went missing or ran away from the unit but the implementation of the lockdown meant that if and when they did disappear, these young people couldn't leave their rooms once they returned for 10 days because of the self-quarantine rules:

> *Martyna*: They then can't leave the room or corridor and we have to wear full PPE as they have been in the community. For these kids it is a massive shock.
> *Interviewer*: How do they deal with it mentally?
> *Martyna*: It has been so strict. We can't have a bond or attachment with them, it has made our relationships more fragile. Can you imagine how a 14-year old boy would react when taken from the streets on drugs and suddenly placed by themselves alone? I see them going through all the feelings. They get lonely. We had one boy who smashed up his whole room [when put into self-isolation] as he just wanted someone to sit next to him. He just wanted that contact. We had to break protocol as we are human, but I got in trouble for that.

The now strained relationships in the unit are further jeopardised by the lack of contact with social workers with whom Martyna says "*the bond has disappeared*". As the weeks went on, staff started to self-isolate and some got ill which further put a strain on the quality of care the unit staff could deliver to the children:

> We have agency staff when people had to shield but this was difficult because people weren't that ill. Mostly it was like a flu although my manager was in hospital for a day. Most people said it was not that bad, some didn't even know they had it.

To avoid possible work absences, and the potential closure of the privately run unit, the senior management did no form of Covid-19 testing:

> I don't know why they have the tests but don't test people, maybe is because they can't afford to lose staff. They are really struggling with getting people to work here, I mean I am a cleaner now doing a care worker job. They are afraid that of ten staff, six will be positive and they lose their contracts and the place closes. Agencies are hit and miss, always asked to cover shifts because people don't want to come in, the staff don't

want to come in, any excuse many people look for not to come in, but I can't afford to do that as I have two small kids.

The consequences for the reduced staffing had drastic implications for staff and youth safety as Martyna says, *"now our kids are hurting themselves more, they already were self-harming but these conditions make it worse for them"*. She also recalls when many safety protocols became compromised:

Martyna: One time we had recently a member of staff beaten unconscious and was on the floor and no one saw it because there is not enough staff. It took two minutes before someone saw it and pressed the alarm but it was very bad, very dangerous. It makes it more dangerous, but our management is focussed on children being safe. Before the management looked after us but now since Covid, they can't afford to do this as there is not many staff.

Interviewer: Since the introduction of lockdown and social distancing, have the kids been more volatile?

Martyna: Yes, I think they are more likely to have these episodes. They are speaking with people with no faces, no relationships, but before it was rare to have violence but now it happens a lot more. They are more angry as they can't go to school, they can't see peers, and they are inside much more. Some teachers agreed to work with them but most didn't bother. They just set work and don't spend time with them. The staff are burnt out now. During the night, we can't even give them snacks, we are not allowed. But its more about attention but we are not allowed to give it to them now because of Covid.

Interviewer: So, the circumstances are much more pressured. How has this all affected the morale of the staff?

Martyna: So, me personally it affects me badly but I tend to get on with it. But I am Polish and I don't moan about my job. But so many have left and changed job. New staff come in, didn't like it and leave. The good staff have had enough. Some don't feel safe, some burnout, some had to shield, some had to look after children. Now I am obliged to stay if there is no one covering a shift. Then they go and put three really disabled people in our unit because one other place closed for vulnerable children and the staff couldn't cope with the extra demand.

Increasingly under pressure to perform long hours in the unit, Martyna is now in no position to say 'no' since the advent of the second UK lockdown saw her partner lose his job. Yet, Martyna is one of millions of people working in awkward and potentially harmful circumstances on the frontline with little recognition apart from some distant claps at 8 p.m. (Chapter 7). Without discounting this frustrating challenge for her, of particular concern in this instance is the impact of public health measures on the functioning of the youth detention centre. During the UK lockdowns, it was estimated that children and minors in detention (around 500) as well as young people aged 18–21 (around 4,000) were locked up for up to 23 hours a day. This has been found to dramatically exacerbate already high levels of anxiety and mental health illness among the young cohort, which, as we saw in Martyna's testimony, pushes some to self-harm and contemplate suicide. Sonya, a youth offending team leader from London, certainly concurred with this when we interviewed her about the lockdowns. In March 2020, her team were sent home to work as they fumbled to try and work out how to support young people online:

> In prison, liberty was taken away but all of a sudden they lost contact with everyone in the outside world. In lockdown, everything was shut down, no one allowed in, no families, no support, no social workers. They went from regular community contact to nothing.

Within a month, online meetings had been set up but "*it wasn't the same*" said Sonya. She estimates half of her team were content with the set up as they "*didn't have to deal with the young people face-to-face*" while others "*recognised how this new mode of working was failing them*". Other problems emerged such as that most of their clients were placed in prisons far away and many families couldn't afford to travel: either that or were "*scared of getting the virus or couldn't because of the lockdowns*". This was jeopardised by fluctuating levels of staff motivation because, as she estimated, "*a good proportion*" of her staff were "*not bothered about seeing the clients and happy to social distance, they didn't want to see young people*". A minority, however, tried to bend rules and find ways to engage them: "*it is like a false compliance where everyone is loving this idea of working from home and having loads of meetings but no real intervention is being given to the young people"*. When the team started to regain face-to-face contact with some of their clients five months later in August 2020, Sonya said the few staff that prepared to return to visits were traumatised by the difference in many of the young people. In a typical scenario that month, she recalls:

> Our main concern was the young peoples' mental health, the lack of services and support so we knew they were suffering in silence. Many felt so abandoned. We had one kid contact us saying he didn't feel safe in prison, was being threatened, and asked to be moved. This was during the lockdown. But we couldn't move him because of the lockdown and he gave up on us. He said *"when I most needed you, you didn't bother so I want nothing to do with you"*. Everything in the sector is now about vaccines and Covid measures, and the emphasis on young peoples' interventions is secondary now.

Life in the 'new normal' was complemented by tense relationships with the police who were, in her view, *"abandoning dealing with serious youth violent crime because it was too **much** paperwork"* and instead *"focussing on the minor Covid-19 infringements like breaking lockdown"*. In addition, the courts also seemed to be prioritising such misdemeanours:

> The police were loving the power because for once they thought 'we have power as the young people are complying' and they were in there when young people were in shops with no masks. The media has scared everyone about this virus and the police are thriving off it and using it and abusing it. There is no need to waste resources and arrest a kid, keep them in a cell when they break lockdown conditions when they could have just walked them home. Then there was the courts who were operating as a means to process things like breach of lockdown while serious offences were just postponed.

She said this was detrimental to the young people and recalled the circumstances of one young man, Billy, only 14, currently on remand for one such serious offence:

There is another kid new to the criminal justice system. Billy was a good kid at school, smart, intelligent, good family, no issues. When they returned to school in Sept 2020 he was 14 and on the way home from school on the bus there was an altercation, and he took out a knife and stabbed someone multiple times. This was completely out of character. No concerns. He was remanded and awaiting sentencing but he has been on remand now for 10 months but he entered a not guilty plea in October 2020 but he won't get a trial until 2021. His teachers described him as happy but he was thrown into prison at the worst moment. 23.5 hours a day in a cell, no real help, it was difficult to access him. He has started self-harming, is on suicide watch 24 hours a day. He was moved to a secure unit so they can watch him in a mental health facility. They started medicating him. He tried to swallow a razor, he is very fragile. There has been no real intervention with him because his family have not been able to travel because we went into lockdown again, workers just give him online meetings and nothing seems to be working. I can see this kid successfully taking his life. I don't think he will make it to his court date. I ask myself would it have been different if we weren't in lockdown because a lot of young people were cooped up for so long and then when they were allowed to go out, things seemed more violent. What has lockdown done to young peoples' feelings and wellbeing? Well Billy was just inside all the time playing Fortnite and saw none of his friends face-to-face for months. Its all he did.

In Fortnite—a game in which you play online with random people from around the world and have to kill everyone else to survive—the violence is cartoony, it doesn't seem real. Perhaps Billy thought he was playing an online game in real life on the bus. We already know that lockdowns significantly increased our affiliation with the digital world of online gaming (Chapter 2) but in this example, we can tentatively conclude that lockdowns:

1. create the conditions by which Billy's social life disappears while;
2. amplify his interest and commitment to a violent video game hours on end, day after day for months;
3. which distorts his perception of real life vs online world and likely contributes to his exaggerated stabbing of another boy on a bus after an altercation; but also lockdowns,

4. are responsible for the delays to his court date with no family visits and the lack of quality intervention he could receive in prison; and, consequently;
5. play a direct role in his fragile mental state, self-harm and suicidal thoughts.

Sonya also thinks the lockdowns may be responsible for more violence. We have speculated in previous work about how lockdowns may be the driver for future youth violence[20] and this is starting to be confirmed in areas of the UK. In one Welsh report, the authors stated how lockdowns:

> ...increased exposure to harm within the home and online, whilst reducing access to care and support from services. In particular, this has placed children and young people at risk, with the potential for increased exposure to Adverse Childhood Experiences (ACEs) and violence to have long term consequences.[21]

In prison, however, Sonya continues to face an uphill struggle to try and repair the relationships and return the support to these very damaged, vulnerable young people. It very much looks in vein, for if anything, lockdowns have driven many of them to desperate measures. Sonya recalled the distressing downward spiral Ismail had taken:

> Ismail is 17 but has been in prison since he was 11 for murder so he has a very strange relationship with his family. He has been diagnosed with serious mental health conditions now as well. His parents are separated but has problems with his mum who thinks he can still recover his life and get a degree or write a book and blocks meetings with his dad. So, he avoids meetings with her. I went to see him three months into the lockdown and it was like starting from scratch with him. Now I have been working with him for six years and much of that work disappeared. Over that time, he was starting to repair. But when I saw him he was back on strong medication, he had assaulted members of staff in the prison. When we sort of got our relationship back on track, he started talking

---

[20] Ellis et al. (2021).
[21] Newbury et al. (2020).

about the dark side of him because he had been locked up 23.5 hours per day. He said to me before that he wasn't bothered about me seeing him but in lockdown he realised he looked forward to seeing me. Now he is telling me *"can you watch this programme"* so we can talk about it and you saw the child in him. It was heart-breaking. Now he refuses to see his parents at all. His mental health has really got worse. He has schizophrenia and bipolar disorder recently and he is now self-harming. One time last week, he was cutting himself and used the blood from his arms to write a hit list on the wall and number 1 was his mum. The violent episodes got worse under lockdown. Then it became self-harm as he described 'voices' in his head to do worse things. *"Like now the voices are telling me I should assault you and I don't want to harm you but when I am by myself for a long time, the dark voices consume me"* he said to me recently.

The UN estimates that around 1.4 million juveniles are locked up in such centres around the world. Many of these young people outside the UK are subject to far worse conditions than we describe here, such as abuse and extortion and, like the prisoners, living in over-crowded and unsanitary conditions and deprived of basic essentials such as food, soap, detergent and toilet paper among others. Youth detention centres around the world have also therefore seen the impact of the withdrawal of teachers, psychologists and social workers, often in many instances leaving only security staff, and barring families from visiting their children in order to prevent the spread of the disease.

Researchers warn of the untold traumas that are evolving in the process of confining such vulnerable children and young people to increased confinement. Early release schemes, which would otherwise be encouraged to monitor the progress a child or young offender makes in the community post sentence, in many instances were cancelled because institutions like social services and probation did not have the capacity to support them. In the USA—where around 43,000 children and young people are held in Juvenile Correctional Facilities (JCF)—overcrowding jeopardises the necessity of self-isolation in the event of positive Covid-19 tests. Even then, and like the UK experience, these children will typically have to self-isolate in cells measuring 6 × 8 feet for 23 hours per day with almost no interaction with anyone. If they are lucky, they may get a short conversation for a couple of minutes through the door with a mental health professional or teacher. This experience, some say, is akin to *punitive solitary confinement which can do irreversible psychological damage.*

Yet, the true picture of how this affects children and minors in custody is unknown largely because authorities are not declaring fundamental elements of what is taking place. American researchers who evaluated 50 state prison agencies—which included all JCFs as well as the federal Bureau of Prisons—on the extent to which they report critical information about Covid-19 found that:

> Some states do not provide sufficient information about tests, cases, and deaths to enable a good understanding of the numbers or to show how the situation is changing over time. And most prison agencies are not reporting other critical information that would help users get a clearer picture of how Covid-19 is affecting people who live and work in the facilities and who is most affected. Additionally, we found that some prison agencies have become less transparent over time insofar as they stopped reporting some critical information. Moreover, we identified several instances where the data that was reported by certain agencies raised questions about the trustworthiness of the information.

These problems aptly summarise the main issues we have found with the arrival of Covid-19 and the public health measures implemented to secure its control: the way information is collated, managed and interpreted drastically negates a complete understanding of the full-scale risk of the virus itself—as a public health threat—against measures taken in the name of reducing transmission such as lockdowns and social distancing which generate multidimensional social harms.

Locked Up and Looking for the Key: Asylum Seekers

"It is the worst place to be, worse than my home country…where I should have died before coming here" says Mohammed, an Iraqi asylum seeker

living in the suburbs of Paris. Mohammed was being processed as an asylum seeker in France in 2019, just before the pandemic, and thought he had done the hard work: *"you don't know the sacrifices I made to come here, what I had to do to leave my country, what I lost to get here, how I got here, the humiliation, the abuse, the insults, and now I am here, I see worse society"*. He feels lucky knowing that many of his friends and others he knows sleep in makeshift encampments or on the streets, often moving on having given up on the Asylum application. Referring to his housing placement in one of Paris' poorest areas, his assimilation into French society and cultural life was stunted by, as he calls it, *"aggressive rejection from the French people"* coupled with the *"constant monitoring from the police"*.

All around Mohammed, the communities of other asylum seekers are also exposed to the same pressures. For example, a study following the long-term integrational progress of the Makasi community[22] in the Parisian suburbs prior to the pandemic concluded that the lockdown had a detrimental impact on various economic and mental health aspects of the community. In particular:

> Among the 100 participants, 68% had no legal residence permit. Food insecurity was more often reported during lockdown than before (62% vs 52%). 9% of participants had a score indicative of severe depression (PHQ9) before lockdown and 17% afterwards. Only 51% knew about the possibility of asymptomatic transmission of the COVID-19 virus.[23]

Mohammed sees it as *"a clear message to asylum seekers like me"* that *"we are not welcome"*. Perhaps he is right. The chronic shortage of housing units for people like Mohammed is very much part of a deliberate national strategy engaged by the French authorities in an effort to try to discourage people from seeking protection in the country. The process is so long-winded and bureaucratic that even with the highest levels of commitment and patience, it still feels like a *"lottery"* in his words. As he was awaiting his application, the country was plunged into lockdown

---

[22] People from the sub-Saharan area of Africa.
[23] Gosselin et al. (2021).

when the government started to shut down movements and activities to reduce the transmission of Covid-19. *"Suddenly, it feels like someone has taken from me the few things I thought I had left"* he says bitterly as he laments the delay it has caused to his asylum application, the lack of freedom as well as the increased discrimination against him: *"there have been days when people throw bricks at the building"* he adds. Sadly, this politically channelled indignation has also spilled over into the discrimination and hate attacks against people of Chinese origin living in France, for one-third of whom, since January 2020 reported having experienced at least one discriminatory act against them because of their association with Covid-19 or the 'China virus' as Donald Trump would say.[24]

Detention centres and housing units for asylum seekers—such as those where Mohammed sits and awaits his fate—became targeted, as asylum seekers were reported by the media to be at a high risk of transmitting the virus which further stigmatised their experiences. Perhaps most poignantly, this was reflected in the high-profile coverage of the 'potential spread of Covid-19' in the Calais Jungle—one of France's most notorious and long-standing improvised refugee hubs—thus tainting the general experience of asylum seekers seeking integration and cultural acceptance. Early in the pandemic, it was reported that Covid-19 was spreading quickly through French refugee camps such as the Calais Jungle *"where over 1,000 people are sheltering without proper sanitation, water supplies or food".*[25]

At a time of border closures, this preceded speculation that asylum seekers fleeing France for the UK shores might arrive and thus infect others.[26] The risk associated with their transmissibility is perhaps unproven though research has concluded that asylum seekers in France are more likely to have certain chronic conditions that appear to be associated with worse Covid-19 outcomes, such as diabetes mellitus, hypertension, and obesity.[27] Yet, it is the high-income countries such

[24] Wang et al. (2020).
[25] Kelly (2020).
[26] Gant (2020).
[27] Lancet Migration (2020).

as France and the UK which foster harmful inequalities and the substandard living conditions which disfavour and handicap populations such as asylum seekers, making them not only (a) at increased risk of infection, but also (b) because of their status, more likely to experience barriers to healthcare including adequate information, language assistance and entitlement.[28]

When compared to previous years, countries such as France as well as UK have reported significantly higher all-cause mortality in migrants from specific countries/regions in 2020 compared with the host residents. Indeed, outbreaks of Covid-19 in detention units and housing centres for asylum seekers have been reported across Europe. But people like Mohammed have also been impacted disproportionately by the restrictions and measures implemented to fight the pandemic. The direct and indirect health and social impacts including increased discrimination, more protracted lockdowns and severe restrictions on movement and travel restrictions and border closures delay important and necessary family reunifications and the asylum process. Consequently, as Mohammed sees it, *"asylum seekers like me have become what French people think is the problem and the coronavirus makes it worse"*.

We find the same in the UK where similar asylum seeker detention centres and housing units have been negatively impacted by the lockdowns. As these people await their asylum decisions, they are temporarily housed and given £37.75 per week for basics like food, clothes and toiletries. Nevertheless, the conditions of their housing as well as the social feeling which envelopes their experience is somewhat traumatic. The 17 centres, which accommodate about 30,000 people each year in the UK, are regularly subject to abuse and violence. In 2017, two such centres—Yarl's Wood and Brook House—came to the public's attention when residents exercised hunger strikes and threatened to commit suicide.[29] The same year saw an undercover report find that one person per day was self-harming in such centres.[30]

---

[28] Hayward et al. (2021).
[29] Dambach (2018).
[30] Ohare (2018).

However, the political decision to lockdown UK society had significant ramifications for these groups already suffering in squalid and pressured circumstances. UK lockdowns as well as border restrictions and political pressure to fast track the asylum seeker population out of the country had seen an increased number of chartered deportation flights as the UK approached the deadline to leave the EU on 31st December 2020. One centre, Brook House, which was specifically processing those who had managed to cross the channel from France in small boats, experienced a 2,000% increase in self-harm among asylum seekers.[31] An impartial report by the Independent Monitoring Board concluded that from July to December 2020, the Home Office treatment and management of Covid-19 in asylum seeker detention centres represented "*inhumane treatment of the whole detainee population*".[32]

In January 2021, Brook House along with other centres in Harmondsworth and Morton Hall were completely cut off because of Covid-19 outbreaks: they were essentially enacting a form of solitary confinement within the wider context of a national lockdown. For the residents—many of whom had escaped war-torn countries, risking their life in an effort to clamber to Europe—experiencing these advanced lockdowns and increased uncertainty resulted in increased self-harm and suicidal thoughts. Despite pleading letters from aid agencies and lobbying groups, there has been no shift from the political elite to ease the restrictions on these groups and, if anything, the government has continued to steam ahead with deporting asylum seekers.

As we write, Napier Barracks—another asylum detention centre which had experienced riots because of a Covid-19 outbreak earlier in the year—was branded overcrowded and unhygienic by independent reports and human rights campaigners. Nevertheless, their continued operation highlights the lack of interest on behalf of the government to make it safe and secure for these people. Indeed, as Refugee Action notes, "*recklessly forcing hundreds of refugees into crowded camps during a killer pandemic was a gamble with people's lives*".[33] But these are the shady consequences

[31] Bulman (2020).

[32] Taylor (2021).

[33] BBC. (2021a, May 3). Napier Barracks: Call to close 'unlawful' asylum centre. *BBC*. Cited online at https://www.bbc.com/news/uk-england-kent-57343968.

of lockdowns which inadvertently exacerbate the life circumstances of those socially excluded and this was also the case with migrant workers, refugees and the homeless.

References

Blair, A., Parnia, A., & Siddiqui, A. (2021, January). A time-series analysis of testing and COVID-19 outbreaks in Canadian federal prisons to inform prevention and surveillance efforts. *Canada Communicable Disease Report, 47*(1), 66–76.

Bulman, M. (2020, November 16). Self-harm incidents surge 2,000% in detention. *The Independent.* Cited online at https://www.independent.co.uk/news/uk/home-news/self-harm-detention-brook-house-asylum-seekers-b1668406.html

Byrne, J., Rapisarda, S. S., Hummer, D., & Kras, K. R. (2020). An imperfect storm: Identifying the root causes of COVID-19 outbreaks in the world's largest corrections systems. *Victims & Offenders, 15*(7–8), 862–909. https://doi.org/10.1080/15564886.2020.1838373

CNA. (2021, May 29). *COVID-19 sweeps through Thailand's overcrowded prisons.* Cited online at https://www.channelnewsasia.com/news/asia/covid-19-thailand-prison-jail-overcrowded-outbreak-14909396

Dambach, K. (2018, April 6). Dire conditions at UK immigration detention centers. *Infomigrants.* Cited online at https://www.infomigrants.net/en/post/8479/dire-conditions-at-uk-immigration-detention-centers

Ellis, A., Briggs, D., Lloyd, A., & Telford, L. (2021). A ticking time bomb of future harm: Lockdown, child abuse and future violence. *Abuse: An International Journal, 2*(1). https://doi.org/10.37576/abuse.2021.017

Fair, H., & Jacobson, J. (2021). *Keeping COVID out of prisons: Approaches in ten countries* (Project Report). ICPR.

Gant, J. (2020, March 17). Border Force officers test 25 migrants for coronavirus after they were intercepted crossing the English Channel today. *Daily Mail.* Cited online at https://www.dailymail.co.uk/news/article-8121813/Border-Force-catches-migrants-Kent-charities-warn-thousands-Calais-risk-coronavirus.html

Gosselin, A., Melchior, M., Carillon, S., Gubert, F., Ridde, V., Kohou, V., Zoumenou, I., Senne, J.-N., & du Loû, A. D. (2021). Deterioration of mental health and insufficient COVID-19 information among disadvantaged immigrants in the greater Paris area. *Journal of Psychosomatic Research, 146*, 110504. https://doi.org/10.1016/j.jpsychores.2021.110504

Hayward, S. E., Deal, A., Cheng, C., Crawshaw, A., Orcutt, M., Vandrevala, T. F., Norredam, M., Carballo, M., Ciftci, Y., Requena-Méndez, A., Greenaway, C., Carter, J., Knights, F., Mehrotra, A., Seedat, F., Bozorgmehr, K., Veizis, A., Campos-Matos, I., Wurie, F., … Hargreaves, S. (2021). Clinical outcomes and risk factors for COVID-19 among migrant populations in high-income countries: A systematic review. *Journal of Migration and Health, 3*, 100041. https://doi.org/10.1016/j.jmh.2021.100041

IDPC. (2018). *Drug dependence treatment in Thailand: Progress against persistent concern.* IDPC.

International Labour Organisation. (ILO). (2020). *ILO brief: COVID-19 employment and labor market impact in Thailand.* ILO.

Kelly, A. (2020, April 9). COVID-19 spreading quickly through refugee camps, warn Calais aid groups. *The Guardian.* Cited online at https://www.theguardian.com/global-development/2020/apr/09/covid-19-spreading-quickly-though-refugee-camps-warn-calais-aid-groups

Kelly, B., & Slattery, G. (2020, May 2). Prisoners take guards hostage in Brazil's Coronavirus-hit Manaus. *Reuters.* Cited online at https://www.reuters.com/article/us-brazil-prison-rebellion-idUSKBN22E0KB

Lai, G. (2021, May 2021). Thailand's prison overcrowding crisis exacerbated by COVID-19. *The Diplomat.* Cited online at https://thediplomat.com/2021/05/thailands-prison-overcrowding-crisis-exacerbated-by-covid-19/

Lancet Migration; Global Collaboration to Advance Migration Health. (2020). *Situational brief: The health of asylum seekers & undocumented migrants in France during Covid-19.* Available at https://www.migrationandhealth.org/migration-COVID19-briefs

Marmolejo, L., Barberi, D., Espinoza, O., Bergman, M., & Fondevila, G. (2020). Responding to COVID-19 in Latin American prisons: The cases of Argentina, Chile, Colombia, and Mexico. *Victims & Offenders, 15*(7–8), 1062–1085. https://doi.org/10.1080/15564886.2020.1827110

Newbury, A., Barton, E., Snowdon, L., & Hopkins, J. (2020). *Understanding the impact of COVID-19 on violence and ACEs experienced by children and young people in Wales.* Violence Prevention Unit.

Ohare, L. (2018, April 2). At least one person a day is self-harming in UK detention centres. *The Independent.* Cited online at https://www.independent.co.uk/news/one-person-day-self-harming-uk-detention-centres-a8285206.html

Oullet, V. (2021, June 16). *Some prisoners not offered COVID-19 shots until months after general public, CBC analysis finds in CBC.* Cited online at https://www.cbc.ca/news/canada/covid-vaccinations-in-jails-1.6066293

Poonsab, W., Vanek, J., & Carré, F. (2020). *Informal Workers in Urban Thailand: A Statistical Snapshot.* WIEGO.

Rapisarda, S., & Byrne, J. (2021). An examination of COVID-19 outbreaks in prisons and jails throughout Asia. *Victims & Offenders, 15*(7–8). https://doi.org/10.1080/15564886.2020.1835770

Ratcliffe, R. (2021). How have Thailand and Cambodia kept COVID cases so low? *The Guardian,* 16 December 2020. Cited online at https://www.theguardian.com/world/2020/dec/16/thailand-cambodia-covid-19-cases-deaths-low

Rodriguez, J. (2021, April 5). 'Public health crisis': Canada's prison conditions during pandemic being investigated. *CTV News.* Cited online at https://www.ctvnews.ca/health/coronavirus/public-health-crisis-canada-s-prison-conditions-during-pandemic-being-investigated-1.5375277

Scott, J. (2020). A pandemic in prisons. *Social Anthropology/anthropologie Sociale, 28*(2), 353–355.

Taylor, D. (2021, May 21). UK asylum seekers at 'unprecedented' risk of suicide amid deportation threat. *The Guardian.* Cited online at https://www.theguardian.com/uk-news/2021/may/21/uk-asylum-seekers-at-unprecedented-risk-of-suicide-amid-deportation-threat

Taylor, J., & Siradapuvadol, N. (2021, May 14). Suicides rise in Thailand as COVID decimates its tourism industry. *The Telegraph.* Cited online at https://www.telegraph.co.uk/global-health/science-and-disease/suicides-rise-thailand-covid-decimates-tourism-industry/

Thawan, T. (2021, June 8). *Nearly 30,000 COVID-19 infections at Thai prisons in recent wave.* The Thaiger. Cited online on https://thethaiger.com/news/national/nearly-30000-covid-19-infections-at-thai-prisons-in-recent-wave

TIJ. (2021). *Research on the Causes of Recidivism in Thailand.* TJI.

UN. (2021). *United Nations System: Common Position on Incarceration.* UN.

UNODC. (2021, June 16). *UNODC supports Thai prisons to respond to COVID-19 outbreak.* Cited on UNODC website at https://www.unodc.org/southeastasiaandpacific/en/2021/06/thai-prison-covid-19/story.html

Wang, S., Chen, X., Li, Y., Luu, C., Yan, R., & Madrisotti, F. (2020). I'm more afraid of racism than of the virus!': Racism awareness and resistance among Chinese migrants and their descendants in France during the COVID-19 pandemic. *European Societies,* 1–22. Available at https://www.tandfonline.com/doi/full/10.1080/14616696.2020.1836384

9

Locked Out: Migrant Workers, Refugees and Stateless Citizens and the Homeless

With borders closed, routes shut and transport ceased in the Global South, migrant workers working in informal sectors could not return home to safety and instead were forced to find alternatives. Similarly, the same sort of worker—often forming part of service industries in many Western countries (Chapters 6–8)—could neither return home nor maintain jobs as casual labour opportunities in precarious sectors evaporated. Likewise, already uprooted by climate ravaged, war torn and politically unstable countries, the worlds' 80 million forcibly displaced and 26 million refugees were unable to continue their journeys and had to find extra money for the 'privilege' of escaping their misery. Lastly, many of the 150 million homeless people around the world could no longer bank on the meagre handouts afforded to them pre-pandemic: lockdowns truly locked them out.

© The Author(s), under exclusive license to Springer Nature
Switzerland AG 2021
D. Briggs et al., *Lockdown*,
https://doi.org/10.1007/978-3-030-88825-1_9

Migrant Workers

In mid-March 2020, Madhuja stopped being paid from a hotel in Calcutta where she was working as a waitress. When the hotel closed, the employees were told to go home and wait until the 14-day lockdown had passed before returning to work. Then *"they said 'stay home and come back to work in September' but I wasn't getting paid but I still had a contract if you see what I mean"* she said. Yet at the end of this two-week period, the lockdown was extended for another 20 days. Feeling the pressure of mounting debts, because in India, as she says, *"when you have a job, you still have to pay taxes and rent"*, she continued to hold out to see if the hotel would reopen and she could resume work. She never returned. It wasn't, however, until June that she was officially made redundant and moved back to Bangalore. She reflected:

> I get depressed, I don't know what to do or what will happen. My situation is not good but many, like those migrant workers, have lives much worse.

In India, she estimates that *"60% of the population live by unorganised work"* or survive by means in the informal sector as 'daily wage migrant workers'. These *"migrant workers"* she described as:

> Leading a minimum lifestyle, have no savings, live by what they earn each day and because of the lockdowns they were stuck in the big cities in Calcutta, Mumbai and they had no way to come back. They were suffering and some were committing suicide. They could not eat and could not feed their family.

She added that these people were stuck living on nothing in big cities around India and that it wasn't until May 2020 that efforts to transport these people home were organised by the governments. Only, on the government trains *"at least 1,000 people went when only 400 was the capacity"*, she said, and consequently, the infection rate increased. *"These workers got scared of this or thought the trains would not start running because of the lockdown and started walking back home, walking 1,000 to*

1,500 km home. Look online and find out how many died" she said. We did so and found that:

> 'Based on the information received from the State Police, 805 people suffered injuries and 8,733 people died on the railway track between January 2020 and December 2020', the Railway Board has said. Many of those who died were home-bound migrant workers who chose to walk along the railway tracks as train routes were considered to be shorter than road or highways, a railway official said, according to PTI. The officials said they also chose to walk along the tracks to avoid the police for violating lockdown norms.[1]

The punishment for violating Covid-19 lockdown measures included a hefty fine or imprisonment or even both. People who violated the lockdown orders could be punished under the following sections of the Indian Penal Code (IPC). It states that under:

> Sec 269 which is a *"Negligent act likely to spread infection of disease dangerous to life"* can result in imprisonment up to six months, or fine, or both.
> Sec 270 which is a *"Malignant act likely to spread infection of disease dangerous to life"* can result in imprisonment up to two years, or fine, or both.
> Sec 188 which is *"Disobedience to order duly promulgated by public servant"* (which is in this case either the police or army) can mean imprisonment up to six months, or a fine of up to 1,000 Indian Rupees, or both.[2]

The authorities were serious as well. In the space of two months in West Bengal, 40,723 people were arrested, and 3,614 vehicles were seized for violation of lockdown measures.[3] In Maharashtra, an Eastern province which hosts the expansive cities of Mumbai, Pune and Nagpur, 60,000 crimes were recorded for various violations of the lockdown, 41,769

---

[1] Scroll (2021).
[2] Jain (2020).
[3] NDTV (2020).

vehicles were seized and 13,381 people were arrested from 22 March to 21 April 2020—just 31 days. And at the height of India's second wave in May 2021, in Delhi alone:

> Nearly 200,000 people were prosecuted during the lockdown between April 19 and May 25 for not following 'Covid-19 appropriate behaviour', of which 171,154 (86.6%) were fined for either not using a mask or wearing it incorrectly.[4]

Yet many of these people were too poor to afford masks so were certainly unable to pay the fines so instead were simply accumulating criminal records and prison time. So, one can perhaps see why thousands of migrant workers opted to walk home, thus avoiding the police and army road controls. Those that made it home, Madhuja said, "*couldn't afford a Covid test*" as they were priced at 3,500 Indian Rupees or about $50. Yet the average earnings of a daily wage migrant worker in India is one tenth of that at 372 Indian Rupees or about $5. The other option Madhuja said was that they could queue for "*two days*" to get a test from a government hospital or centre. "*Many people thought 'I will have the lemon juice and I will be alright'*" she said. Promises were made to give these people free food indefinitely says Madhuja but "*rice and pulses were only available for one month in July 2020*" she said.

With no work, Madhuja returned to Bangalore in the summer of 2020 to try and find work. She used her savings to travel and look for new opportunities. Yet, like her, she encountered many more people without work when she arrived. Indeed, unemployment in Bangalore's province of Karnataka's 64 million had risen to 30% or 19.2 million in April 2020—many of whom were daily wage migrant workers. However, their ongoing plight continues in the shadows of the obscene big tech wealth accumulation under way in Bangalore where Madhuja now lives. Bangalore has been branded the 'world's fastest-growing mature tech ecosystem', and investments expanded 5.4 times from $1.3 billion in

---

[4] Goswami (2021).

2016 to $7.2 billion in 2020.[5] Even in pandemic conditions, it flourished: a sign of the changing times (Chapter 5). Yet just outside her small flat, which she can only afford for two more months before her savings expire, she can see the people she may be joining on the streets:

> If you go around the city now, all these small shops are closed, more homeless people many more on the streets, they are not living a good life. There is no job for them, they have nothing to eat. People don't want to go out and spend, they are scared of the virus so things shut down. No one wants to go out, the remote working culture is taking over, online, takeaways, and the people with money and jobs in big tech are safe in this respect.

All of Madhuja's family have had Covid-19 and, like the 100 people she estimates to know in the city, "*all of them lost their jobs and are sitting at home neck deep in debt*". On reflection, she feels aggrieved and angry as "*all they* [the government] *are doing is giving us loans we can't pay back.*" Perhaps like some of the daily wage migrant workers, she too has contemplated suicide adding "*there are a lot of things going around in my head but there's no one to talk to*". This is made worse when:

> With all these poor people, the governments are investing money in building temples to raise people's pride and they say will help beat Covid? They have the guts to come on Indian television and say things like this when everything like the migrant workers and homeless and you have this feeling of anger burning inside you. No journalist has had the balls to challenge them, no one is questioning anything.

One year on from the advent of Covid-19, nearly half of India's salaried workers now have to survive in the shrinking informal sector as a direct result of pandemic-related lockdowns which caused job losses. In the summer of 2021, about 230 million more people had fallen below the poverty line based on the national minimum wage of 178 Indian Rupees or approximately $2.80 per day.[6] Estimates of child homelessness, which

---

[5] The Times of India (2021).
[6] Centre for Sustainable Employment (2021).

were thought to be in the region of 121,000 pre-pandemic, are almost certainly likely to have increased due to more children being made orphans, having had parents die of hunger, Covid-19 or suicide. India also saw huge cuts in healthcare which impacted basic delivery of nutritional remedies and vaccines: the ramifications of which we now witness across the South Asian area. For example, a recent study found that across the countries of India, Afghanistan, Nepal, Bangladesh, Sri Lanka and Pakistan, 228,000 additional deaths of children under five occurred because crucial services, ranging from food aid, nutrition benefits to immunisation, were halted because of travel restrictions and lockdowns.[7]

Across the border, Hamza's children were almost such victims when they nearly died of starvation in 2020. Born in the rural farming area of Okara—district of Punjab in Pakistan—Hamza lived his early life there until he married and had children. At the best of times, a rural farmer can earn about 24,000 Pakistani rupees a month—which is about $149—but for some years now the surrounding area's work has been diminishing because of climate-change-related droughts and food insecurity.[8] It was not enough to support them so he migrated to the capital Islamabad to work. It took him sometime to establish himself there but eventually found work as a waiter earning a monthly wage of 30,000 Pakistani rupees or about $186. In Pakistan, migration is common in the face of landless farm labour in rural areas like Okara, particularly during floods or droughts. Indeed, between 1995 and 2014, Pakistan experienced 143 extreme weather events and the latest IDMC report estimated 100,000 people were displaced by such disasters in 2019.[9] Finding work then can be difficult but prior to the pandemic, Hamza had found a solid wage to support his family back home, he said:

> There is no life to live for a poor man but this is God's will, especially for a migrated worker like me, even in every circumstance. I had not been living an extraordinary life before covid-19. However, it was quite easy to live compared to the current situation as there were a lot of opportunities

---

[7] BBC (2021a).
[8] Idris (2021).
[9] Actionaid (2020).

to extend my work capacity, to talk with friends and family, and easily go to places I wanted to go.

The two-month lockdown from 1 April to 30 May 2020 changed all that very quickly as aside from his wage shrinking, he could not travel to see his family:

> It came with the worst circumstances [the lockdown]. This not only reduced my work opportunities but also closed the restaurant. It created economic problems for me and the country. At that time, I was completely helpless. Due to lockdowns, I had received only 12,000 rupees instead of my monthly 30,000 as a salary. It hurt me and shattered my relationship with my family because they were depending on me to send them money for food. It forced my whole family into starvation... The lockdown was so harshly imposed by the Federal Government as all types of public transport was sanctioned to stop. I remember that it was the harshest time ever in my life.

12,000 rupees per month is just $75 so Hamza and his family were having to survive on around $2.50 a day. He was perhaps lucky to even receive that meagre wage for studies show that in the April to June quarter of 2020, the labour market in Pakistan shrank 13% quickly rendering 20.7 million people unemployed.[10] These pressures—on top of already pressing environmental and labour circumstances—when combined with the lockdowns were enough to tip many people over the edge for analyses of media-reported suicide cases either pointed to reasons relating to 'lockdown economic recession' or 'fear of infection.'[11] Like these migrant workers, halting social life therefore has many more significant consequences for those already transient and in equally uncertain modes of survival. Many of the harms endured are not simply due to the presence of Covid-19, but the *absence* of employment, stability, security and vital support services resulting, at least in part, from lockdown measures. As we saw in the preceding chapters too, the absence of things like family, supportive care and security can be extremely harmful.

---

[10] Pakistan Bureau of Statistics (2021).
[11] Mamun and Ullah (2020).

Accordingly, it is worth reiterating at this point that while we acknowledge the potential threat of the pandemic, it is also important to consider the harmful absences generated by lockdown.

Refugees and Stateless Citizens

The visual image of Osama fuzzes from time to time: "*the connection is not good from where I am calling you, but the main thing is you can hear me*" he says. Osama, a Syrian refugee who has been floating around Europe for the past five years, is no stranger to these kinds of haphazard communications: "*it is usually much worse when I call my family or my sister in Damascus – there they can cut out at any moment, there is a bomb or no electricity, many things*" he adds. We got to know Osama through previous work we have done with refugees across Europe[12] and have since kept in contact. Before leaving his country, he was a student studying Engineering but abandoned his studies under pressure to join government security services to fight the war against the 'free army'. "*Violence is not in my blood*" he reflects on the reasons why he left Syria as soon as he could.

This was, however, the first time we had been able to contact him since the advent of the Covid-19 pandemic. For someone without formal papers to reside or work, he does his best working cash in hand in a takeaway restaurant run by other Syrians in Munich, Germany. "*They gave me a job because I am Syrian even though I am here illegally*" he says. But there is no time to worry about Covid-19 because he must work to be able to send money to his family back home in Syria:

> You know people here, its funny, I mean the Germans. They are all worried about the coronavirus but people like me who have no money, no status, no existence if you know what I mean, we don't exist, formally, like in the numbers, well they are all worried about this virus and staying at home but I have no choice. I can't sit around and sleep in a shared room because I have to earn money to stay there, to eat, to send to my

---

[12] See Briggs (2020).

family. They listen to the media and government. But I can tell you from my own experience, I have worked every day in the confinement [lockdown] and I didn't get it and the people I work with didn't. Then the weird thing is we deliver food to people and they come to the door with masks and gel their hands to take the food from us as if *we are the infected people.*

For Osama, the whole Covid-19 pandemic issue as well as the public health measures which he sees people follow is surreal. "*I honestly don't understand it, the way people are following it, I am confused by it almost*" he says. This could be perhaps because he attributes minimal risk to the virus, having escaped a war-torn country and has seen people die in front of him from sniper rifle shots and bombs: *he imprints his experience of suffering against what he now sees in the context of Covid-19 and there seems to be a mismatch in his interpretation of risk as he has come to know it* (Chapter 3). He is then keen to point out that Covid-19 is merely exacerbating an already fragile situation in his home country of Syria:

You have to understand that war has brought my country to its knees, we have to understand before we talk about coronavirus. War, violence, illegal activity everywhere, no currency. No hospitals at all. Look how Covid is making it difficult for all the rich countries like USA so imagine in a country that has been in war for 10 years. There are no hospitals they have all been targeted. There is simply no resources to do anything to combat a new virus.

He recalls how rich people escaped when the war started, leaving a scramble for everyone else. In a country characterised by the possibility of being robbed, kidnapped or killed at any moment, there is no one left to trust. In the economic and political instability, inflation is "*through the roof*" as he describes: "*it used to be one dollar to 45 lira now it is 2,700 to the dollar.*" He says now people can't survive in the country "*unless someone from the West, or someone like me who has found work or some money, sends money back, there is no way people can survive with basic things too expensive.*" He is now serving people in Western society, yet now he is on a different kind of frontline—The Covid-19 frontline. Unlike the people in Chapter 6, he has to go out and work for money to be able to eat and support his family and he says Syrians too also still do this, even those that still reside in the country where the danger of death is ever-present:

> Syria did a strict quarantine, a strict one from 6pm to 6pm and if you break it the government imprison you, but many people live day by day if they don't go out and sell they don't have food, do you want to die of hunger or coronavirus? They take their chances, herd immunity it has to be, there is no choice. People can't take it seriously. In my country, people say 'if its not written nothing happens but if it is written then you die'. What I mean is people don't care about coronavirus and with 10 years of war they just do what they can with their lives.

Osama knows a few people who have had Covid-19 back home, "*a few friends of mine*" but he says, "*their situation is super normal and even they are saying it is like a flu*". He recounts how his friend "*got it*" but almost nothing happened. Furthermore, this is not aided by the fact that "*there are no studies and the only people that do statistics are government, 35 cases but who believes them so there is no problem here.*" Because there is no data collection, no media machine driving the worry or hysteria, all one can do, according to Osama is, "*see how the people are: if they carry on, there is no problem but if not, then they don't.*" Mask wearers, he says, are seen as "*strange*" in Syria. He reasons that this could be because people in Syria are "*more philosophical about death and dying*":

> I think people get the ideas about if from media who tell people it is serious but if media say it is ok, people just get on with it like in Syria. My aunt has died of Covid but she was old, over 80.

Osama adds that "*why would people buy disinfectant gel or masks when they cant even afford to eat in Syria?*" Much of this reiterates what we were saying in Chapter 3 about how the machinery of politics and media have converted 'Covid illness and death' into magnified risks to Westerners, who, in their longer lifespans, experience *a sanitised journey to death* rather than something more explicit like being shot or hit by a bomb. In short, Osama has seen graphic, violent suffering on a daily basis so behaviour like hand disinfection and mask wearing to deter a "*hard flu*" are seen as alien:

A lot of people don't understand the word pandemic or epidemic. Do people in Syria stop to wash their hands and wear the masks? No one. It is people saying it is like a hard flu but they lost people, mostly old people or really unhealthy people. It is not as bad. The huge media explosion made it more than it was. But it is about media coverage and government behaviour because if they don't make a deal out of it, it is not a problem. I know a friend working in health, he did four tests, one negative and then one positive, then it was negative again before it was positive. This is not a danger to humanity, but it is dangerous to the economy.

Instead he thinks Syrians have more to worry about and that the whole scenario is "*political and being used to the advantage of powerful people*" (Chapter 5 and 6). The difference, he concludes, is that:

People in the West are trusting of the governments and the pharma companies. Is it the solution? I don't know. Things like masks is more about personal security for people, they just want to be reassured. But it is big business for these companies, Pfizer, Moderna, when these companies bring the solution to the table in the middle of a panic and big money is there to be made. Then, of course, there is the competition between the countries who has the best and quickest vaccine.

We finish our conversation and he puts us in contact with his sister in Damascus. We are not able to interview her due to the unpredictability in the use of electricity so all we can do is exchange a series of messages. LuLu, as she calls herself, said "*at first, when corona started, the country made a lockdown for about two months but it affected everything very negatively and led to the deterioration of the economy.*" By mid-2020, more than 80% of the remaining Syrians had fallen below the poverty line. For many, the lockdowns, closures of borders and domestic travel had forced them into protests because of starvation, prompting speculation that there would be another exodus into Turkey and then Europe.[13]

---

[13] Ozalp (2020).

The money people earn each day is what they need and now a lot of
people cannot afford to bring food for their houses. We hear there are
protests but we ourselves say nothing, it is too dangerous and no one
hears us anyway. We have so many poor people here and they die like
this. They [the government] just don't care. Even if coronavirus affected
us - and we don't know how – there are no masks on buses or in closed
areas.

Official figures at the time of writing in the summer of 2021 indicated
there were 25,404 'cases' of Covid-19 across the country and that 1,897
had died. Yet, as Osama and LuLu testify, this is very much because
of limited testing and healthcare infrastructure. The northeast of the
country in particular suffers much more because there is no cross-border
agreement to enable UN agencies to deliver Covid-19 PPE or vaccines
and, without the permission of the Syrian government, institutions like
the WHO cannot organise deliveries. For example, the only remaining
Covid-19 test centre in the densely populated city of Qamishli—close
to the Turkish and Iraqi border—ran out of PCR testing equipment in
May 2021. Further south, another city, Hassakeh, similarly populated by
around 180,000 people, and Raqqa where another 300,000 people live,
Covid-19 test centres cease to function because of funds and medical
supplies. While many people in Western countries can now call at their
leisure to make an appointment for their vaccine, the five million people
who occupy this north-eastern area of Syria have, to date, only 20,000
vaccines to share between them. Perhaps more concerning is that the
circumstances of famine and compromised sanitary conditions are likely
to make people more vulnerable as a second wave of Covid-19 starts to
spread.[14]

LuLu continues to study in the University of Damascus, one of the
few open in the country. She still receives money sent from Osama who
is essentially illegally working in the margins to pay for her education
and for his parents to be able to afford food. For the other Syrians LuLu
knows in Europe, things are also complex. While most have started to
settle in countries such as Holland, Sweden and Germany, more recent

14 ReliefWeb (2021).

friends attempting to leave via clandestine means because of the Covid-19 lockdowns and lack of food, were equally vulnerable to be caught up in restrictions elsewhere:

> Two of my closest friends finally left their studies and the country to go to Europe after the lockdowns ended in Syria, it was too much for them. They got into Turkey but normally this is not a problem with money as you just pay people to go from place to place, all the police, security people. Then they got on the boats to Greece but got stuck on Lesbos.

In fact, they got stuck at Moria: a refugee camp designed to support, 3,000 refugees. Though its population had swelled in recent years, by the beginning of 2020, the number of people staying there had reached 13,000. When the Greek government started to slowly lift restrictions in May 2020 after its 42-day national lockdown, many of the measures were left in place, particularly those pertaining to the movement of refugees. While the Greek population were allowed to move around the island during the summer of 2020, the thousands of refugees staying in Moria had restrictions on their freedom of movement extended seven times. By August 2020, aid agencies warned of the potential for problems as conditions had started to deteriorate and discontent stirred. When infections started to appear in Mytilene, just 10 km away from the camp, the Greek government – lacking the capacity and interest in investing in adequate support—simply reiterated the need for the refugees to 'keep their hands clean', 'socially distance' and 'self-isolate' if they felt unwell.[15] In the Facebook forums, we found descriptions from Yiannis, an NGO worker, of how desperate things had become:

> What was previously an unsafe environment in Moria is even more so now.
>
> The hygiene conditions in Moria camp are practically non-existent. Its residents suffer from poor sanitation and nutrition, lack of access to water, severe cases of scabies and lice, untreated or inadequately treated chronic conditions, and limited access to medical aid.

---

[15] Schmitz (2020).

With over 20,000 people in Moria camp and easily half that number living in tents in the olive groves, residents are packed so closely together there is little chance for social isolation or distancing to be successful at reducing an outbreak.

And yet, there is an inadequate response to manage the effects of a potential outbreak in Moria.

Following the relevant official government instructions to take all necessary measures and actions for the protection of the population against coronavirus, the Ministry of Migration and Asylum recently announced the following new security measures to counteract virus threats in all RIC areas on the islands.

- The suspension of all visits of individuals and entities, as well as their actions within the Reception and Identification Centers and hosting structures for at least 14 days. Only those who have a job can now enter.
- Requesting compliance with general hygiene rules with daily cleaning of indoor communal areas with detergents and disinfectants as well as continuous disinfection of the doorknobs of these public areas.

The above measures are alarmingly weak as a response to a pandemic and require serious reconsideration.

The camp remains in desperate need of a plan.

That plan never came, and in September 2020, the virus finally reached the camp. To begin with, incidence rates were low, and this is also the case in some of the world's largest refugee camps—such as Cox's Bazaar in Bangladesh where 900,000 people reside. There, low infection rates of Covid-19 are related to the lack of testing and substandard health infrastructure: indeed, estimates indicate that only 1% of the people in Cox's Bazaar have been tested for Covid-19.[16] Refugees similarly are reluctant to get tested because self-isolation limits their ability to work, even by informal means in these closed social networks such as the camps. This may explain why when 35 people tested positive for Covid-19 in Moria, it became difficult for the authorities to persuade people in the small, cramped conditions to self-isolate. They refused, and while the chain of events is unclear, discontent arose, fires broke out and destroyed the

---

[16] Godin (2020).

whole camp.[17] The lockdowns and restrictions were the 'tipping point' for what looked to be a problem which was approaching its climax. LuLu's friends were unhurt and in the coming weeks, they were given asylum in Germany while others foraged what they could from the camp and were made homeless.[18]

Homeless

Over the last few years, one of America's most significant wealth-generating cities—Las Vegas—criminalised homelessness. In the face of generating $22 billion in 2019 from 169 casinos, the authorities still felt obliged to continue to look for ways to remove homeless people from blighting the city's image of luxury and high-stakes gambling. Even before the pandemic took full hold in America, in November 2019, the city council approved a law that made sitting, resting or even 'lodging' on the curb a crime punishable with a fine of up to $1,000 or, depending on the severity of the sitting, resting or 'lodging', six months in jail. Perhaps not seeing enough results, by February 2020, the authorities were looking for additional methods by which they could expel the 6,500 homeless from the city, having seen efforts fail to support them in accommodation supporting only 1,300.[19]

When Covid-19 started to spread across the State of Nevada and indeed the city, however, the homeless shelters and associated support closed leaving the authorities with a potential crisis. They solved it by rounding up all the homeless people they had wanted to eject from the city, opened up an old car park, painted 2 × 2 m white boxes on the floor and instructed the homeless people to go about being homeless in the dedicated spaces. Even though thousands of hotel rooms lay vacant because no tourists could come to the city, the homeless were bundled into this controlled area and were even 'lucky' enough to receive their own sleeping mat/carpet. While professionals such as social workers,

---

[17] BBC (2020b).
[18] Elabdi (2020).
[19] Hernandez (2020).

psychologists and other staff involved in their care and support were now adhering to lockdown and social distancing measures and unable to support them, the only people prepared to do something to help them were volunteer medical and physician students who turned up when they could.[20]

In America, homelessness had increased year on year for the last five years preceding Covid-19 and had reached around 550,000 by 2019. Most of these people lived on the streets, suffered from severe mental health illness, had addiction problems and were left to find a way to survive in the shadows of one of the world's richest nations. As we may expect, homeless people are disproportionately affected by these sorts of health misfortunes but measures taken to control and manage Covid-19 transmission—mostly lockdowns but also social distancing—removed their access to shelters, food and hygiene practices in closed, congregate settings. In 2020, the U.S. Department of Housing and Urban Development's (HUD) published their *Annual Homeless Assessment Report* (AHAR) to Congress which found that homelessness had increased to 580,466 people representing a 2.2% increase from 2019. Not only were *more people becoming homeless*—likely related to the fact that 30 million people had lost their jobs during the national lockdowns—but the risk of the virus had the potential to further compromise their health. One New York study, for example, found that the mortality rate of homeless people was 75% higher than the city's rate.[21]

In Vancouver, Canada, Masie experienced a similar pattern as Covid-19 public health measures closed up the mental health clinic—where she worked as a mental health support worker—and moved its services online. The clinic was one of a few services which helped homeless people on a daily basis. Being a mental health professional, she said she had first noticed a significant difference in peoples' attitudes and behaviours since the lockdowns, as we noted in Chapter 6, but also across the city the visible markers were evident of a society closed for everyone:

---

[20] Koran (2020).
[21] Coalition for the Homeless (2020).

Isolation from the lockdowns is impacting people. We had some Covid at the end of the winter so it wasn't too bad then the summer came and it was fairly liberating, but now to go back into the restrictions and Christmas coming, it is traumatizing for some people. There is more visible unemployment, restaurants and things closed. But now there are a lot more older residents who won't go out because they are scared, won't go to the community centres. They have to force themselves but things are still quite shut down for them.

From April 2020 to June 2021, the authorities detected 144,473 'cases' and 1,703 'deaths' with/from Covid-19 in British Colombia—the province in which Vancouver sits.[22] However, the lockdowns, social distancing and related public health measures doubled the provincial unemployment rate in British Colombia making it the highest in Canada. The worst period was from December 2019 to April 2020, during the first lockdown, which saw the loss of 406,300 jobs and 122,600 of those losses came in Vancouver.[23] Representative surveys in the city show that nearly half of families (44%) experienced worsening mental health due to job losses and occupational pressures created in the wake of lockdowns.[24]

Masie thinks, however, the homeless have been disproportionately affected by these measures for in the clinic, which is in the "*downtown area*", her predominant client base were people with drug addictions, paranoia and psychotic episodes and schizophrenia. The most significant impact from the lockdowns on her client group was the shift in drug supply to her clients—many of whom were coming to terms with their service support being severed as well as drugs with which they were familiar. Like Las Vegas, the networks disappeared and even familiar improvised zones associated with their daily lives were removed. Together, this produced devastating harms for the homeless as Masie recalls that:

---

[22] BC News (2021).
[23] SAFE (2020).
[24] Gadermann et al. (2021).

In April and May 2020, there were the most fentanyl overdoses there had ever been. Those two months, the first lockdown, it increased exponentially. It was because of the isolation. The drug supply changed as well, so a new drug supply some people were using other things and they didn't know about the strength. Then there was a huge tent city which was populated by homeless people but it was bulldozered and they were told to move on. This disrupted the homeless, they were let loose again, cut off and we had yet more overdoses and suicides.

Oppenheimer Park known as 'tent city' evolved during the summer of 2018 as a consequence of collective protests against rising homelessness and the housing affordability crisis. At one point, 300 people were living in the park which is only just over 10% of Vancouver's homeless population ($n = 2,300$). But the authorities had been looking for a way to close it down in 2019 without success. With the arrival of the lockdowns and social distancing, new regulations and laws were passed helping to eradicate them. People started leaving in March 2020, and by May 2020, it had been totally dismantled.[25] During the same period, service providers across the Downtown area, such as those for which Masie worked, closed community drop-in centres, banned guests from attending or presenting at social housing, and scaled back access to some overdose prevention sites—all in the name of physical distancing to fight the virus. In particular, at the height of these closures and cutbacks during the lockdown, there was a spike in overdose deaths. During March 2020, 30 people were thought to have died from these overdoses which represented the highest estimated death rate in a year.[26]

Across the province of British Colombia (BC), there were 1,726 drug overdose deaths in 2020—*a figure that supersedes by 23 those who had died with/from Covid-19*. This was the collateral harms resulting from the lockdowns and social distancing and the damage continued well into the summer of 2021, as a result of the withdrawal of support for street populations because the overdose numbers have reached 680, and Fentanyl has been detected in 86% of those deaths.[27] Pre-pandemic,

---

[25] Winter (2020).
[26] Winter (2020).
[27] Mangione (2021).

Masie was perhaps seeing a few new clients a week but her service—initially aimed at helping street populations with chronic issues—found itself supporting the wider public for now, post-lockdown, "*every day, 8 or 9 new clients are contacting us, asking and pleading us for help with new problems of unemployment, mental illness, debt, a lot more now because of the Covid-19 lockdown.*" Clients with chronic illnesses—many of whom had died off—were now being replaced by a larger swathe of people who were falling into homelessness and drugs having lost their jobs.

> There is a lot more drug use, a lot more visible shooting up, people are outside lying around having overdosed or vomited somewhere, they have nowhere to go now. This is my every day really. They are not the same client profile, these people are the new unemployed. All the public toilets and cafes are closed so these people just take a shit on the streets. We don't realise that by closing those places in the 'name of public health' means those people can't even wash or go to the toilet.

Indeed, at the time of writing, there were reports of people being found dead outside closed toilets and down back alleyways having overdosed from drugs. Support services for the homeless also disappeared in the UK, as Andy—a local outreach worker in the south of England—reported. Reflecting on the onset of lockdowns and the steady rise in Covid-19 fatalities he said:

> When you watched the TV and watched the death rate go up and up…we were losing hundreds a day to a virus 'of the flu'. It was sold to us at the beginning as like a flu and the scientists were just in the pockets in the government. We lost faith in them quickly. Two each side and a politician in the middle. Nothing the government has said has given us security and all that death toll increased, the social distancing was 2m, then 1.5m then you thought 'what are you meant to be doing'. Meanwhile the support for my lads disappeared. Social services hibernated. They all fucked off and disappeared into a cupboard under the stairs with their laptop and pretended to work.

At the height of the first lockdown, Andy was working on the frontline trying to support homeless people at a time when many other services had shut down. At first, he was positive about the solidarity it produced before recognising how it evaporated:

> I think for the people I work with I can see them getting abandoned [homeless people]. There won't be money for my client group, they will slowly die out. I think things will go backwards. I don't think people will come out of this to a brave new world where people are looked after, cared about and accepted. Lockdown has made us less accepting of people. The humanity is gone. There wasn't much to begin with. And what there was is just shrinking and I don't see us coming out of that to be honest. During lockdown, people were nicer, doing shopping for each other and you don't see anything like that now. We are more self-centred than before. We need to blame somebody. I had hopes in lockdown, I thought we'd come out to a better world but it dried up.

Perhaps Andy can say this because provision and support have not returned to pre-pandemic levels and they probably won't. Almost all street support services like food banks, shelters and mental health support seemed to dry up as governmental efforts were instead made to accommodate people who 'couldn't socially distance'. Yet many times housing services struggled to keep up as the demand for homeless services increased. Despite success in bringing people off the streets and rehousing others from shared facilities, a continuing flow of people appeared or reappeared in need of support throughout the pandemic. Suddenly the authorities not only had to accommodate the *traditional and visible homeless* but also the *hidden homeless*—people staying with family members or friends, living in squats or other insecure accommodation on a temporary basis—as well as *new homeless groups* appearing as a consequence of evictions, relationship breakdowns, domestic violence, unemployment or debt or a combination. It didn't mean, however, that everyone was protected as Andy reflects about a vulnerable client of his called Anna. He described her predicament and the role the lockdown had in it:

> Anna comes from a troubled local family, split in two, nine kids, various dads, half are criminals. Anna got into drugs, left the family home, she started drug dealing, became homeless and I managed to house her. She

lost her tenancy, got into debt and more drugs and her life was in danger when she was kidnapped by a gang, she was then sexually exploited by them and turned up on the streets. She had nowhere to go during the lockdown, no service to access so hooked up with an abusive man. Recently, she lost an eye due to domestic violence: she put up with the level of physical abuse to the point that she was blinded just to have a roof over her head. She is only 27.

While already to some degree damaged and exposed, here lockdowns shut out Anna and forced her into a more precarious and harmful situation which results in her victimisation and the partial loss of her sight. The most recent estimates indicate that since the March 2020 lockdown until June 2021, at least 130,000 households in England were made homeless—and this figure discounts those supported by bans on evictions and job furlough schemes.[28] During the summer of 2021, Andy's local council had made significant efforts to house homeless people but were reluctant to invest in their tenancy and welfare support. Andy felt that it would only be a matter of time before they would be on the streets again—along with a new cohort of homeless who had been supported by job furlough schemes and frozen eviction laws, by adding "*When those disappear – which they will because it is the safety net at the moment – everything will collapse. As soon as one part of this structure goes, the rest will come tumbling down after it…and all the government does is bang on about the people not adhering to the restrictions and blaming them for all this*". For us, the rich data presented here and in the preceding chapters speaks for itself in describing the litany of social harms generated by lockdowns. It is clear to see that the absence of numerous mechanisms of support and security have left many in positions of extreme precarity, with some seeing no other solution than to take their own lives. *If this does not scream social harm, then we don't know what does.*

---

[28] Jayanetti (2021).

References

Actionaid. (2020). *Climate migrants pushed to the brink*. Actionaid.

BBC. (2020b). *Peloton sales surge as virus boosts home workouts*. Available at https://www.bbc.co.uk/news/business-54112461. Accessed on 22 June 2021.

BBC. (2021e). *PM must sack Matt Hancock after affair claims—Labour*. https://www.bbc.co.uk/news/uk-politics-57608716. Accessed on 8 July 2021.

BC News. (2021, June 2021). *B.C. reports fewer than 200 new COVID-19 cases, no deaths*. Cited online at https://bc.ctvnews.ca/b-c-reports-fewer-than-200-new-covid-19-cases-no-deaths-1.5451217

Briggs, D. (2020). *Climate changed: Refugee border stories and the business of misery*. Routledge.

Centre for Sustainable Employment. (2021). *State of working in India: One year on from COVID-19*. Centre for Sustainable Employment at Azim Premji University.

Coalition for the Homeless. (2020). *Age-adjusted mortality rate for sheltered homeless New Yorkers*. Cited online at https://www.coalitionforthehomeless.org/age-adjusted-mortality-rate-for-sheltered-homeless-new-yorkers/

Elabdi, F. (2020, December 20). Surviving in the ruins of Moria. *AlJazeera*. Cited online at https://www.aljazeera.com/features/2020/12/29/surviving-in-the-ruins-of-moria

Gadermann, A. C., Thomson, K. C., Richardson, C. G., (2021). Examining the impacts of the COVID-19 pandemic on family mental health in Canada: Findings from a national cross-sectional study. *BMJ Open, 11*, e042871 https://doi.org/10.1136/bmjopen-2020-042871

Godin, M. (2020, October 9). COVID-19 Outbreaks Are Now Emerging in Refugee Camps. Why Did it Take so Long For the Virus to Reach Them? *Time*. Cited online at https://time.com/5893135/covid-19-refugee-camps/

Goswami, S. (2021, June 3). 200,000 people prosecuted in lockdown: Most fines pending. *Hindustan Times*. Cited online at https://www.hindustantimes.com/cities/others/nearly-200-000-violated-covid-rules-in-lockdown-most-fines-yet-to-be-recovered-101622660408771.html

Hernandez, D. (2020, February 13). War on the poor: Las Vegas's homelessness crackdown takes effect. *The Guardian*. Cited online at https://www.theguardian.com/us-news/2020/feb/13/las-vegas-homeless-sleeping-ban-no-lodging

Idris, I. (2021). *Areas and population groups in Pakistan most exposed to combined effects of climate change, food insecurity and COVID-19.* K4D Helpdesk FCDO.

Jain, R. (2020, March 23). These are the penalties for violating Coronavirus lockdown in India. *Business Insider.* Cited online at https://www.businessinsider.in/india/news/these-are-the-penalties-for-violating-coronavirus-lockdown-in-india/articleshow/74778635.cms

Jayanetti, C. (2021, June 13). At least 130,000 households in England made homeless in pandemic. *The Observer.* Cited online at https://www.theguardian.com/society/2021/jun/13/at-least-130000-households-in-england-made-homeless-in-pandemic

Koran, M. (2020, March 31). Las Vegas parking lot turned into 'homeless shelter' with social distancing markers'. *The Guardian.* Cited online at https://www.theguardian.com/us-news/2020/mar/30/las-vegas-parking-lot-homeless-shelter

Mamun, M. A., & Ullah, I. (2020). COVID-19 suicides in Pakistan, dying off not COVID-19 fear but poverty? The forthcoming economic challenges for a developing country. *Brain Behavior and Immunity, 87,* 163–166. https://doi.org/10.1016/j.bbi.2020.05.028

Mangione, K. (2021, June 1). Warning about increasing toxicity follows another record-breaking month for illicit drug overdoses in B.C. *BC News.* Cited online https://bc.ctvnews.ca/warning-about-increasing-toxicity-follows-another-record-breaking-month-for-illicit-drug-overdoses-in-b-c-1.545 1492

NDTV. (2020, May 6). *40,000 arrested since March 25 for lockdown violation in Bengal: Police.* NDTV. Cited online at https://www.ndtv.com/india-news/coronavirus-lockdown-40-000-arrested-since-march-25-for-lockdown-violation-in-bengal-police-2223968

Ozalp, M. (2020, September 17). In war-torn Syria, the Coronavirus pandemic has brought its people to the brink of starvation. *The Conversation.* Cited online at https://theconversation.com/in-war-torn-syria-the-coronavirus-pandemic-has-brought-its-people-to-the-brink-of-starvation-144794

Pakistan Bureau of Statistics. (2021). *Special survey on evaluating the impact of COVID-19.* . Government of Pakistan

ReliefWeb. (2021, May 4). *Northeastern Syria: Hospitals run out of funds and supplies as second COVID-19 wave hits region.* ReliefWeb. Cited online at https://reliefweb.int/report/syrian-arab-republic/northeastern-syria-hospitals-run-out-funds-and-supplies-second-covid-19

SAFE. (2020). *Job market: The unemployment rate doubles in 2020 in BC due to the pandemic.* Cited online at https://hellosafe.ca/en/newsroom/job-market-british-columbia-2020?utm_source=vancouver+is+awesome&utm_campaign=vancouver+is+awesome&utm_medium=referral

Schmitz, F. (2020, August 20). *Europe's largest refugee camp braces for COVID-19 outbreak.* DW. Cited online at https://www.dw.com/en/europes-largest-refugee-camp-braces-for-covid-19-outbreak/a-54640747

Scroll. (2021, June 3). *Covid lockdown: Over 8,700 people, many of them migrant workers, died along railway tracks in 2020.* Scroll. Cited online at https://scroll.in/latest/996519/covid-lockdown-over-8700-people-many-of-them-migrant-workers-died-along-railway-tracks-in-2020

The Times of India. (2021, January 14). Bengaluru world's fastest growing tech hub, London second: Report. *The Times of India.* Accessed from https://timesofindia.indiatimes.com/business/india-business/bengaluru-worlds-fastest-growing-tech-hub-london-second-report/articleshow/80262770.cms

Winter, J. (2020, May 12). *The last days of oppenheimer park, Vancouver's tent city.* Vice. Cited online at https://www.vice.com/en/article/g5ppvq/the-last-days-of-oppenheimer-park-vancouvers-tent-city

10

The Dichotomy of Lockdowns: Covid Compliance and Restriction Refusal

As we approach 18 months of a global pandemic and imposed public health restrictions, some people have continued to follow the rules while others seemingly haven't. This *dichotomy of lockdowns*, as we describe, appears to have split populations along lines of supposed 'compliers' and 'non-compliers'. In Chapter 6, we charted how this divide evolved and played out in the 'new normal' with the culmination of the *responsible* (complier) vs *negligent* (non-complier) citizens. Yet much of the research produced so far about why people comply simply considers their individual characteristics: the fact that they have 'good morals' or 'specific personality traits' and very few researchers and academics consider the immediate, and wider, social contexts in which compliance and non-compliance takes place. Moreover, there is very little mention about the use of particular ideologies which have been exercised for the purpose of compliance (Chapters 2 and 3). By equal measure, studies on refusal to comply only go as far as to suggest someone is inherently 'faulty' or 'being selfish'. The purpose of this chapter is to provide an understanding of Covid-19 compliance and refusal that captures the complexities and nuances of such behaviour and avoids quite individualistic analyses that have, so far, tended to dominate the current literature.

D. Briggs et al., *Lockdown*,
https://doi.org/10.1007/978-3-030-88825-1_10

Non-compliant: Studies on Compliance

Research conducted since the imposition of restrictions upon daily social life as a result of Covid-19 has tended to adopt a more psychologically informed approach to explaining compliance. Ironically, *they don't comply* with a wider consideration of what we identify as a requisite engagement with the social and ideological context generated by the pandemic and through its intersection with existing social, political and economic conditions. For example, recent research has examined the possible association between public compliance with social distancing measures and the spread of Covid-19 in five US states.[1] The study tracked both human mobility and the daily reproduction rate during the first wave of the country's epidemic (March–May 2020) and found reduced compliance with social distancing measures as businesses opened and stay-at-home orders were lifted. The findings confirm an anticipated correlation between public compliance and virus transmissibility, suggesting social distancing measures are a potentially effective means of preventing transmission. However, this study leaves unanswered the question of why individuals' compliance with ongoing advice to remain socially distant from others waned over time, particularly as parts of American society began to open again.

Other studies have sought to address this issue more directly. Another American research project led by Van Rooij and colleagues[2] utilised an online survey to assess the factors that influence compliance with public health measures. While a range of factors are considered in the study, their findings indicate individuals with 'low self-control' and who display 'greater impulsivity' are less likely to follow measures. Researchers drawing upon data from an ongoing cohort study of young people in Switzerland examined the relationship between compliance with public health measures and prior social and psychological risk factors.[3] Their findings, like Rooij et al.'s, suggest that non-compliance was greater among young people, but particularly among those who had scored

---

[1] H. Liu et al. (2021).
[2] Van Rooj et al (2020).
[3] Nivette et al. (2021).

higher on a range of factors indicative of 'antisocial potential', such as low self-control, reduced shame and guilt, previous engagement in delinquent behaviours, and, association with delinquent peers. In these works, there is no context and no mention of ideology and how it has been politically used to galvanise compliance, control and state subservience (Chapters 2 and 3).

Yet these kind of one-dimensional studies are in abundance. In his work, Chan[4] identifies young people in the US as more likely to not comply with restrictions and speculates that this may be partly attributable to a blasé attitude among this group about the potential dangers of contracting the virus. This could be the case since we know that there is a reduced risk of serious illness following infection among younger age groups. Furthermore, Chan argues that the level of compliance with measures is linked, more fundamentally, to innate 'moral intuitions' that guide human behaviour. A similar study in Brazil arrived at the same results: that individualistic outlooks and personality traits have a prominent role in adherence to measures yet *"it was more challenging to people with a pattern of antisociality"*.[5]

Drawing upon an online survey in the US, Wang et al.[6] found that agreement and compliance with preventive measures was the result of respondents' 'desires to protect others' and a 'sense of moral duty'. Disagreement and non-compliance arose from suspicion and mistrust of authority, which was compounded by unclear or mixed messages from authority figures—certainly, we can see this from the many examples of non-compliance to restrictions by members of the political elite. In addition, some respondents believed measures were unnecessary. Harris'[7] study explored the breaking of lockdown rules and utilised semi-structured interviews with a sample of individuals, many of whom admitted breaching imposed restrictions. Harris focuses upon the techniques of neutralisation employed by respondents to assuage guilt or justify their actions and provides a more detailed insight into this

---

[4] Chan (2020).
[5] Miguel et al. (2020).
[6] Wang et al. (2021).
[7] Harris (2020).

behaviour than other studies, particularly through the qualitative data that it presents. Wang et al. and Harris provide insights into (non) compliance behaviour that takes us beyond aspects of personality and towards issues concerning belief, trust and morality in the contemporary era. However, each stops short of a more thorough examination of compliance against the social context in which it is being demanded. Furthermore, Harris seems to accept the inevitability of deviance as a timeless feature of human behaviour that will be accompanied by attempts to justify it, without perhaps asking why the individuals who reported breaking rules actually did so.

While some of the studies mentioned already usefully identify specific individual traits, attitudes and beliefs that might be more liable to influence one's adherence to public health measures, they are largely shorn of the wider social context that might inform the latter, and individual responses more generally, to sudden and very drastic changes in day-to-day social life. In addition, they display a distinct lack of awareness of the context into which the virus emerged and how this has been moulded by recent historical events. As outlined in the opening chapter, Covid-19 arrived into a world experiencing a range of different harmful crises and characterised by polarities along various social as well as economic lines. In areas of the Global South, particularly in middle and low-income nations, the ability of citizens to comply with restrictions is severely compromised in some cases by virtue of their reliance upon the informal economy for work.[8]

In the absence of sufficient financial support to follow measures fully, suggestions of 'antisociality' among those who displayed non-compliance become less tenable. In the West, the pandemic collided with a period in which belief in the possibility of radical political and economic transformation had waned considerably. For the past four decades, people had been routinely told they were personally responsible for their behaviour and that they were 'free' to pursue their own self-interests.[9] Capitalist realism[10] had narrowed the parameters of political debate concerning the

---

[8] Briggs et al. (2021).
[9] Winlow et al. (2015).
[10] Fisher (2009).

future and plugged vast swaths of Western populations into patterns of individual gratification and habitual consumption in the pursuit of pleasure considered indicative of their 'freedom'. To not acknowledge issues like these, we contend, considerably limits any analysis put forward that tries to explain the complexities of compliant behaviour.

The claim that repeated non-compliance with restrictions is possibly the result of specific personality traits, or a predisposition towards a lack of regard for others, is, to some extent, and in particular cases, a potentially plausible one. Yet, one that, firstly, lacks a requisite appreciation of the fact that human action and behaviour is to some extent a reflection of particular socio-historical conditions; and, secondly, omits a nuanced appreciation of potentially complex reasons informing compliance behaviour. As alluded to already, it would not be realistic, nor plausible, to assume that those who broke restrictions did so always and purely for 'selfish reasons', or as a result of particular 'personality traits'. We must also be mindful of the fact that compliance, in all likelihood, was possibly, for many, intermittent, with people following the rules some of the time, but not necessarily consistently. As subjects of capitalism, individuals *"cling feverishly to the image of their own dissatisfaction and to the promise...of a way to escape dissatisfaction"*[11] through repeated consumption and enjoyment. The many reported examples of police breaking up house parties, barbecues, illegal raves and other gatherings[12] while lockdown restrictions were in place, serves as an important reminder of the power of desire and of the belief in contemporary capitalism's promise to satisfy it. The removal of many opportunities to engage in what had been accepted consumption habits and practices symbolic of life under advanced neoliberal capitalism and a marker of social status and inclusion[13] is an issue that requires consideration here.

Furthermore, it remains questionable to what extent political management, or perhaps evident mis-management, of the pandemic affected levels of compliance. For instance, to what extent did the revelations in the UK about the former Prime Ministerial aide Dominic Cummings'

---

[11] McGowan (2016).
[12] Murray and Mistlin (2021).
[13] Hall et al. (2008).

lack of adherence to measures impact upon the public's perception and subsequent adherence to measures? Similarly, how did individuals interpret public health advice and guidance, as well as media coverage about the severity of the virus? Were people basing compliance on their own experiences of the virus? And, to what extent did this impact upon adherence to imposed measures? There are evidently, then, many potential psychological, but also crucially socio-contextual factors that influence Covid-19 compliance and refusal that social science, thus far, has not properly acknowledged. This is what we try to grapple with in the following sections for varying levels of compliance/non-compliance with restrictions reflect highly nuanced explanations and justifications for doing so.

Stories of Compliance and Refusal

Kate was aged in her mid-50s at the time of interview and was working as a Business Trainer in the North West of England. We spoke to Kate as the second wave of Covid-19 infections started to grip the UK in the autumn of 2020. Kate believed both businesses and people had been badly affected by the arrival of Covid-19 and displayed an awareness of the inadvertent harms from the measures that were taken in response, particularly the "*sense of confinement*" resulting from lockdown, which she believed had "*really crushed some people*". As she is in the business of training, she has seen first-hand many of her clients struggle organisationally and with their own mental health. This prompted her to design courses on "*repair, introspection and resilience*" to try to support those experiencing difficulties as a result of the restrictions, while also striving to maintain a viable business and livelihood.

However, Kate sought to position her sense of duty and desire to help others during these difficult times in stark contrast to what she described as an evident and, from her perspective, growing tendency towards self-interest and selfishness among other people, as well as repeated examples of government incompetence. Non-compliers were not following rules for the greater good and welfare of the community. The resurgence of the virus at the time of Kate's interview seemed to be indicative, she believed, of this sense of apathy about the well-being of others and evidence that lessons had not been learned from the devastation caused by the first wave of infections. For Kate, many people evidently didn't care and the gradual rise in cases was not just the result of the virus' behaviour, but symptomatic of a wider malaise within the country rooted in recent tumultuous and divisive events, such as the 2008 economic recession and Brexit (Chapters 1 and 2). Kate was aware of the social and economic inequalities within contemporary Britain and believed "*privilege is advantageous now*" in enabling individuals to insulate themselves from the virus and its socio-economic impact (Chapters 4 and 5). Expressing the point quite bluntly, Kate regarded the UK as a "*shithole*" that had become increasingly characterised by "*poverty, urban deprivation, children suffering, county lines opening up. More violent crime, division*". She continued to express her feelings about Covid-19's interaction with this context that she described:

> Greater Manchester is in local lockdown...so I can't visit people. But people don't care. The measures don't work, people don't care. They should have sacked Cummings earlier, but look it left the door open. People thought 'they know more than we do so it is safe'. It is polarised. There are a lot of people like me, cautious, and we share the same sort of values which is why we get on. My neighbours don't care...people like them just don't care about the rules and that has been going on for months. I think society has been polarised like this for some time and I don't think it is related to class. The mindset is 'all about me' and 'you're on your own'. This came about during Brexit and has not disappeared. It has increased the animosity, demonization, hatred and antagonism. It is really sad this kind of society. People just don't give a toss.

Kate concedes that Covid-19 is more of a risk to the elderly and those with underlying health conditions, but feels it is also a potential risk for other groups because, she reported, knowing people who became seriously ill after contracting the virus. In the main then, her compliance comes from the experiences of people around her who have had Covid-19 because it did not seem to be related to following media updates. Despite differing levels of risk experienced by different groups, she feels that people have adopted, but also rejected the measures because the *"media have not been impartial"* at a time when *"people want to know how do they make sense of it."* She added:

> The media have let us down because of their political agendas, they want to sell they want the clicks, the drama, crisis, hatred, distortion of fact. Social media is just as bad. It is a quagmire of misinformation. BBC is supposed to be impartial, but it isn't. Where is the voice of reason?

Kate's anger and frustration were palpable during the interview. And in her anger, at the situation, she reasoned that the political (mis) management of Covid-19 may have an ulterior, sinister motive:

> If this is about social cleansing, then 'great' surely they will be thinking [government and powerful businesses]. You cut the social care bill. The elderly, the frail, the vulnerable, the socially challenged, people who require intense care we could do without because they cost money. How does having them in society increase the potential business has to increase profit and shareholding? Well they don't.

As we write, Kate still won't go to public places unless they are clean but believes that we should learn to *"assimilate it and work with it* [the virus]". Her position is changing because of the drawn-out nature of the management of the virus. As the country leaves many of its more severe lockdown restrictions behind in the summer of 2021, she reflects:

> I had hoped to start with that there would be a seismic shift in society, but now I am not as optimistic. Behaviour change takes a long time. There are days where I am optimistic when I think humans are resilient and people are caring, but there are more days now where I see people are selfish.

Kate would probably think Carley, another of our participants, could possibly be regarded as 'selfish' because of her supposed 'non-compliance'. Aged in her mid-30s, Carley worked closely with vulnerable adults in the UK. For some time, Carley doubted many of the government and the media's claims about Covid-19 having read up about what many of her friends and colleagues were calling 'conspiracy theories'. Despite this, and having stopped talking to various family members, she has for some time now attended protests in London against the lockdowns and vaccinations where she claims she saw "*people arrested for no reason*". Both Sky News and the BBC on "*many occasions when they have been bothered to report the protests*" only talk about "*a few hundred*". Yet she claims though that there have been "*hundreds of thousands*" in attendance. Indeed, on numerous occasions mainstream media has instead tended to crank up fear about large groups of people socialising without masks instead of focusing on the inherent discontent about the way in which Covid-19 restrictions govern our lives.

> *Carley*: I risk my job every time I go down and protest, it is so important we keep our freedoms. I have never been so passionate about something than this.

Carley apparently sees above the ideology and associates the collective compliance as a darker form of social control which has the potential to spiral out of control in the future. Despite the threat of losing her job, throughout 2021, Carley continued to attend protest events where "*nobody wore masks and there was no social distancing*". While she admits to being initially worried about the virus at the inception of the pandemic, when several of her friends contracted it and said it was nothing more than "*a bad flu*", she became increasingly suspicious about the claims of its severity. Non-compliance is not about personality traits but about how she is subjectively framing the 'risk' against specific contextual information. When her friend showed her some documents about The Great Reset, Carley became further convinced that under the veil of the pandemic core aspects of socio-economic life were being fundamentally altered. Yet, Carley feels the few remaining spaces to say something about it are in the street given that online spaces seem to have been compromised by big tech agendas (Chapter 6):

> I can't be on the Facebook, I am not allowed, my posts are removed, people are trolling me. It is all abuse and criticism and no one is allowed to have an alternative view. Nothing is allowed. All 'anti vaxxers' comments are removed.

She has not seen many friends nor work colleagues for a year. Recently, a colleague of Carley's called her "*selfish*" because she "*didn't wear a mask*". Many of the Covid-19 restrictions intrude on some of the most basic appointments and treatments for some of her clients. At the height of the second UK wave, Carley described the following situation experienced by one of her clients:

> Most colleagues are completely brainwashed. We are not allowed to talk to the elderly clients about it. One of my patients is an 82-year-old man he has been told he has cancer on the phone, no real consultation and his daughter is crying her eyes out. They can't go to hospital as its all Covid. It is important to see my clients but many are not in the day care now, people have died because they have not had the treatment. Deaths of neglect. People not receiving the services they need. Nothing to do with Covid. People who have refused cancer treatments, had clients who have had heart attacks and don't go to A&E, we are told to make appointments for medical emergencies. It's not the NHS, it's the National Covid Service.

Carley's 'non-compliance' therefore also stems from the injustice the public health measures do to other people in need of treatments as well as the apparent lack of care shown to these vulnerable people. What most amazes Carley is the level of "*compliance*" and how she has seen many of her friends, family and colleagues fall into line with public health messages, which, she tried to reason, seemed to come from nowhere:

> It is the compliance which is amazing. A year ago, if someone told you, you couldn't get hospital appointments for life threatening conditions, you couldn't travel, you couldn't hug people, you couldn't go to eat in a restaurant or to a pub, you wouldn't have believed them. In fact, you wouldn't have agreed to it, would you?

Jason, another UK resident who was employed in the construction sector, was, like Carley, similarly suspicious of imposed public health measures and called into question their legitimacy. Furthermore, for Jason, measures designed to reduce transmission in public were not only contradictory, but easy to evade and circumvent, as he explained:

Went to a local pub last week for my auntie's birthday...I turned up with my girlfriend, wasn't much hassle, wasn't wearing a mask, like I normally don't. They half-heartedly said track and trace? I already had the fake track and trace thing opened up, they didn't check it...We walked through to the back no problems, met up with my family. Was all well, was happy to see how close to normal it was. One thing that made me laugh was we were all sitting under a gazebo, and people were walking outside the gazebo to have a fag, masks en route. I was sitting there smoking as I normally do and thinking...'We're already outside for fucks sake?' Is this the level of fucking compliance we're at? So, most of the night I went to the toilet unchallenged without a mask, the bar staff were polite, all good. Nice atmosphere in the pub, then the guvnor of the pub arrived. It soon turned sour. I walked into the pub to go to the toilet like I did all night and got stopped, *"where's your mask?"* I said I'm exempt and carried on about my business. Bear in mind, throughout the night, none of the staff were wearing masks inside the pub, and she and her husband who apparently own the pub weren't either. And she asked me again on my way out. I said what anyone else would say, *"where's yours?"* And, get this, she said *"well I own the pub don't I"*. What? So, you're exempt from these fucking stupid nonsensical rules you're making us abide by 'because you own the pub' yeah? Is that a fucking joke or what? This is what happens when you have a government that has manipulated people in society that can have a job as insignificant as shelf stacking in Tesco, let alone a pub landlord, and turned them into fascist elitists that think they have the authority to have control over your autonomy. This isn't just simple government policy dictating your life, this is social conditioning that, through their record smashing media spending and marketing budgets 10 times over, the government is achieving.

Non-compliance here is based on Jason's interpretation of the illogical design of the public health measures which contradict each other: consequently, Jason rationalises that *measures like mask wearing produce a false sense of protection because the supposed risk exposure remains.* Yet even if the measures may seem extreme or contradictory, compliance is achieved through what we have been told about 'respect for other peoples' welfare' (Chapter 3). On the other side of the globe, from all of these people, retired couple, Geoff and Jan, live in a rural town in Queensland, Australia, several hours drive from the nearest large city. The town, where around 120,000 people live, is the main service centre for surrounding rural communities. Despite this, during the lockdowns, *"schools closed down, some businesses went bust"* said Jan. Even though Geoff and Jan live in an area that has recorded very few positive cases (to their knowledge there have been two confirmed cases), they are concerned about the virus and follow all the governmental public health measures:

> *Geoff*: Big cities have been locked down here. People take it very seriously here, there are a few seeing it as a hoax, but that is a minority. Only one state in Australia that has large numbers even though Australia has the highest land mass, Victoria where Sydney is there was lots of Covid and they shut down, shut borders, a lot of deaths there but we don't have the same population. Borders just recently opened. In our State, Queensland, we have at the moment ten cases. In our town, we have only had two cases since the pandemic. Those people came from the cities. We are an island, we can control our borders. Very restricted numbers.

In a recent report from the Australian Strategic Policy Institute, the Australian government was described as managing the *"crisis as well as any country has, and far better than most"*.[14] O'Sullivan et al.[15] argue similarly that the Australian government's imposition of social distancing, alongside an effective testing programme and the country's geographical isolation have contributed to this success relative to other nations. At the time of writing, the country has recorded 30,378 cases in total, and 910 deaths have been attributed to the disease.[16] While in the state of Queensland, 1,686 cases of Covid-19 had been recorded.[17] As Geoff explained, infections in the country seem to have been largely concentrated in more densely populated urban centres. Yet in reality, the risk is low for Geoff and Jan because they live in a rural, open space: they comply to the measures though because they are approaching the 'most-at-risk' age bracket as they are aged 72 and 73 respectively. In June 2021, in the city of Sydney, measures including a stay-at-home order for particular parts of the city were re-introduced amid an outbreak of the

---

[14] Coyne and Jennings (2020).
[15] O'Sullivan et al. (2020).
[16] Australian Government Department of Health (2021).
[17] Queensland Government (2021).

reportedly more transmissible Delta variant.[18] Yet, in the relatively rural area where Geoff and Jan reside with no such dense populations, and few Covid-19 cases, they display strong compliance by both themselves and much of the local population:

Interviewer: How were people behaving out of lockdown?

Geoff: Few cases of people flocking to beaches on hot days but they were the minority, but people are still cautious like in the supermarket people still dodge around you. They are keeping their distance. The toilet roll aisle and pasta and rice were depleted. You couldn't buy things in the supermarket in the beginning.

Interviewer: How has it affected social relations in the community?

Jan: Not for us, but in the big cities people were getting cabin fever. Much more mental health problems and the economy with the government doing the job seeker plan but I think our generation, we are retired, we are doing ok but young people and those with jobs it would be terribly difficult.

In general, when we compare these levels of infections and deaths to other countries, Australia seems to have done well yet it has instigated the same measures: lockdowns, social distancing, masks, strict self-isolation, border closures, etc. Hardly anyone has died of Covid-19 in Australia in 2021, so could we say the measures work? Is compliance better because of this? This is clearly something pending further investigation, but the problem the country is now facing is that it is difficult to move forward without responding kneejerk to changes to the 'covid normal'. When, for example, 100 'cases' of the Delta variant was detected in Sydney, the country was on the verge of plunging back into lockdowns and mask wearing became obligatory again.[19]

There are also the consequences of lockdowns and other measures to consider in this. O'Sullivan et al.[20] consider some of the emerging evidence on resultant disruption to schooling in Australia as a result of the pandemic and suggest it "*is exacerbating socio-economic differentials in school achievement and proving especially disadvantageous for people*

---

[18] BBC (2021a).

[19] BBC (2021b).

[20] O'Sullivan et al. (2020).

with pre-existing learning difficulties". Furthermore, despite praise for the government's management of the pandemic, early suggestions are that the economic impact will be considerable. In May 2020, almost 600,000 jobs were reported to have been lost in Australia.[21] In contrast to many of our participants' criticisms of the media during the pandemic, Jan stated that Australian *"media did a good job, wasn't scare tactics the government tried to persuade us to be responsible. We had someone reporting every day on the statistics so we followed it"*. Geoff and Jan are not morally superior in this respect because compliance comes from *(a) concern about their age and health, (b) general conformity all around them complimented by ideological messaging and (c) the frequency of exposure and commitment to public health advice*. Yet, at any moment, they anticipate that there might be a sudden Covid-19 wave:

> *Geoff*: There is social distance here, limited numbers at pubs, you can still go but it is limited number and you have to sit apart. All the shops have sanitizers at their doors as precaution - we have been lucky so far as it could hit us at any moment.

Their compliance is bolstered by the collective adherence to the measures in the town—as in the people they know and see around them also practice the same behaviours, no one comes in, no one goes: it is, if you like, a perfect 'new normal' scenario. This is all augmented by the symbolisms of the virus risk in public spaces, in this case sanitizers. This said, with the disruption to education and labour markets coming from the lockdowns, Geoff and Jan foresee a potentially bleak future for young people and think that *"without a vaccine the world will take a long time to recover"*.

Under political regimes in oppressively governed countries, perhaps needing to appear part of the global initiative against Covid-19, there was a sense that public health measures were used as a means to achieve 'global compliance' in order to access funding. At the time of interview, Dave, who we met in Chapter 3, spoke about what he felt was a distinct lack of planning or knowledge of how best to manage the virus, claiming that many of the states that fall under his geographical

---

[21] Ibid.

remit are simply *"copying what the West is doing"*. He suggested that even when *"lockdown measures are there, because of structural healthcare deficiencies, many people just carry on"*. Those healthcare deficiencies are well-documented and have for many years now hindered the ability of states across the African continent to respond adequately to the outbreak of HIV/AIDS, the persistence of Malaria, and the re-emergence of diseases that had previously been brought under control, such as TB.[22] In the light of these deficiencies, severe warnings were issued concerning the potential impact of Covid-19 across the continent; however, public health experts have been left puzzled by fewer reported cases and deaths than first anticipated.[23]

Dave too acknowledged the fear that had initially gripped some public health experts as Covid-19 cases began to appear across the continent, but that this has proved, so far, to have been misplaced. For Dave, public health measures in response to Covid-19 have acted as a smokescreen to enable more oppressive social control over electorates (Chapter 6):

Dave: In Central Africa, there is low-level impact of covid-19 and there is an explanation it is all about systems and how they can cope putting in measures like social distancing, making sure people are wearing masks and ensure people are not gathering but these are practiced differences. Most countries with developed health systems they are more likely to have them in place and police them. The countries in central Africa particularly, as it could lead to further unrest.

Interviewer: Do they see it as a grave disease?

Dave: There is a great divide. A high number of people, the older ones, believe in Covid. The younger ones do not really believe in it. 75% of people in Africa are under 25 so these people are not going to really experience it and they have stronger immune systems compared to people in the Western world. This is the divide. But most people really are not worried about it. The warning signs were wrong as everyone thought the Africans would be badly affected but it is one of the least affected continents. Is that the weather? The ecosystem? The population? I don't know, but what is clear is that you have a lot of people who don't believe in the same severity as the Western media try to paint

---

[22] Sama and Nguyen (2008).
[23] Maeda and Nkengasong (2021).

it. The Western media has run away from reporting Covid here because it is related to some conflict which already exists – the media are interested in conflict in Africa not Covid as there is no story here to tell. The West are doing test and trace because of the health systems. But this is not the case in Africa, no one is overwhelmed here. Every decision about the West is based on science and behaviour of the virus. The reality here is that hospitals are not overwhelmed. People are not dying of Covid by their hundreds.

Dave's observations through his experiences of working in both urban and rural areas of the region during the pandemic led him to feel that compliance with measures, rather than being for the purpose of avoiding contraction of the virus, was, in some cases, the result of an instrumental desire to continue to access shops and amenities (see Chapter 3). Dave also suggested that the imposition of measures was driven by the desire of States in the region to demonstrate international compliance as a means of global participation:

> African society is built on these close social interactions and Covid has been the elephant in the room and everyone is talking about it, the government policies are influenced by international organisations and IMF and WHO and they would see them as not doing well so it becomes like a standard of measuring a country's global compliance. They are things forced on everyone when only a few should do it. What needs to happen is that they need to provide your own measures according to your own version of the problem. There shouldn't be a blanket strategy.

Equally, as we have seen in Chapter 4 and 9, compliance with lockdowns in societies where many citizens rely on the informal economy for work is unrealistic and potentially very harmful, particularly when people have no choice but to leave the house to earn money. Since millions of Africans survive like this, Dave was not surprised that lockdowns seemed to have had little relevance for many people:

> Africans are not accustomed to a system of being locked down, to stay at home and not go anywhere, systems are not structured to support this as people need to leave their house to work, to get food. Lockdowns

really impacted economies, as people rely on small businesses and are not dependent on the state and this economic system has been highly impacted so it was not going to be sustainable. It should not have been a copy and paste and other countries had it more relaxed. If you lockdown, you have to have a solution to open up otherwise you are just incubating the virus.

So, compliance as much as non-compliance with public health measures can't simply be reduced to predisposition or personality traits. Neither is a focus upon justifications or neutralisations for breaching imposed restrictions sufficient either. For us, a complex interaction between the conditions of day-to-day life that emerged as a result of the pandemic's effects and the pre-pandemic social context, evidently informed how people made sense of the demands placed upon them and others. And, as expected, the different nation State contexts in which our respondents were based were relevant, to some extent, in understanding their partic-ular views and their perceptions of others' level of compliance with health measures.

While the 'refusal' of the likes of Carley and Jason might be described by some as a product of selfishness or an antisocial personality, we argue this is reductionist and neglects the fundamental basis of human subjectivity as an emergent and interactive process between the mate-rial body and the external symbolic order[24] (Chapter 1). In short, *people make these decisions based on their particular personal emotional, social and economic situations in tandem with the way in which they interpret the depiction of risk attached to Covid-19 as well as their relationship with wider society and its political apparatus. It is important, therefore, to posi-tion their refusal in context.* The demands for social distancing and the temporary sacrifice of personal liberties and freedoms run counter to the values of Western liberal democracies, which have, for several decades now, exhorted the virtue of personal responsibility and autonomy over reliance upon the State; a stark contrast to societies in parts of the Far East, for example, that were reportedly able to achieve greater compliance

---

[24] Hall (2012) and Hall and Winlow (2015).

among their respective populations.[25] To suddenly demand that citizens should surrender what they have for decades been told are their fundamental rights and way of life was never likely to be met with universal acceptance. In addition, the primacy placed upon Western citizens as consumers, and the role of consumer culture in the maintenance and satisfaction of desire, are enormous and powerful forces against which sudden, and unprecedented in recent times, public health measures were expected to contend and subdue. Yet even this short, sharp, shock to the way of life under neoliberalism has had extraordinary consequences for everyone, which is why lockdowns have left in their wake profound forms of residue as we continue to navigate the 'new normal'.

References

Australian Government Department of Health. (2021). *Coronavirus (COVID-19) current situation and case numbers*. https://www.health.gov.au/news/health-alerts/novel-coronavirus-2019-ncov-health-alert/coronavirus-covid-19-current-situation-and-case-numbers

BBC. (2021a). *COVID: Sydney city centre and Bondi beach to enter lockdown*. https://www.bbc.co.uk/news/world-australia-57590969. Accessed 25 June 2021.

BBC. (2021b, June 28). Australia COVID: Outbreaks emerge across country in 'new phase' of pandemic. *BBC*. Cited online at https://www.bbc.com/news/world-australia-57633457

Briggs, D., Ellis, A., Lloyd, A., & Telford, L. (2021). *Researching the COVID-19 pandemic: A critical blueprint for the social sciences*. Policy Press Rapid Response Series.

Chan, E. (2020). Moral foundations underlying behavioural compliance during the COVID-19 pandemic. *Personality and individual Differences, 171*, 110463. https://doi.org/10.1016/j.paid.2020.110463

Coyne, J., & Jennings, P. (2020). *After Covid-19: Australia and the world rebuild*. Australian Strategic Policy Institute.

Fisher, M. (2009). *Capitalist realism: Is there no alternative?* Zero.

---

[25] Schwab and Malleret (2020).

Hall, S. (2012). *Theorizing Crime and Deviance.* Sage.

Hall, S., & Winlow, S. (2015). *Revitalizing criminological theory: Towards a New ultra- realism.* Routledge.

Hall, S., Winlow, S., & Ancrum, C. (2008). *Criminal identities and consumer culture.* Willan.

Harris, L. C. (2020). Breaking lockdown during lockdown: A neutralization theory evaluation of misbehaviour during the COVID 19 pandemic. *Deviant Behaviour.* https://doi.org/10.1080/01639625.2020.1863756

Liu, H., Chen, C., Cruz-Cano, R., Guida, J. L., & Lee, M. (2021). Public compliance with social distancing measures and SARS-CoV-2 Spread: A quantitative analysis of 5 states. *Public Health Reports, 136* (4), 475–482.

Maeda, J. M., & Nkengasong, J. N. (2021). The puzzle of the COVID-19 pandemic in Africa. *Science Magazine, 371*(6524), 27–28.

McGowan, T (2016). *Capitalism and desire: The psychic cost of free markets.* Columbia University Press.

Miguel, F., Machado, G., Pianowski, G., & Carvalho, L. (2020). Compliance with containment measures to the COVID-19 pandemic over time: Do antisocial traits matter? *Personality and Individual Differences, 168,* 1–8. https://doi.org/10.1016%2Fj.paid.2020.110346

Murray, J., & Mistlin, A. (2021). Police report rise in large COVID lockdown parties in England. *The Guardian.* https://www.theguardian.com/uk-news/2021/feb/19/police-report-rise-in-large-covid-lockdown-parties-in-england. Accessed 28 June 2021.

Nivette, A. et al. (2021). Non-compliance with COVID-19-related public health measures among young adults in Switzerland: Insights from a longitudinal cohort study. *Social Science & Medicine, 268,* 1– 9. https://doi.org/10.1016/j.socscimed.2020.113370

O'Sullivan, D., Rahamathulla, M., & Pawar, M. (2020). The impact and implications of COVID-19: An Australian perspective. *The International Journal of Community and Social Development, 2*(2), 134–151.

Queensland Government. (2021). *Coronavirus (COVID-19).* https://www.qld.gov.au/health/conditions/health-alerts/coronavirus-covid-19 (last accessed 28th June 2021)

Sama, M. T., & Nguyen, V. K. (2008). Governing the health system in Africa. In M. Sama & V. K. Nguyen (Eds.), *Governing health systems in Africa.* Council for the Development of Social Science Research in Africa.

Schwab, K., & Malleret, T. (2020). *COVID 19: The great reset.* World Economic Forum.

Van Rooj, B., Brujin, A., Folmer, C., Kooistra, E., Kuiper, M., Brownlee, M., Olthuis, E., & Fine, A. (2020) *Compliance with COVID-19 mitigation measures in the United States*. C- Lab.

Wang, D., Marmo-Roman, S., Krase, K., & Phanord, L. (2021). Compliance with preventative measures during the COVID-19 pandemic in the USA and Canada: Results from an online survey. *Social Work in Health Care*. https://doi.org/10.1080/00981389.2020.1871157

Winlow, S., Hall, S., Treadwell, J., & Briggs, D. (2015). *Riots and political protest*. Routledge.

11

The Ideological Residue from Lockdown

While the harmful effects of both Covid-19 and the measures taken in response are becoming clearer, there remain many important questions about the respective legacies of the public health measures, in particular, the lockdowns. Already it is becoming evident from research studies that the diversion of significant health resources to address Covid-19, combined with the instruction to remain at home, reduced screening activity and treatment for other health conditions, such as cancer[1] and heart disease.[2] This raises the possibility of increased mortality from these conditions, as well as greater pressure upon health services as much in the immediate future as the medium to long-term. Covid-19 has, to date, been identified as the cause or contributor of mortality in several million people globally. While the discrepancy between recorded 'cases' and 'deaths' indicates many have recovered, and do recover following infection, surviving Covid-19 is evidently not the end of the matter for some. For instance, there is considerable uncertainty around the prognosis of what is being termed as 'long-covid' or 'post-covid syndrome'.

---

[1] Maringe et al. (2020).

[2] Fersia et al. (2020).

While the symptoms of long-covid seem to be debilitating in themselves, there are concerns about its potential impact upon mortality and organ functioning. A recent study of Covid patients discharged from NHS hospitals in England matched with a control group, found they had increased risk of mortality, readmission to hospital and multiorgan dysfunction.[3] Notwithstanding, the immediate and longer-term physiological consequences of Covid-19 remain a significant issue, not just for physical well-being, but peoples' psychological well-being, particularly as restrictions begin to ease across a number of countries while the virus remains in circulation.

As various societies now start to take tentative steps to open up again, how Covid-19 could or should be managed will likely be subject to intense, and likely fierce, contestation. Vaccine programmes are now hastily underway across the world. Indeed, British Prime Minister Boris Johnson ended the most severe restrictions within England in July 2021 and, thereafter, suggested we must learn to coexist with the virus. However, even as we write, division is emerging around the world concerning this strategy and whether masks and social distancing, for example, should remain compulsory indoors, on public transport and in confined spaces. Many remain deeply fearful of contracting the virus, and with perhaps good reason if they comprise groups identified as high-risk of experiencing severe illness. Yet, others are signalling their desire to return to a social life devoid of restrictions, citing collateral damage and the approval and distribution of vaccines as sufficient justification for doing so. The sum of all the different fears concerning the presence of the virus and the harmful effects of measures taken to contain it present significant challenges and even possible threats to collective well-being and social cohesion. This is what we identify as the *residue* from the trauma of the lockdowns and pandemic more widely. By *residue*, we refer to the conditions wrought by the impact of the pandemic and lockdown experience, which continue to affect conditions of daily life and conceptions of our collective future. In the emerging aftermath, what can we now see or what is left?

---

[3] Ayoubkhani et al. (2021).

Opening up...

On the 25th of June 2021, British tabloid newspaper, The Sun, published images of British politician and Health Secretary, Matt Hancock, secretly kissing his aide Gina Coladangelo in his Whitehall office.[4] The newspaper claimed the images were captured on 6 May 2021, when strict restrictions on social distancing, including indoor mixing with those outside of one's household, were in place across the country. Hancock immediately received the backing of Prime Minister Boris Johnson, who insisted he would not remove him from his role as Health Secretary. However, predictably, much political and public outrage at the images followed. Chairwoman of the Labour Party, Annaliese Dodds, described Hancock's position as *"hopelessly untenable"* and said that *"Boris Johnson should sack him."*[5] Outspoken and controversial TV presenter and former newspaper editor, Piers Morgan, called Hancock *"outrageous and pathetic"* on Twitter, and insisted he should resign immediately.[6] Within 24 hours of the release of the images, under mounting political and public pressure, Hancock resigned and was swiftly replaced by former Home Secretary Sajid Javid. Days later, on the 28th of June 2021, amid a considerable rise in recorded positive Covid-19 cases, the newly appointed Health Secretary addressed the House of Commons to discuss restrictions which were due to cease on the 19th of July:

> ...in truth: no date we choose comes with zero-risk for Covid. We know we cannot simply eliminate it – we have to learn to live with it. We also know that people and businesses need certainty. So, we want every step to be irreversible. And make no mistake, Mr Deputy Speaker: the restrictions to our freedoms must come to an end."[7]

It is difficult not to regard this event as symbolic of the end of the British state's legitimacy on Covid-19: the last act that finally eroded already

---

[4] Pattinson and Cole (2021).

[5] BBC (2021e).

[6] O'Connor, R (2021).

[7] Javid, S (2021).

fragile public good-will and confidence, upon which large-scale adherence to restrictions crucially relies (Chapter 10). With Javid's references to the effectiveness of the vaccine programme and the imposing 'wall of immunity' reportedly now within the population during his speech to the Commons, certainly, the new Health Secretary's statement seemed to attempt to position the move to reduce restrictions further as predicated on successful management of the pandemic and that oft used phrase: 'following the science'. Yet, it remains difficult to fully separate this latest example of flagrant disregard of distancing rules by one of those responsible for making them, from the conviction that restrictions must end despite evidence of increasing transmission within the community. Indeed, as some of our participants recognised, these kinds of 'above-the-law' actions were detrimental to trust in government and compliance to public health measures (Chapter 10). The aftermath of this event has further exposed the fault lines that had begun to appear over the course of the pandemic.

Importantly, the announcement seems to have already split opinion considerably, inciting divisions that, as we have argued in previous chapters, have gradually fomented on several fronts throughout the pandemic. Labour's Shadow Secretary for Health and Social Care, Jonathan Ashworth, accused the government of acting too quickly and demanded that the requirement to wear face coverings in shops and on public transport not be relaxed.[8] Labour's leader, Sir Keir Starmer, called the plans "*reckless.*"[9] In a letter to the Lancet, a group of 122 scientists and doctors described the intention to remove restrictions on the 19th of July as 'dangerous and premature'.[10] While several scientific advisers on the government's behavioural science subcommittee warned of the dangers of ending restrictions amid the ongoing roll out of vaccines, arguing that it would lead to greater hospital admissions and possibly the emergence of new variants.[11] We now see this division among the wider public in response to the announced ending of most restrictions and

[8] Nanan-Sen (2021).
[9] BBC (2021f).
[10] Wise (2021).
[11] Allegretti and Geddes (2021).

the reversion to personal responsibility on the matter of mask wearing and social distancing. As we write, conflict continues among the British public over the efficacy of face coverings and the moral fibre of those who indicate a refusal to continue wearing them, or who display vaccine hesitancy: 'anti-vaxxers' as they are known in the Facebook forums.

So far though, evidence remains relatively partial on how individuals will behave as societies begin to open up. Recently, Ipsos, in partnership with the WEF, surveyed adults in nine countries, including the UK, in an attempt to gauge their intentions as societies begin to lift more restrictions.[12] The report indicates some variability across the nine countries sampled, but suggests that, *once vaccinated, around three quarters intend to continue practicing social distancing and will wear face coverings.* Results were more mixed across the sample of countries on the matter of engaging in public activities after vaccination, such as attending sporting events or dining in restaurants, with greater hesitancy evident in some countries than others. Allowing thousands of football supporters into stadiums during the delayed Euro 2020 competition, with accompanying images circulating in national and international media of supporters not practicing social distancing have also drawn fierce criticism from some. Prof Stephen Reicher of the UK government's behavioural science subcommittee, for example, suggested that allowing large numbers of fans into Wembley stadium to watch England matches sends a message that *"the danger has gone away."*[13] Having been vaccinated, perhaps people believe they are protected against future infection.

As the British State seeks to seemingly retract from the greater role it had assumed in the daily life of citizens since March 2020, through recourse to notions of individual responsibility and autonomy, it is fair to say that it effectively leaves a populace divided in crucial respects over the perceived threat of the virus and the appropriate level of mitigation that should be taken against it. In the void generated, lies the genuine possibility for the further deepening of harmful societal divisions, particularly as people seek to orientate themselves to the new

---

[12] Fleming (2021).
[13] Blackall (2021).

demands of social life post-lockdown and post-vaccination, while the virus still remains in circulation. Indeed, at the time of writing, we seem to be in a crucial moment as other countries seek to shed more restrictive measures even if debates begin to re-emerge concerning how Covid-19 should be managed and which, and to what extent, restrictions should remain features of daily life should 'cases', 'hospitalisations' or 'deaths' increase.

What will then remain in this aftermath? The Scottish government, for example, has confirmed legal restrictions will cease on 9 August 2021, but what they refer to as 'baseline measures', such as wearing face coverings, would "*continue for a longer period of time.*"[14] In Spain, restrictions come and restrictions go, and measures are withdrawn and then returned as the government seems to configure the most effective combination of interventions available to them with a seeming lack of knowledge around whether they do much to infection rates which irrespectively rise and fall, then rise then fall.

Such inconsistency between nation states in their approach to post-lockdown social life, as well as the impacts of previous restrictions upon society and economy, also raise important questions about the behaviour and possible reactions of the wider public. While not apparent in mainstream media, there is increasing tension and discontent across the world as a result of these issues and the experience of the pandemic more generally. The Global Peace Index 2020 report warned how we now occupy "*a world in which the conflicts and crises that emerged in the past decade have begun to abate, only to be replaced with a new wave of tension and uncertainty as a result of the COVID-19 pandemic.*" Indeed the report finds that in 2020 alone, 15,000 violent protests took place across the world; 5,000 of which were directly related to Covid-19.[15] In the summer of 2021, there were further protests against the management of Covid-19 and ongoing restrictions involving hundreds of thousands of people from the UK, India, Chile, Italy, France, Germany and South Africa.[16]

---

[14] BBC (2021g).
[15] Institute for Economics & Peace (2020).
[16] Ibid.

The pandemic's impact upon violent behaviour and disorder has been geographically and spatially uneven. Many nations recorded declines in incidents of violence in public spaces as lockdowns were initiated.[17] Evidence from England and Wales suggests that as the restrictions from the first lockdown were eased in the summer of 2020, violent crimes increased in areas experiencing above average unemployment, with levels of violence in impoverished areas reportedly higher than in the period immediately before the pandemic.[18] There are potentially different factors behind these shifts, but certainly as societies seek to increasingly open up and conflicts remain over the nature of post-pandemic life, serious violence and disorder remain distinct possibilities. Indeed, researchers Eisner and Nivette point to proximally closer and more distant 'violence-promoting mechanisms' that will likely exert greater influence at different stages of the pandemic[19]The sudden removal of restrictions and the return of traditional routine opportunities to engage in violence may provide a partial explanation for the sudden rises recorded in more deprived parts of England and Wales. The strain endured as a result of the pandemic and lockdown conditions in poorer communities may add a further explanatory layer to this trend. Importantly though, the threat of immediate and future violent disorder remains, as the more distant 'mechanisms' these researchers identify begin to exert an influence upon populations.

Schwab and Malleret suggest in regards to the social and economic impacts of the pandemic: *"when people have no jobs, no income and no prospects for a better life, they often resort to violence"*.[20] Furthermore, it has already been highlighted in previous chapters that restrictive measures appear to have inadvertently heightened risks for some of experiencing violence in private spaces, specifically intimate-partner, parent-to-child and child-to-parent violence.[21] The trauma of these experiences increases the risks of violence, disorder and unrest in post-lockdown societies.

---

[17] Eisner and Nivette (2020); Kirchmaier and Villa-Llera (2020).
[18] Kirchmaier and Villa-Llera (2020).
[19] Eisner and Nivette (2020).
[20] Schwab and Malleret (2020) p.84.
[21] Condry et al. (2020), Evans (2020), and Evans et al. (2020).

Crucially, as we have argued and evidenced in this book, one of the results of the pandemic is social division on several fronts. We have previously found that some initial solidarity evident at the outset of Covid-19 morphed through collective experience of the pandemic and lockdowns into various forms of division.[22] Our data indicate that, on the one hand, the experience seems to have left some people feeling dejected, distrusting of politics and frustrated at ongoing interruptions to daily life. While other people have become increasingly over-cautious and unwilling to return to the prospect of social life devoid of masks, social distancing and, in some cases, the more restrictive measures applied during the first and second waves of infection.

Residual Division

Generally, all our participants unanimously regarded the pandemic as a damaging and traumatic period of recent history, and this was made most evident to them through the discernible impact upon their familial and personal relationships. Many recounted experiences of conflict, in some cases with significant others, that had arisen in the face of the various challenges and moral quandaries this period had generated. Some believed that lives were being ruined through government-initiated public health measures and were angry about it. For others, common sense, some perspective and proportionality were desperately needed to counter what they perceived to be the hysterical and excessive manner in which the threat of the virus had been regarded and responded to. These Facebook posts typified the division incumbent on such relationships:

Carl: I feel so down about it all. It really is getting to me. The only thing that keeps me going is my family and my determination to see these criminals [the government] get their just deserts. It's like living a bad dream. I'm probably wrong, but I view strangers as hostile opponents most of the time. That's the division these bastards have deliberately caused. (140 likes)

[22] Briggs et al. (2021).

Mary: I know so many that have lost personal relationships through this with family and spouses…including myself losing a 20-year relationship very recently and connections to my family because of my passion for the cause. These are extraordinary times guys and for some reason we know that we can't just let it go as this has been planned for so long and WE were meant to be the generation to deal with it…so we will. (660 likes)

What is wrong with humanity? The mask has become a weapon of such destruction and division ☺(49 likes)

Hopefully people will receive a lengthy sentence and be put into prison, not only for breaking strict local lockdown rules, but for potentially spreading the virus to others. (300 likes)

Division therefore between *responsible* and *negligent citizens* (Chapter 6, 10) revolved mostly around the adherence to measures as well as decisions to take up or reject the vaccine. Evan, a Fitness Instructor based in the US, expressed many of these sentiments and in particular was considerably frustrated and dejected at how divisive the issue of managing the virus had become in his country:

Parents turning against their own children, friends turning against friends, people turning against people, companies turning against their own employees, venues turning against their customers, people losing their livelihoods, families splitting up, people committing suicide, and for what? All of you having a difference of opinion, all having made a different choice, a personal choice about taking a vaccine?

Evan was not alone either. Sarah, an Artist from Australia, and Jake, an American trainee lawyer, echoed many of these sentiments and too felt the vaccine was becoming an unnecessary source of conflict that wasn't regarded as a personal choice but rather an assumed and necessary moral obligation to others:

Sarah: I'm angry with all this rubbish and ruining people's lives, my boyfriend's mum was going through chemo and she's been putting up a great fight to then last year being refused help and now her cancer has spread and told she has a few months left. Another guy, I knew committed suicide over this lockdown and now my family are being pulled apart about taking a vaccine.

Jake: I'm angry today!!! Been to work and was quizzed by a woman working there, who I've never seen before, telling me I SHOULD be getting the vaccine, in order to keep everyone safe. She was basically implying that I'm not keeping people safe because of my decision to not have it. She was looking at me like I was a crazy! Funny thing how before that, she was bragging about which variety of vaccine she had received, whilst talking about how ill she became after receiving it. Give me strength...

Yet, these accounts highlight how many people have absorbed and internalised the public health ideological messaging relating to health, illness and the risk of death from Covid-19 (Chapter 3*): to the point that they feel it necessary to educate others about what they should be doing.* As we discussed previously in this chapter, instances of possible incompetence and wilful disregard of public health measures by politicians and advisors, were often cited as evidence of both hypocrisies, but also valid reasons to not accept the legitimacy of the demands then made by States to prevent viral transmission. Peter, a Doctor from the UK, was particularly scathing of how the pandemic had been managed and believed what had been demanded of the public was neither fair nor proportionate:

It's ok for the Government ministers to do their own thing and many have flouted the rules themselves! I have no problem with people wanting to earn a living, wanting to take responsibility for their own actions and if that means defying ridiculous rules and restrictions so be it. Let us have a conversation in Common Sense Corner - most people are quite sensible, they do not need to be bullied and as in the UK the SAGE Behavioural psychologists have admitted that they deliberately used controlled coercive techniques to instil enough fear and personal threat in the public to manipulate the way people thought and acted! It is wilful dereliction of duty and against the BPS Code of Ethics! Bring on an independent enquiry!

Residual Despair

While the residue of the pandemic appears to have heightened some divisions, particularly exacerbating some pre-existing tensions in certain States, and also contributed to the generation of new conflicts based upon perceived compliance with restrictions and immunisation efforts, many we spoke to had been left with a sense of despair at the way in which their lives had changed so dramatically. These people found little comfort or familiarity in what has been referred to as the 'new normal', and their despair seemed to overshadow their perceptions of the future. For example, Lina and Catherine, two middle-aged women who live in the suburbs of a Spanish city, spoke of the way the pandemic had affected their friendships. Previously, they had enjoyed an active and varied social life that revolved around face-to-face in-person activities, such as playing cards and taking walks in the countryside. Lina and Catherine yearned for those days to return and had hoped that they would soon. However, despite the easing of some restrictions, those days had still not returned and their present day-to-day lives remained tainted by a residual fear and unease engendered during lockdown. Many of their friends remained reticent and reluctant to meet them, or even leave their properties. They spoke with concern and a sense of despair about their friend Yvonne, who they missed dearly. Prior to the pandemic, Yvonne was reported to be a sociable and healthy 60-year-old who would regularly join Lina and Catherine for walks or a game of cards with some drinks. But neither Lina, Catherine, nor their other mutual friends, have seen Yvonne in-person for 14 months.

From what they have been able to glean about Yvonne's situation through occasional phone conversations with her, it seems she has not left her flat at all during the pandemic. All her shopping is delivered online, and when it arrives she ensures that she fully disinfects it. She keeps fit by walking around the living room 200 times and has no intention of leaving her flat until everyone has been vaccinated and the virus has been eradicated. Yet as far as Lina and Catherine are aware, Yvonne has no pre-existing health concerns. When Caroline last talked to Yvonne using Facetime she became worried because Yvonne seemed to have *"a nervous twitch"* and kept *"repeating herself all the time"* during the conversation. For some of our other participants, a sense of despair and hopelessness was becoming palpable, and in some cases visible, within their local communities. On one hand, Vikki is happy to see restrictions ease, but on the other, is most fearful about the future:

> Drove home tonight and near where I live someone has graffiti'd under the bridge 'WHEN WILL IT ALL END?' I thought it was so poignant but oh so sad ☹. People are coming to the end of their tether mentally. You can see so clearly how much happier everyone is now they are back living a more normal life, back with their family and friends etc. But I am scared of what is to come.......

Ashley, similarly, feared that restrictions may imminently return and that individual freedoms may once again be curtailed:

> This is only the beginning just wait until multiple family members are dying, huge inflation, no jobs, UBI, suicides and so much more, it's going to get so, so much worse.

Some anecdotally recounted incidents of suicide in their local areas. In some cases, their suspicions regarding the reason for these self-inflicted deaths fell upon the restrictions associated with lockdowns and a perceived lack of clarity regarding when these might be fully, and indefinitely, removed: Here a discussion in the Facebook forums revolves around suicides:

> *Mandy*: There was a fatality on the railway Wednesday and another on Friday. This is just the Paddington to Swansea line. Suicides are rising it seems.
>
> *Elsa*: Last night a man jumped off a building in [large town in England] opposite the station... My friend who also lives in the area knows two young teenagers who recently committed suicide... And someone very close to me attempted to take their own life last month but luckily failed...Never has there been so much talk about mental health and at the same time so much suffering from mental health issues and a strategic push to accelerate the downward spiral...

Chris: ...we have had at least three fatalities of pedestrians jumping on to our local dual carriage way in the last few weeks.

Among some of the respondents residing in England, the sense of despair they expressed was accompanied by anger, cynicism and suspicion targeted at local and national government:

Beth: I feel like my life is over. I am on house arrest. A person who was 'tagged' five years ago had more freedom than I do. Suicide statistics must be published. But there again, government doesn't care, it's obvious. Economy ruined, rich getting richer, Matt Wankcock raking in his dividends from big pharma shares, they really do not care about us at all...

Pauline: "Lockdowns kill" was sprayed on our local bridge. I've never known the council remove graffiti so fast. Usually it's left until it wears off...

Residual Cynicism: *"They couldn't Give a Shit"*

One year into the pandemic, in April 2021:

It is just after 9pm in the centre of the city of Palma, Majorca. Less than an hour until the nighttime curfew begins. I hurry across the road towards an Indian restaurant to collect my takeaway order. As I cross, I see a police car on patrol further down the road that is driving slowly in my direction. As it reaches me, I notice in the periphery of my vision that the two officers in the vehicle are looking in my general direction. I turn and glance at them briefly and find them both staring at me intently. Ghostly white masks cover the lower half of their faces. The car breaks suddenly to a halt and I can feel their eyes continue to watch me as I stop outside the restaurant. I keep my eyes focused on the menu that is mounted on the wall. After a few seconds they move on up the street, seemingly satisfied that I am a law abider. A waiter, wearing a face mask, asks for my order details and tells me it will be ready soon. As I wait we talk for a few minutes. He explains that business has not been greatly affected as the takeaway service is proving popular. Before heading back inside the restaurant, he says to me *"not the same for my neighbours"*, and points to the now deserted estate agents next door which is already gathering dust.

Restaurants in the city stopped offering sit-down meals several hours ago. What had been, prior to the pandemic, a busy area bustling with people during the evenings is now largely deserted and eerily quiet. The local news has reported that during the last 12 months in the region of 30% of small businesses on the island have permanently closed, many of them small cafes or other hospitality venues. A third of nightlife businesses have closed with losses estimated at €234 million. Around 90,000 people are currently registered unemployed on the island. State support or the furlough scheme does not sufficiently cover many of these people. Payments have also been issued late meaning some people have been waiting months for their money to arrive. I have been hearing about numerous families that have exhausted their savings and are now in debt. Desperate people applying to banks and other lenders for loans, but being refused. I have noticed the queues at local food banks in the city becoming larger, sometimes extended along several streets. The latest statistics on suicide suggest that, on average, one person kills themselves every day in Majorca now, with between 20 and 30 daily suicide attempts.

While I wait for my order, I notice a tired looking man lazily cross the street and walk in my direction. His passage is lit up by the cigarette he inhales deeply. He seems to represent a life I forgot existed before Covid: someone without their face covered-up, smoking in public. As he looks at the menu, I joke *"I am jealous, I wish I smoked so I didn't have to wear this mask."* He turns and looks at me seriously. For a moment I feel, through his facial expression and body language, that I may have somehow offended him. *"What did you say?"* he asks. Unable to facially express the fact that I was making a joke, I add hand gestures and explain: *"I meant that when you smoke, you don't get to wear a mask!"* Again, there is a brief, anxiety-inducing pause, before he visibly relaxes his facial expression and posture, replying *"Ah thank god, you are one of those normal people! Not many of them left"*. He tosses his half-lit cigarette into the street and lights up another. His eyes suddenly widen as he looks at me and says *"well I have seen it all in Austria and Germany, I have seen how people are believing this, how they are behaving now, people are crazy, they are not well…they all have totally bought it"*.

I wonder what he means by *"bought it"*, but before I have a chance to speak he asks me what I have ordered. After I tell him, he whistles over the waiter taking orders and says *"I feel inspired by this man so I too will have what he is having"* before breaking out into what feels like a sense-of-relief bout of laughter. *"This?",* he says as he holds up his mask, *"this is nothing, this is a waste of time. People are believing it and following it like it is the truth, like it will save them and will save other people. I have heard and seen it all from the politicians' lips and they have other ideas"* he adds. He introduces himself as Franz and goes on to tell me that he owned two airline businesses before the outbreak of Covid, both of which went into administration within six months of the pandemic. He shows me photos on his phone of his plane stock before the pandemic and adds *"my charter flights were from Austria and Germany to Spain but of course this was never going to last without the tourists"* he says. He explains that he now offers a bespoke customised and luxury private plane service between the countries. As we talk about the menu, and he shows me what he has tried before, the waiter informs me that my food is ready. As my food is loaded into bags, Franz says to me: *"you know, I transport all the politicians between these countries now, I have heard all their conversations, important and powerful people, wealthy politicians, they tell me things as well, but let me tell you that they don't give a shit about all these poor or unemployed people...they couldn't give a shit."* [Field notes Daniel Briggs 'Waiting for Food']

Residual Compliance: Sanitised Social Life

Some months later during the summer of 2021:

We arrive at the four-star hotel on the outskirts of Palma for the birthday party of one of our daughters friends, Izzy, who turns 8 today. Her family own the hotel and, despite the pandemic, have still managed to stay afloat largely because of domestic tourism. The familiar presence of other parents await us as we walk in with our masks on. Up until 26 July 2021, people had to wear masks both indoors and outdoors but thereafter it has only been a requirement in indoor closed spaces. We walk through and come to an open, outdoor area hoping to then dispense with the masks. But as we come across 12 children and their parents congregating in a socially distanced manner with their masks on, we feel obliged to keep them on. Our daughter Lily stays by our side and waves uncomfortably to her friends.

There is a bizarre and tense atmosphere because no one is buck-
ling to remove their mask in the open space or compromise distancing
restrictions for fear of disrespecting someone else's preference to disease
prevention. Izzy's mum then walks towards us with a hand sanitiser and
we are dutifully disinfected in front of our adult counterparts and kiddy
partygoers. We become cleansed and sanitised as if we were participating
as a religious ritual. Surely now we are safe and can relax but this is not
the case for we quickly learn that there seems to be more preoccupation
for adherence to the covid-19 restrictions and the 'high-risk' of infection
than there is for an eight-year-old to have a normal birthday party.

The sanitised fun begins as we are invited to the buffet food area to
get some snacks. Yet everything has already been set out for each individual. Food choice has already been decided. Each child had a bag full
of nourishments so they don't have to risk infecting someone elses' snack;
an individual popcorn pack, an individual carton of crisps, an individual
biscuit, all individually wrapped in cellophane. Next to this table, there is
a large pick-n-mix sweet stand. Yet the kids can't use it because they can't
touch the stand or the sweets *"due to Covid"* as Izzy's dad says. At this
"Covid-friendly party", as Izzy's mum keeps reiterating, the sweets are pre-
selected and the fun is broken down into sequential bouts of potential
excitement followed by disappointment.

At this point, 10 of the 12 children remove their masks to eat while
two remain committed to their use and seem reluctant to remove them to
enjoy the pre-packed feast. Both their mums privately speak to them and
have to persevere with their encouragement to remove the masks. These
two kids sit together, apart from the others. Suddenly, Lily, our daughter,
sneezes slightly and the girl opposite her picks up chair and moves to
another table. We overhear her feeding it back to her mum while Lily
edges over to us, feeling embarrassed and awkward and says *"Mummy that
girl just stared at me and moved to another table"*. She returns to the table
to find herself adequately distanced from several others in her absence in
case it happens again.

As the games begin, the two masked children remain seated, still
masked up. First up is musical statues then musical chairs both of which
are preceded by further gel disinfection. But the two masked children
sit unmoved by the toned-down fun in front of them, seemingly preoc-
cupied at the level of contact taking place, despite the safety measures
put in place to make them 'feel comfortable'. However, it seems to
have the reverse effect as everyone, including the parents, seem to be

on edge. After further hand disinfection, pass the parcel begins, and the mums of the masked children try to persuade them to join in, but they decline once again. What makes the scenario even more peculiar is that the two mums—masked up—then substitute their own children in the pass-the-parcel game.

In the 35 degree heat, conformity starts to wobble among some of the parents who start to lower their masks when their space is not compromised, only to raise it if someone comes close to talk. Izzy's mum, however, has to relentlessly lower hers to bark orders and instructions to the kids. This time its to announce that the birthday cake will come out. A large and magnificent, homemade unicorn cake is then wheeled out and the children look the most excited they have done all afternoon. But in Covid times, things it seems are different as Izzy's mum says *"just you all know we aren't going to blow out the candles because of Covid"*. Then Izzy's dad has a brainwave and goes to fetch a little cupcake and puts a candle in it so his daughter can blow it out thus allowing the children to be able to enjoy eating the actual cake without having potential Covid particles on it. The 'Covid-friendly' party seems to be in the end a series of procedures organised around adherence to public health measures which collectively seem to remove much of the fun these children may normally have otherwise. Everything related to masks, disinfecting and distancing seem to have stunted the enjoyment evident in the empty and long-faced looks of the children as the party concludes. [Field notes 'Sanitised fun' Daniel Briggs]

Trauma as Residue

An obvious point, but one perhaps worth emphasising regardless, is that a consistent feature of the various accounts offered by our participants on the experience of lockdown, and the pandemic more generally, is that it was, and to some degree still is, akin to a trauma. Another, is that the experience of this traumatic period possesses an indelible quality and leaves behind what we have termed here forms of *residue*, that, even as some restrictions begin to be removed, will continue to shape individual experience and the contours of post-pandemic social life more generally for some considerable time to come.

The concept of trauma has been utilised routinely within psychiatry to account for events that intrude *"into our psychic life and disturbs its balance, throwing out of joint the symbolic coordinates that organise our experience"*[23]. In the wake of a traumatic event, many experience difficulties when trying to comprehend and put into words what has happened to them and evidence indicates traumatised individuals can present an array of symptoms indicative of being trapped in a defensive state, such as avoidance, withdrawal or aggression.[24] Sociologist Piotr Sztompka has attempted to extract the concept of trauma from its individualistic application within the confines of hospitals and psychiatric wards, to address the disruption of social change, which can bring about significant symptoms as well as varying 'costs, pain, and suffering'. For Sztompka, the concept of trauma possesses utility for understanding *"the problem of negative, dysfunctional, adverse effects that major social change may leave in its wake"*.[25] We too contend that the lockdowns are a harbinger of mass, large-scale social change that is traumatic and harmful to many and that has disrupted the established and taken-for-granted coordinates of social life, leaving human populations struggling to come to terms with what has taken place and how best to move on from it. A major obstruction to understanding where it may go is related to the fact that we are still experiencing it.

The traumatic intrusion of the pandemic and the uneven impact of the virus and the measures taken in response, have split human populations on several fronts, with derogatory and harmful labels such as 'sheeple' and 'covidiots' emblematic of the new fault lines that have emerged. Some remain fearful and anxious about the presence of the virus within the community, and understandably so in some cases. Others remain fearful of the return of lockdown and what this means for their familial life, their employment, their children's education and their mental well-being. While there are those whose fear has morphed into anger and

---

[23] Zizek (2006).
[24] Greenwald (2002).
[25] Sztompka (2000).

cynicism, who see restrictions as unnecessary overkill, or a veil to conceal more sinister intentions. The enduring issue remains how these issues that emanate from the damage wrought by the virus and the measures taken against it, might be overcome in a manner that minimises as much as possible various harms.

References

Allegretti, A., & Geddes, L. (2021). PM to confirm 19 July end to COVID rules despite scientists' warnings. *The Guardian.* https://www.theguardian.com/politics/2021/jul/04/pm-confirm-19-july-end-covid-restrictions-scientists-warnings-england (last accessed 8th July 2021)

Ayoubkhani, D., Khunti, K., Nafilyan, V., Maddox, T., Humberstone, B., Diamond, I., & Banerjee, A. (2021). Post-COVID syndrome in individuals admitted to hospital with COVID-19: Retrospective cohort study. *BMJ, 372.* https://doi.org/10.1136/bmj.n693

BBC. (2021e). *PM must sack Matt Hancock after affair claims—Labour.* https://www.bbc.co.uk/news/uk-politics-57608716 (last accessed 8 July 2021)

BBC. (2021f). *COVID-19: 'Lifting all protections at once is reckless'—Keir Starmer.* https://www.bbc.co.uk/news/av/uk-57728368 (last accessed 8 July 2021)

BBC. (2021g). *COVID in Scotland: Restrictions to end as planned.* https://www.bbc.co.uk/news/uk-scotland-scotland-politics-57732436 (last accessed 14 July 2021)

Blackall, M. (2021). *Euro 2020 crowds like eat out to help out on steroids' and encourages fans to ditch rules, Sage adviser warns.* https://inews.co.uk/news/uk/euros-wembley-fans-covid-rules-eat-out-to-help-out-sage-adviser-1080772 (last accessed 8 July 2021)

Briggs, D., Ellis, A., Lloyd, A., & Telford, L. (2021). *Researching the Covid-19 pandemic: A critical blueprint for the social sciences.* Policy Press.

Condry, R., Miles, C., Brunton-Douglas, T., & Oladapo, A. (2020). *Experiences of child and adolescent to parent violence in the COVID-19 pandemic.* University of Oxford. https://www.law.ox.ac.uk/sites/files/oxlaw/final_report_capv_in_covid-19_aug20.pdf

Eisner, M., & Nivette, A. (2020). *Violence and the pandemic: Urgent questions for research*. Harry Frank Guggenheim Foundation. https://hfg.org/Vio lence%20and%20the%20Pandemic.pdf

Evans, D. P. (2020). COVID-19 and violence: A research call to action. *BMC Women's Health, 20*(249), 1–3.

Evans, M. L., Lindauer, M., & Farrell, M. E. (2020). A pandemic within a pandemic—Intimate partner violence during COVID-19. *The New England Journal of Medicine, 383,* 2302–2304.

Fersia, O., Bryant, S., & Nicholson, R., (2020). The impact of the COVID-19 pandemic on cardiology services. *Open Heart, 7,* e001359. https://doi.org/ 10.1136/openhrt-2020-001359

Fleming, S. (2021). *How will behaviour change after COVID vaccination? New survey reveals post-pandemic trends*. World Economic Forum. https://www. weforum.org/agenda/2021/07/ipsos-behaviour-change-covid-vaccine/

Greenwald, R. (2002). The role of trauma in conduct disorder. *Journal of Aggression Maltreatment & Trauma, 6*(1), 5–23. https://doi.org/10.1300/J14 6v06n01_02

Institute for Economics & Peace. (2020, June). *Global peace index 2020: Measuring peace in a complex world*. Available from: http://visionofhuma nity.org/reports

Javid, S., (2021). *Oral statement to parliament: 19 July remains our target date for ending restrictions*. https://www.gov.uk/government/speeches/19-july-rem ains-our-target-date-for-ending-restrictions (last accessed 8th July 2021)

Kirchmaier, T., & Villa-Llera, C. (2020). *COVID-19 and changing crime trends in England and Wales* (Centre for Economic Performance, No.013). http:// doi.org/10.2139/ssrn.3700329

Maringe, C., Spicer, J., Morris, M., Purushotham, A., Nolte, E., & Sullivan, R. (2020). The impact of the COVID-19 pandemic on cancer deaths due to delays in diagnosis in England, UK: A national, population-based, modelling study. *The Lancet, 21*(8), 1023–1034. https://doi.org/10.1016/ S1470-2045(20)30388-0

Nanan-Sen, S. (2021). 'Keep masks!' Jon Ashworth erupts at Sajid Javid as labour demands Covid 'U-turn'. *The Express*. https://www.express.co. uk/news/politics/1459029/Jon-Ashworth-Sajid-Javid-health-secretary-face-masks-covid19-latest-Labour-Party-news-vn (last accessed 8th July 2021)

O'Connor, R. (2021). Piers Morgan calls for 'outrageous and pathetic' Matt Hancock to step down over aide scandal. *The Independent*. https://www. independent.co.uk/arts-entertainment/tv/news/piers-morgan-matt-hancock-sack-b1873287.html (last accessed 8th July 2021)

Pattinson, R., & Cole, H. (2021). Cheating Hancock: Matt Hancock's secret affair with aide Gina Coladangelo is exposed after office snogs while COVID raged on. *The Sun*. https://www.thesun.co.uk/news/15388014/matt-hancock-secret-affair-with-aide/ (last accessed 8th July)

Schwab, K., & Malleret, T. (2020). *COVID 19: The great reset*. World Economic Forum.

Sztompka, P. (2000). Cultural trauma: The other face of social change. *European Journal of Social Theory, 3*(4), 449–466.

Wise, J. (2021). COVID-19: Ending all restrictions in England on 19 July "dangerous and premature" say experts. *BMJ, 374*. https://doi.org/10.1136/bmj.n1751

Zizek, S. (2006). *How to read Lacan*. Norton.

12

Endgames

At the time of writing, Covid-19 continues to dominate our social land-scape. In the UK, the Americas, Europe, Australia and elsewhere, the more transmissible 'Delta' variant has polarised opinion on easing restric-tions, and while the global vaccine rollout shows significant efficacy against serious illness, hospitalisation and death, it does not necessarily prevent infection. The ongoing public response to some governments' decisions to open up society indicate this new and troubling fault line between those who feel restrictions are still required and those who feel the vaccine allows us to live with the virus (Chapter 11). Each side can call upon scientific experts to support their position and, in its extremes, both sides shout past each other and demonstrate Alasdair MacIntyre's[1] perceptive reflection that morality today exemplifies 'emotivism'—'good' and 'right' are located within individual perception rather than any external authority or objective position (Fig. 12.1).

---

[1] MacIntyre (2011).

Fig. 12.1 Guaranteed compliance: A model for the future?[2]

What we deem to be good is based on how we think and feel: face masks and vaccinations are seen to keep other people safe and are therefore the sign of a good and caring person. Vaccine efficacy makes restrictions increasingly unnecessary, and we need to learn to live with the virus. These positions are irreconcilable; we can call on science to support both sides and there is no external adjudicating authority upon which we can rely or place our faith. We rely on how we think and feel on the subject. It is difficult to know which side is right, particularly given the mountain of information, expert opinion and conflicting evidence circulating in the public domain, let alone any suggestion of government spin, vested interest or conspiracy. This example tells us that Covid-19 and the measures imposed to tackle the crisis have had a significant *sociological* impact on the world in which we live. It also tells us that while the virus will become endemic and the crisis will pass, the sociological

---

[2] Photo. Daniel Briggs.

implications will linger for some time into the future. Here we conclude the key themes from our book, return to the social harm framework to weigh up the balance of harm argument and offer a forward-facing look at the new world we have entered.

Lockdown Realities

As mentioned, a global pandemic should not have come as a surprise.[3] In the last forty years, AIDS, SARS, MERS, Swine Flu, Zika and Ebola have killed thousands around the world. The constant erosion of the natural environment coincides with the regular emergence of new disease and is reflective of a wider process of capitalist expansion that shaped the world into which Covid-19 arrived. Exploitation of the natural environment has been at the heart of capitalist political economy and although the neoliberal countries of the Global North and West had outsourced its dirty industries to the South and East, particularly Africa and China,[4] the global system of capitalism has accelerated the destruction of the natural environment in the name of profit and progress. An increasingly fragile and deaptive neoliberal capitalism, unable to resolve its own contradictions and provide a coherent narrative, further destroyed social institutions and social cohesion in the name of market share, competition and progress.[5] Neoliberalism had hollowed out civic institutions, including political systems as well as the very idea of the social, and had instilled market principles in sectors previously run in the public interest and thus distorted their goal and mission. When the pandemic hit, global supply chains, pharmaceutical companies and healthcare systems, not to mention government itself, were unable to respond in a way that adequately protected people.[6] Despite detailed plans to deal with a global pandemic, Covid-19 appears to have caught most governments by surprise; their response will be the subject of future public inquiries,

---

[3] Honigsbaum (2020).
[4] Pitron (2020).
[5] Streeck (2016).
[6] Jones and Hameiri (2021).

but we can already begin to see the consequences, whether intended or otherwise.

National lockdowns were not part of the WHO's guidance on pandemic response and were not a recommended course of action. However, following China's lead, countries around the world enacted restrictive non-pharmaceutical interventions that varied in severity and length and while a few avoided 'lockdown' entirely, much of the world effectively participated in a novel social experiment. Rather than a long-term solution, evidence seems to suggest that lockdown, if used at all, should have been a very short-term measure while other measures including mass testing or contact tracing were established. The efficacy of lockdown is hard to measure as it is difficult to isolate the effects of lockdown from other public health measures such as hand washing, social distancing and self-isolation. Places that did not lock down, such as Sweden, and places that removed restrictions entirely, such as Florida, appear to show similar or even better patterns of cases, hospitalisations and deaths as those who enacted stringent and repeated lockdowns. As we stated in the opening chapter, we are not epidemiologists, virologists or public health experts and therefore the efficacy of lockdown versus other interventions is not our area of expertise. What we have tried to demonstrate is the impact of lockdown policies on the political, social, cultural and economic landscapes of countries and its citizens around the world.

And for us, these lockdown realities paint a harrowing picture because they sit within a pre-existing context and factor in already-active inequalities, many of which we have outlined throughout this book. Those previously at the bottom of the socio-economic hierarchy almost uniformly, despite geographic variation, suffered far greater consequences than those at the top of the ladder.[7] While some have suggested that a virus does not discriminate, the reality is that exposure to, and the health impact of, Covid-19 mostly followed existing social and health inequalities. As we have demonstrated through our own data and the existing research, racial, class-based, economic and geographic

---

[7] Bambra et al. (2021).

inequalities had a significant determining factor in who caught Covid-19, who required hospitalisation and, ultimately, who died. While age was a significant determining risk factor, those already unequal—the truly disadvantaged—were most at risk. Those deemed 'essential' or 'key' workers, often in low-paid occupations, were more at risk while middle class professionals like us stayed at home. Those who lived in crowded conditions, were homeless, in prison, in care homes, or stuck somewhere as a refugee or stateless citizen were also at greater risk of the virus. Ironically, those for whom life pre-Covid-19 was one of immense suffering and upheaval—as demonstrated in Chapter 9 by our Syrian contact Osama—saw Covid-19 as less important than the effects of prolonged civil war. However, his story showed that the economic inequality resulting from the hollowing out of Syrian society propelled Osama into working in high-risk occupations in order to send money home to his family. While he felt the virus was of minimal importance, the *reality* of his family's situation *put him at greater risk* of the virus than someone in a stable home-based occupation and a secure home environment.

As noted in Chapter 5, there were significant 'lockdown winners' as the elite consolidated their wealth and those in key industries—pharmaceuticals, logistics and online shopping, and digital technologies—realised huge profits. Others were able to exploit the panic and secure (often seemingly without oversight or due process) government contracts to supply PPE and other equipment. For many in secure forms of professional work that could transition into homeworking, lockdown afforded a more modest consolidation of finances, a better work-life balance and more time for pursuits that could be characterised as higher order human flourishing—learning new skills and spending meaningful time with loved ones. Meanwhile, many more suffered in multifaceted ways.

Lockdown shattered entire labour market sectors and forced unemployment rates up significantly. While governments intervened in their economies in ways that dismantled neoliberal shibboleths of fiscal spending and the non-existence of magic money trees, evidence suggests that furlough schemes, unemployment insurance and government payments were not always timely, adequate or universal.[8] Millions of people lost jobs or were asked to survive on a percentage of their usual wage. Local economies dependent on tourism collapsed overnight. Hospitality closures has seen significant levels of business failure. The personal and social impacts of unemployment have long been noted, regardless of whether we believe unemployment to be a structural problem or a personal failing. In the immediate aftermath of lockdown, millions around the world were laid off. The consequences of that will reverberate for some time.

We welcome the measures implemented to support workers, despite the inequalities in access and delays in payment because it demonstrated that the nation state has more tools in its economic toolbox than it had previously been prepared to admit. The destruction of neoliberal fiscal orthodoxy creates space in which marginal positions such as Modern Monetary Theory (MMT) and previously fringe policy ideas such as UBI and, more profitably, a Job Guarantee Programme can break through. Although employment rates began to climb again following the initial lockdown, the significant levels of unemployment, labour market uncertainty and employment insecurity have very real consequences for individuals, families, communities and society. These are unambiguously the *result of lockdown policies and not the pandemic* because the decision to shut down large parts of society to tackle the pandemic created the conditions we have outlined in earlier chapters.

We have also seen the emergence of trauma, depression and anxiety throughout the pandemic which will have significant consequences in the present and future. The forceful concentration of health and illness into our lives, through government messaging, public health measures and sensationalised media reporting has reshaped feelings about health, illness and death. New fears about illness permeated the responses we received, as demonstrated in our chapters. Fears of getting sick prevented Luis in Spain (Chapter 3) from leaving the house without his anxiety rising. In South Africa, Steve (Chapter 3) got angry at those refusing to comply with restrictions because his grandmother had died with

---

[8] Tcherneva (2020).

Covid-19. Indeed, Prolonged Grief Disorder and Persistent Complex Bereavement Disorder (PCBD) appear to be more severe among those who have lost loved ones to Covid-19.

Children are displaying higher levels of anxiety, depression and panic attacks. While we present evidence of Covid-19 related suicides, Laura Dodsworth's[9] research suggests that it might be too early to see the full extent of the relationship between Covid-19 and suicide. In addition to mental ill-health, anxiety and depression, experience of trauma has grown, and not just in relation to bereavement. Statistical evidence and qualitative insights from Child Protection Officers Fiona and Sonya (Chapter 7) show the future challenges around child abuse and domestic violence. The data indicates that reported incidents have risen in many countries and can be connected to the enforced proximity of offender and victim within the home. Fiona and Sonya also indicate that Covid-secure working practices, namely remote and online sessions, has hampered their ability to engage with hard-to-reach children. Abuse and trauma in childhood is a contributory factor in the future violent behaviour among *some* men in certain contexts, which tells us that rising levels of abuse is both an immediate and future issue.[10] In our data from healthcare workers and care home staff, we can also see the residue of traumatic experiences in their prolonged exposure to significant levels of illness and death.

We have also presented significant evidence that signals further inequalities in lockdown experience which indicate a wide range of harms and challenges faced by marginalised groups. Despite the governments' insistence that a 'protective bubble' was thrown around the elderly, many in care homes in various countries were separated from families and the outside world. In some cases, as evidenced in Chapter 7, this accelerated mental ill-health and was as important in subsequent deaths as Covid-19. Healthcare systems were placed under significant strain which forced cancellation of routine procedures, face-to-face services and public health initiatives, such as routine vaccinations in some African countries. The elderly and vulnerable, in particular, suffered as a result. The

---

[9] Dodsworth (2021).
[10] Ellis et al. (2021).

overall fear of the virus, recalibrated health systems and government messaging also resulted in people too afraid to go to hospital, which led to missed appointments and potentially life-saving treatment. Excess death tolls across countries are made up of far more than Covid-19 victims. Evidence from prisons across the world, particularly Brazil and Thailand, reinforce Wacquant[11] and Bauman's[12] assertions that prisons of poverty house what many regard as wasted humans, easily disposable and neglected when the pandemic struck.

Asylum seekers, already buffeted by the increasing hostile environment across much of the West, suffered further stigma and aggression and became the 'diseased other' who spread the virus and therefore must be denied entry or deported. Refugee camps appeared to have limited exposure to the virus, but evidence suggested this was due to low levels of testing and a reluctance to test as self-isolation limited the ability to work, even by informal means. The same hardening attitudes towards refugees and asylum seekers was also evidenced towards precarious migrant workers who were multiply impacted by lockdown. Immediately thrown out of work, many were denied payments or support from host governments due to their migrant status. Those who remained in work were likely to be in low-paid, precarious forms of employment that required face-to-face contact and therefore risk of viral exposure. Finally, we explored the shocking example of homeless people being relocated to a disused car park with 'designated' spots in which they were told to be homeless. Vital services for the homeless, often charity based, have been suspended due to public health measures and additionally data suggests there has been an increase in drug overdose deaths. Indeed, in some areas such as British Columbia in Canada the death toll from drug overdoses in 2020 exceeded the deaths with/from Covid-19.

It is clear that lockdown inequalities also extend to newly emergent fault lines and social antagonisms. Overall, a general disparity in belief and trust exists which, we argue, represents the post-political age of cynicism. We simply don't trust our leaders, our experts or each other. This

---

[11] Wacquant (2009).
[12] Bauman (2004).

is characterised by the distinction between *responsible* and *negligent* citizens, between 'Covidiots' and 'Sheeple'. The rise in conspiracy theory predates the pandemic and is reflective of a desire to believe, in a world shorn of belief. In an age of objectless anxiety and ontological insecurity, the subject requires immersion in a symbolic order that gives life meaning and makes sense of the world. In such a fragmented and cynical age as ours, the idea that life is contingent and random, that God no longer exists and faith in mass movements is misguided, conspiracy theories, like New Age spiritualism, yoga or other belief systems, provide comfort, reassurance and order.

It is easy to dismiss people who look for underlying explanations for events as cranks or weirdos. Agenda 2030 and the Great Reset, Bill Gates, 5G and microchips are all dismissed by many and in some cases with very good reason, however, it further demonstrates the absence of consensus and cohesion as well as the growth in antagonism and anti-social sentiment. We no longer hear each other out and search for consensus. We dismiss those who rigidly follow the rules as 'bed wetters' and 'sheeple'. We castigate those who criticise lockdown as 'covid-deniers' and 'corona clowns'. Covid-19 and the debate over lockdown represents the latest in a series of divisions that characterise our society. From Brexit to Trump, from lockdowns to face masks. The debate around lockdown shows us that our society is divided, polarised and antagonistic, and this disequilibrium is particularly harmful in terms of trying to overcome all of the other inequalities outlined here.

The Balance of Harm

We started this book with the intention to consider the consequences and effects of lockdown from a social harm perspective. In doing so, we positioned our ultra-realist harm framework as a useful tool for understanding what we have seen during the pandemic. Ultra-realism facilitates a more integrated approach towards the study of crime and harm and allows us to explore and explain both the negative and positive motivation to harm.[13] It has been put to work here as an overarching theoretical framework precisely because it does not demand that we separate the harms emanating from 'up there' in the board rooms from those 'down there' on the streets. Instead, it actively encourages a more holistic view of harm production and suffering. Indeed, we have seen how government restrictions imposed in response to the pandemic have caused a range of unintended harms because they exacerbated existing—and even created new—forms of inequality. This we connected to the negative motivation to harm associated with the smooth functioning of neoliberalism.

However, there were also examples of people showing a willingness to inflict harm on others to satisfy their own expressive or instrumental interests. For example, tussling to bulk buy vital supplies and medicine which put others, particularly the most vulnerable, at risk. The early panic buying shattered the myth of social solidarity and resembled a 'me-first' attitude reflective of a neoliberal society focused on the cult of the individual. Other examples include the increases in hate crime, sexual and domestic abuse, non-compliance with Covid-19 rules—hosting house parties during lockdown or breaking social distancing rules to carry on extra-marital affairs, for instance. Many of these demonstrate a libertarian impulse to act outside of the rules through a sense of entitlement or disregard for the well-being of others, something that ultra-realism refers to as 'special liberty'.[14] These are the positive motivations to harm rather than the unintended or unfortunate consequences of benign processes. The unintended consequences of lockdown and the positive motivation to harm tell the full story of the myriad consequences of this social experiment and help us understand the full extent of the harms generated and inflicted during the pandemic—and most likely, for some years to come.

It begs the question—has lockdown been worth it? We have tried to ask critical questions in this book and consider all of the evidence. This includes the scientific evidence about Covid-19, its effects and the threat it poses, the evidence on various public health interventions and their

---

[13] Hall and Winlow (2015) and Kotzé (2021).
[14] Hall (2012).

efficacy, including lockdown, and the impact and consequences of lockdowns around the world. As criminologists with an interest in social harm, we have approached this from a simple 'balance of harm' position. On a societal level, is the disease more harmful than the cure, or vice versa? We have come to the conclusion that the consequences and outcomes of lockdown policies have been far more harmful than the threat posed by Covid-19. Lockdowns have inadvertently generated multiple social distress which is largely absent from nations that did not lock down. It has also created new fault lines and social antagonisms that we will be dealing with for some time to come. Many of the public health measures, including lockdown, appear to have been implemented based on a fundamental assumption of harmlessness.[15] There seems to have been little appreciation for the causative potential of absence—in employment, in healthcare, in support services and in social contact—to produce harm. If harm represents those barriers and impediments that prevent us from striving towards individual and collective flourishing and leading a good life, then the pandemic and lockdown are both harmful. On the balance of harm, lockdown has been unintentionally but catastrophically harmful. In the final section, we turn to the future and consider the implications of the pandemic and lockdown.

Where Do We Go from Here?

The question everyone is thinking but perhaps not asking is 'where the pandemic and lockdown will take us in the coming years?' As social scientists, we predict that the social experiment we have lived through, lockdown, will have consequences great and small for people all over the world, in some ways we can already see and in others that are yet to manifest. Most obviously, we now live in a world where locking down a country has become part of the suite of measures available to tackle a public health crisis. In March 2020, before the Italian government implemented a national lockdown, UK government advisors suggested that they 'couldn't get away with it' in liberal democracies such as the

---

[15] Raymen (2021).

UK. That is no longer the case and we now live in a world where any existential crisis, from a pandemic to climate change, will see calls for the implementation of lockdown measures. We have outlined the numerous harms felt in countries around the world but we have crossed that invisible line. As we write these final words, restrictions are easing in a number of countries but emergency legislation remains in place, officials warn of a 'difficult' winter ahead and the threat of 'variants of concern' lead some to speculate that restrictions, including full lockdown, will return.

The government has intervened in daily life in a way not seen for almost a century. It remains to be seen whether emergency interventions will be transient or a precursor to new forms of governance, principally built on the foundations of biosecurity. Rather than conspiracy theory, a political-economic analysis tells us that capitalism never lets a good crisis go to waste. Measures to fight terrorism, passed in the wake of the September 11 attacks, have become routine; increased security at airports, the massive expansion of surveillance, geopolitical realities in the Middle East. We do not yet know whether measures implemented to tackle Covid-19 will remain or be further embedded, from test and trace apps to vaccine certification to health passports right up to the Chinese social credit system. *Only time will tell*, but the social scientific implications of such changes will require further study and critical scrutiny.

These measures are possible due to the development of new digital technologies, and the pandemic has accelerated the centralisation of technology within our lives.[16] Could lockdowns have been enacted across Western countries without the ability of a large percentage of the labour force to work remotely? Businesses and labour market sectors that were slowly integrating digital technology into their business model and culture[17] were forced to move much more quickly to meet the requirement to work from home. Online platforms such as Zoom and Microsoft Teams have transformed patterns of work, eliminated daily commutes, and opened up new avenues in education and healthcare. Consumption and entertainment have also further relied on technology for online

---

[16] Schwab and Malleret (2020).
[17] Schildt (2020).

shopping and deliveries, gaming, and streaming TV and movies. For some, this sounds like a positive development. However, as we have demonstrated here, this has the potential to reinforce and create new forms of inequality and suffering.

Disparities exist between those who can work from home and those occupations that require physical presence; informal labour often cannot be done from home, couriers and delivery drivers, supermarket workers, takeaway staff and many other low-paid and insecure workers facilitate the comfortable existence for many who can remain at home. Labour market inequality has always existed, but the pandemic has and will continue to heighten these disparities. As economies slowly recover from the lockdown restrictions, many business failures leave harmful residues in terms of debt, unemployment and the stress and anxiety that accompanies these uncertainties. Employees who have been unable to work during lockdown—those in informal sectors, tourism and hospitality, for example—have been paid a fraction of their normal wage and have slipped into precarious and uncertain circumstances. Sectors such as tourism and hospitality will require consumer confidence in order to recover. The economic consequences of lockdown will be disastrous for many who slide towards precarity and insecurity but bountiful for some who will find new opportunities to grow and profit.

On a political-economic level, the pandemic response may represent the final nail in the coffin for neoliberalism. The Global Financial Crisis undermined its ideological legitimacy and demonstrated its limitations in providing a coherent and stable narrative.[18] After a decade of austerity, governments everywhere turned on the spigot in a set of emergency measures that contradicted everything we had been told up to that point. There *was* a magic money tree after all. On an economic level, MMT has begun to move from the margins, and some of its key principles about the reality of our monetary system are proving right. For example, the UK, USA and other countries with sovereignty over its money supply can always find the money it needs for anything—military spending, education, unemployment insurance and healthcare—as shown in the emergency spending on pandemic support. While some still cling to

---

[18] Mitchell and Fazi (2017).

what Stephanie Kelton[19] calls the 'deficit myth', proving the intransigent nature of ideology, space has opened up for alternative perspectives. MMT's one policy initiative, a state-backed Job Guarantee Programme, has been debated as part of the Green New Deal in the USA.[20]

In political terms, there appears to be a rejection of neoliberalism and a recognition that we may be in a transitional moment. Grace Blakely[21] argues that the 'corona crash' represents a movement towards monopoly capitalism. Klaus Schwab,[22] head of the WEF, argues that this moment allows for not only the acceleration of the fourth industrial revolution (around clean energy and digital technology) but also the transition from shareholder to stakeholder capitalism. Schwab has become a shadowy figure wrapped up in conspiracy theories surrounding the Great Reset. Many have mocked those who have connected Covid-19 and the Great Reset which we would suggest is short-sighted. However, we also reject the idea of sinister Machiavellian plotting; conspiracies are by nature secret and the fact that Schwab published a book in 2020 setting out his entire agenda seems to negate that point. However, it is important for us to remember that capitalism, as a system, has always responded to a crisis in order to both reproduce itself and to stave off threats. The slow disintegration of neoliberalism and the increased dissatisfaction we have seen in recent years demonstrates a system in crisis; the Great Reset presents an opportunity to reshape the world in a way that both maintains the position of those in power and addresses the challenges that our system has created—particularly climate change. In this respect, it is what you might call a double-edged sword. Indeed, the Great Reset proposes changes that will transform every aspect of our society—increased use of Artificial Intelligence and digital technology, transition to clean energy sources, deglobalisation and on-shoring, shortening supply chains. The pandemic has created the momentum to push through changes and the economic crash has created the fiscal headroom required to invest significantly in new technologies, carbon capture, hydrogen batteries and clean energy.

---

[19] Kelton (2020).

[20] Tcherneva (2020).

[21] Blakeley (2020).

[22] Schwab. and Malleret (2020).

Some of these changes are likely to be more welcomed than others and may generate points of friction. One thing is for sure, we must be cautious in presenting the Great Reset as some sort of panacea.

Alex Hochuli, George Hoare and Philip Cunliffe[23] suggest we have reached the 'end of the end of history' and are moving from post-politics to anti-politics. The post-politics period that emerged with the end of the Cold War, characterised by cynicism, apathy and the acceptance of globalisation and neoliberalism, is ending and we have entered an age of anti-politics. People have become angry and vocal but increasingly focused on the failings of the political system and its actors rather than presenting an alternative vision. They see the emergence of a centre-right nationalism likely to dominate in places like the UK, Europe and beyond while the Left holds on to a technocracy of experts severely undermined by the handling of the pandemic:

> With the abdication of British leadership before Covid-19, we saw the last flare-up of technocratic rule – even as it disintegrated into warring academic factions based on competing methodologies, assumptions and models. The unsustainability of technocracy as a mode of governance was plainly revealed in the unevenness and mismanagement of lockdown policies across the Western world. (p. 156)

Although commentators do not agree on where we are going, they are in agreement that the post-pandemic world will be different, politically, economically, culturally and socially. Inequalities and harms have grown significantly across the pandemic and are juxtaposed against grotesque increases in wealth among the elite. Existing problems—food insecurity, insecure and precarious forms of work, educational inequality, inadequate housing, cultural antagonisms around migration and asylum seekers, crime and anti-social behaviour—have grown since the onset of the pandemic and lockdown. The economic, cultural and social fault lines and antagonisms exemplified by Donald Trump and Brexit have now been joined by disagreement and division over Covid-19 rules, mask wearing, vaccination, compliance and freedom.

---

[23] Hochuli et al. (2021).

As stated at the start of this chapter, these are ethical and moral questions without resolution in an emotive age with no adjudicating authority to settle moral debates. The fault lines and antagonisms over Covid-19 represent a further fraying of social cohesion. Simon Winlow and Steve Hall[24] persuasively suggested that we had moved into a 'post-social' era and the pandemic reinforces this point. The ties that bind us have broken and we defensively filter out those we disagree with, those who do not think or look or act like us. The divides are racial, gendered, nationalist and above all class-based. The consequences of this are troubling and when viewed from a criminological viewpoint, the erosion of social cohesion alongside the myriad other inequalities is a recipe for an explosion of expressive and instrumental crime, violence and anti-social behaviour. Challenging people for not respecting social distance or for wearing or not wearing masks will result in assaults, violence and harm.

If harm represents those barriers that prevent us from individually and collectively striving towards a good life and flourishing,[25] the unintended harms of lockdown are manifold. These pages attest to that. According to this definition, Covid-19 is also incredibly harmful and required a measured response to protect those most vulnerable and at risk. However, in implementing non-recommended measures like lockdown, the balance of harm is skewed and lockdown appears to have unleashed harms that we will have to face in the coming decades. We require politics in its true sense in order to overcome this and the first step has to be a willingness to listen to those we disagree with. If we are to truly recover from the pandemic, we will have to do it together. We may not have all been equal in our experience of the pandemic, but the stakes are too high to be divided as we move into a post-pandemic future.

---

[24] Winlow and Hall (2013).

[25] Raymen (2019) The Enigma of Social Harm and the Barrier of Liberalism: Why Zemiology Needs a Theory of the Good. *Justice, Power and Resistance*. 3(1) 134–163.

References

Bambra, C., Lynch, J., & Smith, K. E. (2021). *The unequal pandemic*. Policy Press.

Bauman, Z. (2004). *Wasted lives: Modernity and its outcasts*. Polity.

Blakeley, G. (2020). *The Corona crash*. Verso.

Dodsworth, L. (2021). *A state of fear*. Pinter & Martin Ltd.

Ellis, A., Briggs, D., Lloyd, A., & Telford, L. (2021). A ticking time bomb of future harm: Lockdown, child abuse and future violence. *Abuse: An International Journal, 2*(1). https://doi.org/10.37576/abuse.2021.017

Hall, S., & Winlow, S. (2015). *Revitalizing criminological theory: Towards a New ultra- realism*. Routledge.

Hall, S. (2012). *Theorizing crime and deviance*. Sage.

Hochuli, A., Hoare, G., & Cunliffe, P. (2021). *The end of the end of history: Politics in the twenty-first century*. Zero.

Honigsbaum, M. (2020). *The pandemic century: A history of global contagion from the Spanish Flu to COVID-19*. Penguin.

Jones, L., & Hemeiri, S. (2021). COVID-19 and the failure of the neoliberal regulatory state. *Review of International Political Economy*, 1–25. Online First. https://www.tandfonline.com/doi/epub/10.1080/09692290.2021.189 2798?needAccess=true

Kelton, S. (2020). *The deficit myth: Modern monetary theory and how to build a better economy*. John Murray.

Kotzé, J. (2021). On researching harm: An ultra-realist perspective. In P. Davies, P. Leighton, & T. Wyatt (Eds.), *The Palgrave handbook of social harm*. Palgrave Macmillan.

MacIntyre, A. (2011). *After virtue*. Bloomsbury.

Mitchell, W., & Fazi, T. (2017). *Reclaiming the state*. Pluto Press.

Pitron, G. (2020). *The rare metals war*. Scribe.

Raymen, T. (2021). The assumption of harmlessness. In P. Davies, P. Leighton, & T. Wyatt (Eds.), *The Palgrave handbook of social harm*. Palgrave Macmillan.

Schildt, H. (2020). *The data imperative: How digitalization is reshaping management, organizing, and work*. Oxford University Press.

Schwab, K., & Malleret, T. (2020). *COVID 19: The great reset*. World Economic Forum.

Streeck, W. (2016). *How will capitalism end?* Verso.

Tcherneva, P. (2020). *The case for a job guarantee*. Polity.

Wacquant, L. (2009). *Prisons of poverty*. University of Minnesota Press.
Winlow, S., & Hall, S. (2013). *Rethinking social exclusion*. Sage.

Bibliography

Abassi, K. (2020). COVID-19: Politicisation, "corruption", and suppression of science. *British Medical Journal, 371*, 1–2. https://doi.org/10.1136/bmj. m4425

ABC Australia. (2012). Another 50,000 Australians take out private health cover. *International Journal of Health Care Quality Assurance, 25*(7). https:// doi.org/10.1108/ijhcqa.2012.06225gaa.006

Abuhammad, S., Alzoubi, K., & Khabour, O. (2020). Fear of COVID-19 and stigmatization towards infected people among Jordanian people. *International Journal of Clinical Practice, 75*(4), e13899.

Acs, G., & Karpman, M. (2020, June). *Employment, income, and unemployment insurance during the COVID-19 pandemic* (Urban Institute Report).

Actionaid. (2020). *Climate migrants pushed to the brink*. Actionaid.

Allegretti, A., & Geddes, L. (2021). PM to confirm 19 July end to COVID rules despite scientists' warnings. *The Guardian*. https://www.theguardian. com/politics/2021/jul/04/pm-confirm-19-july-end-covid-restrictions-scient ists-warnings-england. Accessed 8 July 2021.

Almeida, F., & Duarte Santos, J. (2020). The effects of COVID-19 on job security and unemployment in Portugal. *International Journal of Sociology and Social Policy, 40*(9/10), 995–1003. https://doi.org/10.1108/IJSSP-07-2020-0291

© The Editor(s) (if applicable) and The Author(s), under exclusive license to Springer Nature Switzerland AG 2021
D. Briggs et al., *Lockdown*,
https://doi.org/10.1007/978-3-030-88825-1

Altena, E., Baglioni, C., Espie, C., Ellis, J., Gavriloff, D., Holzinger, B., Schlarb, A., Frase, L., Jernelov, S., & Riemann, D. (2020). Dealing with sleep problems during home confinement due to the COVID- 19 outbreak: Practical recommendations from a task force of the European CBT-I Academy. *Journal of Sleep Research, 29*(4), 1–7.

Ambrose, J. (2020). Investors plan major move into renewable energy infrastructure. *The Guardian.* https://www.theguardian.com/environment/2020/nov/23/investors-plan-major-move-into-renewable-energy-infrastructure. Accessed 25 June 2021.

American Cancer Society. (2021). *Cancer facts & figures 2021.*

Amnesty International. (2020a). *As if expendable: The UK government's failure to protect older people in care homes during the Covid-19 pandemic.*

Amocida, B., Formenti, B., Ussai, S., Palestra, F., & Missoni, E. (2020). *The Italian health system and the COVID-19 challenge.* https://www.researchgate.net/publication/340180459_The_Italian_health_system_and_the_COVID-19_challenge. Accessed 5 June 2021.

Amnesty International. (2020b). *Spain: Older people in care homes abandoned during COVID-19 pandemic.* Amnesty International

Arahan, R., Doan, D., Dornan, M., Muñoz, A., Parsons, K., Yi, S., & Vergara-Hegi, D. (2021). *Pacific Island countries in the era of Covid-19.* World Bank Group.

Arenas-Arroyo, E., Fernandez-Kranz, D., & Nollenberger, N. (2021). Intimate partner violence under forced cohabitation and economic stress: Evidence from the COVID-19 pandemic. *Journal of Public Economics, 194,* 04350.

Arevalo-Rodriguez, I., Buitrago-Garcia, D., Simancas-Racines, D., Zambrano-Achig, P., Del Campo, R., Ciapponi, A., Sued, O., Martinez-Garcia, L., Rutjes, A. W., Low, N., Bossuyt, P. M., Perez-Molina, J. A., & Zamora, J. (2020). False-negative results of initial RT-PCR assays for COVID-19: A systematic review. *PLoS One 15*(12), 14. e0242958. https://doi.org/10.1371/journal.pone.0242958

Armocida, B., Formenti, B., Ussai, S., & Missoni, E. (2020). The Italian health system and the COVID-19 challenge. *The Lancet Public Health.* https://doi.org/10.1016/S2468-2667(20)30074-8

Arndt, C., Davies, R., Gabriel, S., Harris, L., Makrelov, K., Robinson, S., Levy, S., Simbanegavi, W., Van Seventer, D., & Anderson, L. (2020). COVID-19 lockdowns, income distribution, and food security: An analysis for South Africa. *Global Food Security, 26,* 100410. https://doi.org/10.1016/j.gfs.2020.100410

Arshed, N., Meo, M., & Farooq, F. (2020). Empirical assessment of government policies and flattening of the COVID19 curve. *Journal of Public Affairs* *20*(4), e2333. https://doi.org/10.1002%2Fpa.2333

Asmundson, G., & Taylor, S. (2020). How health anxiety influences responses to viral outbreaks like COVID-19: What all decision makers, health authorities, and healthcare professionals need to know. *Journal of Anxiety Disorders, 71,* 1–2.

Associated Press. (2021, February 16). *As the COVID-19 crisis drags on, hard-hit French youth struggle.* Cited online at https://www.euronews.com/2021/02/16/as-the-covid-19-crisis-drags-on-hard-hit-french-youth-struggle

Assouad, L., Chancel, L., & Morgan, M. (2018). Extreme inequality: Evidence from Brazil, India, the Middle East, and South Africa. *AEA Papers and Proceedings, 108,* 119–123. https://www.aeaweb.org/articles?id=10.1257/pandp.20181076

Atkinson, R. (2020). *Alpha City.* Verso.

Atkinson, R., & Rogers, T. (2016). Pleasure zones and murder boxes: Online pornography and violent video games as cultural zones of exception. *British Journal of Criminology, 56*(6), 1291–1307.

Australian Government Department of Health. (2021). *Coronavirus (COVID-19) current situation and case numbers.* https://www.health.gov.au/news/health-alerts/novel-coronavirus-2019-ncov-health-alert/coronavirus-covid-19-current-situation-and-case-numbers

Ayati, N., Saiyarsarai, P., & Nikfar, S. (2020). Short and long term impacts of COVID-19 on the pharmaceutical sector. *DARU Journal of Pharmaceutical Sciences, 28,* 799–805.

Ayoubkhani, D., Khunti, K., Nafilyan, V., Maddox, T., Humberstone, B., Diamond, I., & Banerjee, A. (2021). Post-COVID syndrome in individuals admitted to hospital with COVID-19: Retrospective cohort study. *BMJ, 372.* https://doi.org/10.1136/bmj.n693

Badiou, A. (2012). *The rebirth of history.* Verso.

Bakhit, M., Krzyzaniak, N., Scott, A. M., Clark, J., Glasziou, P., & Del Mar, C. (2021). Downsides of face masks and possible mitigation strategies: A systematic review and meta-analysis. *BMJ Open, 11*(2), e044364. https://doi.org/10.1136/bmjopen-2020-044364

Balogun, J. (2020). Lessons from the USA delayed response to the COVID-19 pandemic. *African Journal of Reproductive Health, 24*(1), 14–21.

Bambra, C., Lynch, J., & Smith, K. E. (2021). *The unequal pandemic.* Policy Press.

Bambra, C., Munford, L., Alexandros, L., Barr, A., Brown, H., Davies, H., Konstantinos, D., Mason, K., Pickett, K., Taylor, C., Taylor-Robinson, D., & Wickham, S. (2020). *COVID-19 and the Northern powerhouse*. Northern Health Science Alliance.

Bambra, C., Riordan, R., Ford, J., & Matthews, F. (2020). The COVID-19 pandemic and health inequalities. *Journal of Epidemiology and Community Health, 74*(11), 964–968.

Bamji, A. (2020). COVID-19: What's going wrong with testing in the UK? *British Medical Journal, 370*. https://doi.org/10.1136/bmj.m3678

Banerjee, D., & Bhattacharya, P., (2021). The hidden vulnerability of home-lessness in the COVID-19 pandemic: Perspectives from India. *International Journal of Social Psychiatry, 67*(1), 3–6. https://doi.org/10.1177%2F0020 764020922890

Baral, S., Chandler, R., Prieto, R., Gupta, S., Mishra, S., & Kulldorff, M. (2021). Leveraging epidemiological principles to evaluate Sweden's COVID-19 response. *Annals of Epidemiology, 54*, 21–26.

Baron, E. J., Goldstein, E. G., & Wallace, C. T. (2020). Suffering in silence: How COVID-19 school closures inhibit the reporting of child maltreat-ment. *Journal of Public Economics, 190*, Article 10425. https://doi.org/10.1016/j.jpubeco.2020.104258

Barry, C., & Lazar, S. (2020). Justifying lockdown. *Ethics & International Affairs*, 1–7.

Bauman, Z. (2004). *Wasted lives: Modernity and its outcasts*. Polity.

BBC. (2020a, April 5). *Coronavirus fears linked to Illinois pair's murder-suicide*. Cited online at https://www.bbc.com/news/world-us-canada-52192842

BBC. (2020b). *Peloton sales surge as virus boosts home workouts*. https://www.bbc.co.uk/news/business-54112461. Accessed 22 June 2021.

BBC. (2020c). *COVID-19: Euro 2020 tickets offered as part of vaccine push*. *BBC*. 6 July 2021. Cited online at https://www.bbc.com/news/uk-england-london-57732002

BBC. (2020d, July 7). *Coronavirus: Boris Johnson criticised over 'cowardly' care home comments*. Cited online at https://www.bbc.com/news/uk-politics-533 15178

BBC. (2020e, September 9). Moria migrants: Fire destroys Greek camp leaving 13,000 without shelter. *BBC*. Cited online at https://www.bbc.com/news/world-europe-54082201

BBC. (2021a, May 3). Napier Barracks: Call to close 'unlawful' asylum centre. *BBC*. Cited online at https://www.bbc.com/news/uk-england-kent-57343968

BBC. (2021b, March 17). COVID-19 disruptions killed 228,000 children in South Asia, says UN report. *BBC*. Cited online at https://www.bbc.com/news/world-asia-56425115

BBC. (2021c). *COVID: Sydney city centre and Bondi beach to enter lockdown.* https://www.bbc.co.uk/news/world-australia-57590969. Accessed 25 June 2021.

BBC. (2021d, June 28). Australia COVID: Outbreaks emerge across country in 'new phase' of pandemic. *BBC*. Cited online at https://www.bbc.com/news/world-australia-57633457

BBC. (2021e). *PM must sack Matt Hancock after affair claims—Labour.* https://www.bbc.co.uk/news/uk-politics-57608716. Accessed 8 July 2021.

BBC. (2021f). *COVID-19: 'Lifting all protections at once is reckless'—Keir Starmer.* https://www.bbc.co.uk/news/av/uk-57728368. Accessed 8 July 2021.

BBC. (2021g). *COVID in Scotland: Restrictions to end as planned.* https://www.bbc.co.uk/news/uk-scotland-scotland-politics-57732436. Accessed 14 July 2021.

BC News. (2021, June 2021). *B.C. reports fewer than 200 new COVID-19 cases, no deaths.* Cited online at https://bc.ctvnews.ca/b-c-reports-fewer-than-200-new-covid-19-cases-no-deaths-1.5451217

Bega, S., Smillie, S., & Ajam, K. (2020, May 16). *Spike in child abandonments and the physical abuse of youngsters during lockdown.* IOL. https://www.iol.co.za/saturday-star/news/spike-in-child-abandonments-and-the-physical-abuse-ofyoungsters-during-lockdown-48012964

Begum, M., Farid, M., Alam, M., & Barau, S. (2020). COVID-19 and Bangladesh: Socio-economic analysis towards the future correspondence. *Asian Journal of Agricultural Extension, Economics & Sociology, 38*(9), 143–155.

Berenson, A. (2020). *Unreported truths about COVID-19.* Amazon.

Berniell, I., & Facchini, G. (2021). COVID-19 lockdown and domestic violence: Evidence from internet-search behavior in 11 countries. *European Economic Review, 136,* 1–13.

Bhattacharya, J., Gupta, S., & Kulldorff, M. (2020). *Focused protection: The middle ground between lockdowns and "let it rip".* The Great Barrington Declaration. https://gbdeclaration.org/focused-protection/. Accessed 17 June 2021.

Bhopal, S., Bagaria, J., Olabi, B., & Bhopal, R. (2021). Children and young people remain at low risk of COVID-19 mortality. *The Lancet Child and*

Adolescent Health. Published online 10 March 2021. https://doi.org/10. 1016/S2352-4642(21)00066-3

Bhorat, H., Oosthuizen, M., & Stanwix, B. (2021). Social assistance amidst the COVID-19 epidemic in South Africa: A policy assessment. *South African Journal of Economics, 89*(1), 63–81. https://doi.org/10.1111/saje.12277

Blackall, M. (2021). *Euro 2020 crowds like eat out to help out on steroids' and encourages fans to ditch rules, Sage adviser warns.* https://inews.co.uk/news/uk/euros-wembley-fans-covid-rules-eat-out-to-help-out-sage-adviser-108 0772. Accessed 8 July 2021.

Blair, A., Parnia, A., & Siddiqui, A. (2021, January). A time-series analysis of testing and COVID-19 outbreaks in Canadian federal prisons to inform prevention and surveillance efforts. *Canada Communicable Disease Report, 47*(1), 66–76.

Blakeley, G. (2020). *The Corona crash.* Verso.

Blanchard, S. (2021, May 14). Sage models warn COVID hospital admissions could be higher than second wave if Indian variant is 40% more infectious than Kent strain as UK cases double in a week. *Daily Mail.* Cited online at https://www.dailymail.co.uk/news/article-9578503/Coronavirus-SAGE-models-warn-hospital-admissions-soar-India-variant-infectious.html

Bloodworth, J. (2019). *Hired: Six months undercover in low-wage Britain.* Atlantic Books.

Blumenthal, D., & Hamburg, M. (2021, February 20). US health and health care are a mess: Now what? *The Lancet, 397,* 647–648.

Blundell, R., Joyce, R., Keiller, A. N., & Ziliak, J. P. (2018). Income inequality and the labour market in Britain and the US. *Journal of Public Economics, 162,* 48–62. https://doi.org/10.1016/j.jpubeco.2018.04.001

Brandén, M., Aradhya, S., Kolk, M., Drefahl, S., Malmberg, B., Cederström, A., Andersson, G., & Mussino, E. (2020). Residential context and COVID-19 mortality among adults aged 70 years and older in Stockholm: A population-based, observational study using individual-level data. *Lancet Healthy Longevity, 1*(2), e80-88. https://doi.org/10.1016/S2666-756 8(20)30016-7

Brant, L. C. C., Nascimento, B. R., Teixeira, R. A., Lopez, M. A. C. Q., Malta, D. C., Oliveira, G. M. M., & Ribeiro, A. L. P. (2020). Excess of cardiovascular deaths during the COVID-19 pandemic in Brazilian capital cities. *Heart, 106,* 1898–1905.

Brendau, A., Petzold, M., Pyrkosch, L., Maricic, L., Betzler, F., Rogoll, J., Große, J., Ströhle, A., & Plag, J. (2021). Associations between COVID-19 related media consumption and symptoms of anxiety, depression and

COVID-19 related fear in the general population in Germany. *European Archives of Psychiatry and Clinical Neuroscience, 271*, 283–291.

Briggs, D. (2020). *Climate changed: Refugee border stories and the business of misery*. Routledge.

Briggs, D., Ellis, A., Lloyd, A., & Telford, L. (2020). New hopes or old futures in disguise? Neoliberalism, the Covid-19 pandemic and the possibility of social change. *International Journal of Sociology and Social Policy, 40*(9/10), 831–848. https://doi.org/10.1108/IJSSP-07-2020-0268

Briggs, D., Ellis, A., Lloyd, A., & Telford, L. (2021). *Researching the COVID-19 pandemic: A critical blueprint for the social sciences*. Policy Press Rapid Response Series.

Briggs, D., Ellis, A., Telford, L., & Lloyd, A. (2021). *Working, living, and dying in COVID times: Perspectives from frontline residential care workers in the UK' in safer communities*. https://doi.org/10.1108/SC-04-2021-0013

Briggs, D., & Gamero, R. M. (2017). *Dead-end lives*. Policy Press.

Bristow, J., & Gilland, E. (2021). *The Corona generation*. Zero.

British Heart Foundation. (2021). *UK Factsheet*. British Heart Foundation.

Brown, H. (2021, May 14). *Ohio's $1 million COVID vaccine lottery is bribery at its best*. MSNBC News Online. Cited online at https://www.msnbc.com/opinion/ohio-s-1-million-covid-vaccine-lottery-bribery-its-best-n1267276

Bulman, M. (2020, November 16). Self-harm incidents surge 2,000% in detention. *The Independent*. Cited online at https://www.independent.co.uk/news/uk/home-news/self-harm-detention-brook-house-asylum-seekers-b1668406.html

Burgen, S. (2020, April 28). Women killed in Spain as Coronavirus lockdown sees rise in domestic violence. *The Guardian*. Cited online at https://www.theguardian.com/global-development/2020/apr/28/three-women-killed-in-spain-as-coronavirus-lockdown-sees-rise-in-domestic-violence

Buck, H. J. (2019). *After geoengineering*. Verso.

Bundgaard, H., Bundgaard, J. S., Raaschou-Pedersen, D. E. T., von Buchwald, C., Todsen, T., Norsk, J. B., Pries-Heje, M. M., Vissing, C. R., Nielsen, P. B., Winsløw, U. C., Fogh, K., Hasselbalch, R., Krisrtensen, J. H., Ringgaard, A., Andersen, M. P., Goecke, N. B., Trebbien, R., Skovgaard, K., Benfield, T., … Iversen, K. (2020, November). Effectiveness of adding a mask recommendation to other public health measures to prevent SARS-CoV-2 infection in Danish mask wearers: A randomized controlled trial. *Annals of Internal Medicine*. https://doi.org/10.7326/M20-6817

Byrne, J., Rapisarda, S. S., Hummer, D., & Kras, K. R. (2020). An imperfect storm: Identifying the root causes of COVID-19 outbreaks in the world's largest corrections systems. *Victims & Offenders, 15*(7–8), 862–909. https://doi.org/10.1080/15564886.2020.1838373

Calcea, N. (2021). Pandemic winners and losers: How Big Tech's gains mask a struggling economy. *New Statesman.* https://www.newstatesman.com/politics/2021/02/pandemic-winners-and-losers-how-big-techs-gains-mask-struggling-economy. Accessed on 23 June 2021.

Campbell, A. (2020). An increasing risk of family violence during the COVID-19 pandemic: Strengthening community collaborations to save lives. *Forensic Science International: Reports, 2,* Article 100089. https://doi.org/10.1016/j.fsir.2020.100089

Campbell, D. (2019, November 25). Hospital beds at record low in England as NHS struggles with demand. *The Guardian.* Cited online at https://www.theguardian.com/politics/2019/nov/25/hospital-beds-at-record-low-in-england-as-nhs-struggles-with-demand

Campbell, P., & Miller, J. (2021). Electric cars surge in popularity after manufacturers' late dash. *Financial Times.* https://www.ft.com/content/e9a6aa4f-4a8b-4c80-a89b-13e8fbde2c43. Accessed 25 June 2021.

Canning, V. (2018). Zemiology at the border. In A. Boukli, & J. Kotzé (Eds.), *Zemiology: Reconnecting crime and social harm.* Palgrave Macmillan.

Canning, V., & Tombs, S. (2021). *From social harm to zemiology: A critical introduction.* Routledge.

Carrington, D. (2021). Global sales of electric cars accelerate fast in 2020 despite pandemic. *The Guardian.* https://www.theguardian.com/environment/2021/jan/19/global-sales-of-electric-cars-accelerate-fast-in-2020-despite-covid-pandemic. Accessed 25 June 2021.

Cartabellotta, N., Cottafava, E., Luceri, R., & Mosti, M. (2019, September). *Il definanziamento 2010–2019 del Servizio Sanitario Nazionale.* https://www.gimbe.org/osservatorio/Report_Osservatorio_GIMBE_2019.07_Definanziamento_SSN.pdf. Accessed 20 March 2020.

Carter, P. (2016). *Operational productivity and performance in English NHS Acute hospitals: Unwarranted variations. independent report for the department of health.* Accessed from https://www.gov.uk/government/publications/productivity-in-nhs-hospitals

Case, A., & Deaton, A. (2020). *Deaths of despair and the future of capitalism.* Princeton University Press.

Castillo, I., Mato-Diaz, F., & Alvarez-Rodriguez, A. (2021). Furloughs, teleworking and other work situations during the COVID-19 lockdown: Impact on mental well-being. *International Journal of Environmental Research and Public Health, 18,* 1–16.

Catalan News. (2020, June 19). Spain's COVID-19 death toll revised up by 1,177 to 28,313. *Catalan News.* Cited online at https://www.catalannews. com/society-science/item/spain-s-covid-19-death-toll-revised-up-by-1177-to-28313

Catana, S., Toma, S., & Gradinaru, C. (2020). The economic and social impact of COVID-19 pandemic: Evidence from Romania. *University Annals, Economic Sciences Series, 20*(2), 273–277.

CDC. (2016). *2014–2016 Ebola Outbreak in West Africa.* Cited online at https://www.cdc.gov/vhf/ebola/history/2014-2016-outbreak/index.html

CDC. (2021). *Symptoms of anxiety or depressive disorder and use of mental health care among adults during the COVID-19 pandemic—United States, August 2020–February 2021.* CDC.

Centre for Sustainable Employment. (2021). *State of working in India: One year on from COVID-19.* Centre for Sustainable Employment at Azim Premji University.

Conticini, E., Frediani, B., & Caro, D. (2020). Can atmospheric pollution be considered a co- factor in extremely high level of SARS-CoV-2 lethality in Northern Italy? *Environmental Pollution, 261,* 114465.

Chaiuk, T., & Dunaievska, O. (2020). Producing the fear culture in media: An examination of Coronavirus discourse. *Journal of History, Culture and Art Research, 9*(2), 184–194. https://doi.org/10.7596/taksad.v8i4.2316

Chan, E. (2020). Moral foundations underlying behavioural compliance during the COVID-19 pandemic. *Personality and individual Differences, 171,* 110463. https://doi.org/10.1016/j.paid.2020.110463

Chan, J. (2013). A suicide survivor: The life of a Chinese worker. *New Technology, Work and Employment, 28*(2), 84–99. https://doi.org/10.1111/ntwe.12007

Chaudhry, R., Dranitsaris, G., Mubashir, T., Bartoszko, J., & Riazbi, S. (2020). A country level analysis measuring the impact of government actions, country preparedness and socioeconomic factors on COVID-19 mortality and related health outcomes. *EClinicalMedicine, 25,* 1–8.

Chomsky, N., & Pollin, R. (2020). *Climate crisis and the global green new deal.* Verso.

Choudhari, R. (2020). COVID-19 pandemic: Mental health challenges of internal migrant workers of India. *Asian Journal of Psychiatry, 54,* 102254.https://doi.org/10.1016/j.ajp.2020.102254

Choudhary, S. (2021, August 9). *Charts show that COVID is hitting parts of Asia harder now than when the pandemic began.* CNBC. Cited online at https://www.cnbc.com/2021/08/10/covid-is-hitting-parts-of-asia-harder-now-than-beginning-of-pandemic.html

Chen, S. (2020, December 24). *China has a huge wealth-gap problem—And it's getting worse.* Bloomberg. https://www.bloomberg.com/news/storythreads/2020-12-24/china-has-a-huge-wealth-gap-problem-and-it-s-getting-worse

Chen, J., Shi, L., Zhang, Y., Wang, X., & Sun, G. (2021). A cross-country core strategy comparison in China, Japan, Singapore and South Korea during the early COVID-19 pandemic. *Globalization and Health, 17*(22), 1–10.

Chin, V., Ioannidis, J., Tanner, M., & Cripps, S. (2020). Effects of non-pharmaceutical interventions on COVID-19: A tale of three models. *medRxiv*, 1–45.

Churchill, B. (2020). COVID-19 and the immediate impact on young people and employment in Australia: A gendered analysis. *Gender, Work & Organization, 28*(2), 783–794.

Claeson, M., & Hanson, S. (2021). Comment: COVID-19 and the Swedish enigma. *The Lancet, 397*, 260–261.

Clarke, L. (2021, May 18). Covid Bolton: Vaccine surge as Indian variant remains a concern. *The Bolton News.* Cited online at https://www.theboltonnews.co.uk/news/19309873.covid-bolton-vaccine-surge-indian-variant-remains-concern/

CNA. (2021, May 29). *COVID-19 sweeps through Thailand's overcrowded prisons.* Cited online at https://www.channelnewsasia.com/news/asia/covid-19-thailand-prison-jail-overcrowded-outbreak-14909396

Coalition for the Homeless. (2020). *Age-adjusted mortality rate for sheltered homeless New Yorkers.* Cited online at https://www.coalitionforthehomeless.org/age-adjusted-mortality-rate-for-sheltered-homeless-new-yorkers/

Cohen, A., Kessel, B., & Milgroom, M. (2020). Diagnosing COVID-19 infection: The danger of over- reliance on positive test results. *medRxiv: The Preprint Server for Health Sciences*, 1–11. https://doi.org/10.1101/2020.04.26.20080911

Collins, C., Ocampo, O., & Paslaski, S. (2020). *Billionaire bonanza 2020: Wealth windfalls, tumbling taxes, and pandemic profiteers.* Institute for Policy Studies.

Condry, R., Miles, C., Brunton-Douglas, T., & Oladapo, A. (2020). *Experiences of child and adolescent to parent violence in the COVID-19 pandemic.* University of Oxford. https://www.law.ox.ac.uk/sites/files/oxlaw/final_report_capv_in_covid-19_aug20.pdf

Coyne, J., & Jennings, P. (2020). *After Covid-19: Australia and the world rebuild.* Australian Strategic Policy Institute.

Costello, H., Cooper, C., Marston, L., & Livingston, G. (2020). Burnout in UK care home staff and its effect on staff turnover: MARQUE English national care home longitudinal study. *Age and Ageing, 49*(1), 74–81.

Collins, C. (2020). Let's stop pretending billionaires are in the same boat as us during the pandemic. *The Guardian.* https://www.theguardian.com/commentisfree/2020/apr/24/billionaires-coronavirus-not-in-the-same-boat. Accessed 22 June 2021.

CRRC. (2020). *Armenia: Citizens' perceptions on COVID-19 pandemic.* The World Bank.

Cullen, W., Gulati, G., & Kelly, B. (2020). Mental health in the COVID-19 pandemic. *QJM: An International Journal of Medicine, 113,* 311–312.

Czeisler, M., Lane, R., Petrosky, E., Wiley, J., Christensen, A., Njai, R., Weaver, M., Robbins, R., Facer-Childs, E., Barger, L., Czeisler, C., Howard, M., & Rajaratnam, S. (2020, June 24–30). Mental health, substance use, and suicidal ideation during the COVID-19 pandemic—United States. *Centers for Disease Control and Prevention: Weekly Report, 69,* 1049–1057.

Czeisler, M. É., Marynak, K., Clarke, K. E., Salah, Z., Shakya, I., Thierry, J. M., Ali, N., McMillan, H., Wiley, J. F., Weaver, M. D., & Czeisler, C. A. (2020, June). Delay or avoidance of medical care because of COVID-19–Related concerns—United States. *MMWR Morbidity and Mortality Weekly Report, 69,* 1250–1257. http://doi.org/10.15585/mmwr.mm6936a4

Dahel, M., Khanal, P., Maharajan, S., Panthi, B., & Nepal, S. (2020). Mitigating violence against young women and girls during COVID-19 induced lockdown in Nepal: A wake up call. *Globalisation and Health, 16,* Article 84. https://doi.org/10.1186/s12992-020-00616-w

Dalglish, S. L. (2020). COVID-19 gives the lie to global health expertise. *Lancet, 395,* 1189.

Dalsania, A. K., Fastiggi, M. J., Kahlam, A., Shah, R., Patel, K., Shiau, S., Rokicki, S., & DallaPiazza, M. (2021). The relationship between social determinants of health and racial disparities in COVID-19 mortality. *Journal of Racial and Ethnic Health Disparities.* Online First. https://doi.org/10.1007%2Fs40615-020-00952-y

Daly, M. (2020). COVID-19 and care homes in England: What happened and why? *Social Policy Administration, 54*(7), 985–998.

Dambach, K. (2018, April 6). Dire conditions at UK immigration detention centers. *Infomigrants.* Cited online at https://www.infomigrants.net/en/post/8479/dire-conditions-at-uk-immigration-detention-centers

Dapić, M., Flander, G., & Prijatelj, K. (2020). Children behind closed doors due to COVID-19 isolation: Abuse, neglect and domestic violence. *Archives of Psychiatry Research, 56* (2), 181–192. https://doi.org/10.20471/dec.2020. 56.02.06

Das, M., Das, A., & Mandal, A. (2020). Examining the impact of lockdown (due to COVID-19) on domestic violence (DV): An evidences from India. *Asian Journal of Psychiatry, 54*, 1–2.

Day, M. (2021). Amazon sales skyrocket as pandemic shopping habits persist. *Al Jazeera.* https://www.aljazeera.com/economy/2021/4/29/amazon-sales-skyrocket-as-pandemic-shopping-habits-persist. Accessed 22 June 2021.

De, A. (2020, April 17). India's top infectious disease killed over 440,000 people in 2018. *Indian Express.* Cited online at https://indianexpress.com/article/india/coronavirus-india-top-infectious-disease-tuberculosis-6365732/

De Cao, E., & Sandner, M. (2020, May 8). *The potential impact of the COVID-19 on child abuse and neglect: The role of childcare and unemployment.* Vox Eu CEPR. Retrieved from: https://voxeu.org/article/potential-impact-covid-19-child-abuse-and-neglect

Desmond, M. (2017). *Evicted: Poverty and profit in the American city.* Penguin.

Devi, R., Hinsliff-Smith, K., Goodman, C., & Gordon, A. (2020). The Covid-19 pandemic in care homes—Revealing the cracks in the system. *The Journal of Nursing Home Research Sciences, 6*, 58–60.

Dlamini, J. (2021). Gender-based violence, twin pandemic to COVID-19. *Critical Sociology, 47* (4/5), 583–590. https://doi.org/10.1177%2F0896920 520975465

Dodsworth, L. (2021). *A state of fear.* Pinter & Martin Ltd.

Dorling, D. (2015). *Inequality and the 1%.* Verso.

Dsouza, D. D., Quadros, S., Hyderabadwala, Z. J., & Mamun, M. A. (2020). Aggregated COVID-19 suicide incidences in India: Fear of COVID-19 infection is the prominent causative factor. *Psychiatry Research*, 113145. https://doi.org/10.1016/j.psychres.2020.113145

Dumitrache, L., Stanculescu, E., Nae, M., Dumbraveanu, D., Simion, G., Talos, M., & Mareci, A. (2021). Post-lockdown effects on students' mental health in Romania: Perceived stress—The impact of missing daily social interactions and boredom proneness. *Preprints.* https://doi.org/10.20944/preprints202107.0473.v1

Duncan, P. (2021, May 11). More care home residents died of COVID in second wave than first in England and Wales. *The Guardian.*cited online on https://www.theguardian.com/world/2021/may/11/more-care-home-residents-died-of-covid-in-second-wave-than-first-in-england-and-wales

Dzinamarira, T., Dzobo, M., & Chitungo, I. (2020). COVID-19: A perspective on Africa's capacity and response. *Journal of Medical Virology, 92*(11), 2465–2472. https://doi.org/10.1002/jmv.26159

ECDC. (2021, June 4). *COVID-19 situation update for the EU/EEA.*

Eger, L., Komarkova, L., Egerova, D., & Micik, M. (2021). The effect of COVID-19 on consumer shopping behaviour: Generational cohort perspective. *Journal of Retailing and Consumer Services, 61*, 1–11.

Egger, D., Miguel, E., Warren, S., Shenoy, A., Collins, E., Karlan, D., Parkerson, D., Mobarek, A., Fink, G . C., Walker, M., Haushofer, J., Larreboure, M., Athey, S., Lopez-Pena, P., Benhachmi, S., Humphreys, M., Lowe, L., Meriggi, N., Wabwire, A., Davis, C., ... Vernot, C. (2021) Falling living standards during the COVID-19 crisis: Quantitative evidence from nine developing countries. *Science Advances, 7*(6), 1–12.

Ehnts, D., & Paetz, M. (2021). COVID-19 and its economic consequences for the Euro Area. *European Economic Review, 11*, 227–249.

Eisma, M. C., Boelen, P. A., & Lenferink, L. I. M. (2020). Prolonged grief disorder following the Coronavirus (COVID-19) pandemic. *Psychiatry Research, 288*, 113031. https://dx.doi.org/10.1016%2Fj.psychres.2020.113031

Eisner, M., & Nivette, A. (2020). *Violence and the pandemic: Urgent questions for research.* Harry Frank Guggenheim Foundation. https://hfg.org/Violence%20and%20the%20Pandemic.pdf

Ejang, H. M. (2020). *Protecting children from a distance: An ongoing experience in virtual child protection during COVID-19.* UNICEF.

Elabdi, F. (2020, December 20). Surviving in the ruins of Moria. *AlJazeera.* Cited online at https://www.aljazeera.com/features/2020/12/29/surviving-in-the-ruins-of-moria

El-Osta, A., Alaa, A., Webber, I., Sasco, E., Bagkeris, E., Millar, H., Vidal-Hall, C., & Majeed, A. (2021). How is the COVID-19 lockdown impacting the mental health of parents of school-age children in the UK? A cross-sectional online survey. *British Medical Journal Open, 11*, 1–11.

Ellis, A. (2016). *Men, masculinities and violence.* Routledge.

Ellis, A. (2019). A decivilizing reversal or system normal? Rising lethal violence in post-recession austerity United Kingdom. *The British Journal of Criminology, 59*(4), 862–878. https://doi.org/10.1093/bjc/azz001

Ellis, A., Briggs, D., Lloyd, A., & Telford, L. (2021). A ticking time bomb of future harm: Lockdown, child abuse and future violence. *Abuse: An International Journal, 2*(1). https://doi.org/10.37576/abuse.2021.017

Epifanio, M., Andrei, F., Mancini, G., Agostini, F., Piombo, M., Spicuzza, V., Riolo, M., Lavanco, G., Trombini, E., & Grutta, S. (2021). The impact of COVID-19 pandemic and lockdown measures on quality of life among Italian general population. *Journal of Clinical Medicine, 10*, 1–19.

Euronews. (2021, June 10). EU anti-fraud office identified nearly €300m in misused public funds last year. *Euronews.* Cited online at https://www.euronews.com/2021/06/10/eu-anti-fraud-office-identified-nearly-300m-in-misused-public-funds-last-year

European Commission. (2020). *EU support for vaccines.* https://ec.europa.eu/info/research-and-innovation/research-area/health-research-and-innovation/coronavirus-research-and-innovation/vaccines_en. Accessed 24 June 2021.

European Centre for Disease Prevention and Control. (2020). *COVID-19 in children and the role of school settings in transmission—First update.*

Evans, D. P. (2020). COVID-19 and violence: A research call to action. *BMC Women's Health, 20*(249), 1–3.

Evans, M. L., Lindauer, M., & Farrell, M. E. (2020). A pandemic within a pandemic—Intimate partner violence during COVID-19. *The New England Journal of Medicine, 383*, 2302–2304.

Every-Palmer, S., Jenkins, M., Gendall, P., Hoek, J., Beaglehole, B., Bell, C., Williman, J., Rapsey, C., & Stanley, J. (2020). Psychological distress, anxiety, family violence, suicidality, and wellbeing in New Zealand during the COVID-19 lockdown: A cross sectional study. *PLoS ONE, 15*(11), 1–19.

Faggioni, M., Melado, F., & Di Pietro, M. (2021). National health system cuts and triage decisions during the COVID-19 pandemic in Italy and Spain: Ethical implications. *Journal of Medical Ethics, 47*, 300–307.

Fair, H., & Jacobson, J. (2021). *Keeping COVID out of prisons: Approaches in ten countries* (Project Report). ICPR.

Ferguson, N., Laydon, D., Gilani, G., Imai, N., Ainslie, K., Baguelin, M., Bhatia, S., Boonyasiri, A., Cucunuba, Z., Dannenburg, G., Dighe, A., Dorigatti, I., Fu, H., Gaythorpe, K., Green, W., Hamlet, A., Hinsley, W., Okell, L., Elsland, S., Thompson, H. … Ghani, A. (2020). *Report 9: Impact of non-pharmaceutical interventions (NPIs) to reduce COVID-19 mortality and healthcare demand.* Imperial College COVID-19 Response Team.

Ferguson, N., Laydon, D., & Nedjati-Gilani, G. (2020) *Impact of non-pharmaceutical interventions to reduce COVID-19 mortality and health care.* Imperial College London, 1–20. https://doi.org/10.25561/77482

Fersia, O., Bryant, S., & Nicholson, R., (2020). The impact of the COVID-19 pandemic on cardiology services. *Open Heart, 7*, e001359. https://doi.org/10.1136/openhrt-2020-001359

Fielding, S. (2020, April 3). In quarantine with an abuser: Surge in domestic violence reports linked to coronavirus. *The Guardian*. https://www.theguardian.com/us-news/2020/apr/03/coronavirus-quarantine-abuse-domestic-violence

Filho, W., Lütz, J., Sattler, D., & Nunn, D. (2020). Coronavirus: COVID-19 transmission in Pacific small island developing states. *International Journal of Environmental Research on Public Health, 17*, 5409. https://doi.org/10.3390/ijerph17155409

Fisher, M. (2009). *Capitalist realism: Is there no alternative?* Zero.

Flaherty, G. T., Hession, P., & Liew, C. H. (2020). COVID-19 in adult patients with pre-existing chronic cardiac, respiratory and metabolic disease: A critical literature review with clinical recommendations. *Trop Dis Travel Med Vaccines, 6*, 16. https://doi.org/10.1186/s40794-020-00118-y

Flaxman, S., Mishra, S., Gandy, A., Unwin, H. J. T., Mellan, T. A., Coupland, H., & Bhatt, S. (2020). Estimating the effects of non-pharmaceutical interventions on COVID-19 in Europe. *Nature, 584*, 257–261. https://doi.org/10.1038/s41586-020-2405-7

Fleming, S. (2021). *How will behaviour change after COVID vaccination? New survey reveals post-pandemic trends*. World Economic Forum. https://www.weforum.org/agenda/2021/07/ipsos-behaviour-change-covid-vaccine/

Freier, L. F., & Espinoza, M. V. (2021). COVID-19 and immigrants' increased exclusion: The politics of immigrant integration in Chile and Peru. *Frontiers in Human Dynamics, 3*, 6. https://doi.org/10.3389/fhumd.2021.606871

Fukuyama, F. (1992). *The end of history and the last man*. The Free Press.

Gadermann, A. C., Thomson, K. C., Richardson, C. G., (2021). Examining the impacts of the COVID-19 pandemic on family mental health in Canada: Findings from a national cross-sectional study. *BMJ Open, 11*, e042871 https://doi.org/10.1136/bmjopen-2020-042871

Gambin, M., Sekowski, M., Wozniak-Prus, M., Wnuk, A., Tomasz, O., Cudo, A., Hansen, K., Huflejt-Lukasik, M., Kubicka, K., Lys, A., Gorgol, J., Holas, P., Kmita, G., Lojek, E., & Maison, D. (2021). Generalized anxiety and depressive symptoms in various age groups during the COVID-19 lockdown in Poland. Specific predictors and differences in symptoms severity. *Comprehensive Psychiatry, 105*, 1–10.

Ganesan, B., Al-Jumaily, A., Fong, K., Prasad, P., Meena, S., & Kai-Yu Tong, R. (2021). Impact of Coronavirus disease 2019 (COVID-19) outbreak quarantine, isolation, and lockdown policies on mental health and suicide. *Frontiers in Psychiatry, 12*, 1–12.

Gant, J. (2020, March 17). Border force officers test 25 migrants for Coronavirus after they were intercepted crossing the English channel today. *Daily Mail*. Cited online at https://www.dailymail.co.uk/news/article-8121813/Border-Force-catches-migrants-Kent-charities-warn-thousands-Calais-risk-coronavirus.html

Garthwaite, K. (2016). *Hunger pains*. Policy Press.

Gastroenterol, A. (2020). COVID-19: Mitigation or suppression. *Arab Journal of Gastroenterology, 21*, 1–2.

Gaythorpe, K. Bhatia, S., Mangal, T., Unwin, H. J. T., Imai, N., Cuomo-Dannenburg, G., Walters, C. E., Jauneikaite, E., Bayley, H., Kont, M. D., & Mousa, A. (2020, November 19). *Children's role in the COVID-19 pandemic: As systematic review of early surveillance data on susceptibility, severity, and transmissibility*. Imperial College London. https://doi.org/10.25561/84220

Godefroy, J. (2020). Recommending physical activity during the COVID-19 health crisis. Fitness Influencers on Instagram. *Frontiers in Sports and Active Living, 2*, 1–7.

Godin, M. (2020, October 9). *COVID-19 outbreaks are now emerging in refugee camps: Why did it take so long for the virus to reach them? Time*. Cited online at https://time.com/5893135/covid-19-refugee-camps/

Golechha, M. (2020). COVID-19, India, lockdown and psychosocial challenges: What next? *International Journal of Social Psychiatry, 66*(8), 830–832.

Gómez-Beccara, I., Flujas, J., Andrés, M., Sánchez-López, P., & Fernández-Torres, M. (2020, September). Evolución del estado psicológico y el miedo en la infancia y adolescencia durante el confinamiento por la COVID-19. *Revista de Psicología Clínica con Niños y Adolescentes, 7*(3), 11–18.

Gordon, A., Goodman, C., Achterberg, W., Barker, R., Burns, E., Hanratty, B., Martin, F. C., Meyer, J., O'Neill, D., Schols, J., & Spilsbury, K. (2020). Commentary: COVID in care homes—Challenges and dilemmas in healthcare delivery. *Age and Ageing, 49*(5), 701–705.

Gosselin, A., Melchior, M., Carillon, S., Gubert, F., Ridde, V., Kohou, V., Zoumenou, I., Senne, J.-N., & du Loû, A. D. (2021). Deterioration of mental health and insufficient COVID-19 information among disadvantaged immigrants in the greater Paris area. *Journal of Psychosomatic Research, 146*. 110504. https://doi.org/10.1016/j.jpsychores.2021.110504

Goswami, S. (2021, June 3). 200,000 people prosecuted in lockdown: Most fines pending. *Hindustan Times*. Cited online at https://www.hindustan times.com/cities/others/nearly-200-000-violated-covid-rules-in-lockdown-most-fines-yet-to-be-recovered-101622660408771.html

GOV. (2020a). *Does the use of face masks in the general population make a difference to spread of infection?*. https://assets.publishing.service.gov.uk/government/uploads/system/uploads/attachment_data/file/890039/s0117-rapid-review-face-masks-070420-sage24.pdf. Accessed 15 June 2021.

GOV. (2020b). *Government takes historic step towards net-zero with end of sale of new petrol and diesel cars by 2030*. Accessed 25 June 2021. Available at: https://www.gov.uk/government/news/government-takes-historic-step-tow ards-net-zero-with-end-of-sale-of-new-petrol-and-diesel-cars-by-2030

Gover, A. R., Harper, S. B., & Langton, L. (2020). Anti-Asian hate crime during the COVID-19 pandemic: Exploring the reproduction of inequality. *American Journal of Criminal Justice 45*, 647–667.https://link.springer.com/content/pdf/10.1007/s12103-020-09545-1.pdf

Graham, P., Martin, E. H., McCartney, M., & Dingwall, R. (2020). Science, society, and policy in the face of uncertainty: Reflections on the debate around face coverings for the public during COVID-19. *Critical Public Health, 30*(5), 501–508. https://doi.org/10.1080/09581596.2020.1797997

Green, P. (2020). Risks to children and young people during COVID-19 pandemic. *British Medical Journal, 369*(8244), https://doi.org/10.1136/bmj.m1669

Greene, T., Harju-Seppänen, J., Adeniji, M., Steel, C., Grey, N., Brewin, C. R., Bloomfield, M. A., & Billings, J. (2021). Predictors and rates of PTSD, depression and anxiety in UK frontline health and social care workers during COVID-19. *European Journal of Psychotraumatology, 12*(1), 1882781. https://doi.org/10.1080/20008198.2021.1882781

Greenberg, J. (2020, March 20). Timeline: How Donald Trump responded to the Coronavirus pandemic. *PolitiFact*. https://www.politifact.com/art icle/2020/mar/20/howdonald-trump-responded-coronavirus-pandemic/. Accessed 3 April 2020.

Greenwald, R. (2002). The role of trauma in conduct disorder. *Journal of Aggression Maltreatment & Trauma, 6*(1), 5–23. https://doi.org/10.1300/J14 6v06n01_02

Grierson, J. (2021, May 16). Fake COVID vaccine and test certificate market is growing, researchers say. *The Guardian*. https://www.theguardian.com/world/2021/may/16/fake-covid-vaccine-and-test-certificate-market-is-gro wing-researchers-say

Grigg-Damberger, M., & Yeager, K. (2020). Bedtime screen use in middle-aged and older adults growing during pandemic. *Journal of Clinical Sleep Medicine, 16*(1), 25–26.

Gruzd, A., & Mai, P. (2020). Going viral: How a single tweet spawned a COVID-19 conspiracy theory on Twitter. *Big Data & Society, 7*(2), 1–19.

Guerin, O. (2021). *COVID-19 pandemic: Everything you should not do, Brazil has done*. https://www.bbc.co.uk/news/world-latin-america-57733540

Guilmoto, C. (2020). *COVID-19 death rates by age and sex and the resulting mortality vulnerability of countries and regions in the world*. CEPED Université de Paris.

Haider, N., Osman, A., Gazekpo, A., Akipede, G., Asogun, D., Ansumana, R., Lessels, R., Khan, P., Hamid, M., Yeboah-Manu, D., Mboera, L., Shayo, E., Mmbaga, B., Urassa, M., Musoke, D., Kapata, N., Ferrand, R., Kapata, P., Stigler, F., … McCoy, D. (2020). Lockdown measures in response to COVID-19 in nine sub-Saharan African countries. *British Medical Journal Global Health, 5*(1–10), 2.

Hall, P. A., & Soskice, D. (2001). *Varieties of capitalism*. Oxford University Press.

Hall, S. (2012). *Theorizing crime and deviance*. Sage.

Hall, S., & Winlow, S. (2015). *Revitalizing criminological theory: Towards a New ultra- realism*. Routledge.

Hall, S., Winlow, S., & Ancrum, C. (2008). *Criminal identities and consumer culture*. Willan.

Hanafiah, M. H., Balasingam, A. S., Nair, V., Jamaluddin, M. R., & Zahari, M. S. M. (2021). Implications of COVID-19 on tourism businesses in Malaysia: Evidence from a preliminary industry survey. *Asia-Pacific Journal of Innovation in Hospitality and Tourism, 10*(1), 81–94.

Hanratty, B., Burton, J., Goodman, C., Gordon, A., & Spilsbury, K. (2020). COVID-19 and the lack of linked datasets for care homes. *British Medical Journal, 369*, m2463.

Harris, L. C. (2020). Breaking lockdown during lockdown: A neutralization theory evaluation of misbehaviour during the COVID 19 pandemic. *Deviant Behaviour*. https://doi.org/10.1080/01639625.2020.1863756

Harvey, D. (2005). *A brief history of neoliberalism*. Oxford University Press.

Harvey, D. (2010). *The enigma of capital*. Profile.

Hasanbayli, A. (2021). *Nascent consumer behaviors in the platform economy during COVID-19 pandemic*. 7th ITEM Conference—"Innovation, Technology, Education and Management", 80–89.

Hayward, S. E., Deal, A., Cheng, C., Crawshaw, A., Orcutt, M., Vandrevala, T. F., Norredam, M., Carballo, M., Ciftci, Y., Requena-Méndez, A., Greenaway, C., Carter, J., Knights, F., Mehrotra, A., Seedat, F., Bozorgmehr, K., Veizis, A., Campos-Matos, I., Wurie, F., ... Hargreaves, S. (2021). Clinical outcomes and risk factors for COVID-19 among migrant populations in high-income countries: A systematic review. *Journal of Migration and Health, 3*, 100041. https://doi.org/10.1016/j.jmh.2021.100041

Hazeldine, T. (2020). *The Northern question.* Verso.

Hell, A., Kampf, L., Kaulet, M., & Kohrsal, C. (2020, May 6). Hausliche Gewalt in der CoronaKrise. Wenn das Kind verborgen bleibt. *Süddeutsche Zeitung.* www.sueddeutsche.de/politik/coronavirus-haeusliche-gewalt-jugendaemter-1.4899381

Hernandez, D. (2020, February 13). War on the poor: Las Vegas's homelessness crackdown takes effect. *The Guardian.* Cited online at https://www.theguardian.com/us-news/2020/feb/13/las-vegas-homeless-sleeping-ban-no-lodging

Hillis, S., Mercy, J., Amobi, A., & Kress, H. (2016). Global prevalence of past-year violence against children: A systematic review and minimum estimates. *Pediatrics, 137*, e20154079. https://doi.org/10.1542/peds.2015-4079

Hillyard, P., & Tombs, S. (2004). Beyond criminology? In P. Hillyard, C. Pantazis, S. Tombs, & D. Gordon (Eds.), *Beyond criminology: Taking harm seriously.* Pluto Press.

Hilton, S., & Hunt, K. (2011). UK newspapers' representations of the 2009–10 outbreak of swine flu: One health scare not over-hyped by the media? *Journal of Epidemiology and Community Health, 65*, 941–946.

Hochuli, A., Hoare, G., & Cunliffe, P. (2021). *The end of the end of history: Politics in the twenty-first century.* Zero.

Honigsbaum, M. (2020). *The pandemic century: A history of global contagion from the Spanish Flu to COVID-19.* Penguin.

Hope, C. (2020). *COVID-19 death rate is higher in European countries with a low flu intensity since 2018.* Cambridge University Press.

HM Treasury. (2021, March 8). *Build back better: Our plan for growth.*

Huff, C. (2020). COVID-19: Americans afraid to seek treatment because of the steep cost of their high deductible insurance plans. *The British Medical Journal, 371*, 1–2.

Human Rights Watch. (2021, April 23). *Cameroon: Ensure credible inquiry on COVID-19 funds.* Cited online at https://www.hrw.org/news/2021/04/23/cameroon-ensure-credible-inquiry-covid-19-funds

IDPC. (2018). *Drug dependence treatment in Thailand: Progress against persistent concern*. IDPC.

Idris, I. (2021). *Areas and population groups in Pakistan most exposed to combined effects of climate change, food insecurity and COVID-19*. K4D Helpdesk FCDO.

IHME COVID-19 Health Service Utilization Forecasting Team. (2020, March 26). Forecasting COVID-19 impact on hospital bed-days, ICU-days, ventilator days and deaths by US state in the next 4 months. *MedRxiv*. https://doi.org/10.1101/2020.03.27.20043752.

Indian Express. (2020, April 5). *No seats in special rescue flight, Malaysian couple attempts suicide*. Cited online at https://www.newindianexpress.com/states/tamil-nadu/2020/apr/05/no-seats-in-special-rescue-flight-malaysian-couple-attempts-suicide-2125937.html

International Energy Agency. (2021). *Renewable energy market update: Outlook for 2021 and 2022*. IEA.

International Labour Organisation. (ILO). (2020). *ILO brief: COVID-19 employment and labor market impact in Thailand*. ILO.

International Labour Organisation. (ILO). (2021). *ILO Monitor: COVID-19 and the world of work* (7th ed.). ILO.

Institute for Economics & Peace. (2020, June). *Global peace index 2020: Measuring peace in a complex world*. Available from: http://visionofhumanity.org/reports

Ioannidis, J., Cripps, S., & Tanner, M. (2020). Forecasting for COVID-19 has failed. *International Journal of Forecasting*, 1–16.

Islam, N., Shkolnikov, V. M., Acosta, R. J., Klimkin, I., Kawachi, I., Irizarry, R. A., Alicandro, G., Khunti, K., Yates, T., Jdanov, D. A., White, M., Lewington, S., & Lacey, B. (2021). Excess deaths associated with COVID-19 pandemic in 2020: Age and sex disaggregated time series analysis in 29 high income countries *BMJ, 373*, n1137. https://doi.org/10.1136/bmj.n1137

Ismangil, M., & Lee, M. (2021). Protests in Hong Kong during the COVID-19 pandemic. *Crime, Media and Culture, 17*(1), 17–20. https://doi.org/10.1177%2F1741659020946229

Jain, R. (2020, March 23). These are the penalties for violating Coronavirus lockdown in India. *Business Insider*. Cited online at https://www.businessinsider.in/india/news/these-are-the-penalties-for-violating-coronavirus-lockdown-in-india/articleshow/74778635.cms

Jain, R., Budlender, J., Zizzamia, R., & Bassier, I. (2020). *The labor market and poverty impacts of COVID-19 in South Africa.* (SALDRU Working Paper No. 264). Saldru.

Jain-Chandra, M. S., Khor, N., Mano, R., Schauer, J., Wingender, M. P., & Zhuang, J. (2018). *Inequality in China: Trends, drivers and policy remedies* (IMF Working Paper. WP/18/127).

Javid, S., (2021). *Oral statement to parliament: 19 July remains our target date for ending restrictions.* https://www.gov.uk/government/speeches/19-july-remains-our-target-date-for-ending-restrictions. Accessed 8 July 2021.

Jayanetti, C. (2021, June 13). At least 130,000 households in England made homeless in pandemic. *The Observer.* Cited online at https://www.theguardian.com/society/2021/jun/13/at-least-130000-households-in-england-made-homeless-in-pandemic

Jetten, J., Mols, F., & Selvanthan, H. P. (2020). How economic inequality fuels the rise and persistence of the yellow vest movement. *International Review of Social Psychology, 33*(1), 1–12. https://doi.org/10.5334/irsp.356

Jia, R., Ayling, K., Chalder, T., Massey, A., Broadbent, E., Coupland, C., & Vedhara, K. (2020). Mental health in the UK during the COVID-19 pandemic: Cross-sectional analyses from a community cohort study. *BMJ Open, 10,* e040620. https://doi.org/10.1136/bmjopen-2020-040620

Jinnah, Z. (2017). Silence and invisibility: Exploring labour strategies of Zimbabwean farm workers in Musina, South Africa. *South African Review of Sociology, 48*(3), 46–63.

Jiao, W. Y., Wang, L. N., Liu, J., Fang, S. F., Jiao, F. Y., Pettoello-Mantovani, M., & Somekh, E. (2020). (Behavioral and emotional disorders in children during the COVID-19 epidemic. *The Journal of Pediatrics, 221,* 264–266.

Jones, L., & Hemeiri, S. (2021). COVID-19 and the failure of the neoliberal regulatory state. *Review of International Political Economy,* 1–25. Online First. https://www.tandfonline.com/doi/epub/10.1080/09692290.2021.1892798?needAccess=true

Josefsson, K. (2021). Perspectives of life in Sweden during the COVID-19 pandemic. *Journal of Clinical Sport Psychology, 15,* 80–86.

Katana, E., Amodan, B. O., Bulage, L., Ario, A. R., Fodjo, J. N. S., Colebunders, R., & Wanyenze, R. K. (2021). Violence and discrimination among Ugandan residents during the COVID-19 lockdown. *BMC Public Health, 21*(1), 467. https://doi.org/10.1186/s12889-021-10532-2

Katz, A. P., Civantos, F. J., Sargi, Z., Leibowitz, J. M., Nicolli, E. A., Weed, D., Moskovitz, A. E., Civantos, A. M., Andrews, D. M., Martinez, O., & Thomas, G. R. (2020). False-positive reverse transcriptase polymerase chain reaction screening for SARS-CoV-2 in the setting of urgent head and neck surgery and otolaryngologic emergencies during the pandemic: Clinical implications. *Head & Neck, 42,* 1–8. https://doi.org/10.1002%2Fhed.26317

Kaur, A. (2020, September 20). Residents against COVID-19 lockdown protest again. *Pacific Daily News.* Cited online at https://eu.guampdn.com/story/news/local/2020/09/10/residents-against-covid-19-lockdown-protest-again/5765533002/

Kaur, H., Singh, T., Arya, Y., & Mittal, S. (2020). Physical fitness and exercise during the COVID-19 Pandemic: A qualitative enquiry. *Frontiers in Psychology, 11,* 1–10.

Kaushal, V., & Srivastava, S. (2021). Hospitality and tourism amid COVID-19 pandemic: Perspectives on challenges and learnings from India. *International Journal of Hospitality Management, 92,* 102707. https://doi.org/10.1016/j.ijhm.2020.102707

Kelly, A. (2020, April 9). COVID-19 spreading quickly through refugee camps, warn Calais aid groups. *The Guardian.* Cited online at https://www.theguardian.com/global-development/2020/apr/09/covid-19-spreading-quickly-though-refugee-camps-warn-calais-aid-groups

Kelly, B., & Slattery, G. (2020, May 2). Prisoners take guards hostage in Brazil's Coronavirus-hit Manaus. *Reuters.* Cited online at https://www.reuters.com/article/us-brazil-prison-rebellion-idUSKBN22E0KB

Kelton, S. (2020). *The deficit myth: Modern monetary theory and how to build a better economy.* John Murray.

Khanijahani, A., & Tomassoni, L. (2021). Socioeconomic and racial segregation and COVID-19: Concentrated disadvantage and black concentration in association with COVID-19 deaths in the USA. *Journal of Racial and Ethnic Health Disparities,* 1–9. Online First. https://doi.org/10.1007/s40615-021-00965-1

King, E. (2020). Rapid response: COVID-19: Science, conflicts and the elephant in the room. *BMJ, 371,* m4425.

Killgore, W. D. S., Cloonan, S. A., Taylor, E. C., Miller, M. A., & Dailey, N. S. (2020). Three months of loneliness during the COVID-19 lockdown. *Psychiatry Research, 293,* 113392. https://doi.org/10.1016/j.psychres.2020.113392

Kirchmaier, T., & Villa-Llera, C. (2020). *COVID-19 and changing crime trends in England and Wales* (Centre for Economic Performance, No.013). http://doi.org/10.2139/ssrn.3700329

Kisielinski, K., Giboni, P., Prescher, A., Klosterhalfen, B., Graessel, D., Funken, S., Kempski, O., & Hirsch, O. (2021). Is a mask that covers the mouth and nose free from undesirable side effects in everyday use and free of potential hazards? *International Journal Environment Research Public Health, 18*(8), 4344. https://doi.org/10.3390/ijerph18084344

Klein, N. (2014). *This changes everything: Capitalism vs the climate.* Allen Lane.

Kollewe, J. (2021). From Pfizer to Moderna: Who's making billions from COVID-19 vaccines? *The Guardian.* https://www.theguardian.com/business/2021/mar/06/from-pfizer-to-moderna-whos-making-billions-from-covid-vaccines. Accessed 24 June 2021.

Kolmes, S. (2020). Employment-based, for-profit health care in a pandemic. *The Hastings Center Report, 50*(3), 22–22.

Kontopantelis, E., Mamas, M. A., Webb, R. T., Castro, A., Rutter, M., Gale, C. P., Ashcroft, D. M., Pierce, M., Abel, M. K., Price, G., Faivre-Finn, C., Van Spall, H. G. C., Graham, M. M., Morciano, M., Martin, G., & Doran, T. (2021). Excess deaths from COVID-19 and other causes by region, neighbourhood deprivation level and place of death during the first 30 weeks of the pandemic in England and Wales: A retrospective registry study. *The Lancet Regional Health—Europe.* https://doi.org/10.1016/j.lanepe.2021.100144

Koran, M. (2020, March 31). Las Vegas parking lot turned into 'homeless shelter' with social distancing markers'. *The Guardian.* Cited online at https://www.theguardian.com/us-news/2020/mar/30/lasvegas-parking-lot-homeless-shelter

Kostev, K., & Lauterbach, S. (2020). Panic buying or good adherence? Increased pharmacy purchases of drugs from wholesalers in the last week prior to COVID-19 lockdown. *Journal of Psychiatry Research, 130*, 19–21.

Kott, M. (2021, May 7). Free beer offered as US vaccine drive turns to bribes. *The Sydney Morning Herald.* Cited online at https://www.smh.com.au/world/north-america/pots-shots-and-pot-for-shots-us-vaccine-drive-turns-to-bribes-20210507-p57pom.html

Kotzé, J. (2018). Criminology or zemiology? Yes, please! on the refusal of choice between false alternatives. In A. Boukli & Kotzé, J. (Eds.), *Zemiology: Reconnecting crime and social harm.* Palgrave Macmillan.

Kotzé, J. (2019). *The myth of the 'crime decline.'* Routledge.

Kotzé, J. (2020). The commodification of abstinence. In S. Hall, T. Kuldova, & M. Horsley (Eds.), *Crime, harm and consumerism.* Routledge.

Kotzé, J. (2021). On researching harm: An ultra-realist perspective. In P. Davies, P. Leighton, & T. Wyatt (Eds.), *The Palgrave handbook of social harm*. Palgrave Macmillan.

Kotzé, J., & Antonopoulos, G. A. (2019). Boosting bodily capital: Maintaining masculinity, aesthetic pleasure and instrumental utility through the consumption of steroids. *Journal of Consumer Culture*. https://doi.org/10.1177/1469540519846196

Kotzé, J., Richardson, A., & Antonopoulos, G. A. (2020). Looking 'acceptably' feminine: A single case study of a female bodybuilder's use of steroids. *Performance Enhancement and Health, 8*(2–3), 100174. https://doi.org/10.1016/j.peh.2020.100174

Kulldorff, M., (2021). Why i spoke out against lockdowns. *Spiked*. https://www.spiked-online.com/2021/06/04/why-i-spoke-out-against-lockdowns/. Accessed 17 June 2021.

Kumar, A. (2020, May 4). *Coronavirus lockdown 3.0: Unable to repay loan, couple commits suicide in Bihar*. Cited online at https://www.deccanherald.com/national/east-and-northeast/coronavirus-lockdown-30-unable-to-repay-loan-couple-commits-suicide-in-bihar-833285.html

Lal, A., Erondu, N., Heymann, D., Gitachi, G., & Yates, R. (2021). Fragmented health systems in COVID-19: Rectifying the misalignment between global health security and universal health coverage. *The Lancet, 397*, 61–67.

Lai, G. (2021, May 2021). Thailand's prison overcrowding crisis exacerbated by COVID-19. *The Diplomat*. Cited online at https://thediplomat.com/2021/05/thailands-prison-overcrowding-crisis-exacerbated-by-covid-19/

Lancet Migration; Global Collaboration to Advance Migration Health. (2020). Situational brief: The health of asylum seekers & undocumented migrants in France during Covid-19. Available at https://www.migrationandhealth.org/migration-COVID19-briefs

Landauro, I. (2021). *Health policies a shot in the arm for west European insurers hit by COVID-19*. Reuters. https://www.reuters.com/article/us-healthcoronavirus-insurance-idUSKBN2AW0KE. Accessed 24 June 2021.

Lapavitsas, C. (2019). *The left case against the EU*. Polity.

Large, J. (2018). Spot the fashion victim(s): The importance of rethinking harm within the context of fashion counterfeiting. A. Boukli & J. Kotzé (Eds.), *Zemiology: Reconnecting crime and social harm*. Palgrave Macmillan.

Laudette, C. (2021, January 20). *The silent epidemic: Abuse against Spanish women rises during lockdown*. Cited online at https://www.reuters.com/article/us-health-coronavirus-spain-women-idUSKBN29P1WU

Lazzerini, M. (2020). Delayed access or provision of care in Italy resulting from fear of COVID-19. *The Lancet Child & Adolescent Health, 4*(5), e11-12.

Leigh, G. (2020). Why private are all the rage during a pandemic. *Forces.* https://www.forbes.com/sites/gabrielleigh/2020/08/25/why-private-jets-are-all-the-rage-during-a-pandemic/?sh=744d7ae778f7. Accessed 22 June 2021.

Lewis, M. (2021). *The premonition: A pandemic story.* Allen Lane.

Li, Y., Yao, L., Jiawei, L., Lei, C., Song, Y., Cai, Z., & Yang, C. (2020). Stability issues of RT- PCR testing of SARS-CoV-2 for hospitalized patients clinically diagnosed with COVID-19. *Journal of Medical Virology, 92*(7), 903–908. https://doi.org/10.1002/jmv.25786

Liang, S., Liang, L., & Rosen, J. (2021). COVID-19: A comparison to the 1918 influenza and how we can defeat it. *Postgraduate Medical Journal, 97*(1147), 273–274.

Lintern, S. (2020, May 31). Coronavirus: Care homes mentioned only twice in five months of Sage minutes. *The Independent.* Cited online at https://www.independent.co.uk/news/health/coronavirus-sageme etings-care-homes- a9541321.html

Liu, H., Chen, C., Cruz-Cano, R., Guida, J. L., & Lee, M. (2021). Public compliance with social distancing measures and SARS-CoV-2 Spread: A quantitative analysis of 5 states. *Public Health Reports, 136*(4), 475–482.

Liu, M., & Tsai, K. S. (2020). Structural power, hegemony and state capitalism: Limits to China's global economic power. *Politics and Society, 49*(2), 235–267. https://doi.org/10.1177%2F0032329220950234

Lloyd, A. (2013). *Labour markets and identity on the post-industrial assembly line.* Ashgate.

Lloyd, A. (2018). *The harms of work.* University Press.

Lloyd, A. (2020a). Harm at work: Special liberty and bullying in the retail sector. *Critical Criminology, 28*(4), 669–683. https://doi.org/10.1007/s10 612-019-09445-9

Lloyd, A. (2020b). Efficiency, productivity and targets: The gap between rhetoric and reality in the call centre. *Critical Sociology, 46*(1), 83–96. https://doi.org/10.1177/0896920518794251

Lloyd, A., Devanney, C., Wattis, L., & Bell, V. (2021). "Just tensions left, right and centre": Assessing the social impact of international migration on dein-dustrialised locale. *Ethnic and Racial Studies, 44*(15), 2794–2815. https://doi.org/10.1080/01419870.2020.1854813

MacIntyre, A. (2011). *After virtue.* Bloomsbury.

Maeda, J. M., & Nkengasong, J. N. (2021). The puzzle of the COVID-19 pandemic in Africa. *Science Magazine, 371*(6524), 27–28.

Mairhofer, A., Peucker, C. H., Pluto, L., van Santen, E., & Seckinger, M. (2020). *Kinder- und Jugendhilfe in Zeiten der Corona-Pandemie.* DJI Publication.

Mamun, M., Bhuiyan, A., & Manzar, M. (2020). The first COVID-19 infanticide-suicide case: Financial crisis and fear of COVID-19 infection are the causative factors. *Asian Journal of Psychiatry, 54,* 102365. https://doi.org/10.1016/j.ajp.2020.102365

Manduca, R. A. (2019). The contribution of national income inequality to regional economic divergence. *Social Forces, 98*(2), 622–648. https://doi.org/10.1093/sf/soz013

Mangione, K. (2021, June 1). Warning about increasing toxicity follows another record-breaking month for illicit drug overdoses in B.C. *BC News.* Cited online https://bc.ctvnews.ca/warning-about-increasing-toxicity-follows-another-record-breaking-month-for-illicit-drug-overdoses-in-b-c-1.5451492

Maringe, C., Spicer, J., Morris, M., Purushotham, A., Nolte, E., & Sullivan, R. (2020). The impact of the COVID-19 pandemic on cancer deaths due to delays in diagnosis in England, UK: A national, population-based, modelling study. *The Lancet, 21*(8), 1023–1034. https://doi.org/10.1016/S1470-2045(20)30388-0

Marmolejo, L., Barberi, D., Espinoza, O., Bergman, M., & Fondevila, G. (2020). Responding to COVID-19 in Latin American prisons: The cases of Argentina, Chile, Colombia, and Mexico. *Victims & Offenders, 15*(7–8), 1062–1085. https://doi.org/10.1080/15564886.2020.1827110

Marmot, M., Allen, J., Goldblatt, P., Herd, E., & Morrison, J. (2020). *Build back fairer: The COVID-19 Marmot review: The pandemic, socioeconomic and health inequalities in England.* Institute of Health Equity.

Massie, G. (2021). Zoom increased profits by 4000 per cent during pandemic but paid no income tax, report says. *The Independent.* https://www.independent.co.uk/news/world/americas/zoom-pandemic-profit-income-tax-b1820281.html. Accessed 25 June 2021.

Mauricio, J., Pereyra, A., & Carbajal, D. (2020, July–December). Análisis de políticas públicas en el Peru ante la crisis derivada de la COVID-19. *Semestre Económico, 23*(55), 113–138.

McGowan, T (2016). *Capitalism and desire: The psychic cost of free markets.* Columbia University Press.

Mellor, P., & Shilling, C. (1993). Modernity, self-identity and the sequestration of death. *Sociology, 27*(3), 411–431.

Melnick, E., & Ioannidis, J. (2020). Head to head: Should governments continue lockdown to slow the spread of COVID-19? *British Medical Journal, 369*, 1–3.

Mamun, M. A., & Ullah, I. (2020). COVID-19 suicides in Pakistan, dying off not COVID-19 fear but poverty? The forthcoming economic challenges for a developing country. *Brain Behavior and Immunity, 87*, 163–166. https://doi.org/10.1016/j.bbi.2020.05.028

Menton, M., Milanez, F., de Andrade Souza, J. M., & Cruz, F. S. M. (2021). The COVID-19 pandemic intensified resource conflicts and indigenous resistance in Brazil. *World Development, 138*, 105222. https://doi.org/10.1016/j.worlddev.2020.105222

Menzies, R. E., & Menzies, R. G. (2020). Death anxiety in the time of COVID-19: Theoretical explanations and clinical implications. *The Cognitive Behaviour Therapist, 13*(e19), 1–11. https://doi.org/10.1017%2FS1754470X20000215

Meo, S., Abukhalaf, A., Alomar, A., Beeshi, I. Z., Alhowikan, A., Shafi, K. M., Meo, A. S., Usmani, A. M., & Akram, J. (2020). Climate and COVID-19 pandemic: Effect of heat and humidity on the incidence and mortality in world's top ten hottest and top ten coldest countries. *European Review for Medical and Pharmacological Sciences, 24*, 8232–8238.

Mercer, P. (2021, May 3). Papua New Guinea Covid-19: Mistrust fuels crisis as infections rise. *BBC*. Cited online at https://www.bbc.com/news/world-asia-56926131

Miguel, F., Machado, G., Pianowski, G., & Carvalho, L. (2020). Compliance with containment measures to the COVID-19 pandemic over time: Do antisocial traits matter? *Personality and Individual Differences, 168*, 1–8. https://doi.org/10.1016%2Fj.paid.2020.110346

Miles, D., Stedman, M., & Heald, A. (2021). "Stay at home, protect the national health service, save lives": A cost benefit analysis of the lockdown in the United Kingdom. *The International Journal of Clinical Practice, 75*(3), 1–14.

Milkman, R. (2020). *Immigrant labor and the new precariat*. Polity.

Ministry of Equality. (2020). *GBV helpline calls*. Data obtained from the website of the Ministry of Equality of Spain.

Mitchell, W., & Fazi, T. (2017). *Reclaiming the state*. Pluto.

Moderna. (2021). *U.S government purchases additional 100 million doses of Moderna's COVID-19 Vaccine*. Moderna. https://investors.modernatx.com/node/10991/pdf. Accessed 24 June 2021.

Moustsen-Helms, I. R., Emborg, H.-D., Nielsen, J., Nielsen, K. F., Krause, T. G., Mølbak, K., Møller, K. L., Berthelsen, A.-S.N., & Valentiner-Branth, P. (2021). Vaccine effectiveness after 1st and 2nd dose of the BNT162b2 mRNA Covid-19 vaccine in long-term care facility residents and healthcare workers—A Danish cohort study. *MedRxiv*. https://doi.org/10.1101/2021.03.08.21252200

Muller, S. (2021). The dangers of performative scientism as the alternative to anti-scientific policymaking: A critical, preliminary assessment of South Africa's COVID-19 response and its consequences. *World Development, 140,* 1–14.

Murray, J., & Mistlin, A. (2021). Police report rise in large COVID lockdown parties in England. *The Guardian*. https://www.theguardian.com/uk-news/2021/feb/19/police-report-rise-in-large-covid-lockdown-parties-in-england. Accessed 28 June 2021.

Mutz, M., Muller, J., & Reimers, A. (2021). Use of digital media for home-based sports activities during the COVID-19 pandemic: Results from the German SPOVID survey. *International Journal of Environmental Research and Public Health, 18*(9), 4409.

Nagle, A. (2017). *Kill all normies*. Zero.

Nanan-Sen, S. (2021). 'Keep masks!' Jon Ashworth erupts at Sajid Javid as labour demands Covid 'U-turn'. *The Express*. https://www.express.co.uk/news/politics/1459029/Jon-Ashworth-Sajid-Javid-health-secretary-face-masks-covid19-latest-Labour-Party-news-vn. Accessed 8 July 2021.

Nanuqa, J. (2021, March 16). Social issues major cause of suicide. *FBC News*. Cited online at https://www.fbcnews.com.fj/news/social-issues-major-cause-of-suicide/

Neate, R. (2021). Amazon had sales income of £44bn in Europe in 2020 but paid no corporation tax. *The Guardian*. https://www.theguardian.com/technology/2021/may/04/amazon-sales-income-europe-corporation-tax-luxembourg. Accessed 22 June 2021.

NDTV. (2020, May 6). *40,000 arrested since March 25 for lockdown violation in Bengal: Police*. NDTV. Cited online at https://www.ndtv.com/india-news/coronavirus-lockdown-40-000-arrested-since-march-25-for-lockdown-violation-in-bengal-police-2223968

Nechifor, V., Ramos, M. P., Ferrari, E., Laichena, J., Kihiu, E., Omanyo, D., Musamali, R., & Kiriga, B. (2021). Food security and welfare changes under COVID-19 in Sub-Saharan Africa: Impacts and responses in Kenya. *Global Food Security, 28,* 100514.

Net Zero Teesside. (2020). *System value to the UK power market of carbon capture and storage*. Net Zero Teesside.

Nettle, D., Johnson, E., Johnson, M., Saxe, R. (2021). Why has the COVID-19 pandemic increased support for universal basic income? *Humanities and Social Sciences Communication, 8*(79). https://doi.org/10.1057/s41599-021-00760-7

Newbury, A., Barton, E., Snowdon, L., & Hopkins, J. (2020). *Understanding the impact of COVID- 19 on violence and ACEs experienced by children and young people in Wales*. Violence Prevention Unit.

Neyra-Leon, J., Huancahuari-Nunez, J., Diaz-Monge, J. C., & Pinto, J. A. (2021). The impact of COVID-19 in the healthcare workforce in Peru. *Journal of Public Health Policy, 42*, 182–184. https://doi.org/10.1057/s41 271-020-00259-6

Nicola, M., Alsafi, Z., Sohrabi, C., Kerwan, A., Al-Jabir, A., Losifidis, C., Agha, M., & Agha, R. (2020). The socio-economic implications of the Coronavirus pandemic (COVID- 19): A review. *International Journal of Surgery, 78*, 185–193. https://doi.org/10.1016/j.ijsu.2020.04.018

Nivette, A. et al. (2021). Non-compliance with COVID-19-related public health measures among young adults in Switzerland: Insights from a longitudinal cohort study. *Social Science & Medicine, 268*, 1– 9. https://doi.org/10.1016/j.socscimed.2020.113370

Nkwayep, C., Bowong, S., tewa, T., & Kurths, J. (2020). Short-term forecasts of the COVID-19 pandemic: A study case of Cameroon. *Chaos, Solitons and Fractals, 140*, 110106. https://doi.org/10.1016/j.chaos.2020.110106

Nnaji, C. A., & Moodley, J. (2021). Impact of the COVID-19 pandemic on cancer diagnosis, treatment and research in African health systems: A review of current evidence and contextual perspectives. *Ecancermedicalscience, 15*, 1170. Published 2021 January 14. https://doi.org/10.3332/ecancer.2021. 1170

Nørgaard, S., Vestergaard, L., Nielson, J., Richter, L., Schmid, D., Bustos, N., Brave, T., Athanasiadou, M., Lytras, T., Denissov, G., Veideman, T., Luomala, O., Möttönen, T., Fouillet, A., Caserio-Schönemann, C., Heiden, M. A. D., Uphoff, H., Gkolfinopoulou, K., Bobvos, J., ... Mølbak, K. (2021). Real- time monitoring shows substantial excess all-cause mortality during second wave of COVID-19 in Europe, October to December 2020. *Euro Surveillance, 26*(2). https://doi.org/10.2807/1560-7917.ES.2021.26.1. 2002023

O'Connor, R. (2021). Piers Morgan calls for 'outrageous and pathetic' Matt Hancock to step down over aide scandal. *The Independent*. https://www.

independent.co.uk/arts-entertainment/tv/news/piers-morgan-matt-hancock-sack-b1873287.html. Accessed 8 July 2021.

OECD. (2021, April). *Unemployment rates*. OECD.

O'Hara, M. (2014). *Austerity bites*. Policy Press.

Ohare, L. (2018, April 2). At least one person a day is self-harming in UK detention centres. *The Independent*. Cited online at https://www.indepe ndent.co.uk/news/one-person-day-self-harming-uk-detention-centres-a82 85206.html

Ojong, N. (2020). The COVID-19 pandemic and the pathology of the economic and political architecture in Cameroon. *Healthcare, 8*, 176. https://doi.org/10.3390/healthcare8020176

Oliver, D. (2020). Let's not forget care homes when COVID-19 is over. *British Medical Journal, 369*, 1629.

ONS. (2020a). *Excess winter mortality in England and Wales: 2018 to 2019 (provisional) and 2017 to 2018 (final)*. ONS.

ONS. (2020b, November). *Domestic abuse during the Coronavirus (COVID-19) pandemic, England and Wales*. https://www.ons.gov.uk/peoplepopulationan dcommunity/crimeandjustice/articles/domesticabuseduringthecoronavirus covid19pandemicenglandandwales/november2020

Oronce, C. I., Scannell, C. A., Kawachi, I., & Tsugawa, Y. (2020). Association between state-level income inequality and COVID-19 cases and mortality in the USA. *Journal of General Internal Medicine, 35*(9), 2791–2973. https:// doi.org/10.1007/s11606-020-05971-3

O'Sullivan, D., Rahamathulla, M., & Pawar, M. (2020). The impact and impli-cations of COVID-19: An Australian perspective. *The International Journal of Community and Social Development, 2*(2), 134–151.

Oullet, V. (2021, June 16). *Some prisoners not offered COVID-19 shots until months after general public, CBC analysis finds in CBC*. Cited online at https://www.cbc.ca/news/canada/covid-vaccinations-in-jails-1.6066293

Ozalp, M. (2020, September 17). In war-torn Syria, the Coronavirus pandemic has brought its people to the brink of starvation. *The Conversation*. Cited online at https://theconversation.com/in-war-torn-syria-the-coronavirus-pan demic-has-brought-its-people-to-the-brink-of-starvation-144794

Pacific Community. (2021, May 24). *COVID-19: Pacific community updates*. Cited online at Updates https://www.spc.int/updates/blog/2021/05/covid-19-pacific-community-updates

Pacific News Centre. (2020, September 5). *15 suicides on Guam in the past three months of COVID year*. Cited online at https://www.pncguam.com/ 15-suicides-on-guam-in-the-past-three-months-of-covid-year/

Pakistan Bureau of Statistics. (2021). *Special survey on evaluating the impact of COVID-19.*. Government of Pakistan

Papadopoulou, A., Efstathiou, V., Yotsidi, V., Pomini, V., Michopoulos, I., Markopoulou, E., Papadopoulou, M., Tsikaropoulou, E., Kalemi, G., Tournikioti, K., Douzenis, A., & Gournellis, R. (2021). Suicidal ideation during COVID-19 lockdown in Greece: Prevalence in the community, risk and protective factors. *Psychiatry Research, 297*, 1–8.

Parenti, C. (2011). *Tropic of chaos: Climate change and the new geography of violence.* Basic Books.

Parker, R. M. (2006, December 24). What an informed patient means for the future of healthcare. *Pharmacoeconomics, 2*, 29–33. https://doi.org/10.2165/00019053-200624002-00004. PMID: 23389486.

Patel, S., & Kariel, J. (2021). Universal basic income and Covid-19 pandemic. *British Medical Journal, 372.* https://doi.org/10.1136/bmj.n193

Pattinson, R., & Cole, H. (2021). Cheating Hancock: Matt Hancock's secret affair with aide Gina Coladangelo is exposed after office snogs while COVID raged on. *The Sun.* https://www.thesun.co.uk/news/15388014/matt-hancock-secret-affair-with-aide/. Accessed 8 July 2021.

Pemberton, S. (2016). *Harmful societies.* Policy Press.

Pietrykowski, B. (2017). Revaluing low-wage work: Service-sector skills and the fight for 15. *Review of Radical Political Economics, 49*(1), 5–29. https://doi.org/10.1177%2F0486613416666543

Piketty, T. (2014). *Capital in the twenty-first century.*

Pillai, A. (2021, May 21). *How virtual tourism can rebuild travel for a post pandemic world.* World Economic Forum. Cited online at https://www.weforum.org/agenda/2021/05/covid-19-travel-tourism-virtual-reality/

Pitron, G. (2020). *The rare metals war.* Scribe.

Plott, C., Kachalia, A., & Sharfsterin, J. (2020). Unexpected health insurance profits and the COVID-19 crisis. *Journal of the American Medical Association, 324*(17), 1713–1714.

Podder, S., & Mukherjee, U. (2020). Ascending child sexual abuse statistics in India during COVID-19 lockdown: A darker reality and alarming mental health concerns. *Indian Journal of Psychological Medicine, 42*(5), 491–493. https://doi.org/10.1177%2F0253717620951391

Poonsab, W., Vanek, J., & Carré, F. (2020). *Informal workers in urban Thailand: A statistical snapshot.* WIEGO.

Posel, D., Oyenubi, A., & Kollamparambil, U. (2021). Job loss and mental health during the COVID-19 lockdown: Evidence from South Africa. *PLoS ONE, 16*(3), 1–15.

Pulla, P. (2020). What counts as a COVID-19 death? *British Medical Journal*. https://doi.org/10.1136/bmj.m2859

Queensland Government. (2021). *Coronavirus (COVID-19)*. https://www.qld. gov.au/health/conditions/health-alerts/coronavirus-covid-19.Accessed   28 June 2021.

Quinones, S. (2016). *Dreamland*. Bloomsbury.

Raifman, J., Bor, J., & Venkataramani, A. (2021). Association between receipt of unemployment insurance and food insecurity among people who lost employment during the COVID-19 pandemic in the United States. *JAMA, 4*(1), e2035884 . .. https://jama.jamanetwork.com/article.aspx?doi= 10.1001/jamanetworkopen.2020.35884&utm_campaign=articlePDF% 26utm_medium=articlePDFlink%26utm_source=articlePDF%26utm_con tent=jamanetworkopen.2020.35884

Rao, C. (2020). Medical certification of cause of death for COVID-19. *Bulletin World Health Organisation, 98*(5), 298. https://www.who.int/bulletin/vol umes/98/5/20-257600.pdf

Rapisarda, S., & Byrne, J. (2021). An examination of COVID-19 outbreaks in prisons and jails throughout Asia. *Victims & Offenders, 15*(7–8). https:// doi.org/10.1080/15564886.2020.1835770

Ratcliffe, R. (2021). How have Thailand and Cambodia kept COVID cases so low? *The Guardian*. 16 December 2020. Cited online at https://www. theguardian.com/world/2020/dec/16/thailand-cambodia-covid-19-cases-dea ths-low

Razavi, A., Erondu, N., & Okereke, E. (2020). The global health security index: What value does it add? *BMJ Glob Health, 5*, e002477

Reiss, K., & Bhakdi, S. (2020). *Corona, false alarm?* Chelsea Green Publishing.

ReliefWeb. (2021, May 4). *Northeastern Syria: Hospitals run out of funds and supplies as second COVID-19 wave hits region*. ReliefWeb. Cited online at https://reliefweb.int/report/syrian-arab-republic/northeastern-syria-hospit als-run-out-funds-and-supplies-second-covid-19

Robbins, I., Gordon, A., Dyas, J., Logan, P., & Gladman, J. (2013). Explaining the barriers to and tensions in delivering effective health in UK care homes: A qualitative study. *British Medical Journal Open, 3*, 1–9.

Rodriguez, J. (2021, April 5). 'Public health crisis': Canada's prison condi tions during pandemic being investigated. *CTV News*. Cited online at https://www.ctvnews.ca/health/coronavirus/public-health-crisis-canada-s- prison-conditions-during-pandemic-being-investigated-1.5375277

Rasul, G., Nepal, A., Hussain, A., Maharjan, A., Joshi, S., Lama, A., Prakriti, G., Ahmad, F., Mishra, A., & Sharma, E. (2021). Socio-economic implications of COVID-19 pandemic in South Asia: Emerging risks and growing challenges. *Frontiers in Sociology, 6*, 1–14.

Raymen, T. (2019). The Enigma of social harm and the barrier of liberalism: Why zemiology needs a theory of the good. *Justice, Power and Resistance, 3*(1), 134–163.

Raymen, T. (2021). The assumption of harmlessness. In P. Davies, P. Leighton, & T. Wyatt (Eds.), *The Palgrave handbook of social harm.* Palgrave Macmillan.

Raymen, T., & Kuldova, T. (2021). Clarifying ultra-realism. *Continental Thought and Theory, 3*(2). http://doi.org/10.26021/10709

Reiner, R. (2021). *Social democratic criminology: New directions in criminology* (p. 154). Routledge.

Reiss, K., & Bhakdi, S. (2020). *Corona: False alarm?* Chelsea Green Publishing.

Reuters. (2020, June10). *Denmark sees no rise in COVID-19 cases after further easing of lockdown.* Cited online at https://www.reuters.com/article/us-hea lth-coronavirus-denmark-idUSKBN23H1DU

Ricci, G., Pallotta, G., Sirignano, A., Amenta, F., & Nittari, G. (2020). Consequences of COVID-19 outbreak in Italy: Medical responsibilities and governmental measures. *Frontiers in Public Health, 8*, 588852. https://doi.org/10.3389/fpubh.2020.588852

Richards, M., Anderson, M., Carter, P., Ebert, B. L., & Mossialos, E. (2020). The impact of the COVID-19 pandemic on cancer care. *Nature Cancer, 1*(6), 565–567. https://doi.org/10.1038/s43018-020-0074-y

Robinson, E., Gillespie, S., & Jones, A. (2020). Weight-related lifestyle behaviours and the COVID-19 crisis: An online survey study of UK adults during social lockdown. *Obesity, Science and Practice, 6*(6), 735–740.

Rogerson, C. M., & Rogerson, J. M. (2020). COVID-19 and tourism spaces of vulnerability in South Africa. *African Journal of Hospitality, Tourism and Leisure, 9*(4), 382–401.

Romanou, E., & Belton, E. (2020). *Isolated and struggling: National society for the prevention of cruelty to children.* NSPCC. https://learning.nspcc.org. uk/media/2246/isolated-and-struggling-social-isolation-risk-child-maltreatm ent-lockdown-and-beyond.pdf

Romei, V. (2020, December 31). How the pandemic is worsening inequality. *Financial Times.* https://www.ft.com/content/cd075d91-fafa-47c8-a295-85bbd7a36b50

Roozenbeek, J., Schneider, C., Dryhurst, S., Kerr, J., Freeman, A., & van der Bles, S. (2020). Susceptibility to misinformation about COVID 19 around the world. *Royal Society of Open Science, 7*, 1–15. https://doi.org/10.1098/rsos.201199

Rudenstine, S., McNeal, K., Schulder, T., Ettman, C. K., Hernandez, M., Gvozdieva, K., & Galea, S. (2021). Depression and anxiety during the COVID- 19 pandemic in an urban, low-income public university sample. *Journal of Traumatic Stress, 34*(1), 12–22. https://doi.org/10.1002/jts.22600

Rushworth, S. (2021). *COVID: Why most of what you know is wrong.* Karneval Publishing.

SAFE. (2020). *Job market: The unemployment rate doubles in 2020 in BC due to the pandemic.* Cited online at https://hellosafe.ca/en/newsroom/job-mar ket-british-columbia-2020?utm_source=vancouver+is+awesome&utm_cam paign=vancouver+is+awesome&utm_me dium=referral

Sama, M. T., & Nguyen, V. K. (2008). Governing the health system in Africa. In M. Sama & V. K. Nguyen (Eds.), *Governing health systems in Africa.* Council for the Development of Social Science Research in Africa.

Santos, S., & Chiesa, M. (2020). *PCR positives: What do they mean?* The Centre for Evidence- Based Medicine. https://www.cebm.net/covid-19/pcr-positives-what-do-they-mean/

Sanyaolu, A., Okorie, C., Marinkovic, A., Patidar, R., Younis, K., Desai, P., Hosein, Z., Padda, I., Mangat, J., & Altaf, M. (2020). Comorbidity and its impact on Patients with COVID-19. *SN Comprehensive Clinical Medicine*, 1–8. https://doi.org/10.1007%2Fs42399-020-00363-4

Sarwal, R., & Sarwal, T. (2020, March 29). *Mitigating COVID-19 with lock-downs: A possible exit strategy.* Available at SSRN https://ssrn.com/abstract=3563538 or http://dx.doi.org/10.2139/ssrn.3563538

Sayce, L. (2021, February 21). *The forgotten crisis: Exploring the dispropor-tionate impact of the pandemic on disabled people.* The Health Foundation. Cited online at https://www.health.org.uk/news-and-comment/blogs/the-for gotten-crisis-exploring-the- disproportionate-impact-of-the-pandemic

Schalkwyk, M., Maani, N., & McKee, M. (2021). Public health emergency or opportunity to profit? The two faces of the COVID-19 pandemic. *The Lancet: Diabetes & Endocrinology, 9*(2), 61–63.

Schildt, H. (2020). *The data imperative: How digitalization is reshaping manage-ment, organizing, and work.* Oxford University Press.

Schmitz, F. (2020, August 20). *Europe's largest refugee camp braces for COVID-19 outbreak.* DW. Cited online at https://www.dw.com/en/europes-largest-refugee-camp-braces-for-covid-19-outbreak/a-54640747

Schwab, K. (2017). *The fourth industrial revolution*. Penguin.

Schwab, K., & Malleret, T. (2020). *COVID 19: The great reset*. World Economic Forum.

Scott, J. (2020). A pandemic in prisons. *Social Anthropology/anthropologie Sociale, 28*(2), 353–355.

Scott, S. (2017). *Labour exploitation and work-based harm*. Policy Press.

Scott, S., McGowan, V. J., & Visram, S. (2021). 'I'm gonna tell you about how Mrs Rona has affected me': Exploring young people's experiences of the Covid-19 pandemic in North East England: A qualitative diary-based study. *International Journal of Environmental Research and Public Health, 18*, 3837. https://doi.org/10.3390/ijerph18073837

Scroll. (2021, June 3). *Covid lockdown: Over 8,700 people, many of them migrant workers, died along railway tracks in 2020*. Scroll. Cited online at https://scroll.in/latest/996519/covid-lockdown-over-8700-people-many-of-them-migrant-workers-died-along-railway-tracks-in-2020

Sediri, S., Zgueb, Y., Ouanes, S., Ouali, U., Bourgou, S., Jomli, R., & Nacef, F. (2020). Women's mental health: Acute impact of COVID-19 pandemic on domestic violence. *Archives of Women's Mental Health, 23*, 749–756. https://doi.org/10.1007/s00737-020-01082-4

Seerwanja, A., Kawuki, J., & Kim, J. (2020). Increased child abuse in Uganda amidst COVID-19 pandemic. *Journal of Paediatrics and Child Health*. Advance Online Publication. https://doi.org/10.1111/jpc.15289

Sharov, K. (2020). Adaptation to SARS-CoV-2 under stress: Role of distorted information. *European Journal of Clinical Investigation, 50*(9), 1–7.

Shell. (2020). *Responsible energy: Sustainability report 2020*. Shell.

Shields, K. (2021). Free school meals and governmental responsibility for food provision. *Edinburgh Law Review, 25*(1), 111–117. https://doi.org/10.3366/elr.2021.0678

Shutes, I. (2012). The employment of migrant workers in long-term care. *Journal of Social Policy, 41*(1), 43–59.

Silva, J. (2019). *We're still here*. Oxford University Press.

Sim, K., Chua, H., Vieta, E., & Fernandez, G. (2020). The anatomy of panic buying related to the current COVID-19 pandemic. *Psychiatry Research, 280*, 113015.

Singh, R., Rai, C., & Ishan, R. (2021). Impact of COVID-19 lockdown on patients with cancer in North Bihar, India: A phone-based survey. *Cancer Research, Statistics and Treatment, 4*(1), 37–43.

Singh, S., Roy, D., Sinha, K., Parveen, S., Sharma, G., & Joshi, G. (2020). Impact of COVID-19 and lockdown on mental health of children and adolescents: A narrative review with recommendations. *Psychiatry Research*, *293*, 1–10.

Singhari, S., & Madheswaran, S. (2017). Wage structure and wage differentials in formal and informal sectors in India. *The Indian Journal of Labour Economics*, *60*, 389–414. https://doi.org/10.1007/s41027-018-0110-y

Slobodian, Q. (2019). *Globalists*. Harvard University Press.

Smart, B. (2010). *Consumer society*. Sage.

Smith, O. (2019). Luxury, tourism and harm: A deviant leisure perspective. In T. Raymen & O. Smith (Eds.), *Deviant leisure: Criminological perspectives on leisure and harm*. Palgrave Macmillan.

Smith, S. G., Zhang, X., Basile, K. C., Merrick, M. T., Wang, J., Kresnow, M., & Chen, J. (2018). *The National Intimate Partner and Sexual Violence Survey (NISVS): 2015 data brief—Updated release*. National Center for Injury Prevention and Control, Centers for Disease Control and Prevention.

So, A. Y. (2019). The rise of authoritarianism in China in the early 21st century. *International Review of Modern Sociology*, *45*(1), 49–70.

Soltesz, K., Gustafsson, F., Timpka, T., Jalden, J., Jidling, C., Heimerson, A., Schon, T., Spreco, A., Ekberg, J., Dahlstrom, O., Carlson, F., Joud, A., & Bernhardsson, B. (2020). The effect of interventions on COVID- 19. *Nature*, *588*, 26–28.

Southworth, P. (2021). Lockdowns are 'the single biggest public health mistake in history', says top scientist. *The Telegraph*. https://www.telegraph.co.uk/news/2021/06/10/lockdowns-single-biggest-public-health-mistake-history-says/. Accessed 17 June 2021.

Standing, G. (2011). *The precariat*. Bloomsbury.

Stang, A., Standl, F., Kowall, B., Brune, B., Böttcher, J., Brinkmann, M., Dittmer, U., & Jöckel, K.-H. (2020). Excess mortality due to COVID-19 in Germany. *Journal of Infection*, *81*(5), 797–801.

Stanley, E., & Bradley, T. (2020). Pandemic policing: Preparing a new pathway for Māori? *Crime, Media and Culture*, *17*(1), 53–58. https://doi.org/10.1177%2F1741659020946228

Statista. (2021a). *Unemployment rate in selected European countries as of April 2021*. https://www.statista.com/statistics/1115276/unemployment-in-europe-by-country/. Accessed 17 June 2021.

Statista. (2021b). *Coronavirus (COVID-19) in Brazil*. Statista.

Streeck, W. (2016). *How will capitalism end?* Verso.

Surkova, E., Nikolayevskyy, V., & Drobniewski, F. (2020). False-positive COVID-19 results: Hidden problems and costs. *The Lancet*, *8*, 1167–1168. https://doi.org/10.1016/s2213-2600(20)30453-7

Szajnoga, D., Klimen-Tulwin, M., & Piekut, A. (2021). COVID-19 lockdown leads to changes in alcohol consumption patterns. Results from the Polish national survey. *Journal of Addictive Diseases, 39*(2), 215–225.

Sztompka, P. (2000). Cultural trauma: The other face of social change. *European Journal of Social Theory, 3*(4), 449–466.

Tavares, F., & Betti, G. (2021). The pandemic of poverty, vulnerability, and COVID-19: Evidence from a fuzzy multidimensional analysis of deprivations in Brazil. *World Development, 139*, 24.

Taylor, D. (2021, May 21). UK asylum seekers at 'unprecedented' risk of suicide amid deportation threat. *The Guardian.* Cited online at https://www.theguardian.com/uk-news/2021/may/21/uk-asylum-seekers-at-unprecedented-risk-of-suicide-amid-deportation-threat

Taylor, J., & Siradapuvadol, N. (2021, May 14). Suicides rise in Thailand as COVID decimates its tourism industry. *The Telegraph.* Cited online at https://www.telegraph.co.uk/global-health/science-and-disease/sui cides-rise-thailand-covid-decimates-tourism-industry/

Taylor, M., Watts, J., & Bartlett, J. (2019, September 27). Climate crisis: 6 million people join latest wave of global protests. *The Guardian.* https://www.theguardian.com/environment/2019/sep/27/climate-crisis-6-million-people-join-latest-wave-of-worldwide-protests

Tcherneva, P. (2020). *The case for a job guarantee.* Polity.

Telford, L. (2021). 'There is nothing there': Deindustrialization and loss in a coastal town. *Competition & Change.* Online First. https://doi.org/10.1177/10245294211011300

Telford, L., & Briggs, D. (2021). Targets and overwork: Neoliberalism and the maximisation of profitability from the workplace. *Capital & Class.* Online First. https://doi.org/10.1177/03098168211022208

Telford, L., & Lloyd, A. (2020). From "infant hercules" to "ghost town: Industrial collapse and social harm in Teesside. *Critical Criminology, 28*, 595–611.

Telford, L., & Wistow, J. (2020). Brexit and the working class on Teesside: Moving beyond reductionism. *Capital & Class, 44*(4), 553–572.

Thawan, T. (2021, June 8). *Nearly 30,000 COVID-19 infections at Thai prisons in recent wave.* The Thaiger. Cited online on https://thethaiger.com/news/national/nearly-30000-covid-19-infections-at-thai-prisons-in-recent-wave

The Times of India. (2021, January 14). Bengaluru world's fastest growing tech hub, London second: Report. *The Times of India.* Accessed from https://tim esofindia.indiatimes.com/business/india-business/bengaluru-worlds-fastest-growing-tech-hub-london-second-report/articleshow/80262770.cms

The White House. (2021). *Fact sheet: G7 to announce joint actions to end public support for overseas unabated coal generation by end of 2021.* Briefing Room. https://www.whitehouse.gov/briefing-room/statements-releases/2021/06/12/fact-sheet-g7-to-announce-joint-actions-to-end-public-support-for-ove rseas-unabated-coal-generation-by-end-of-2021/. Accessed on 25 June 2021.

TIJ. (2021). *Research on the causes of recidivism in Thailand.* TJI.

Tombs, S. (2014). Health and safety 'crimes' in Britain: The great disappearing act. In P. Davies, P. Francis, & T. Wyatt (Eds.), *Invisible crimes and social harms.* Palgrave Macmillan.

Troya, M. (2021, March 2). *El Gobierno certifica que 29.408 personas han muerto por coronavirus en residencias desde el inicio de la pandemia.* La Sociedad. Cited online at https://elpais.com/sociedad/2021-03-02/en-esp ana-han-muerto-29408-mayores-que-vivian-en-residencias-desde-el-inicio-de-la-pandemia.html

Tudor, K. (2018). Toxic sovereignty: Understanding fraud as the expression of special liberty within late-capitalism. *Journal of Extreme Anthropology, 2*(2), 7–21. https://doi.org/10.5617/jea.6476

UN. (2021). *United Nations system: Common position on incarceration.* UN.

UNDP. (2020). *Socio-economic impact assessment of COVID-19 on Papua New Guinea* (p. 8). UNDP.

UNODC. (2016). *Global report on trafficking in persons 2016.* United Nations Publication.

UNODC. (2021, June 16). *UNODC supports Thai prisons to respond to COVID-19 outbreak.* Cited on UNODC website at https://www.unodc.org/southeastasiaandpacific/en/2021/06/thai-prison-covid-19/story.html

Unni, J. (2020). Social effects of COVID-19 pandemic on children in India. *Indian Journal of Practicing Pediatricians, 22*(2), 102–104.

Vainshelboim, B. (2021). Facemasks in the COVID-19 era: A health hypothesis. *Medical Hypotheses, 146,* 110411.

Van Lancker, W., & Parolin, Z. (2020). COVID-19, school closures and child poverty: A social crisis in the making. *The Lancet Public Health, 5*(5), e243-244. https://doi.org/10.1016/S2468-2667(20)30084-0

Van Rooj, B., Brujin, A., Folmer, C., Kooistra, E., Kuiper, M., Brownlee, M., Olthuis, E., & Fine, A. (2020) *Compliance with COVID-19 mitigation measures in the United States.* C- Lab.

Varoufakis, Y. (2013). *The global minotaur.* Zeb Books.

Vives-Cases, C., Parra-Casado, D. L., Estévez, J. F., Torrubiano-Domínguez, J., & Sanz-Barbero, B. (2021). Intimate partner violence against women during the COVID-19 lockdown in Spain. *International Journal Environment Research and Public Health, 18*, 4698. https://doi.org/10.3390/ijerph18094698

Vogl, A., Fleay, C., Loughnan, C., Murray, P., & Dehm, S. (2020). COVID-19 and the relentless harms of Australia's punitive immigration detention regime. *Crime, Media and Culture, 17*(1), 43–51. https://doi.org/10.1177%2F1741659020946178

Wacquant, L. (2009). *Prisons of poverty*. University of Minnesota Press.

Walter, T. (2017). *What death means now: Thinking critically about dying and grieving*. Policy.

Wang, C., Horby, P. W., Hayden, F. G., & Gao, G. F. (2020). A novel coronavirus outbreak of global health concern. *The Lancet, 395*(10223), 470–473. https://doi.org/10.1016/S0140-6736(20)30185-9

Wang, D., Marmo-Roman, S., Krase, K., & Phanord, L. (2021). Compliance with preventative measures during the COVID-19 pandemic in the USA and Canada: Results from an online survey. *Social Work in Health Care*. https://doi.org/10.1080/00981389.2020.1871157

Wang, S., Chen, X., Li, Y., Luu, C., Yan, R., & Madrisotti, F. (2020). 'I'm more afraid of racism than of the virus!': Racism awareness and resistance among Chinese migrants and their descendants in France during the COVID-19 pandemic. *European Societies*, 1–22. Available at https://www.tandfonline.com/doi/full/10.1080/14616696.2020.1836384

Warren, G., Lofstedt, R., & Wardman, J. (2021). COVID-19: The winter lockdown strategy in five European nations. *Journal of Risk Research, 24*(3/4), 267–293.

Waterhouse, D., Harvey, R., Hurley, P., Levit, L., Kim, E., Klepin, H., Mileham, K., Nowakowski, G., Schenkel, C., Davis, C., Bruinooge, S., & Schilsky, R. (2021). Early impact of COVID-19 on the conduct of oncology clinical trials and long-term opportunities for transformation: Findings from an American society of clinical oncology survey. *American Society of Clinical Oncology, 16*(7), 417–422.

Wegerif, M. C. A. (2020). 'Informal' food traders and food security: Experiences from the COVID-19 response in South Africa. *Food Security, 12*(4), 797–800. https://doi.org/10.1007/s12571-020-01078-z

Weinberger, D., Chen, J., Cohen, T., Crawford, F., Mostashari, F., Olson, D., Pitzer, V. E., Reich, N. G., Russi, M., Simonsen, L., & Watkins, A. (2021). Estimation of excess deaths associated with the COVID-19 pandemic in the United States, March to May 2020. *JAMA*

Internal Medicine, 180(10), 1336–1344. doi:https://doi.org/10.1001/jam ainternmed.2020.3391 Published online July 1, 2020.

White, R. (2013). *Environmental harm.* Policy Press.

White, R. D., & Heckenberg, D. (2014). *Green criminology: An introduction to the study of environmental harm.* Routledge.

Wilkinson, R., & Pickett, K. (2009). *The spirit level.* Penguin.

Winter, J. (2020a, May 12). *The last days of oppenheimer park, Vancouver's tent city.* Vice. Cited online at https://www.vice.com/en/article/g5ppvq/the-last-days-of-oppenheimer-park-vancouvers-tent-city

Winter, J. (2020b, April 30). *Deadly overdoses are rocking Canada's poorest neighbourhood under lockdown.* Vice. Cited online at https://www.vice.com/en/article/akw5aa/deadly-overdoses-are-rocking-canadas-poorest-neighbour hood-under-coronavirus-lockdown

Winlow, S., & Hall, S. (2013). *Rethinking social exclusion.* Sage.

Winlow, S., Hall, S., Treadwell, J., & Briggs, D. (2015). *Riots and political protest.* Routledge.

Winlow, S., Hall, S., & Treadwell, J. (2017). *The rise of the right.* Policy Press.

Wise, J. (2021). COVID-19: Ending all restrictions in England on 19 July "dangerous and premature" say experts. *BMJ, 374.* https://doi.org/10.1136/bmj.n1751

Withers, M., Henderson, S., & Shivakoti, R. (2021). International migration, remittances and COVID-19: Economic implications and policy options for South Asia. *Journal of Asian Public Policy.* https://doi.org/10.1080/175 16234.2021.1880047

Wood, M., Anderson, B., & Richards, I. (2020). Breaking down the pseudo-pacification process: Eight critiques of ultra-realist crime causation theory. *British Journal of Criminology, 60*(3), 642–661. https://doi.org/10.1093/bjc/azz069

Wood, H., & Skeggs, B. (2020). Clap for carers? For care gratitude to care justice. *European Journal of Cultural Studies, 23*(4), 641–647. https://doi.org/10.1177%2F1367549420928362

Woodward, B. (2020). *Rage.* Simon and Schuster.

Wootton, H., & Mizen, R. (2021). Victorian teenage suicide threats jump 184pc amid pandemic. *Financial Review.* https://www.afr.com/policy/hea lth-and-education/victorian-teenage-suicide-threats-jump-184pc-amid-pan demic-20210607-p57ypu. Accessed 21 June 2021.

World Health Organization. (2005). *WHO global influenza preparedness plan: The role of WHO and recommendations for national measures before and during pandemics.* World Health Organization.

World Health Organization. (2020a). *WHO characterises Covid-19 as a pandemic.* https://www.who.int/emergencies/diseases/novel-coronavirus-2019/events-as-they-happen

WHO. (2020b, May 22). *At least 80 million children under one at risk of diseases such as diphtheria, measles and polio as COVID-19 disrupts routine vaccination efforts, warn Gavi, WHO and UNICEF.* Cited online https://www.who.int/news/item/22-05-2020-at-least-80-million-children-under-one-at-risk-of-diseases-such-as-diphtheria-measles-and-polio-as-covid-19-disrupts-routine-vaccination-efforts-warn-gavi-who-and-unicef

WHO. (2020c, June 8). *The true death toll of COVID-19.* Cited online at https://www.who.int/data/stories/the-true-death-toll-of-covid-19-estimating-global-excess-mortality

WHO (2020d, October 12). *Q&A on Coronavirus disease (COVID-19).* Cited online at https://www.who.int/emergencies/diseases/novel-coronavirus-2019/question-and-answers-hub/q-a-detail/coronavirus-disease-covid-19#:~:text=symptoms

Xue, J., Chen, J., Chen, C., Hu, R., & Zhu, T. (2020). The hidden pandemic of family violence during COVID-19: Unsupervised learning of tweets. *Journal of Medical Internet Research, 22*(11), e24361. https://doi.org/10.2196/24361

Yanez, J. A., Jahanshahi, A. A., Alvarez-Risco, A., Li, J., & Zhang, S. X. (2020). Anxiety, distress and turnover intention of healthcare workers in Peru by their distance to the epicenter during the COVID-19 crisis. *American Journal of Tropical Medicine and Hygiene, 103*(4), 1614–1620. https://doi.org/10.4269/ajtmh.20-0800

Yar, M. (2012). *Critical criminology, critical theory and social harm.* In S. Hall & S. Winlow (Eds.), *New directions in criminological theory.* Routledge.

Young, A. (2021). Locked-down city. *Crime, Media and Culture, 17*(1), 21–25.

Yu, Q., Salvador, C., Melani, I., Berg, M., Neblett, E., & Kitayama, S. (2021). Racial residential segregation and economic disparity jointly exacerbate COVID-19 fatality in large American cities. *Annals of the New York Academy of Sciences, 1–14.*

Zamin, M. (2020, April 24). *Marido y mujer se suicidan con una cuerda en Keshabpur.* Cited online at https://mzamin.com/article.php?mzamin=223588

Zhang, H. (2020). The influence of the ongoing COVID-19 pandemic on family violence in China. *Journal of Family Violence.* Advance Online Publication. https://doi.org/10.1007/s10896-020-00196-8

Zizek, S. (2006). *How to read Lacan.* Norton.

Zizek, S. (2020). *Pandemic: COVID-19 shakes the world*. OR Books.

Zizek, S. (2021). *Pandemic 2: Chronicles of a lost time*. Polity.

Zussman, R. (2020. May 11). Reports of child abuse down amid COVID-19, as B.C. advocates remind public of duty to report. *Global News*. https://glo balnews.ca/news/6929622/child-abuse-reporting-coronavirus

Index